CW01513085

MARGARET DE FLAHAUT
(1788–1867)

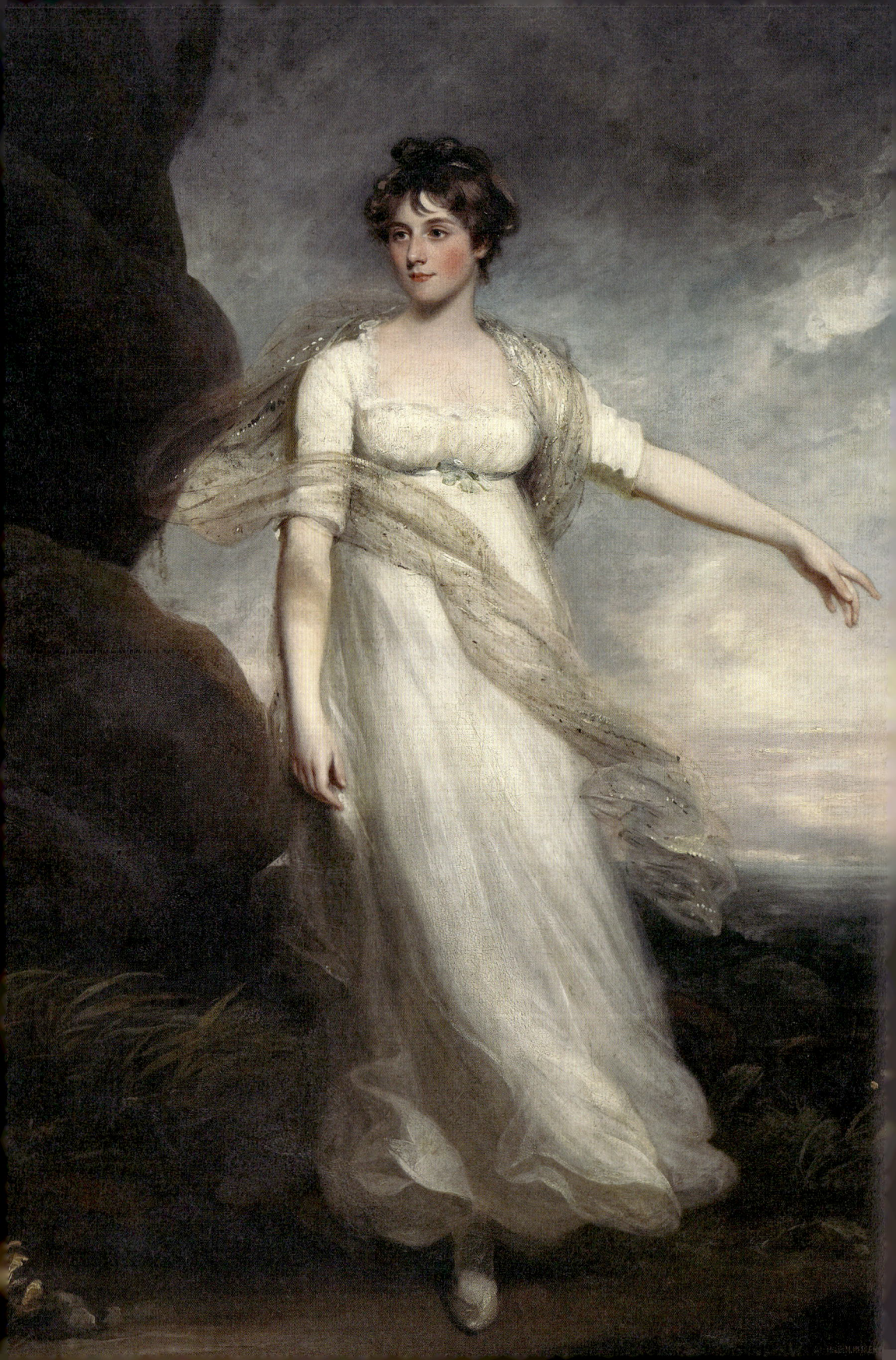

MARGARET DE FLAHAUT

(1788–1867)

A Scotswoman at the French Court

DIANA SCARISBRICK

A

John Adamson
Cambridge

First published in the United Kingdom
in 2019 by John Adamson Books
90 Hertford Street
Cambridge CB4 3AQ

British Library Cataloguing-in-Publication Data
A catalogue record for this book is available
from the British Library

ISBN 978-1-898565-16-1

Generously sponsored by the Drummond Foundation

Designed and typeset in Granjon by Chris Jones, Design4Science Ltd, London
Printed on Tatami White 115 gsm and bound in Italy by Opero S.r.l., Verona

FRONTISPIECE
**John Hoppner (1758–1810): full-length portrait of Margaret
as Shakespeare's Miranda, 1801**

This book is dedicated to
Jane Willoughby de Eresby

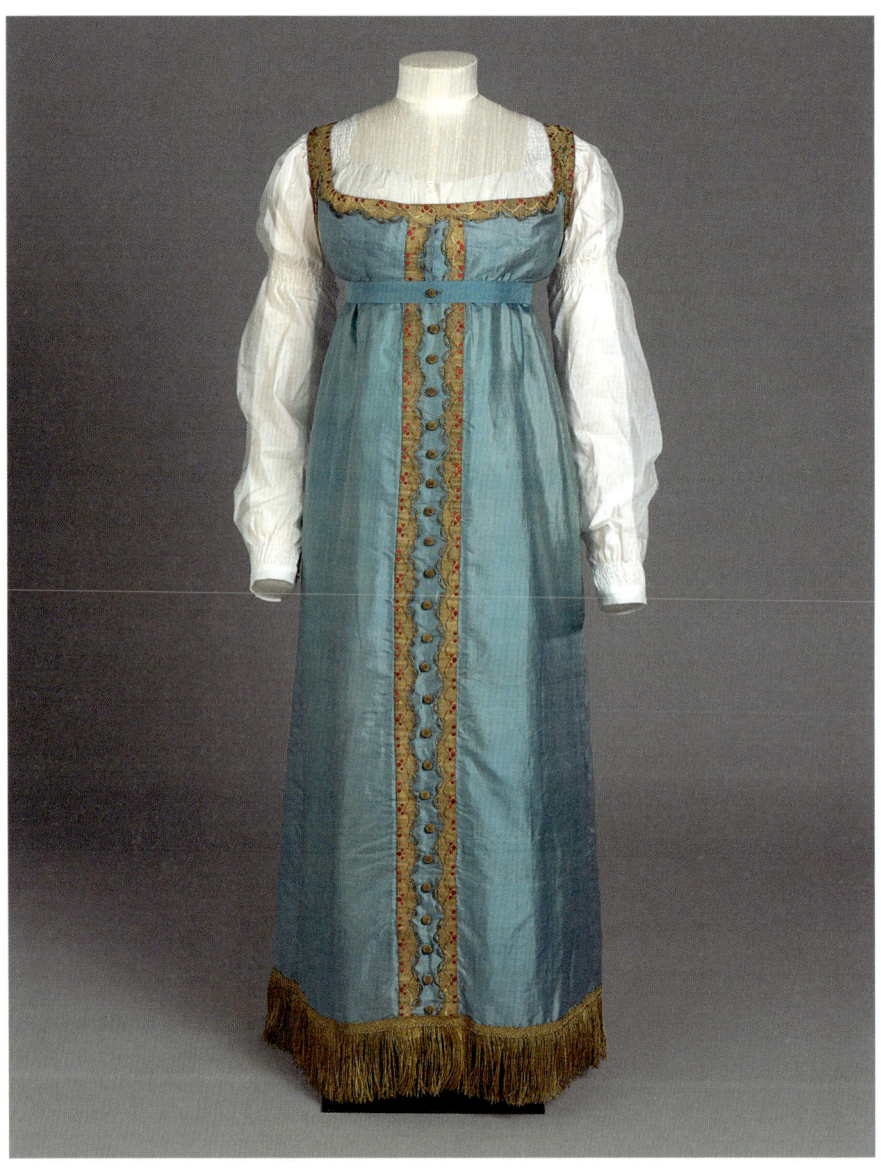

1 This high-waisted Russian-style dress, in blue silk trimmed with scalloped gold lace, was made for Charlotte, Princess of Wales, in around 1817. Margaret wears another version in her portrait by Thomas Lawrence (p. 118, no. 20).

CONTENTS

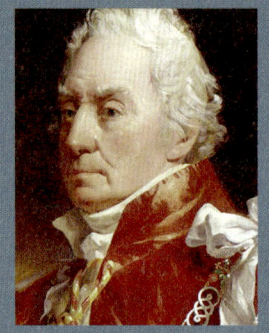

CHAPTER I

The Admiral's Ambitious Daughter

. . . a shock had then been given
To old opinions: and the minds of all men
Had felt it

Wordsworth, *The Prelude*, Book Tenth: Residence in France and
French Revolution

Scotland has produced some memorable women both in history and literature, each of them remarkable in her own way. First comes Mary Stuart, the model of queenly dignity, charm and generosity, then the cool-headed Flora MacDonald, who saved Prince Charles Edward Stuart from captivity in 1745, followed by Sir Walter Scott's heroine, the passionate Lucy Ashton, who inspired Donizetti's opera *Lucia di Lammermoor*, and more recently, by Muriel Spark's dedicated teacher, Jean Brodie. Named after Scotland's patron saint, Margaret Mercer Elphinstone (1788–1867), with her powerful mind and independent spirit, deserves a place among these famous characters. Seeking to realize her ambitions for her family against the background of intellectual upheaval and social and political change which followed the French Revolution and the end of the *ancien régime*, she was never daunted by adversity. The turning point in her life was her controversial marriage in 1817 with the general Charles de Flahaut (1785–1870), which, contrary to all expectations, resulted in one of the most successful partnerships in the "auld alliance" between France and Scotland.

Her choice of a French husband was a great blow to her father, Admiral George Keith Elphinstone (1745/6–1823), created Viscount Keith in 1814. His career was devoted to maintaining British maritime supremacy and thus preventing the invasion threatened by Napoleon, who estimated that "it is necessary for us to be masters of the sea for six hours only and England will have ceased to exist". Two important episodes made the admiral famous. The first was when, as commander-in-chief of the Mediterranean Fleet, he participated in the victory of Aboukir Bay and the capture of Alexandria in 1801, which effectively blocked Napoleon's advance into the Middle East.

9

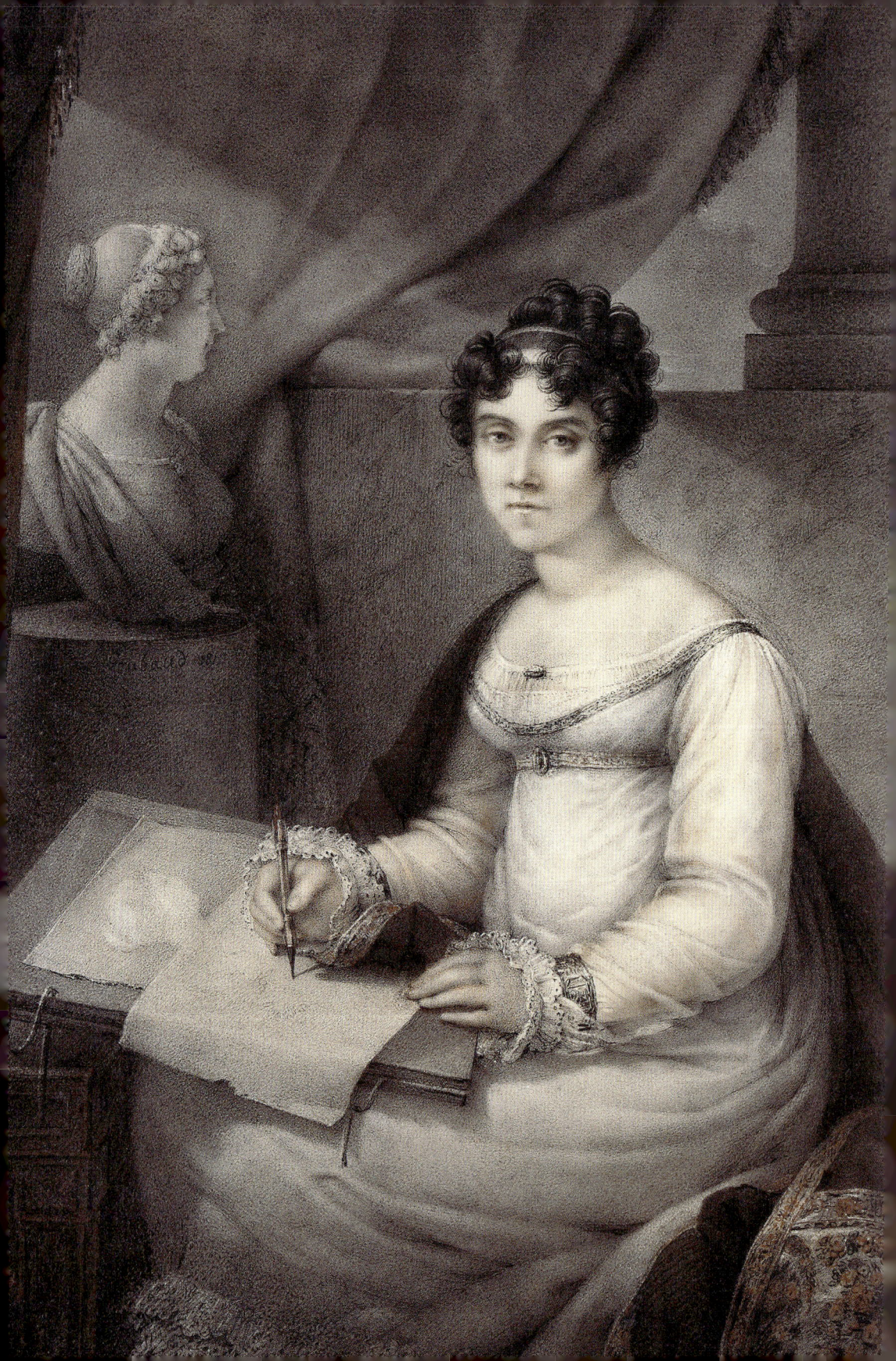

The second came on 27 July 1815 when, in charge of the Channel fleet, he was responsible for sending Napoleon from Torbay to the island of Saint Helena. Firm and intransigent, this "fine-looking old man, with perfect manners", refused to negotiate the terms of exile with the "brutal monster".[1] The young Margaret shared this view, and, after visiting the works of the émigré engineer Marc Isambard Brunel at Portsmouth in 1807, remarked, "How provoking it is that all Frenchmen will be so ingenious and such villains."

Not only had Margaret been brought up to agree with her father's anti-French attitudes, which she was to abandon, but she also inherited his fighting spirit, aristocratic hauteur and his Whiggish politics,[2] to which she remained faithful. Known by the derogatory term applied to the seventeenth-century Scottish Covenanters and Presbyterians who rebelled against the attempts of Charles II and James II to enforce religious conformity, the Whigs, with their rivals the Tories, came to dominate British politics during the eighteenth century. However, being divided within, the Whig party had to remain, powerless, in opposition from 1790.

After the battle of Waterloo had been won and the long period of war and revolution was over, there were signs at last that the nation wanted a change from the Tory government, and Lord Macaulay's nephew Sir George Trevelyan affirmed that "the last cannon shot fired on the 18th June 1815 was in truth the death-knell of the golden age of Toryism". Arising from the strong demand for Parliamentary Reform and wider political representation, which was accompanied by social unrest in the cities of London and Manchester, a crisis seemed imminent. However, those who, under the leadership of Lord Grey, hoped to carry through political reform, however limited, faced a serious constitutional obstacle in the person of the Prince Regent, the future George IV, who by his refusal to agree to any measures in that direction kept the Tories in power until his reign ended in 1830. Margaret, who by birth, inclination and upbringing belonged to the Whig party, began to show her allegiance by wearing the blue ribbon of the very liberal-minded Sir Francis Burdett at his first election for Middlesex in 1802.

Though very well born, and successful in his career, Admiral Keith was not rich, having joined the Navy in 1761 with just £5 in his pocket. Instead,

2 Innocent-Louis Goubaud (1780–1840): portrait
of Margaret with her sketch-book

Margaret's money came from her mother, Jane, co-heiress of the banker William Mercer of Aldie, co. Perth, son of the Honorable Robert Mercer, second son of William, Lord Nairne.[3] This marriage, which took place in 1787, was brief, for Jane, known as the Princess of Aldie, died in 1789 leaving the eighteen-month-old Margaret in the care of her father's three sisters, the unmarried Primrose and Mary Elphinstone, and Clementina, Lady Perth. Margaret loved them all, but was particularly attached to Mary, who "showed me all the affection and kindness of a parent and to whom I owed every feeling and attachment". From them Margaret learnt the old Scottish legends and imbibed the romantic family history, which she describes in a letter of 26 January 1824 to her neighbour and friend, the Whig politician Edward Ellice:

> Memories transmitted to us by my grandmother and her
> family who all lived to be remarkably old people . . . these
> tales of other times were the gossip of my childhood, and
> having no younger playfellows than old maids of three score,
> Frederick the Great and Marischal Keith occupied the vacant
> places of Bluebeard and Jack the Giant Killer in my
> imagination.[4]

When at home with her father, the young Margaret enjoyed the company of the outstanding political personalities of the time, and so, as an adult, she was ready to hold her own with whomsoever was in power. After reading Lord Malmesbury's *Diaries and Correspondence IV* (1844) she recalled how as a child she

> . . . lived much in the intimacy of the families whose names
> are so often mentioned. The description too of Mr Pitt and
> Lord Melville who [*sic*] I at that time saw continually at
> Ramsgate, of the coalition and the political scene is so well
> described. My young companions were Herries, Elliot, Eden,

3 **George Sanders (1774–1846): portrait of**
Admiral Viscount Keith

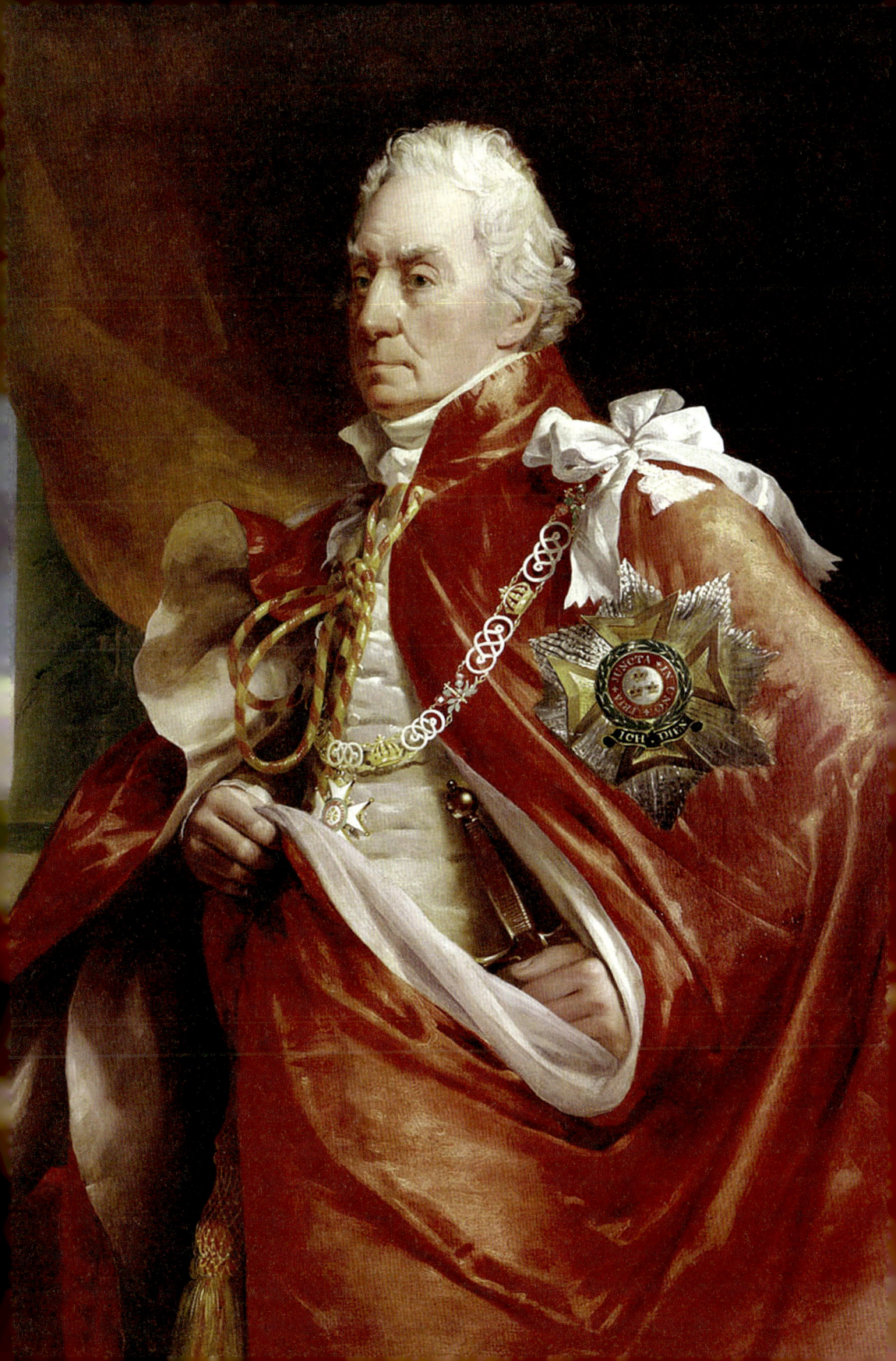

Palmerston, Carnegie, Woronzow and so, you may suppose,
I felt myself quite at home in the houses he mentions, besides
having heard all the violent discussions which the events of
the day gave rise to in a large military and political society
composed of people of all parties and opinions, and now,
having been so long drilled to foreign reserve and intrigues,
I look back with astonishment at the very independent and
hostile way Lord Sidmouth's government was canvassed and
attacked at my father's table, *the whole party in uniform.*

Well-read and clever, Margaret also had artistic talents alluded to in a
miniature showing her at the age of fourteen, holding a lyre.[5] Encouraged
by her aunts, she was an accomplished pianist, entertaining her friends with
the latest German waltzes, polonaises and music from Russian composers.
As a painter, miniatures were her speciality and she obtained good likenesses
of her cousin Clementina Sarah and husband, Peter Robert Burrell, of friends
such as Mary Fox and Lord Byron, and of the outstanding political personalities, Napoleon and the Russian Grand Duke Nicholas. She copied Old
Masters, and Lord Holland said he "never saw a prettier drawing" than the
portrait of the Spanish playwright and poet Lope de Vega (1562–1635) which
she executed as the frontispiece of a new edition of his works for the library
at Holland House. She also excelled at painting porcelain plaques for furniture and the cups and saucers which she gave as mementoes.

Although Admiral Keith was away for months on the high seas, his
daughter remained very close to him. When he was in England she stayed
at his official residences in Portsmouth and Plymouth and in his Hampshire
and London houses. His letters from abroad were accompanied by exotic
presents, some from himself, such as a beautiful box of perfumes, others from
his allies. Thus, he wrote on 12 April 1801 from Aboukir – "a most beautiful
sublime bay but now in Bad gale" – that

Captain Pacha sends you 2 shawls and three pieces of stuff
such as are in use here and boots such as ladies in Turkey
wear via Captain Middleton. Mr. Pacha has your picture
copied if the Sultana should depart this life I think you may
become Madame Pacha and sit on a cushion. The sultana is

sister to the Emperor. I send you a little diamond box which you may keep as I do not take snuff.

In return, she went shopping

> for things some of the ladies that come on board your ship will like, some English paper, so I send you some quires [sheets of paper in bulk] for those to whom you do not have to give expensive presents . . . For Madame Pacha a dejeuner of Wedgwood coffee pot, cups, and a very pretty Roman lamp . . . more for beauty than use . . . from Gray's the Bond Street jewellers, a letter case embroidered in steel and filled with all sorts of instruments . . . we have chosen a very handsome sword hilt for Captain Pacha.

Impressed with her excellent judgment he entrusted Margaret with his own commissions asking her to

> Tell Mr. Jackson I want a very handsome repeating telescope and Atlas also Case of Instruments for myself and two good day glasses – I have given all to the Turks. I would also have a Woodstock steel handled Sword hilt Diamond cut, to be well packed up via Captain Perth.[6]

Thus, from an early age, Margaret showed a real talent for shopping, choosing articles which would give pleasure to her friends and family.

In 1808, after a long friendship, Admiral Keith married "Queeney" Thrale (1762–1857), daughter of Hester Lynch Piozzi, the brilliant conversationalist much admired by Dr Samuel Johnson. On hearing the news of this unexpected event, Queen Charlotte observed to Lady George Murray that "Miss Mercer's fortune will be large enough from her mother's side . . . the young lady I am told adores her father and should she get a brother I believe her good principles will not let her grieve at the pleasure it would give her father." However, instead of a son, it was a daughter, Georgy, who was born in 1809. Margaret, who came of age that year and had succeeded to her estates, continued to live at the Keith houses at 45 Harley Street

London, Purbrook Lodge in Hampshire and Meikleour in Scotland, though she had her own independent income and staff.

Meanwhile, Queeney, who was a patroness of Almack's[7] and loved entertaining, encouraged Margaret to enjoy balls and fêtes, and wear smart clothes. They got on so well that Margaret relied on her to buy French gloves, silk handkerchiefs, bonnets, and a new gown to wear at a ball held in honour of the Emperor Alexander in June 1814. In return, Margaret entertained her father and Queeney with glowing accounts of the emperor, the festivities, held "morning, noon and night" and described the other foreign visitors, who included the King of Prussia,

> a good looking man but is either mad, stupid or melancholy,
> he stalks around continually without speaking to anybody or
> appearing to hear or see or understand what is going on
> nothing can be more uncouth,

and commented on the most attractive

> Six Princes of Prussia all particularly handsome and
> agreeable in their manners – 2 sons, 2 brothers, a nephew and
> a cousin, Prince Augustus the handsomest man I ever saw
> (please tell Lady K[eith] he is quite her style) 2 Princes of
> Wurtemberg, Duke of Saxe Weimar, Prince Charles of
> Mecklenberg, Prince of Bavaria, Prince Radziwill, a beautiful
> Prince of Saxe Coburg who I think might also endanger
> Lady K's peace of mind were she to see him.

This easy going, slightly teasing relationship was threatened during the crisis over Margaret's marriage to Charles de Flahaut, but when it was over she thanked Queeney for "the sentiments of friendship and kindness which you formerly professed towards me and which contributed so much to my happiness during the nine years I remained under your roof".

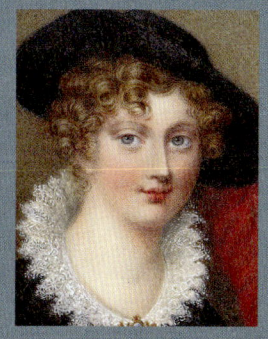

CHAPTER 2

Friendship with Princess Charlotte

The fair-hair'd Daughter of the Isles . . .
The love of millions! How did we intrust
Futurity to her!

Lord Byron, *Childe Harold's Pilgrimage*, Canto IV, stanza CLXX

In 1811, the 23-year-old Margaret, firmly established in London society, began an important but demanding friendship with the 15-year-old Princess Charlotte, daughter of the Prince Regent, future George IV, and his estranged wife, Princess Caroline of Brunswick-Wolfenbüttel. The two young women may have got to know each other either through Admiral Keith, who in 1809 was appointed treasurer to the household of the Regent's younger brother, the Duke of Clarence, and future William IV, or through William Adam, adviser to the latter, married to Margaret's aunt Eleonor, and a great favourite with Princess Charlotte. While the Prince Regent was never entirely happy about Margaret's influence on his daughter because of her Whig politics, most people, such as Lord Yarmouth, considered her an "agreeable, clever and a very proper intimate", implying that she not only had brains but also the excellent manners required of a companion to royalty.

As for the young Princess Charlotte, the Grand Duchess Ekaterina, visiting London with her brother, the Emperor Alexander I, thought her quite the most interesting of all the women in the British royal family:

> She is a little shorter than I, too big made, especially about the hips, fair, fresh, appetising as need be, fine arms, pretty feet, great, intelligent eyes of pale blue, though with at times the fixed look of the House of Brunswick, fair-haired, a good nose, delightful mouth and good teeth, some slight marks of small-pox, scarcely to be seen, much wit and doggedness in her nature, seeming to have a will of bronze in the least things, a searching reasoning power and manners so odd that

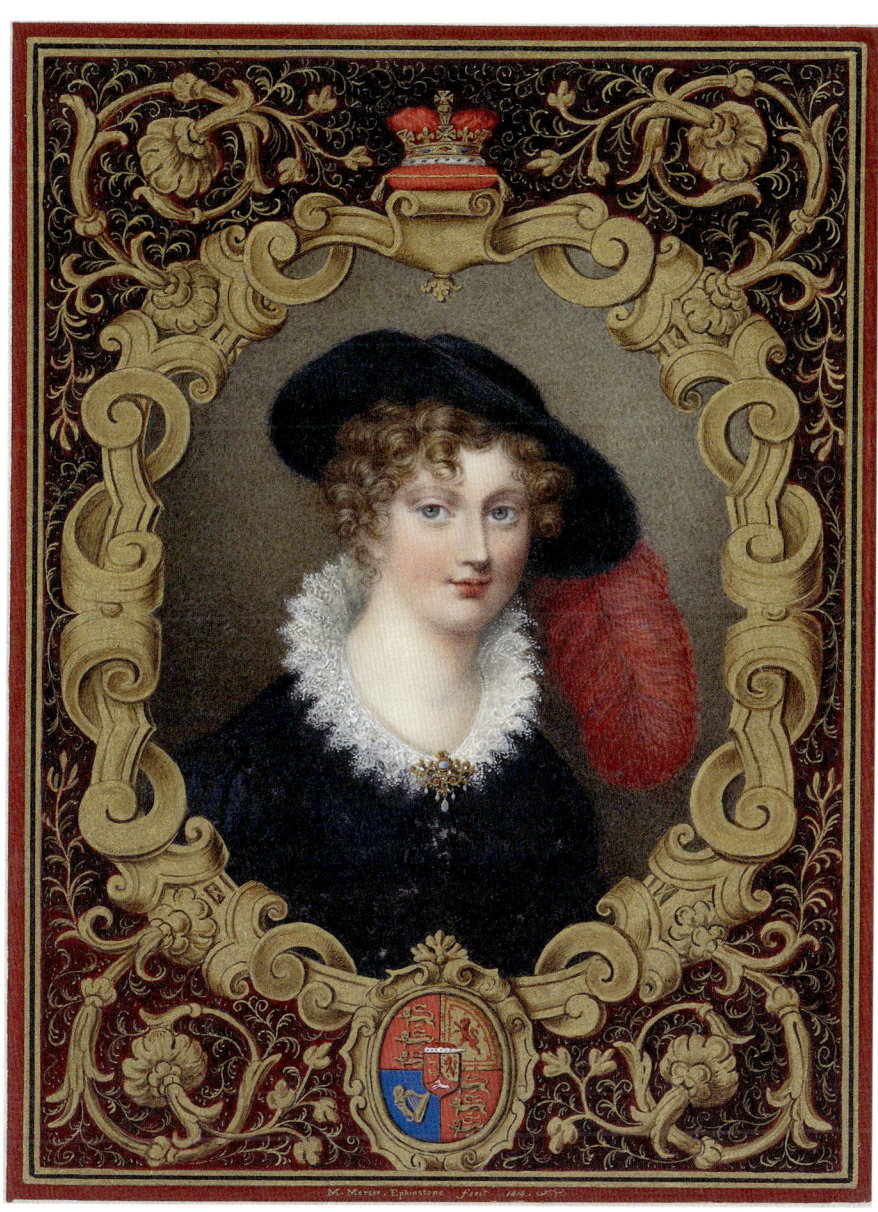

4 Miniature of Princess Charlotte by Margaret

they take your breath away; no exaggeration I vow to you. She goes up to each man, young or old no matter, or more properly the latter have the preference, and takes his hand which she shakes with all her might, and she seems to have a good deal of it. In walking, she takes bounds or strides so that you don't know which way to look, her clothes cling to her and don't come down to the calf, so that at every movement they threaten to let the knee be seen. She looks like a boy, or rather, a young rascal dressed as a girl. I swear to you I am within the truth, far from exceeding it. She is seductive, and it is a crime to have let her acquire such ways.[1]

Shamefully neglected by an indifferent father and irresponsible mother, disliking her grandmother Queen Charlotte, suspicious of her father's four unmarried sisters, Charlotte led an isolated and unhappy existence at Warwick House, her London residence. She made friends with Whig politicians, such as Henry Brougham and Samuel Whitbread, who might support her in battles with father, and took to Margaret immediately. When they could not be together, Charlotte poured out her devotion in letters. Hearing that Margaret had chilblains she wrote:

I wish I could fly in a little birdcage as I would be a very good nurse and take a great deal of care of you,

and when a visit was cancelled in 1811 she expressed her

... deep disappointment at not seeing you tomorrow. I have often said how much happiness seeing you gives me but now I feel it more than ever. Your kindness to me will be in my solitary hours and reflections most soothing, and may I add, the hope of not being forgotten nor out of your memory ... you will never be out of mine and that on my return I shall with open arms receive the one I love so dearly.

Charlotte, who resented being "always on the road", complained in August 1812 from Lower Lodge, Windsor:

> My residence is deplorable and irksome deprived of all
> possibility of seeing my friends, surrounded by spies that
> detail everything and surrounded by people who can neither
> be trusted or liked – a perfect prison.

Forbidden by her father to dine with her mother, Princess Caroline, on her birthday, she confided:

> She is still my mother whether acting right or wrong and I
> cannot bear to think of her unhappy, for too well do I know
> the smarts and cuttings of a wounded heart not to feel for her
> or anyone that has a secret grief preying on them.

Desperately lonely, she longed for Margaret to reply; "I tear every letter open expecting it from you", and declared that their friendship consoled her "for the bitter pills I have to swallow".[2]

Not only did Margaret and the princess, who in her own words, was "a decided Jacobin", share the same Whig political views but they had much else in common. Charlotte asked Margaret to "Recommend a piece of music that you like, that I may follow your taste, your advice in everything", and they discussed the merits of the Italian Angelica Catalani as a singer and individual. Books were another common interest, and Charlotte asked, "Reading is now a great passion of mine . . . can you recommend any books both serious and light?" When Margaret lent her copy of *The Life of Sir John Moore*, about the hero of the Peninsular War, in return Charlotte offered the correspondence of Denis Diderot with Baron von Grimm, and the history of France by Charles de Lacretelle. Greatly interested in Jane Austen's *Sense and Sensibility*, Charlotte said it made her feel "quite one of the company and very like the character of the 'imprudent' Mary Anne, though I am not so good".

Both were fascinated by Lord Byron, and seized on each new publication. Captivated by the *Bride of Abydos*, Charlotte went over it twice in one sitting, and felt so strongly about his "new and best poem *The Corsair*" that she sent Margaret an advance copy; "I cannot resist being the first person from whom you will receive it – and read its passages written in gold". Smitten by Byron's appearance as well as his poetry she continued:

> Have you seen new print just come out of Lord B? I have got
> it and look at it very often. I admire it so much and think it so
> very beautiful. I try to trace the man and his mind in it but
> cannot: it belies what he is, for it looks so loving and loveable
> & something so very much above the common sort of beauty
> or what is regularly handsome.

Later, she promised to send Margaret a cast of Lord Byron's bust. Ever more
dependent, she could not make a decision on her own without referring to
Margaret, and when offered studio copies of the Van Dyck portraits of
Charles I, Henrietta Maria, their three children and dog, consulted her before
buying them. Throughout their correspondence she appealed to the lively
minded Margaret for an opinion not just on literature and works of art but
on everyone and everything, from the intellect of her uncle, the Duke of
Sussex, to her choice of jewellery. They shared the same taste in clothes, and
were painted wearing identical Russian-style dresses.

Bereft of family support, Charlotte opened her heart to Margaret:

> I most firmly believe that there are few if any thoughts of
> mine concealed from you. You know how entirely I consulted
> you . . . at all times you entered into it so fully – perfect and
> undisguised confidence – I feel justice and truth of your
> observations.

This trust inevitably involved Margaret in the princess's love affairs, and here
she had to tread very carefully indeed. The first crisis came in 1812 when,
encouraged by her irresponsible mother, Charlotte fell for Captain Charles
Hesse (1792–1832), reputed son of the Duke of York by a German lady of
high rank. After their first meeting at Windsor, where he was serving in the
18th Hussars, they saw each other in London and exchanged letters. When
the affair, "this unfortunate folly of mine", had blown over, Charlotte, who
had prudently burnt his letters, wanted him to return hers, "the living records
of my weakness". She begged Margaret to help and enlist the support of
Admiral Keith. Yet, in spite of the pressure put on him by the redoubtable
admiral and his daughter, Hesse proved very reluctant to co-operate, leaving
letters unanswered or else making excuses for not complying. After denying

the existence of the letters, he said that they were in the safekeeping of a friend. He went on to hint at blackmail in a letter of 11 March 1816 and demanded that the admiral arrange sea passages for him so he could meet Charlotte's mother in Italy.[3]

While Margaret and her father were still making every effort to persuade Hesse, Charlotte confessed their flirtation to her father. Alarmed by the revelation, determined to remove her from the baleful influence of her mother, the Prince Regent decided that it was time for her to marry. Her husband was to be the Prince of Orange (1792–1849, later William II of the Netherlands), who as an undersized "little hero" of the Peninsular War, had arrived in London on 7 September 1813 with dispatches from the Duke of Wellington. Anxious to strengthen the connection with the Netherlands, and supported by the Government, the young prince had emerged as the most suitable candidate. Although he was considered "excessively plain, thin as a needle, with fair hair, brown burnt skin, eyes with no expression at all, and his fine teeth stick out excessively in front", Charlotte accepted him on 12 December at a Carlton House dinner. The marriage seemed to offer a welcome escape from her father's domination, as she explained to Margaret:

> God knows I have never been happy in my life and I have
> had every object of my love taken from me by force or by
> artifice or unforeseen fate and have rather proved a source of
> misery to me than happiness but considering the life of
> seclusion of deprivation and of ill treatment and being a man
> of good character and principle it is at least a change for the
> better as I shall not be as much confined and as obliged to
> submit to every caprice of the Prince and his family.

Two days later, the Prince Regent informed his mother, Queen Charlotte, of the proposed alliance and the couple exchanged portraits, rings and other "remembrances".

However, a problem arose over the time and duration of the princess's residence in Holland each year. Charlotte turned once again for advice from Margaret, who had already questioned "the necessity of marrying one man to apologise for writing love letters to another" and had her doubts about the proposed bridegroom. The situation was so serious that Margaret then turned to the Whig statesman Lord Grey for guidance. This had to be done in secret because the Prince Regent detested Lord Grey for his politics. Yet for Margaret the consequences of this consultation were far reaching as it led to her great friendship with Lord and Lady Grey and brought her right into the centre of the Whig party socially and politically.[4] On the subject of Princess Charlotte's difficulties Lord Grey advised caution. However, he was clear that spending half the year in Holland was unacceptable, and that the terms of residence abroad should be decided by the princess herself. He emphasized that her principal home must be in England since she had had such limited opportunities of getting to know the society of which she would one day be head. He also pointed to the dangers of the unsettled state of Holland. While the negotiations continued, Margaret found herself shouldering the full burden of advising Charlotte. As she told her father:

> I have a difficult part to play, she leaves everything to
> me. I feel uneasy at the situation she places me in and the
> responsibility attached to it but I am consoled by the certainty
> that if I withdrew or shrank from it in the least degree she
> would fall into the hands of worse advisers and probably be
> the victim of her mother's dangerous and vindictive plans.

Meanwhile, the Prince of Orange did not help his cause by getting drunk on various public occasions as well as at dinner at Carlton House. His undignified behaviour, combined with the debates on the subject of residence not being resolved, gave the princess an excuse to break off their engagement on 18 June 1814.[5] Predictably, the Prince Regent reacted to the ending of the engagement with "violent displeasure, grief and astonishment", and, believing that the princess was surrounded by bad advisers he decided to dismiss her entire household and banish her to Windsor. Charlotte panicked, and during the night of 12 July ran away to join her mother at her house in Connaught Place. After a night of drama, her uncle, the Duke of York, together with Margaret, persuaded her to return home to Warwick House. There she was subjected to further repression; as Margaret duly reported the next day: "Something very unpleasant has happened. Poor Princess Charlotte is treated with utmost hardship and is in the most cruel situation imaginable". Many years later Margaret gave the diarist, Henry Greville, a full account of this famous flight, and told him that the Prince Regent, who had always disliked her, was much more civil after it.[6] As for Charlotte, recognizing how much she owed to Margaret's tact and diplomacy, wrote, "Never can I express half I feel towards you nor my deep sense of obligation."

As Charlotte's confidante, Margaret was one of the few who knew that the real reason for the ending of the engagement with the Prince of Orange was that only nine days before she had met Prince Frederick of Prussia (1794–1863) and fallen madly in love with him. One of six handsome princes of Prussia, he had arrived in England in June 1814 with the victorious Allied sovereigns led by the Emperor of Russia to be entertained to a round of celebrations, fêtes and receptions. Young and flattered, he encouraged the princess, who remained hopelessly attached to him, waiting anxiously for letters after he returned to Germany. Although Charlotte told Margaret that she would continue "to love Frederick long after he may have ceased to think of or to regard me", yet when she learnt – from Margaret – that he had decided to break off their correspondence, she declared: "He is dead for ever to me now."

Even before the dénouement, Charlotte, recognizing that marriage was the only means of escape from her miserable situation, had admitted to Margaret that if she were disappointed by Frederick, then "the Prince of Saxe Cobourg decidedly would be accepted by me in preference to any other Prince that I have seen". This candidate was the handsome Leopold of Saxe-Coburg who on 14 July 1814 had made clear his desire to marry when he accompanied the Emperor Alexander to London, but had been ignored on account of Charlotte's sudden passion for Prince Frederick.

He had also been suspected by her father, angry at the breaking off of the Orange marriage, as having been received at Warwick House as an aspirant, encouraged by the governess, Miss Knight.[7] As Charlotte begged her to "Assist me with your good head, advice and heart", for the last time, Margaret was obliged to act as an intermediary, though now with the full support of the Duke and Duchess of York. It was not so easy to make any contact with Prince Leopold, who, while attending the Congress of Vienna, on hearing the news of Napoleon's escape from Elba had immediately returned to his Russian regiment of the Grand Duke Constantine's cuirassiers.

Not until after Waterloo (18 June 1815) could Margaret suggest he come

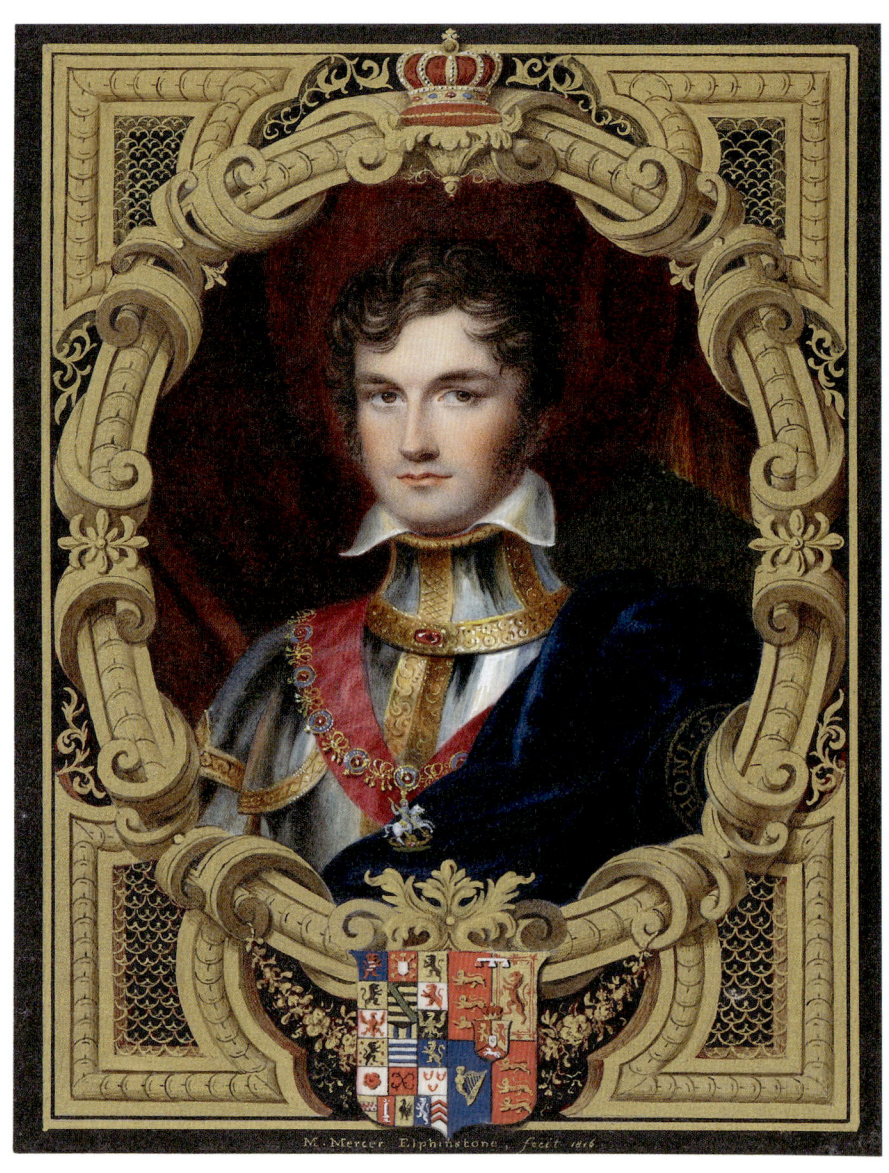

5 Miniature of Prince Leopold by Margaret

to England, an invitation which was followed on 26 July by a letter from Charlotte herself. As the cunning Leopold took his time before replying, Charlotte urged Margaret to "make him write to you soon, and never forget to let me know when you hear". On receiving the letter he finally sent, she was delighted and hoped he would come to England soon "to push the matter further". However, as Leopold continued to take his time and Charlotte, fearing that he had been hearing rumours about her, instructed Margaret "to see him for me. You have done everything for me, therefore I have only to entreat you will continue to do so, and leave no doubts, no tales uncleared or undiscovered to him." Ignoring Margaret's appeals, he still refused to commit himself to a visit, leaving Charlotte annoyed because "he has danced us ladies up and down for him when he has done nothing himself in turn". On 14 November Margaret asked Lady Grey to inform her husband that she had not "heard one word of Prince Leopold since I last wrote to him. It seems very singular that he should have given up his intention of coming to England without accounting for it after having so positively announced it. Princess Charlotte is extremely fidgety about it."[8] They were left in suspense until, after having received formal invitations from both the Prince Regent, written on 10 January 1816, and from Charlotte, Leopold appeared in London on 21 February 1816. Thereafter, all went smoothly, the young couple were delighted with each other, Parliament voted them a handsome establishment and they married on 2 May at Carlton House at a private ceremony, as was then customary.

Margaret, who had done so much to bring this about and had risked involving herself in a royal-family quarrel by helping Charlotte resist the Orange marriage, now found that their friendship was coming to an end. Warned by the Prince Regent that Charlotte was too easily influenced by female friends and advice, Leopold determined that he should be in total control of his wife. He acted quickly, for as early as 26 February 1816, on his instructions, Charlotte reproved Margaret for her "intimacy with de Flahaut. He knows him personally and disapproves highly of him and thinks his acquaintance is likely to do you no good, altho' he readily admits his many agréments in society." Although in the next letter of 2 March Charlotte affirmed: "You know I must love you always just as much and just the same independently of who you live with", they were seeing far less of each other. In the months leading up to Charlotte's death in childbirth on 6 November

1817 there was a further bone of contention when Margaret refused to return the 575 letters sent her by the princess, feeling that as they fully justified her conduct, especially during the negotiations over the Orange marriage, she might need them should she ever be accused of meddling in affairs of state. According to Queeney, Lady Keith, Margaret's stepmother, the princess

> has been awakened to the danger of letting the volumes of letters which she used to write and which would fill a large folio I have no doubt get into hands of such people as this man and his mother who have lived by and upon intrigues of court and know to an atom the value of such.

After this hostile reference to Margaret's suitor, Charles de Flahaut, and to his mother, Adèle, she continued:

> How often have I longed to put them on the fire when they arrived knowing well that she [the princess] would be rejoiced at some future time if I had done so.[9]

Lord Keith was also of this opinion, calling Margaret's refusal "a blackguard business". In the hope of getting her letters returned, the princess invited Margaret at least once to dine and sleep in the couple's beautiful home at Claremont near Esher in Surrey. Margaret stood firm and by June 1817 the princess was so upset that she refused to have any further communications with her.

After Charlotte died in November 1817, Leopold did not give up, claiming ownership of an oil portrait of the princess as well as the letters, but Margaret remained adamant. Now married to Charles de Flahaut, she told Lady Grey in June 1818 that Prince Leopold, who had offered to give her a miniature of Princess Charlotte by George Sanders, had also suggested that "she and Lord Grey will now think it right to deliver the letters of the Princess". She went on:

> In this, however, he is mistaken, for I shall neither receive the miniature from Prince Leopold nor deliver the letters to him. I have the only miniature which Princess Charlotte ever sat

for to Sanders and half a dozen others which she gave me herself and which are valuable to me as her gifts: for the same reason I wished to have the oil painting which for so many years I considered my own and if Prince Leopold has not the honour or feeling to give it to me, I can only say that I think myself very ill used and I feel rather obliged to him for confirming my bad opinion and dislike of him. As for the letters I am now determined to keep them as memorials of his ingratitude. Therefore I do beg that Lord Grey will not 'think it right' for me to give them to this odious man. You see I am very angry so perhaps I had better leave off.[10]

The dispute which continued for some years, culminated in an agreement that the boxes of letters should be kept in a bank, the keys to be kept by Lord Grey. Nonetheless, they remained in Margaret's possession and were part of the archive of her descendants, the marquesses of Lansdowne until acquired by the British Library.[11]

Leopold, who never forgave her, refused to acknowledge the part Margaret had played in bringing about his marriage, and continued to dismiss her as a bad influence. As late as May 1845, when, as King of the Belgians, he sent his niece, Queen Victoria, a miniature of Princess Charlotte as a birthday present, he stated that although the princess

> was particularly determined to be a *good* and *obedient* wife, some of her friends were anxious she should *not*: amongst these Madame de Flahaut must be mentioned *en première ligne*. This became even a subject which severed the intimacy between them. Madame de Flahaut who was much older than Charlotte and of a sour and determined character, had gained an influence which partook on Charlotte's part a little of fear. She was afraid of her but when once supported took courage.[12]

His attack, intended to prejudice Queen Victoria against her, fully justifies Margaret's decision to keep the letters, which provide incontrovertible proof of her disinterested, responsible and loving relationship with the unhappy princess. Two months after the death of Lord Grey in July the same year, Leopold tried again, asking whether the letters contained "accurate though rather hard opinions on contemporary events". Three days later Margaret assured him that she had destroyed any such as he described, and declared that she had kept only those that "me touchent personnellement" [concern me].[13]

For the rest of her life, Margaret, who much regretted the premature death of the princess, treasured mementoes of their friendship. She set a cameo portrait of the princess in the clasp of her pearls and to the end of her life wore a bracelet containing a miniature and a locket containing her hair. On 15 May [1858], when ill in bed, on the birthday of her eldest daughter, Emily, she parted with another royal souvenir as a remembrance. It was, she wrote,

> . . . the last gift I received from poor P[ss] Charlotte on her
> marriage – it will be only of historical interest to you, but to
> me was the sad memento of the close of a devoted and deep
> attachment that had existed between us for eight years!
> Receive it kindly and value it, for it came from one of the best
> of hearts, and grandest natures that God ever created. Alas!
> There was no one to clean away the weeds, which grow on
> the same soil, and checked a perfect development.

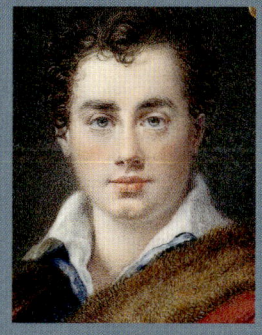

CHAPTER 3

Margaret's Man Friends and Suitors

Adieu dear maid! I must not speak
Whate'er my secret thoughts may be;
Though thou art all that man can seek
I dare not talk of Love to thee

Lord Byron, *Love and Gold*

While guiding Princess Charlotte through her entanglements until finally seeing her married, Margaret also had to deal with suitors of her own. As the daughter of Admiral Lord Keith, with a large fortune, "not handsome but with fine and gentle eyes, attractive, not at all shy", she was exceptionally well placed in London society to find a suitable husband. However, this took her a long time. Named "The Fop's Despair", because she had rejected so many offers, she inspired the character of Miss Broadhurst in Maria Edgeworth's novel *The Absentee* (1812). This fictional heiress also "had received all the advantages of education which money could procure, and had profited by them in a manner uncommon among those for whom they are purchased in such abundance; she not only had had many masters, and read many books, but had thought of what she read, and had supplied, by the strength and energy of her own mind, what cannot be acquired by the assistance of masters." . . . She "might marry whom she pleased . . . she was the person to decide and reject . . . every thing was to depend upon her . . . inclinations". She wanted a lover, not a suitor, but had "too lofty and independent a spirit to stoop to coquetry . . . perfectly aware of her want of beauty, yet with a just sense of her own merit . . ."

In 1811, Margaret turned down the Duke of Clarence, later William IV, and her name was also linked with the Duke of Gloucester (1776–1834) and with Lord Dundonald Cochrane – all men of rank who needed to marry money. There were others too, and after visiting Downham Hall as guest of the Assheton family she told her daughter Emily on 21 November 1850, "It is the ugliest country I ever saw but the House has been rebuilt and is comfortable. I looked at the place with some curiosity and thought how I

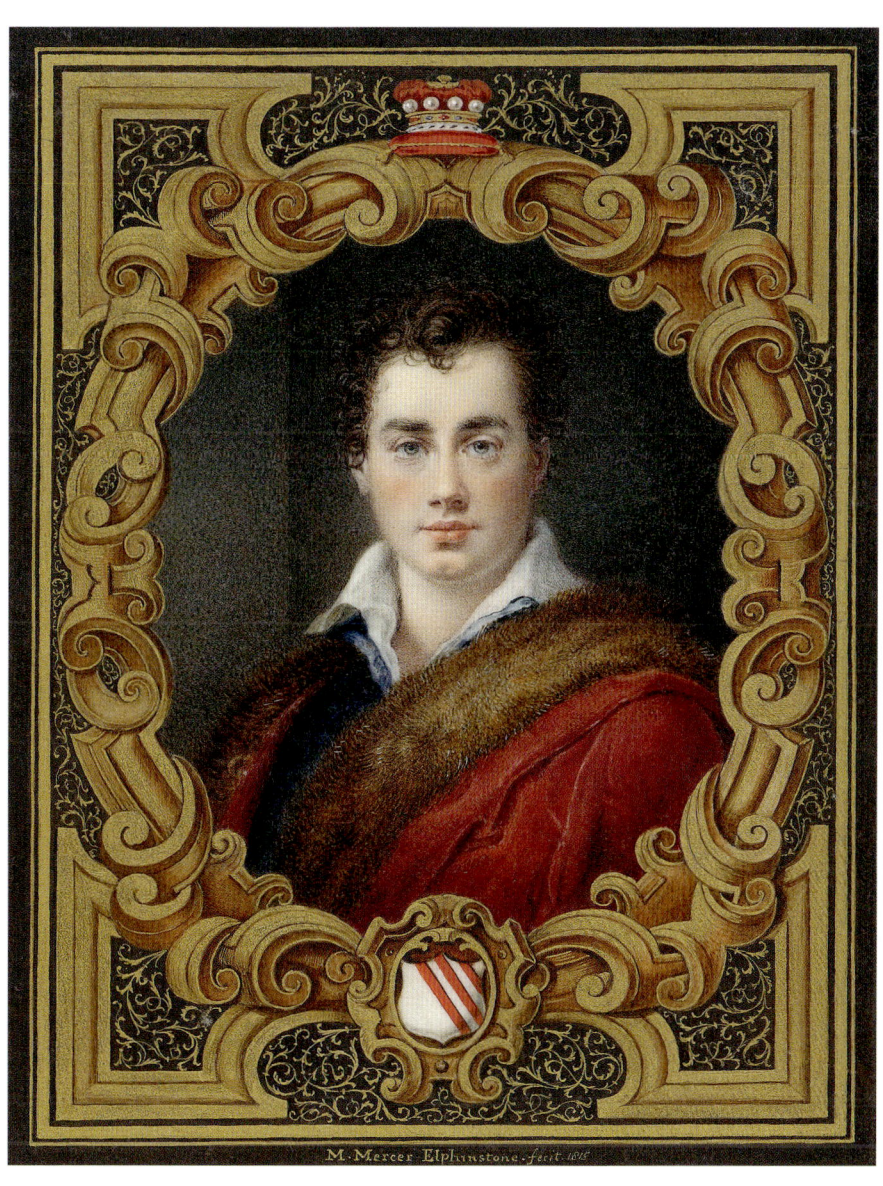

6 **Miniature of Lord Byron by Margaret**

should have hated it if I had accepted Col. Cadogan's kind offer of becoming its mistress!"

It is clear from his satirical account of London society in *Don Juan* that Byron sympathized with the heiresses in the "Smithfield Show", or marriage market, targeted by the fortune-hunters who, he wrote,

> Buzz round "the Fortune" with their busy battery,
> To turn her head with waltzing and with flattery!

continuing:

> While the poor rich wretch, object of these cares,
> Has cause to wish her sire had had male heirs

and concluding:

> Some are soon bagg'd, and some reject three dozen
> 'Tis fine to see them scattering refusals[1]

It is therefore not surprising that even at the height of his fame, Byron should have felt that Margaret's wealth imposed an insurmountable barrier between them, as he expresses in his poem *Love and Gold* (1813): "Adieu dear maid! I must not speak / Whate'er my secret thoughts may be; / Though thou art all that man can seek / I dare not talk of Love to *thee*". After they first met in Melbourne House, the "young and free and fair" Margaret seems to have given him every encouragement. Declaring himself "Half a Scot by birth and bred / A whole one", Byron had much in common with Margaret. They shared the same Whig politics, both disliked the Duke of Wellington, the "Great Captain", and "best of cut-throats", and came to admire Napoleon's character and career. In July 1812, after Byron complained in a letter that London was dull, she invited him to join her in Tunbridge Wells, and accompany

> . . . our expeditions mounted on donkies [*sic*] with Swiss
> saddles and followed by two or three little boys and half a
> dozen dogs – I have left all my late hours and whirligig

propensities to my friends in London while I accommodate myself to the more wholesome fashions of this place getting up at 8 o'clock and going to bed at 10, by which means I find my appetite has got far beyond the prohibited wing of chicken.

On 3 August he announced that he "will set out for Mecca or Tunbridge Wednesday . . . I shall not much embarrass myself with the brilliant society at Tunbridge but I shall do honour to your donkey cavalcade in which I may most appropriately join".[2]

Nothing is known of what followed except that their correspondence continued. On 3 May 1814 from 2 Albany he sent her the "Albanian costume. It is put on in a few minutes. If you like the dress – keep it," and he explained his reluctance to pursue her:

> You must recollect that from your situation you can never be sure you have a friend (as somebody has said of sovereigns I believe) and that any apparent anxiety on my part to cultivate your acquaintance might have appeared to yourself like importunity – and as I happen to know – would have been attributed to a motive not very creditable to me – and agreeable to neither.

She replied:

> How can I thank you half enough for your note and the splendid dress you have been so kind as to send me with it. My eyes are quite dazzled with its beauty but I really do not have the impudence to keep it though I feel equally grateful to you for offering it to me.

And acknowledging his avowal wrote:

> . . . the latter part of your letter is too flattering for me not to thank you most sensibly for it. I am but too well aware of the desagrements of our situation. I am certain no woman of real

feeling could value such a one. However, with regard to our
acquaintance I can only say that I must ever think of it with
pleasure and trust that all the nonsense that has been said or
may be said will not prevent its continuance.[3]

Margaret showed her independent spirit in an incident which occurred
at Lady Jersey's party on 8 April 1816, after the scandal of Byron's separation
from his wife.

Byron's entry was the signal for 'Countesses and ladies of
fashion' to leave the room 'in crowds'. Only one woman,
besides his hostess, consented to speak to him. As he stood
leaning against a mantelpiece, lonely and defiant, and heard
the petticoats of outraged fashion go sweeping past, 'a little
red-haired, bright-eyed coquette' – Miss Mercer Elphinstone
– 'came flirting up . . . and with a look that was exquisitely
insolent, said, "You had better have married me. I would
have managed you better."'[4]

Byron agreed, and later that month on his departure from England, he
gave her one of his Harrow school prizes – a copy of the poetry of Virgil –
for her loyalty and friendship, and wrote, again implying that he feared being
accused of fortune-hunting:

I thank you truly for y[r]. kind acceptance of my memorial,
more particularly as I felt a little apprehensive that I was
taking a liberty of which you might disapprove. A more
useless friend you could not have but still a very sincere and
by no means a new one – although from circumstances you
never knew (nor would it have pleased you to know how
much . . .). These have long ceased to exist – I breathe more
freely on this point – because now no motive can be
attributed to me with regard to you of a selfish nature . . .
neither my vanity nor my wishes ever induced me at any time
to suppose that I by any chance have become more to you
than I now am . . . This may account for you for that which –

however little worth accounting for, must otherwise appear inexplicable in our former acquaintance I mean those 'intermittents'.[5]

She thanked him:

> As you already know the desire I have to possess any volume that had occupied a place in your library, it is needless for me to repeat it, still less how much I must value this one chosen by your own hand and in a way so flattering!

Before boarding ship, he asked his friend Scrope Davies to "Tell her that had I been fortunate enough to marry a woman like her I should not now be obliged to exile myself from this country",[6] and in a letter to the poet Thomas Moore admitted that he had always loved her and "always shall, not only because I really did feel attracted to her personally but because she and about a dozen others of that sex were all who stuck by me in that grand conflict of 1815".[7]

Another reference to her appears in his poem *Don Juan*, as Haidée: "greatest heiress of Eastern lands / Rejected several suitors just to learn / How to accept a better in his turn". Margaret spoke of him many times afterwards in Paris, and in January 1867 told her eldest daughter Emily that she had had a correspondence and a visit from the tactless Mad[me] d'Haussonville,

> more inquisitive than friendly, who is writing a notice on the life of Lord Byron, and has put me to the question as to my rapports with him!

She then related the conversation:

> Did he want to marry you? Did you turn him down? What was he really like? Was he really so good looking and fascinating etc. etc.

Her answer was:

> . . . I have always been proud to have been his friend and
> deeply appreciative of the last sad token he sent me, writing
> a touching letter of farewell when about to leave England
> for ever.[8]

It is impossible to guess how many were attracted to her as she kept letters from only two of her suitors. Certainly, these two were so very different that we can only assume that her appeal must have been wide-ranging. The first was a highly civilized man of the world, the Russian Aleksandr Antonovich, Count Balmain, whom she met at the receptions given in honour of Alexander I by Princess Lieven, wife of the Russian ambassador in 1814. Descended from the Ramsay family of Balmain, Jacobites loyal to James II who emigrated to Russia, Balmain, with his Scottish sense of humour and lively wit was a great social success.[9] A friend of her cousins Clementina Sarah and Peter Burrell, he admired how Margaret waltzed and danced the polonaises of Saint Petersburg when they were together at Brighton. However, he complained, in excellent French, that she was always surrounded by friends "whose presence intimidated him so much that he hardly dared even look in her direction". These circumstances making it difficult to converse, he proposed to her, somewhat apprehensively, in a letter, 5 October 1814:

> Since you are already aware of my feelings, which are only
> too well known, and they deserve, if not your approval, at
> least your sympathy, then kindly let me open my heart to you.
> Today I have no other intention but to put my fate in your
> hands – in other words, to decide on my future – and while it
> will be painful for me to hear the 'No' I am expecting, yet I
> prefer this misery to the torments of uncertainty and
> therefore beg you to be frank with me.

When Margaret turned him down, he replied:

> I was glad to get the assurance of your friendship and
> promise that mine, which I offer in return, will remain
> sincere and will never be found wanting. I shall be

impatiently awaiting your return to London.

However, on the same date he confessed his disappointment to Margaret's cousin, Clementina Sarah Burrell:

> As promised I accept the decision of Miss Mercer as final, and can only reproach her for the disdainful manner in which she disposed of me, as if I was no more than a nuisance who could not be gently treated in case I began bothering her all over again. It is my own fault for not taking to heart Mr. Sayn's warning, but at least I shall never have to reproach myself for not being hurt by your cousin's attitude to me.[10]

Shortly after this he was appointed Russian Commissioner on the island of Saint Helena, where he married Miss Johnson, the stepdaughter of Sir Hudson Lowe, the governor during Napoleon's captivity. On the boat to Saint Helena he made an excellent impression on Margaret's cousin, Lady Malcolm, who wrote home: "Balmain has conducted himself with more good sense and propriety than any of them . . . Everybody likes Balmain, clever, interesting, and perfectly well bred . . . a superior man".[11]

More persistent was Count Bothmer, from Mecklenberg-Schwerin, of the King's German Legion, a great enthusiast for all that was English. His approach, direct and clumsily expressed, was quite different from that of his elegant and correct Russian rival. He first saw her in August 1806 at the Canterbury races, then at a ball in Ramsgate, and after leaving her at Petersfield proclaimed his devotion:

> Celestial girl, divine farewell. Never, for the rest of my life, shall I forget the sight of your eyes and that divine curtsy as you bade me goodbye. My thoughts will always be with you, and I hope that you will always be happy in this paradise which is England, and that when I am dead and buried for the benefit of mankind that you will remember me as one not destined to enjoy the fruits of peace. With all my adoration and deepest respect.

He sent her the latest German waltzes, which from 1813 had supplanted the French quadrille, the traditional English country dances, Scotch steps and the occasional Highland reel in the ballrooms of London. There were also other well-chosen gifts, whose significance he explained in broken English:

> The ink-horn is from Gibraltar made from that ancient rock, the melon seeds, the incense powder, belonging to the roman katholic religion, the whist-marks (Spanish pesa doros) & the music from the Isle of Leon and Cadix . . . Between the music are two Spanish favourite marches with songs, but only the principal ton; I could them not translated for the pianoforte. I am no more musician enough to arrange them for other instruments and I thought it would be for you a little satisfaction to be the first Lady, who got this music before I brought such in other hands. I hope in a short time I shall have the honour to deliver to you some Fandango's or Bolero's, or from Germany and France new music.

In 1810 he was obliged to return to Germany but after the death of his brother he inherited the family estates and proposed to Margaret, his tutelary deity, in the following letter:

> My lady,
> I hope you will recollect me or mine existence as officer in the King's German Legion, since the year 1806 than it was the first time that I did see you at the Canterbury races in the month of August; in the same year I went by an election in the month of November, from our quarters with the second regiment of light dragoons King's German Legion to Ramsgate, where I got the honour at the ball & the high place where our band was playing to see you again I didn't speak your language well enough to let me present to you. Since that period my mind saw you always but never my eyes again till the year 1811 I remained in the English service then I went home & took service in the Russian army. I have had the

happiness to save [serve] you & your own country & since that time I have been so lucky to make a very good fortune, to be one of the first men of this part of Germany & now I can wish to know if it is allowed for you to give your hand to a foreigner. Europe is now liberated & I am now through the death of my brother in such a happy situation that I can beg for the hand of a fortunate [rich] Lady . . . My lady are you free, could you give your hand to a foreigner, then tell it to me with some lines. I [take it upon?] myself to make your acquaintance to show my endeavour to gain your friendship & love. I flatter myself to have gained your estime & affection . . . I saved [served] the Kingdom in stopping the theatre tumult at Coventgarden & many other dangers, I did show very often how dearly England was to me . . . I did give, 6 months before Bonaparte escaped from the Isle of Elba the first advice to the prince regent & the first idea to him to send him for the tranquility [sic] of the world to St Helena. Pray lovely Miss have the gracious kindness to give to me a few words for answer. I beg you tau send [sic] pardons that I speak so much about me, but I wish to gain your favour blessing [. . .?] to have the gracious permission to do homage to you & to undersign as your greatest venerator."[12]

In contrast to this persistent pursuit, it was Margaret who took the initiative in her relationship with the 6th Duke of Devonshire (1790–1858), the greatest parti in England, for she really did set her cap at Byron's "cautious Duke". At the Whig houses they both frequented and where they might enjoy waltzing together, he and Margaret could meet as equals – no one could accuse him of being a fortune-hunter! He cut a romantic figure, and at the coronation of William IV in 1831, according to Lord Macaulay, "looked as if he came to be crowned instead of his master. I never saw so princely a manner and air". In the opinion of the 9th Duke of Argyll, writing in his *Passages from the Past*, he was

the model of the old English noble of his time. Very tall, very benignant, full of poetic spirit, delighting in doing good, full

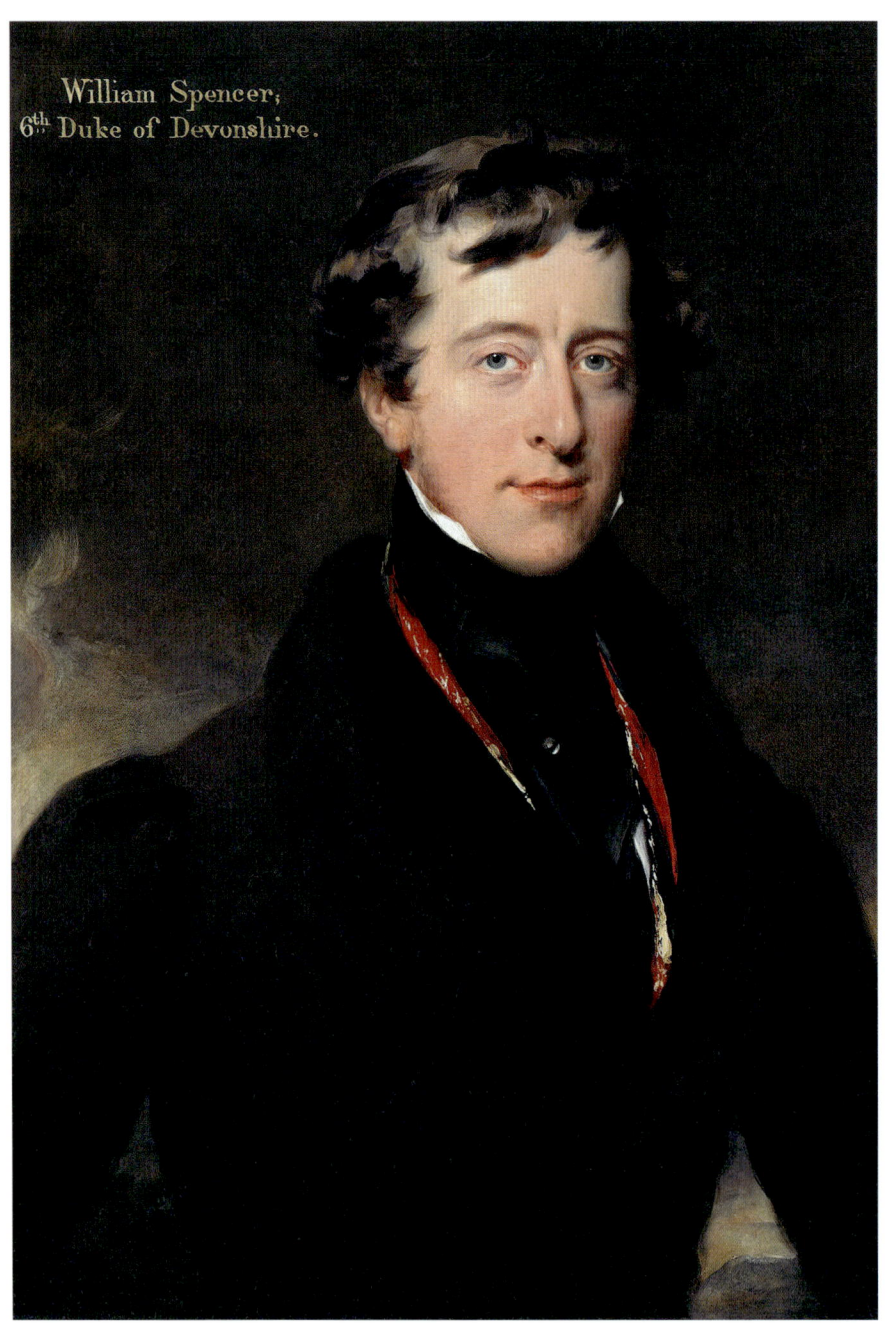

William Spencer,
6th Duke of Devonshire.

of schemes for the improvement of the people on his immense property and generous almost to a fault, and to his own kith and kin, however remote, he was an earthly providence.

Rumours about their friendship reached such a pitch that on 17 January 1814 Princess Charlotte, who knew the duke very well, but was not attracted to him herself, advised Margaret: "For heaven's sake do not mind the abominable and wicked reports of London about yourself and D o D. I should hope London and the old greedy mothers will be more charitable this season." She must have made her intentions too obvious as the publisher John Murray told Byron that the "Grand Duke Nicholas has enchanted everyone and has just gone carrying off with him the Duke of Devonshire – to the great grief of Miss Mercer who has never smiled since". The duke's sister Harriet, married to Lord Granville, the future ambassador in Paris, approved his efforts to extricate himself from the flirtation, writing on 17 July 1815:

> My brother was very good and gave no encouragement to
> Poor Dear [the nickname given to Margaret by his sisters],
> who had supped with us en famille the night before, owing to
> her good Genius coming to her aid in the shape of a Torrent
> of which made it impossible to turn her from the Door. I am
> at last brought to pity her – she has so committed and
> exposed herself – People laugh at her so openly that she must
> see and hear them . . .[13]

They remained in touch and in a letter of 16 February 1817, Margaret confided that she had resolved not to give up Princess Charlotte's letters. This was because they vindicated her advice over various matters, especially the marriage with the Prince of Orange, and that Charlotte was *very* angry at this point stating that she was "totally deceived in a person's character", and the issue, which ended their friendship, was much talked about. Margaret explained to the duke:

7 **Thomas Lawrence (1769–1830):**
William Cavendish, 6th Duke of Devonshire

I send you the letters which you were so good to say last night you would take the trouble of reading. Pray do so with indulgence and do not attribute my wish of your seeing them to any worse motive than the desire of returning your good opinion. I know that what has hitherto been the strongest link in the chain of our friendship is broken, and I should be sorry that you were led to suppose that I had idly sacrificed a sentiment so long and so dearly cherished to the first feelings of disappointed affection and mortified pride. I will not deny that the first of these feelings have [sic] made me very unhappy, more so perhaps than the cause deserved but there are weaknesses of the heart which are uncontrollable and for which we are willing to excuse ourselves if even the better judgment of our friends should teach them to be more severe. From the latter I have received all the consolation they were capable of affording and I only hope you will not think it has induced me to act harshly towards a person for whom I still feel an undiminished affection. Adieu, I often think there has been a strange sympathy between us on this subject – it is very disagreeable to think of the hostility of the human mind and very foolish to be annoyed or surprised by it.[14]

Some, such as the comtesse de Boigne, were of the opinion that it was Margaret's intention to bring – like a dowry – her close friendship with the Princess Charlotte to the marriage with the duke, knowing what a great coup this would be for the Whig party, but the attitude of Prince Leopold put an end to the plan.[15] This may have been so, but their friendship endured well into old age. Soon after her marriage, she wrote in connection with the death of Princess Charlotte of the "sad feelings equally shared, in midst of my own affliction yours was not forgotten and it can never be indifferent to me". They shared a love of literature, and in 1818 she offered him an edition of the *Lusiads,* the masterpiece of the Portuguese poet Luis Vaz de Camões, for his library "as a remembrance of an old friend". The book, edited by the Marquis de Souza, husband of Adèle, the mother of Charles de Flahaut, was soon in the library at Chatsworth: "beautifully bound here in brown and gold with a D and the coronet in diamonds".

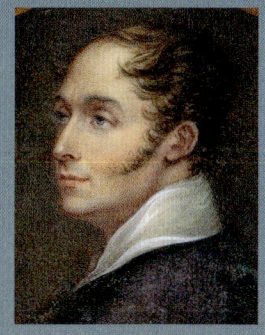

CHAPTER 4

Charles de Flahaut before
his Marriage

Un homme fait pour aller à tout

Napoleon Bonaparte

By the time Margaret first met Charles de Flahaut (1785–1870) early in 1816, he had already made a name for himself as a general. Closely associated with Napoleon, he had accompanied him back to Paris after Waterloo. Having been the lover of Caroline Murat, Queen of Naples, and of Hortense, Queen of Holland, Flahaut had the reputation of being a ladies' man, famed for his charm and agreeable manners.

His background was unconventional. His penniless mother, Adèle (1761–1836), the ambitious, talented and unscrupulous daughter of an adventurer, was the sister of Julie, wife of the influential marquis de Marigny. In 1779 Adèle had married an older man, Charles-François, comte de Flahaut de la Billarderie (1728–1794), brother of the talented comte d'Angiviller, appointed by Louis XVI in 1774 as "directeur général des bâtiments, arts, jardins et manufactures de France". Through Angiviller the comte de Flahaut was appointed "intendant" of the Jardin des Plantes, in the household of the comte d'Artois, brother of Louis XVI, and given a "grace and favour" apartment in the Louvre. There, the young and attractive Adèle, with her white skin, brown eyes and chestnut wavy hair, entertained English visitors including Lord and Lady Holland, who remembered her enjoyable supper parties and games of chess.[1] She had other admirers, principally the American representative in Paris, Gouverneur Morris, and the club-footed Bishop of Autun, Talleyrand, always regarded as the father of Adèle's son, Charles, nicknamed Nené. Adèle's brother-in-law, the comte d'Angiviller, disapproved: "This child who means nothing to me has the misfortune to be the son of a woman for whose treachery and wickedness, for her affair with the mitred monster who is her lover and the father of her child, I have unlimited contempt."[2]

The Revolution of 1789 brought the Flahauts many problems including loss of income. The husband remained in France, where he escaped from prison with the help of his lawyer, who was subsequently put on trial and condemned to death. On hearing this, the chivalrous comte de Flahaut gave himself up in exchange for the life of his rescuer and was executed at Arras in January 1794.[3] Meanwhile, Adèle and her son had left for England in 1792, expecting assistance from Talleyrand, who was already there, but was soon to emigrate to America. As he did nothing for them, she realized that she must now fend for herself. Although very short of money, she found herself lodgings in Half Moon Street in Southwark, London, and sent Charles to boarding school in Hounslow, a hard decision but one which laid the foundations of his command of the English language and understanding of English institutions, which was to prove such an asset in later life. At the same time, she made contact again with the Hollands and Lord Wycombe, heir to the marquessate of Lansdowne. With their help she published in 1794 her autobiographical novel, *Adèle de Sénange*, on the theme of incompatibility in marriage. It was praised by Lord Holland:

> Your most attractive talent as a novelist is to show the effect little details, bagatelles, have on the heart and imagination. As an author you have feelings, powers of observation and wit – if I must make a criticism it is that you are too kind to everybody – there is not one bad person in your story.[4]

With support at this level, the book was a great success and brought in much needed funds.

However, she decided to leave England for the émigré colonies of Germany and Switzerland, where life was much cheaper. In 1797, under the protection of Talleyrand, now minister of foreign affairs, they returned to Paris, where she had to face more money troubles and the problem of her status as a returned émigré. To make ends meet, she continued to write and in 1799 published *Émilie et Alphonse*, the novel which is read by Pierre Bezukhov in *War and Peace*, Leo Tolstoy's epic of Russia during the Napoleonic wars. Her manœuvres to establish herself during these years were observed by Madame de Staël, who depicts her as the scheming Madame d'Arbigny in her novel *Corinne* (1807): "... her countenance was very agreeable, her figure all grace and faultless elegance. She said not a word that was unbecoming; failed in no species of attention, and, without exaggerated politeness, flattered self-love by an address which showed with what she was pleased, but never committed her."[5]

Thanks to the recommendation of Talleyrand, the 15-year-old Charles was employed at the ministère de la Marine, where he was so impressed by the extraordinary rise of Bonaparte that he offered to serve as his aide-de camp. His request being ignored by Napoleon, he was taken up instead by General Dumas in 1800, and then by Louis Bonaparte, "who was always singing his praises".[6] They fought side by side in the battle of Marengo and in Prussia, where they were received by Frederick Wilhelm III, who remembered Charles thirty years later, when he was sent on a mission to Berlin by Louis-Philippe, then King of the French.[7] In spite of being wounded nine times in the campaigns of the Grande Armée, notably at Austerlitz in 1805, he was rapidly promoted. His courage and leadership so impressed the dashing cavalry leader Joachim Murat, then grand duc de Berg, that he appointed him as aide-de camp. At this stage Charles was supported by Talleyrand, who was very friendly and took a great interest in his career, writing in 1807:

> I wrote again to the GD de Berg asking him to appoint you.
> It is a very personal request. When you can find a bit of paper
> do let me know how you are, what you are doing, and what
> you want. You are one of the greatest interests of my life –
> there are only about three of them – Holding you close to my
> heart with love and kisses.[8]

Next, through Marshal Berthier, came the long-desired appointment of aide-de-camp to Napoleon, whom he served with total devotion. After the defeat of the battle of Leipzig in 1813 he was promoted general with the title of comte de l'Empire and granted a good income. But these rewards meant nothing to him, for his only wish was to stay close to Napoleon. His admiration knew no bounds: "No-one has a mind like his, nobody can compare with him. He is quite amazing," and he admitted that "To be noticed by him is in my eyes the highest reward." In his turn Napoleon recognized Charles's talents, as "un homme fait pour aller à tout". He sent him with Marshal Ney on diplomatic missions and in 1809 employed him to negotiate informally

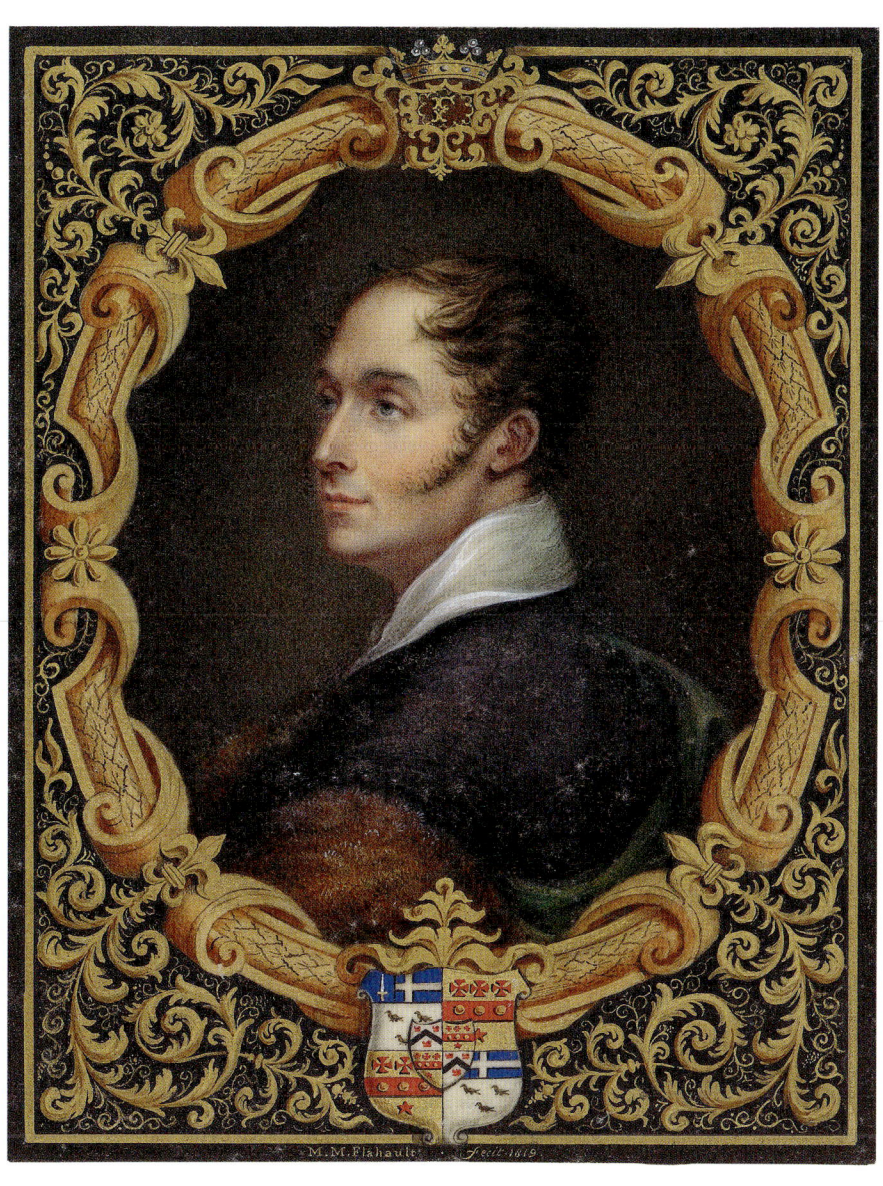

8 Miniature of Charles by Margaret

with the English and German allies. With his good manners and handsome presence, he made an excellent impression on every occasion, demonstrating diplomatic skills, presumably inherited from Talleyrand.

He endured the Russian campaign: the victory of Smolensk; then the taking of Moscow, followed by fire; and the devastating winter retreat. Thereafter he remained close to Napoleon while the peace talks came to nothing, the victorious Allies entered Paris, and events led to the emperor's abdication at Fontainebleau in April 1814. Although he did not follow Napoleon into exile at Elba he did rally to him immediately when he returned for the Hundred Days; he helped organize the army, fought beside him at Waterloo, and afterwards escorted him back to Paris. He took part in the five hard days of negotiations on the terms of defeat, and on leaving Malmaison, Napoleon embraced him four times in recognition of his loyalty. It was perhaps under pressure from his mother that Charles did not accompany Napoleon to Saint Helena, and his devotion cannot be compared with that of General Bertrand and Baron Gourgaud. Yet, as his later career shows, his admiration for Napoleon remained strong and he appointed himself guardian of his memory. Now, in July 1815, after having been an "eye witness and sharer in events of the greatest moment" at the age of thirty, he was faced with the reality that his brilliant career was over, and that he had no future in Restoration France.

Meanwhile, in 1802, his mother had married the Portuguese diplomat José Maria, marquis de Souza Botelho, recently widowed with a son, José Luis, created conde de Vila Real, who became friends with Charles. On account of his disagreements with Talleyrand, the marquis de Souza resigned his post to devote himself to literature and settled permanently in Paris with Adèle. For the next twenty years they received a mixture of foreign and French guests at their fine mansion and rose garden in the Grande-Rue-Verte.[9]

Although she continued writing novels, enjoyed entertaining, and looked after her husband, the main purpose of Adèle's existence was Charles, for whom she planned a brilliant future. From his childhood nothing gave her more pleasure than to hear him praised, and she ignored any suggestions that she was spoiling him. Nowhere was her obsession more evident than in his many love affairs, which she, being no moralist, actively encouraged. It was inevitable that while enjoying the social life of Empire society Charles, with his fine figure, good looks and charm, should have soon become involved with women; in his own words, "lancé fort jeune dans une société légère".[10] While acting as aide-de-camp to Joachim Murat, he had caught the eye of his wife, Caroline, sister of Napoleon, and they became lovers. Then there was Léontine, wife of Alfred de Noailles, who fell in love with him "jusqu'à la folie" and, in spite of his many infidelities, remained attached to him all her life. The Polish countess Anna Potocka, who also had a great passion for him, resented Adèle's influence: "she was infatuated with her son, it went far beyond pride in him which one might forgive: in addition I was taken aback by her desire to participate in his love affairs, making it a threesome." She went on to describe the many attractions of the young Charles:

> He spoke very well, and without being strictly handsome he had a charming face. His slightly melancholy expression seemed to indicate some hidden sorrow. He understood the art of conversation like a true Frenchman, exploring every subject and then smoothly going on to another topic. Nobody could equal his singing of the most enchanting romantic songs.

He acted like the hero of one of his mother's novels, for when indisposed and they could not meet he sent a bouquet of violets plus a programme for her day – what she should see, whom she should visit. Nothing came of this brief but intense encounter: she went back to Poland and they met again fleetingly in Warsaw, and in Paris in 1830.[11]

More serious and lasting was his love affair with Hortense, daughter of the Empress Josephine, unhappily married to Louis Bonaparte, King of Holland. Their story was romanticized in the novel Adèle published in 1808, *Eugène de Rothelin*: Charles is the hero Eugène, and Hortense is the heroine Athénaïs. According to Hortense's version they met while singing but she did not take to him at first, "Not my style at all, not serious enough". She admitted he had "distinguished looks, ready wit, agreeable, brilliant, sensitivity, easy manners, and was more anxious to please and to charm than to be loved". She also noticed how many women were attracted to him.[12] However, by 1805 they had become close, though they had to be very discreet. Here Adèle, impressed by her son's conquest, was delighted to act as go-

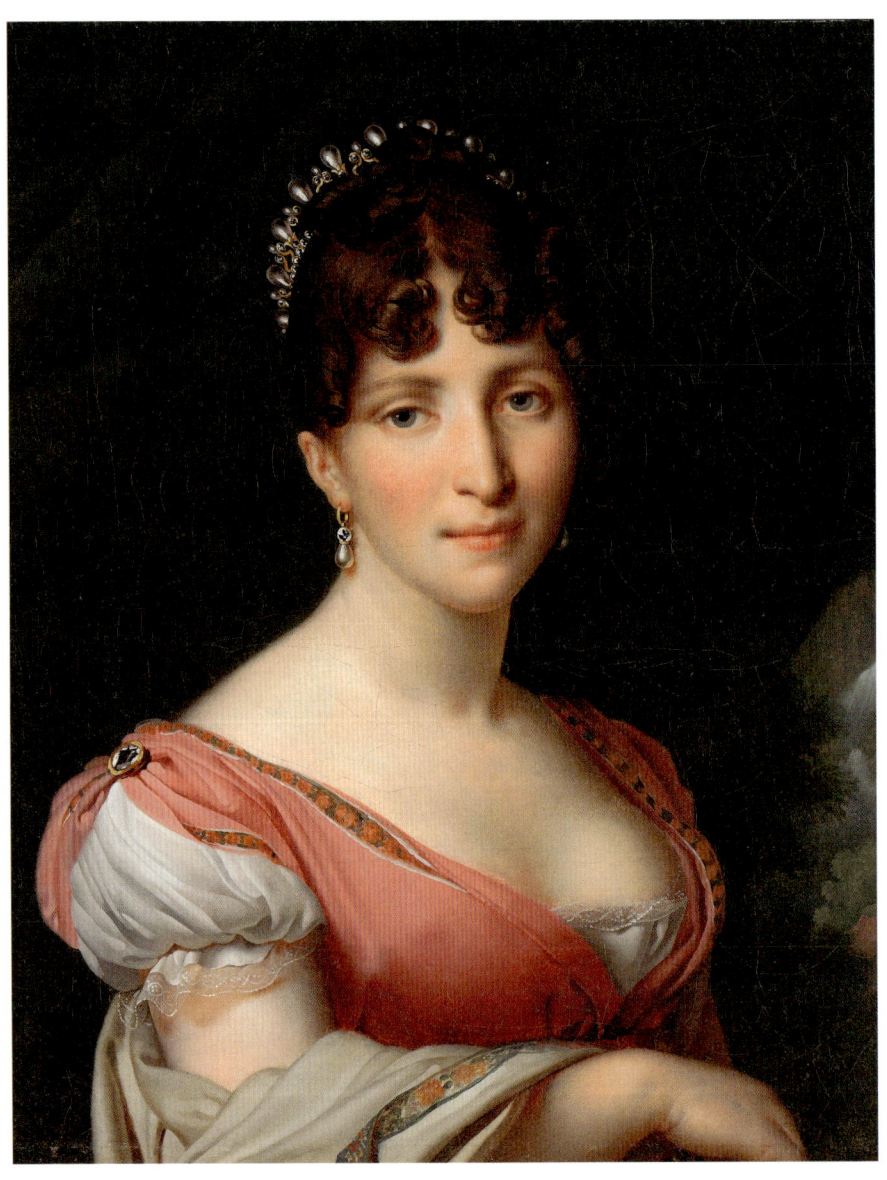

9 Anne Louis Girodet-Trioson (1767–1824): portrait of
Hortense de Beauharnais, Queen of Holland, c. 1805–c. 1809

between. Charles sent Hortense messages via his letters to his mother from Germany in 1807, and, using the code names "ma cousine Sophie" and "Henriette de Capellis", declared, "I love her with all my heart and the note she has sent me has made me very happy." They exchanged gifts, and significantly, from Bayonne, on 21 July 1808, he asked Adèle to have a seal made for Hortense, full of allusions to their love. On one side an aloe leaf is engraved, with the flower, which only blooms after a long period of waiting, between a Latin motto and *Fuira-t-il jamais.* The other side is inscribed *Soleil je t'implore* invoking the sun to show itself from behind a mass of clouds with anchor in the centre.[13] This could allude to the great masked ball held at the Tuileries when Hortense triumphed as the High Priestess of the Sun dressed in silver with white diamonds, white feathers, surrounded by eight priestesses wearing black masks. Her position as Queen of Holland, wife of Louis Bonaparte and as a mother made it very difficult for them to meet. The situation eased after her separation from Louis in 1809, and in 1811 she gave birth to her son by Charles, Auguste Morny. Almost immediately Auguste was given code names of his own: Henri; ma nièce; ma petite filleule; ma famille; le protégé de papa. He lived with Adèle, who spoilt him and gambled away the funds provided by Hortense.

Charles had always hoped that he and Hortense could marry. After Napoleon's first abdication on 7 April 1814 he told his mother, "My whole life belongs to her and with her I would be the happiest of mortals", and then after the defeat at Waterloo in June they planned a life together in America.[14] However, Hortense refused to divorce Louis, fearing that it would create difficulties for their two sons if she did so. When the Restoration government obliged Hortense to leave Paris in July, she went first to Geneva, then after her expulsion from Switzerland she moved on to Aix-la-Chapelle. When Charles appeared there on 12 August, declaring that he wished to dedicate his life to her, she begged him to leave because his presence not only compromised her reputation, but also because her company was prejudicial to his. He therefore made for Lyons, where, under police surveillance as a noted Bonapartist, he awaited permission to go elsewhere.

Meanwhile, Hortense opened letters which had arrived for him at Aix and was shocked to read the passionate outpourings of another woman, the famous actress Mademoiselle Mars (1779–1847), who also believed herself his only love. Effectively, this deception brought the affair with Hortense to an

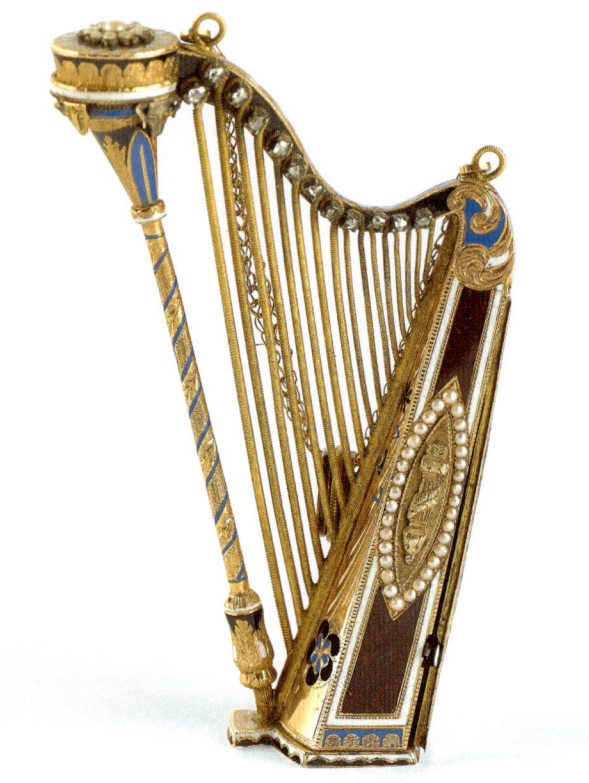

10 Harp automaton given by Queen Hortense
to Auguste Morny

end.[15] He begged her forgiveness, said he wished he had died at Waterloo, made new promises and pledges, but the charm had vanished. In October, Charles, who told Adèle how upset Hortense had been, had to admit that "Ma cousine is better but our happiness is destroyed." He was right, for they were fated not to see each other again until 1829 at Aix-la-Chapelle when Charles introduced her to Auguste, then 18 years old.

Although still very attached to Charles but disillusioned by the discovery of the affair with Mademoiselle Mars, the lonely Hortense, after many months' reflection, decided to release him. Their correspondence continued after his departure from Aix and when, months later in England, he mentioned that he had met a rich young woman who seemed to like him, she understood that she might be regarded as an obstacle to his chance of making a brilliant marriage. She therefore begged him forget his promises to her and look after his own interests. Her mind made up, she went at the end of October on a pilgrimage to the Benedictine shrine of Our Lady of the Hermits at Einsiedeln, near Zurich, where she prayed to the Black Madonna. Next day, she returned and after making a full confession, a priest helped her break with the past and release Charles from his feelings of obligation, while keeping her friendship. In thanksgiving, she sent a bouquet of diamond hydrangeas to the Virgin and a ring for the abbot, having been blessed with "so many consolations, such happiness at Einsiedeln not to wish that my memory remain there after I had left."[16]

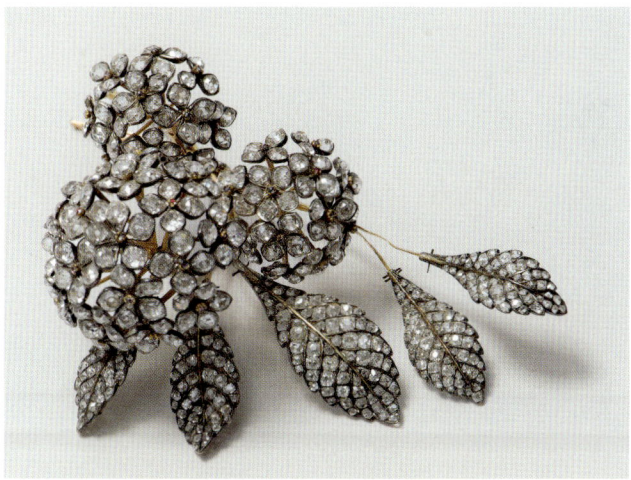

11 Hortensia brooch presented to statue of the Black Madonna at the Abbey of Einsiedeln by Hortense after renouncing her claims on Charles de Flahaut

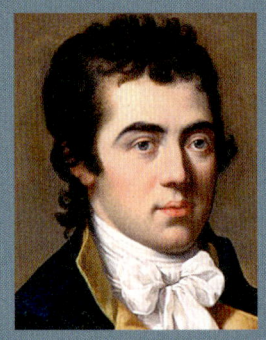

CHAPTER 5

Charles in England
November 1815–December 1816

*The Whig leaders liked him . . . It was rather as if he had
been to some French Eton and Christ Church*

E. Tangye Lean, *The Napoleonists* (1970)

C harles's military career came to an end with the Restoration of 1814. Living on half-pay, he had nothing to do except hunt, frequent the salon of Madame Alexandre Girardin and see his friends, Charles de la Bedoyère among them. Although his father had been guillotined, he was not welcome at the court of Louis XVIII; the king could not bring himself to utter one kind word to him. It was worse after the Hundred Days and the defeat of Waterloo when Paris was occupied by foreign troops, for his movements were restricted and, on the orders of Fouché, the chief of police, he was spied on everywhere. When the minister Decazes pressed by Adèle, at last issued a passport for his departure, he travelled to Holland and wrote to his mother that there was nothing he wanted more than "to go to England, to sit in the first armchair he found there and never get up from it".[1] However, although he was now free to leave France, he had to wait for another passport so as to enter England. This he obtained on 5 November 1815 through Lord Kinnaird, a Scottish peer with Whig connections, who suggested that Charles should spend some months in Scotland enjoying the shooting at Rossie Priory, the Kinnaird family estate, get in touch with the Hollands and also with the Duke of Bedford, to whom he sent letters of introduction.[2]

Charles, as the son of their old friend Adèle, then made himself known to the Hollands who accepted him as a favourite member of their liberal-minded circle. Well-known as a champion of civil and religious liberty, Lord Holland was also a great admirer of Napoleon, whose bronze bust was placed in the Dutch Garden at his Kensington mansion, Holland House. Adèle wrote at once to thank them for their kindness and in return undertook to shop in Paris for the imperious Lady Holland. Except for a special type of oil lamp, these requests were all for dresses and fashion accessories. Seeking out the very newest designs, she copied one made for the trousseau of the duchesse de Berry, chose others from Lenormand and Madame Fosse, bought sets of sleeves "dernière mode", gloves from Houbigant, fichus and under-wear from Madame La Bourdette. In the hope that Lady Holland would wear it "en souvenir de moi", she embroidered a scarf for her, and took more trouble over this gift than she did over writing her novels. She also made herself useful to the Duchess of Bedford, sending her a veil which could be worn as a dress, and also arranging the purchase of furniture. A letter from the Duke of Bedford thanked her for nursing his son, Lord William Russell, who fell ill during a visit to Paris.

Although she claimed that spending so much time shopping for Lady Holland and the Duchess of Bedford helped her forget Charles's absence, this was not true. He was the centre of her life, and she admitted, "I love, have never ever loved anyone more than you." This overwhelming love is expressed in a series of letters advising him on how to succeed in English society. She was grateful not only to friends like the Hollands but to the entire English nation for welcoming him when he was obliged to leave his own country, and declared that if she came to England she would stop people in the streets to thank them personally. Even the briefest note from him made her rejoice in their perfect friendship and mutual confidence, which she compared to Montaigne's feelings for his friend La Boétie, "because it was he, because it was I!" and concludes, "Goodbye, dear one, you know that you are the reason for my existence."[3]

From the beginning she planned his progress in England like a military campaign. On 25 October 1815 she told him that he should leave cards with Lord Castlereagh, the foreign secretary, with Lord and Lady Granville (who were to live in Paris for many years as British ambassador and ambassadress), and with Lord Grey to remind him that she had met him with Lord Lansdowne. He should go on paying visits to the Hollands, talk with Alexander Baring, the banker, and spend time at Woburn with the Duke and Duchess of Bedford. She suggested that he should see the influential, art-loving Lord Yarmouth, who could introduce him to the Prince Regent, as this would impress everyone in Paris. In his conversation he should not run down France or his former benefactor Napoleon, but speak of him with

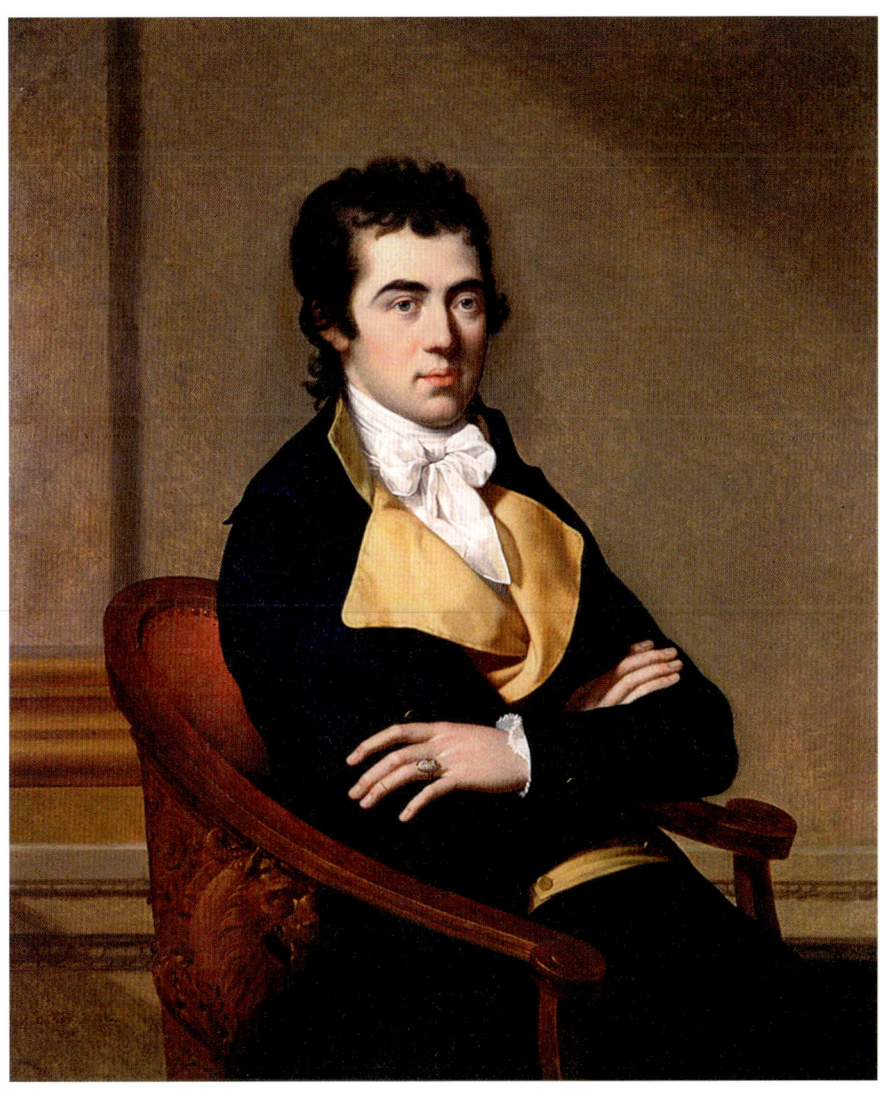

12 François-Xavier Fabre (1766–1837): Henry Richard Fox (later
Vassall Fox), 3rd Baron Holland, 1795 [4]

regret when talking to a small group of friends. She advised him not to show off his singing except in the country at small parties, and then only with people friendly to France. He should play games of whist, hunt, fish, and remain straightforward with men, and not make up to the women, remembering that the English make a great thing of morality. In order to get a good reputation as a statesman in France he should perfect his knowledge of the English language, commerce, laws and institutions, attend the debates in the Houses of Parliament, read and improve his vocabulary. She reminded him that he owed his excellent English to her "barbarous" decision to plunge him, "poor little creature, into that English school not understanding a single word that was said". Always shrewd, she warned him against self-deprecation, for she knew that the English, who would take this literally, would think less well of him, and begged him to be always correct. She thought of everything, and collected amusing stories which might help him shine in society.

Meanwhile, Charles had lost no time in getting in touch with the Duke of Bedford, for on 11 December 1815, Lord Holland wrote to Adèle, "Charles is quite safe from all perils including those of the *chasse* from which he is just returned after slaughtering 8 hares, 7 pheasants & one rabbit." He congratulated her on the way she had brought him up, said how much his conversation interested them and added that his good looks and military bearing were of course great advantages.[5] From London on 2 February 1816 Charles answered his mother's concerns about his warm clothing, his footwear and told her how he spent his time. He described the agreeable daily routine of a guest at Woburn:

> Like Papa [M. de Souza, his stepfather] I don't rise with the sun, but between 10 and 11 o'clock, and go downstairs between 11 and midday. As you must know breakfast is available until everybody has been served, and I usually took mine with the Duchess and the other ladies in the house. After that I either play tennis or go hunting, until about 4 when I sit with the party until it is time to take my bath before dinner. The dinner which is always excellent lasts from 6 until 9.30. Afterwards there is music, or billiards until 11 when supper is brought in, bowls of punch or mulled wine to keep us going until about 2 in the morning when I go to

bed, so as to start all over again on the next morning.[6]

Then he told her about his London engagements. There were visits to the theatre, as the guest of Lady Bessborough in the Duke of Devonshire's box, and in November he watched the Lord Mayor's show. He was impressed by Parliament:

> Yesterday I went to the opening of the House of Commons, very well placed in the gallery thanks to Lord Tavistock and Mr. Seymour, the Serjeant at Arms. It was not at all what I expected, for I was surprised by the freedom with which political matters were discussed and by the simplicity of the proceedings. The best speakers of the opposition, George Tierney, Samuel Romilly, Henry Brougham, Francis Horner, all spoke so well in defence of the principles of liberty and of national honour that it was a pleasure to listen to them.

He went back to hear Lord Brougham propose a motion on the problem of the Spanish exiles, and a few days later went to the House of Lords when Lord Granville was speaking. Another time he was present when the Lords were debating on the current situation in France, which he said made France appear like a sick man at the mercy of the quack doctors – Saugrado and Cuchillo – in Alain-René Lesage's picaresque novel *Gil Blas*. Frustrated at not being able to get up and speak his mind he decided to keep away from Parliament for a while.[7]

Knowing how every detail of his existence in England meant so much to her, in another letter of 19 February 1816 he listed the people he had met during the previous few days:

> Dinner on Thursday with Mr. Burrell, in company with Lord and Lady Jersey, Lord and Lady Cowper, Lord Gower and others, who could not have been kinder to me. Then, on Friday at Lord Kinnaird's brother's house I met the Duke of Sussex, to whom I gave a message from Papa. Saturday with Lord Yarmouth, with a great gathering of dandys [*sic*] – the British version of what we call 'incroyables' and even better,

a perfect meal. There was quite a different atmosphere at Lord Lansdowne's on the Sunday, but of course I was delighted to find myself a guest once again in that great house.

He assured her that he was learning from these encounters and tried not to get involved in political issues.

Adèle, not content with watching over Charles's interests in Paris, also chose presents for his English friends. For Lord Holland, "that good man who has done so much for you", she sent a book of music and then on 28 December 1815, she wrote of a discovery which would make a charming gift: a porcelain vase with portraits of the emperor and his family which she could not resist on account of the superb quality and future historic interest. Always keen for Charles to resume his affair with Hortense, she continued: "the sight of all those pretty women with their crowns made me feel so sad, for it reminded me of that poor little person stranded on Lake Constance at the mercy of the Swiss peasantry".

Not everybody found Charles irresistible. The Regent, who blamed Margaret for the collapse of the projected marriage between Princess Charlotte and the Prince of Orange, disliked the idea of her own union with a Bonapartist, and wondered what Charles was doing in England. Prince Leopold, who married Princess Charlotte in April 1816, had a very poor opinion of him, perhaps because Charles had flirted with one of his sisters. Byron, who met him several times with the writer Benjamin Constant, wrote how he compared unfavourably with the Corsican general Sébastiani, being "more of a petit maître and younger, but I should think not of the same intellectual calibre".[8] Ultra Tories such as Lady Mansfield and Lady Hamilton were very hostile and at a grand dinner given by Lord Bathurst all the Scots present shouted their antagonism to the possibility of his marriage. Lord Bathurst asked them to "Calm down, calm down", and promised, "we will put Mac before Flahaut and you will all be happy".[9]

His chief opponent was the French ambassador, the marquis d'Osmond, who accused Charles of marrying for money and disseminating Bonapartist propaganda. The duc d'Orléans, his wife, Marie-Amélie, and sister, Adélaïde, warned Charles about this and diplomats were well aware of his animosity. Madame Narishkine, the beautiful Russian named the Polar Star, told Adèle that M. d'Osmond had made a dreadful scene and insisted that neither Princess Lieven nor Prince Esterházy should invite Charles to their respective embassies.[10] However, that did not prevent Charles and the princess, both excellent musicians, from meeting in other people's houses.

Charles admitted that his circle belonged to the Whig opposition. As a favourite of Lady Holland he was constantly at Holland House, and he often stayed at Woburn, where he encountered the Whig grandees, Lord Grey, Lord Granville, Francis Horner, Lady Charleville, Lord Alvanley, George Lamb and Lord William Bentinck. Of particular interest was his meeting with Sir Robert Wilson and Michael Bruce, who had helped the comte de Lavalette, condemned to death for his loyalty to Napoleon, make a dramatic escape from prison in Paris.[11]

Not all his friends were English. At Holland House he met: Ugo Foscolo, "so knowledgeable, so original and high spirited, everyone likes him"; the Spanish ambassador Fernán Nuñez; the Portuguese statesman the Duke of Palmela; the Sicilian Count Sant Antonio; and the Danish diplomat Bourcke, who became a close friend. He moved around the country. With the witty Casimir de Montrond he visited Newmarket, went north to Edinburgh, staying on the way with the Earl and Countess of Durham at Lambton Hall, and with the Kinnairds at Rossie Priory, then south again with Lord and Lady Rancliffe, to Brighton with the Hollands, then to Windsor, leaving again to Cumberland for the Lake District scenery, and to the industrial cities of Manchester and Liverpool in his desire to know the country well. In July 1816 he spent a month with Lord and Lady Grey at Howick, their mansion on the Northumberland coast, and it was then that he and his fellow guest, Margaret Mercer Elphinstone, decided that they loved each other.

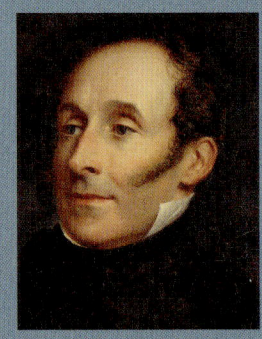

CHAPTER 6

A Mutual Attraction

Love, the supreme power of the heart, mysterious
enthusiasm that encloses in itself all poetry, all heroism,
all religion

Madame de Staël, *Corinne*

Although the exact circumstances of the first meeting of Charles and Margaret are not clear, the most likely place was at the London home of her cousin, Clementina Sarah Burrell, the future Lady Willoughby de Eresby. Charles alludes to it in a letter dated 8 December 1816: ". . . it is rumoured that another of your cousins will soon be here. Will you be calling on her? That was how I first saw you, exactly a year ago." Then, after saying how much he liked her recollection of that occasion, he mentioned that a few days beforehand, he had passed in front of the Burrells' house with Lady Holland, who had remarked that Clementina Sarah had "a cousin whom you should marry". Then, as he felt still bound to Hortense he had strongly rejected the idea. However, he and Margaret were soon seeing each other frequently at balls, at the opera, at the theatre, and at dinners in the houses of the many friends in Whig society they had in common. People were quick to notice them together. One of the first was Lady Granville, who observed on 3 February 1816 that "there is a little novel going on – Miss Mercer affichera desperate love for Flahaut which he acts a most assiduous return to but is really épris with Lady Cowper", and a few days later, on 11 February, continued, "I hear that Miss Mercer is desperately in love and that Charles de Flahaut acts it quite like somebody in a play: the most extravagant speeches before everybody which Margaret swallows."[1] In her *Mémoires* Madame de Boigne, always unfriendly, suggested that it was because Margaret was on the rebound after her disappointment with the Duke of Devonshire that she was particularly susceptible to so much flattery.[2] Rumours reached Paris, and Adèle reported on 15 February 1816 that Lady Kinnaird had heard of an Englishwoman who was so much in love with him that he could marry her if he wished, and that he had charmed everyone with his melancholy looks, which reflected the sad state of things in France. In spite of his immediate denial, "Mon mariage est un non-sens", his mother persisted, writing in March, ". . . everyone here talks of your marriage, and the Ultras are furious because the lady is a friend of Princess Charlotte".[3]

Through the long and numerous – more than eighty – letters written by Charles to Margaret until their marriage, the course of their love affair can be traced from flirtation to commitment as he rejoices in its high points and laments the misunderstandings, separations, illnesses and obstacles put in their way. Although it is a one-sided correspondence because no letters to Charles during their courtship have survived in the copious family archives, a picture emerges of the many interests they shared, their pleasure in each other's company and their determination to stay together in spite of the world "qui juge et qui blâme" and the increasingly ferocious opposition of Admiral Lord Keith, encouraged by the hostility of the French ambassador, the marquis d'Osmond. Moreover, it is a masterclass on how an attractive and experienced suitor, by means of charm and flattery, can, against all the odds, make a brilliant marriage. The force with which he expressed his love and his misery when they were apart could not have failed to appeal to the imagination and feelings of a woman responsive to the romantic poetry of Lord Byron.[4] She never regretted her "grande passion", and years later, when their cautious daughter Emily was considering marriage, she declared that there could be no real happiness without "ce sentiment violent".[5]

His earliest surviving letter, written in March 1816, began with a light-hearted semi-declaration: "I am truly attached to you and consider that you are quite different from anybody else." Unlike Byron, he soon (in June) dared to confess, "You will never know how much I love you", and reminded her of a brief but significant meeting; "that wonderful occasion when you made me feel a happiness I never believed possible". He went on to reflect how this sudden unexpected moment of bliss now seemed like a dream, for it was so quickly followed by a separation, owing to their both falling ill with measles.

Next month, in July, their relationship was sealed. This turning point was reached thanks to the hospitality of Lord and Lady Grey, who invited them to spend almost five weeks together at their mansion at Howick on the Northumberland coast. There they enjoyed the privacy of long seaside walks, bathing, woods, beautiful gardens and each other's company, alone with the

Greys and their "sweet-faced" children. In this happy family atmosphere Margaret could freely admit that she too was in love, and years later she told Lady Grey, "I always look back to my Howick days as the most joyous of my life and feel how much of my happiness I have owed to the friendship and affection of you and Lord Grey."

On his travels around England Charles revisited Howick, where, "seeing everything again, our walk, the bathing cabin, the hedge where you nearly fell, the sea front, evoked tender thoughts but also left me feeling hopelessly sad". He continued to pour out his sufferings in his letters, begged her assurance that his love was returned, and that he now lived only for her, and would only find happiness with her.

During their separations, so frequent for the rest of their courtship, he said that as letters were the only pleasure that fate permitted, he regarded them like a conversation. He wrote at length, telling her about his visits to the theatre, how he was disappointed in Kean's performance in *The Iron Chest* but how much he admired Miss O'Neill in *King John*. Books were another shared interest. Struck by the phrase, "always consider improbabilities as impossibilities", from Anna Maria Porter's *The Recluse of Norway* (1814), he raised the question of whether he was right to have pursued her as he had and in so doing risk making her unhappy. In spite of knowing how much Byron meant to Margaret he dared criticize the poem *Ode* on account of the allusions to Napoleon. Challenged to justify his view, while admitting that there were some fine passages, such as "the eagle escaping the debris with the chains of the world", he declared that Byron had said nothing new about his character, and moreover had repeated the calumny that the man who had ruled the world was incapable of controlling himself.

In return, Margaret, now a supporter of Napoleon, sent him an account of the very sympathetic meeting of her cousin, Admiral Sir Pulteney Malcolm and his wife, with "le pauvre prisonnier" in Saint Helena. His reply defends Napoleon's truculent attitude to British authority, subject as he was to a governor as limited as Sir Hudson Lowe.

Music, which was another bond between them, was his greatest pleasure and consolation. Whereas he found reading difficult since his concentration went after a few pages and he was too distracted to join in the after-dinner conversations at Holland House, only music, which demanded no intellectual effort, could calm his restless heart. Not only did he send Margaret all the new waltzes, and songs, such as "The Marquis de Carabas", but he described his musical evenings when with friends, particularly the three Liddle sisters, singing favourites from Mozart's operas. Always reluctant to sing on his own, as he thought it made him seem pretentious, he now refused to do so in front of large gatherings, especially if he owed the audience nothing. When obliged to sing at a musical evening, on 11 December 1816, accompanied by Princess Lieven at the piano, he cursed having to perform "in front of all the monkeys in Europe" and resolved in future to do so only for the private amusement of his friends.

More confidences were exchanged, and he mentioned his worries about the health of his mother, his despair over the political situation in France, and gave his opinion of the people he met – the affectations of Madame Narishkine, the elderly "cabinet des antiques" at Lady Perth's whist party and Lady Holland's mischief-making and contrariness. In a long passage, written on 15 November 1816, he explained why he considered his military career now finished. In spite of volunteering so young, he admitted he was never happy in the army, and thoroughly disliked military life. Having to mix with uncongenial company, to give orders or carry them out was contrary to his tastes. All he had ever wanted was a tiny share in the glory of the French army and nothing more. He was now determined, whatever happened, never to serve again.[6] Announcing that a miniature copy of his portrait as a colonel painted by Gérard in 1810, before the military campaigns had taken their toll on his young looks, had just arrived from Paris, he said he was putting it in box for which she alone would have key, so that both this copy and original sitter would belong only to her. He then said that the best way of showing that she was pleased to have his portrait would be to send her own in return.

That October, he asked for a sketch showing her seated in her own room while staying in the country at Wood End. A few weeks later he thanked her for sending a beautiful drawing, saying he had spent so many hours looking at it that he had come to feel he had always known what her room was like. Next, he told her how much he would like to have a catalogue of her collection of portrait busts of monarchs and statesmen, and whether he was right in recognizing that of Charles James Fox on the chimneypiece. Reading her letter, the words "take me with you" made his heart beat fast, and made him wish that he could offer her all the good things of this world for them to enjoy together. Imagining that he was there in her room, he quoted Jean de La Fontaine's "Éloge de la Peinture" in which the poet claims that painting can console lovers suffering the pain of separation. Then, in December, he worried when the turquoise set in the ring she had given him fell out, and a pin broke, for when a pledge of love is broken it could be a portent that things will turn out badly.

When she referred to her predicament as an heiress, always suspicious that she was being courted for her money and not for herself, he answered that it also posed a problem for a sensitive man who preferred to remain silent rather than run the risk of being accused of fortune-hunting. On another personal note, when she asked him whether a new summer dress suited her, he flattered, "As long as you look just as you did when I last saw you, I will think you quite perfect." He said he was miserable when she did not write, and that when he left home he longed to return in case a letter was awaiting him. If not, he was miserable for the rest of the day. If there was one, then he was blissfully happy.

He seems to have made a clean breast of his love affairs, but after Lady Grey mentioned that Margaret knew all about them, he accused her of repeating the secrets "which I would not like you to reveal to your dearest friend". When she retaliated that as his past was already only too well known, he could hardly accuse her of being indiscreet, he said how much he disliked having this reputation. It was now, in November 1816, that he justified his relations with Hortense, the mother of his son, with whom he had been linked for so long, but who had nobly released him from any feelings of obligation towards her.

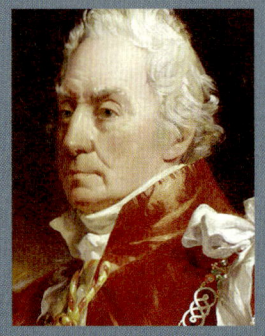

CHAPTER 7

Weathering the Storm

Omnia vincit Amor

Virgil, *Eclogues*

While Margaret and Charles drew closer together, the opposition to their romance grew stronger. Since she was so well-known and he had a controversial reputation, all London society was talking about them – even suggesting they were secretly married – and when the gossip inevitably reached Lord Keith, who had a disliking for all Frenchmen and particularly Bonapartists, he reacted vehemently. So, having at last found a man after her own heart, Margaret had to face ferocious opposition. On 22 October 1816, she told Charles that the endless family rows were making her life intolerable, and this situation intensified over the following months. Although at first Charles reproached her for not standing up to her father, he became more sympathetic, observing that as the years advanced, the ideas and attitudes of elderly parents hardened so they became both unjust and demanding. Aware of her unhappiness, Charles offered to free her from their engagement if she felt there was no alternative to submission to her father's will, adding that he could give no better proof of his love for her, though he would only have the strength to make this sacrifice if he could be sure it would make her happy. Matters were made worse by the slanders spread by the French ambassador, the marquis d'Osmond, and also by an agent of the French police, Beaumont de Brivesal, who in conversation and perhaps through anonymous letters, attributed Charles's rise in the army over sixteen years' active service to his success with women – "ses galanteries". This accusation was indignantly rebutted by Charles, who said there was nothing the emperor loathed more and that he was surprised that Lord Keith had been taken in by such calumny.

Furthermore, as the situation had become so embarrassing and difficult now she was the target of the gossips, it was clear that the time had come to bring it to a halt. From Woburn,[1] he revealed the state of his finances, and estimated that with her disposable income as well his military pension they could live comfortably together in Paris. Then followed an exchange of letters between Margaret and her father. On 28 March 1817 she wrote:

> My dearest Father
> No one can be as much interested or more anxious than I am to be fully satisfied of the honour and character of Gen[l] Flahaut, and certainly if it could be proved to me that there was any truth in the various calumnies which have been repeated to you, or that he has deceived one in the smallest particular respecting his family or fortune, I should consider myself perfectly justified in breaking an engagement which from his unworthiness I should feel convinced could no longer form my happiness. But as I cannot sacrifice my attachment for him or give up the good opinion I have formed of him upon false grounds or anonymous authorities, I most willingly agree to your proposal of referring the matter to Lord Grey. If he is satisfied of the truth of the allegations against Gen[l] Flahaut and considers that the information of the persons you will in confidence name to him is to be depended upon, I shall abide by his opinion, and consider myself fortunate in having escaped the misfortune of forming a connection with a person whose conduct would then appear to me in the most contemptible light. There is one point which I beg may be distinctly understood by you and explained to L[d] Grey which is that I have quite made up my mind to every sacrifice of fortune and interest which the circumstances may exact as well as to all the objections and inconveniences which may arise to me from his being a foreigner. It is with the greatest pleasure that I have entered into this proposal of submitting one different opinion to the investigation and judgment of a third person, as it would have been equally painful to me to have betrayed your confidence to Gen[l] Flahaut or to have withheld mine from

him, upon a subject of so much delicacy and such deep
interest to us both. I have no wish to hurry either Lord Grey
in giving his opinion or you in making up your mind upon
the subject. On the contrary, I should wish that every enquiry
should be made that could satisfy you, or undeceive me as to
the merits of Genl Flahaut. I enclose Genl Flahaut's letter
stating the circumstances of his family, which I beg may be
shown to Ld Grey. [This enclosure she read aloud to her
father, who could hardly bear listening to it.[2]]

Lord Keith then answered, setting out his objections:

The family and fortune of General Flahaut can be of no
concern to me neither can mine be of the least importance to
him ... My own objections are that the Genl is a foreigner
and of a different religion from that of this country and
yourself that of course all his natural feelings must be adverse
to this country that his whole connections have been and still
are inimical to this nation and its Government. He openly
professes the same sentiments. That so far as I have been able
to learn his habits of life have not been satisfactory. Nor such
as to induce me to suppose he is calculated to make a good
husband and render you happy according to the notions of
this country which differ wildly from those of others and I
feel it my duty as a parent to bring this before your eyes. As
for that attachment upon his past, you forgive me for
entertaining strong doubts upon that subject, your fortune is
very considerable and may be large so is your rank in life ...
As a parent I cannot approve of General Flahaut's proceeding
so far without consulting myself or some of your relations
who take interest in your future welfare. Nor can I forgive
his persisting in his attentions after I had signified my
disapproval of his doing so. Towards you his conduct has
been unpardonable by making you the common subject of
conversation and even causing your company to be avoided
by many valuable friends who respected you, even among the

> highest circles . . . All your relations are sorely grieved at the
> thoughts of such a connection and I earnestly pray that you
> put an end to it. His plea of disinterestedness is ridiculous on
> the score of not getting my property he knows your own is
> very large even to become an object to most men in this
> country much more to one of his where fortunes are not so
> considerable.[3]

In another letter he rebutted the idea that he favoured Georgina, the daughter of his second marriage:

> I hope I love her as I ought to do my daughter and a
> charming child but if you imagine I love her better than you
> or even put her in competition with you it is a sad mistake
> indeed. An experience of twenty years might have shown you
> the contrary.

After receiving these letters, Margaret, desperate, begged her father to consult Lord Grey immediately and promised:

> If it is the opinion of Lord Grey that a parent's authority is
> unlimited, and that my happiness and future prospects in life
> should be forever sacrificed to the reasons you give for
> opposing the marriage, or the feelings which the idea of it has
> excited, it certainly is a sacrifice my mind may in time be
> brought to make from a sense of moral and religious duty.

However, her attachment

> has been founded upon the highest opinion of the qualities
> both of heart and mind, which Gen[l] F. possesses, and from a
> thorough conviction of his love for me; as well as from being
> sensible that his talents, habits and pursuits are suitable to my
> tastes, and such as to render him an agreeable companion to
> me. My actions may be governed, but my mind never, my
> affections are entirely devoted to him, and if ever separation

is exacted as a point of duty he will before we part voluntarily [underlined twice] receive my most solemn promise and assurance never to give myself to another.

She insisted, before any decision was made,

> upon the most thorough investigation taking place of all the points upon which the truth and honor of General Flahaut has been represented to you as doubtful. I ask it, not only as an act of justice, which I am sure you will not refuse to a man whose greatest fault towards you has been liking me too well, but also as a satisfaction to my feelings, that it may be distinctly known to you and all my family that my affections were not placed upon a person unworthy of having gained them or undeserving of still possessing them.

Always well disposed towards the young couple, Lady Grey defended Charles, saying how much they liked him and that their only reservation was on account of his being a foreigner. Similarly, her husband made his support of Margaret clear in a letter promising Charles that should Lord Keith continue to believe all the allegations made against him he must produce facts, evidence and sources and give Charles the chance to refute them. He promised to act as arbitrator as requested, describing it as a most agreeable duty, for he hoped it would lead to the happiness of both.[4]

Further light is thrown on the "threatened alliance" of Charles and Margaret by the letters Queeney, Margaret's stepmother, wrote to the novelist Fanny Burney, married to General d'Arblay, a Frenchman living in Paris.[5] Fanny, who disliked Adèle, also remembered the young Charles, then the protégé of Louis Bonaparte, "who never let him out of his sight", and added, "What I have known of him, favourable, honourable, and truly interesting, has left a strong impression on my mind and memory to his advantage – but I have never seen him since!" and she predicted, "If he can reform he will certainly be one of the most aimable husbands in the world but what an IF!" Queeney, invidiously placed in the middle of the fight between the imperious father, "angry, irritated, disappointed", and the strong-minded daughter, reported in February 1817 to Fanny that

Margaret had condescended to say:

> . . . she had not yet nor would she enter into any possible
> engagement without his consent. He is hurt and she has more
> regard for her father than for anyone else and cannot help
> respecting his character. . . . He had expressed the horror of
> this possible connection so very strongly saying he would
> rather see her dead, that he would rather she married her
> footman (far worse) than this man.

Queeney was reluctant to show him the letter from her friend, but when she
did, he dismissed it, saying he had heard it all before and remarked that
Fanny had only known him as a boy. The old Admiral seemed to know far
more about Adèle, whom he described as belonging to a group of

> Belles of no Rank or Distinction in Paris: one of them, her
> sister, managed to get Monsieur de Marigny and because of
> this connexion Monsieur de Flahaut thought he might rise in
> the world, but soon after was guillotined. She led a life of
> intrigue in all the bustle of a corrupt court. As for her son,
> here he was let loose upon society to exert his talents which
> no doubt were well adapted to his present situation.

Queeney continued:

> I can from your account easily give credit to his being better
> off for money than I had imagined – royal personages
> [meaning Caroline Murat and Hortense, respectively Queen
> of Naples and Queen of Holland] may have amply repaid his
> assiduities.

Then she gave her considered opinion:

> Between ourselves, and only ourselves, I think she would like
> him far better than anyone on earth they are so entirely
> d'accord upon all subjects – his politics are hers, his foreign

manners, his music, his dancing, his singing, the whole of
him is exactly what she likes and admires and if she is not
already too far gone no doubt his petits soins and artifice will
achieve the business. So great is her capacity to wound and
twist Lord Keith's heart that I almost think he could hardly
survive the blow.

Queeney then confided her fears of bringing her own daughter, Georgy, in
contact with "such a totally unprincipled lot of people".

Queeney learnt that the "proscribed person" had been meeting with
Margaret somewhere or other every day and night, as if nothing was wrong.
She described how in public "he spoke to me in the most unconcerned
easy manner and was hovering around her and talking the whole night",
and another time, when Margaret was waltzing, "to my horror they spun
round and round the room greatly to the amusement of all the beholders and
immediately fell back amidst the crowd when I saw them seated afterwards
together in the most conspicuous manner". When Queeney remonstrated
with her, Margaret retorted that if her disgrace was so terrible why were they
publishing it over the town, making her ridiculous, treating her like a child.
This put Queeney in a dilemma. She wished to remain on good terms with
Margaret, but neither did she want to upset Lord Keith, who would rather
see Margaret dead than married to such a scoundrel, believing him "a bastard
of Talleyrand!" He predicted it would end badly: "she might be planting
larches in Scotland while he was keeping a gaming house and an Opera girl",
and Queeney, who thought Charles "all artifice and hackneyed in intrigues
of all description – thinking of what a Prize he would seize on her", was of
the same opinion.

Meanwhile Margaret enlisted support from her friends, as Queeney
informed Fanny:

> The storm has blackened and thickened around us
> wonderfully since I last wrote and has now taken quite a new
> character and she has made it quite a party business. The
> heroine of the drama has worked up all the leaders of the
> Opposition into her interest and having met first with this
> Paragon at Lord Holland's and Lord Grey's has certainly

been encouraged in it most decidedly by them and their families They are so committed that they are determined to carry it on and Lord Lauderdale who is a great favourite of the Duchess of York has got her to patronise the hero by her notice and marked civilities, so he is always to be seen in her Box at the Opera, play etc. Now Lord Erskine she has got to attack Lord Keith upon it. And now for my trouble. The marriage is quite determined upon. She has been completely deaf and blind to any remonstrance or representation that could be made from any quarter whatsoever. Whenever she was told anything against him she always replied, 'Who says this and with what authority' But at last an authority came and presented himself willingly and said always she was more than welcome to make any use of his authority and who should this be but the Duke of Wellington. He called on Lord Keith, and said how sorry he was, how he hoped something, someone, anything, might prevent what he thought almost a national disgrace that the daughter of a British admiral should demean herself to marry one of these detestable Bonapartist crew. That Charles was quite a Roué about Paris, not respected in any society whatsoever and could get into no society there that she could form any idea of the profligacy in which they live – and much more.

Enraged, Margaret said she did not see why the Duke of Wellington was to interfere in her concerns, that she could not suppose he could be any judge of the subject because he had been lucky enough to win an unfortunate battle, that she thought all he said extremely impertinent and should not listen to such calumnies.

Queeney continued:

She was then attacked by Princess Charlotte who [*sic*] I used to think she loved, if she could love anyone . . . Now she is totally lost in every one's opinion but her Father's who, as drowning men clutch at straws, cannot help still thinking it

> within possibility to save her . . . it keeps us lingering here,
> pitied by our friends and laughed at by our enemies.

After declaring that "Everybody repeats private conversations", she ended by saying that the day before the Regent himself had given Lord Keith a word-for-word account of a long talk between herself and Margaret![6] The court sided with the Keiths, who were invited without Margaret, to Claremont, Carlton House and Brighton.

Matters got worse. Lord Keith was permanently in a state of great agitation, "unable to believe a word of Charles's fancied perfections", and Margaret, on her side, insisted that only her father's dislike of him would prevent her marriage. At home, Queeney, hoping to act as a peacemaker, found Margaret in the "highest state of irritation, vexation, with rage boiling over in her heart. Volumes would not hold the torrent of things she let forth". She began by saying "she thought herself extremely ill-used" and that her father's abuse and vilification of the person she liked best in the world was painful to her feelings. She went on to assert that Charles had "instantly engaged her decided preference" from the first moment she had seen him, and her partiality had increased the more she saw of his talents, his mind, his charming qualifications, his love and attachment. She then turned to other grievances. First, if Lord Keith attacked Adèle for not being nobly born, why then, she asked, had he married Queeney? Secondly, she made it clear that she had never been worried about the financial provisions for her half-sister Georgy: if her father chose to give her his fortune she did not care, as she had a competence of her own; Flahaut had £2,000 in stocks, and his mother's house in Paris. They could live happily there if she was to be driven out of father's house by ill usage, and if her father thought he could frighten her into submission by disinheriting her he was much mistaken.

Next, she made the point that as her father had married for money he wanted her to do same, but she considered herself above such conduct. Then she demanded to know why her happiness should be sacrificed to her family and went on to describe them as "a parcel of insignificant people she cared nothing for except her father". However, his prejudices and cruelty showed he did not feel the same for her and he had made his disregard obvious by marrying Queeney. Flahaut, on the other hand, would marry her with no view to her fortune at all. When able to get a word in at last, Queeney pointed out that "he well knew it to be an estate of her own of £6,000 annually. 'This was denied:' Pooh! What with taxes expenses etc it is never more than half that", and in any case she was heavily in debt. This admission came as no surprise to Queeney, who told Fanny that Margaret kept no accounts, flung money about without an idea as to where it all went and although cheated and robbed on all sides, considered it "mean and vulgar to pay attention to such low concerns". Finally, she said that rather than settle for marriage with a foxhunting, farming, country landowner she would be much happier travelling on the continent with him and living in Paris, "which her imagination paints with such delight with her charming companion". Showing great fairness, Queeney thought she was right: "I really do think that if he behaved well to her she would be happier with him than with any other but what an IF! She has by no means beauty or the Agremens with people."[7]

Across the Channel Adèle did everything in her power to further the match. She sought out the company of Alexander Baring, Lady Dalrymple Hamilton and Madame Rumford, who took the side of the lovers; she found Charles's certificate of baptism and lobbied the ministers Decazes and Richelieu to obtain other documents needed to legalize the marriage.[8] When told that Louis XVIII would not authorize the marriage of a French lieutenant general without the permission of the bride's father, she blamed M. d'Osmond for urging the king to refuse, wishing that he with the other enemies – Lady Mansfield and the Countess of Hertford – would all drown. Since the authorization from Lord Keith was not forthcoming, Charles was obliged to resign from the army, considering it a small price to pay for his future happiness.[9] His Portuguese diplomat stepfather, M. de Souza, explained the financial arrangements for the marriage contract, which were made through Alexander Baring, and urged them to get married as soon as this was signed. He pointed out that whether this took place in an Anglican or Roman Catholic church, in either case the marriage would be valid.

Having received a message from Margaret, Adèle, who had shed many tears over the difficulties faced by the couple, asked Charles to tell Margaret "how much I love her noble character, so elevated, so generous, knowing she will make you happy, and also me, for now, right up to my last hours I can think of her looking after you, so I can die, sure that her affection will take the place of mine". These effusions were not well received by Margaret, who, after reading one of her letters, shocked Queeney by remarking, "what a tiresome woman – I hope I shall never hear any more of her, for such a correspondence would be intolerable". Deprived of her mother's love and protection so early in life, such tender feelings were quite beyond Margaret's understanding.

In the last weeks of May neither father or daughter would speak to each other. While Margaret was busy packing up all her possessions there were inevitably arguments about ownership, carried on by notes which were usually received on both sides with cries of rage and anger. Amidst all the confusion, agitation and anxiety it was finally agreed that they should travel to Scotland, where Lord Keith most reluctantly gave his consent to the marriage, though he adhered to his decision of disinheriting Margaret, and made it clear that he wished for nothing more to do with her. On 19 June the marriage took place at St Andrew's Church, Edinburgh, attended by John Murray, lawyer and future Lord Advocate, his sister, a Mr Pollen, solicitor or Writer to the Signet, a Mr Thomson, and Sir Harry Moncrieff. None of Margaret's family were present, but she, in token of her Scottish descent, was triumphantly arrayed in green gloves and ribbons. Lord Keith had travelled on to Perth to his estate at Tulliallan on the banks of the Firth of Forth, where building a mansion took his mind off his anger and grief. For Queeney, who had borne the brunt of the quarrel between father and daughter, it was "like landing in a quiet pool after being thrown down a waterfall and dashed against the rocks". As for Charles and Margaret, they left Edinburgh to stay at Drummond Castle, home of her aunt, Lady Perth, and cousin, Clementina Sarah Burrell. From there Charles wrote to the comtesse d'Albany, widow of Prince Charles Edward Stuart, Pretender to the throne of England and a friend of Adèle. He told her how strongly the marriage had been opposed, and declared that he would do his best to prove that a Frenchman could make a good husband, contrary to the national reputation.[10]

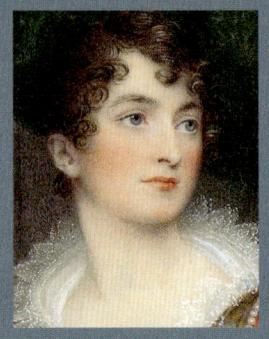

CHAPTER 8

Early Married Life
in Scotland

Thou hast affections too, as pure
As thine one Scottish mountain sun
Affections which for aye endure
When all things perish here below

Poem to Margaret from Mr Bouverie (1842)

Married at last, where did Charles and Margaret make their home? Since he had no prospects of employment either in Louis XVIII's Paris, or in London, they decided to live on her mother's family estate at Meikleour in Perthshire, varied with visits to Edinburgh, the legal, fashionable, intellectual and business capital of Scotland. But, although happy in Scotland, they came to miss the great world, and so occasionally journeyed south, staying in Northumberland with the Greys at Howick and from thence to Brighton, to London and to Woburn for the Duke of Bedford's shooting parties. In 1819 they spent some months in Paris, which from 1827 to 1841 became their main residence. During these years Margaret spent less time in London, and by 1824 admitted that she would feel "quite a stranger there and have all the younger part of the Society to make acquaintance with", and, in 1826, that "I have so many friends in London who I have been long separated from and should feel so bustled and strange on my reappearance in the world." As she grew older, she found London life taxed her health even more, and in 1838 dismissed the social round as being "little suited to her age and inclination", but eventually, once she found a good house, she was there more often and for longer periods, though she always needed to recuperate afterwards in Scotland.

Against this background Margaret produced five daughters. After a succession of miscarriages she gave birth to Emily in 1819, to Clementina in 1821, to Georgina in 1822, to Adelaide in 1824, and finally, to Louise in 1825. It took her months to recover from her last confinement. Lady Holland described the failure to produce a son as "a misfortune", and from her home on Lake Constance, Queen Hortense commiserated with Charles:

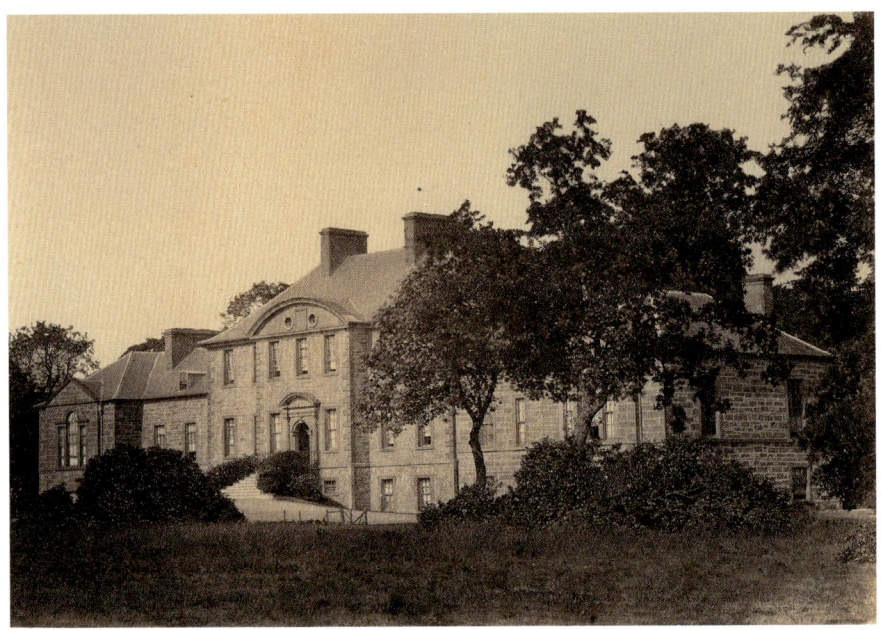

13 Old Meikleour House, Perthshire

> I was much distressed to learn that there are only girls in your
> family – this is indeed hard. I have never heard how the
> grandfather disposed his fortune or whether there would
> have been any chance of it being inherited by a son. It must be
> embarassing to have such a lot of girls and it is sad to think
> that this is the case.

However, the couple did not mind and in 1846, from Vienna, after giving
Emily the news that Princess Liechtenstein had just produced her eighth
daughter but had hoped for a boy, Charles added, "I've never regretted not
having had a son and am quite happy with the children I've got, and only
ask God to let me keep them."

Throughout her life Margaret fussed about her health, but never more
so than when expecting her babies, complaining that she never could understand why these sufferings should be called a "happy state", and regretting

that the invention of chloroform came too late to help her through her confinements. With each pregnancy she lost a tooth – "a sad tribute which I pay to every child", and considered herself a martyr to permanent toothache. Her bouts of excessive tiredness, violent colds, neuralgia, rheumatism, and bilious attacks led to a dependence on Dr Hamilton, the oracle of Edinburgh. When he prescribed a course of electric shocks followed by sea bathing she obeyed him to the letter:

> I begin my day with 30 shocks of electricity and as these thunderbolts have not yet proved fatal I tempt fate in another shape by rushing into the sea three miles from Edinburgh from whence I return half dead with fatigue into a house like a cheese toaster with a boiling sun upon it.

Charles, who was more sceptical, commented to Lady Grey:

> He must be a great man, for Margaret felt better the first time she saw him. As soon as he uttered the divine command: 'Take up thy bed and walk', she did so and I wouldn't be surprised if she was completely recovered within the next fortnight.

Margaret, who was a great believer in water treatments, especially "the warm baths in Dover", recommended thermal baths at Aix and Spa for Lord Grey's rheumatism. Her favourite resort was Brighton, where the "air was so good, there were nice houses close to sea with full southern exposure where you might bask in sun all day long, and good company every evening from 8–11." There she convalesced for several months after the birth of Louise, and in 1826 bought a new house in Brunswick Terrace, three doors away from her friends the Bedfords, near the Tankervilles, the Hollands and her cousins, Clementina Sarah and Peter Robert Burrell. Not only was her own health a constant preoccupation but that of the children was too, as they succumbed to head colds, whooping coughs, typhus, and teething problems. They also benefited from staying in Brighton with their governesses and nurses. This was a penance for Charles, who hated the "nice sea air", and, as the house got into a very bad state over the years, begged Margaret to give it up. Nor could he understand how she could endure the cold sea bathing, and for his own peace of mind and body longed to be back in Scotland.

The first years of the marriage were blighted by Lord Keith's refusal to have anything to do with them. Charles blamed the rift on Queeney, "an odious monster & I am glad, as an observer & a physiognomist, that I discovered that from the very first day I saw her weasel face and hoped that the world would repay her for it". Queeney, who was in a difficult situation, ignored Margaret's letters, while Lord Keith remained adamant. When his sister, Lady Perth, attempted to bring them together, he categorically refused "once for all I will not come nor be harpooned into any situation which will give me much pain". However, after many appeals for forgiveness, cancelled meetings and disappointments, the old man relented and the reconciliation came at last. Charles, aware that he was the cause of the trouble, expressed his relief to Margaret on 17 July 1820 and advised her to be

> all kindness & gratitude & avoid all discussion upon past events or future plans. Don't find fault with the new house, nor with Scotland, nor with Scotchmen, try to avoid all points upon which you differ & try to forgive me all this impertinent advice, which our affection alone can render tolerable.

A few weeks later Margaret confided to Lady Grey:

> I am sure you will be glad to hear that my Father is very kind to me and seems quite at his ease and in good spirits. He saw the little girl yesterday and seemed very much pleased with her but Mr. de Flahaut's name has not yet *been pronounced*, however I hope that Time which has already done so much, may *work this miracle* too before we leave town.

That winter, so as to be in easy reach of London where she could meet her father but also so that Charles could shoot, they stayed in Bedfordshire at Ampthill Park lent them by the Hollands. The miracle happened and by 4 July 1821, Charles had been accepted, Lord Keith writing to him:

> My dear Sir, I received your letter yesterday with much

satisfaction by the account you gave of my daughter . . .
complete recovery ere long . . . My love to Mrs de Flahaut and
believe me Yours faithfully.

Thereafter, relations remained good, and while living at Meikleour House
they kept closely in touch with Lord Keith, who was living in the new house
on his estate at Tulliallan, which they – husband, wife, nurses, children, bag-
gages – could reach within a day. Once arrived there, Queeney received them
hospitably, and, in December 1822, with her daughter, Georgy, visited them
in Edinburgh for the christening of Georgina.

Afterwards the observant Queeney sent her verdict on the state of the
ménage to Fanny d'Arblay:

> He is charming with her, sings, plays games, all her cousins
> there . . . he is extremely sagacious . . . having a daughter
> must be a sad disappointment, as she always said Lord Keith
> was to make her son his heir which I daresay he will do if she
> will assure him that Mr de Flahaut is not the père. As for the
> state of the marriage - he keeps her in good order. She does
> not speak French before him . . . he criticises her
> pronunciation so severely, and she dares not play piano before
> him - he criticises her style in that too.[1]

When Lord Keith died in March 1823, it was found that, in spite of the
reconciliation, he had not altered the terms of his will, which excluded
Margaret and her children from their share of his property, even though he
had expressed his intention of doing so on his next visit to Edinburgh. For
her part, Queeney claimed that she had been promised a larger sum for
housekeeping than the one mentioned in the will, and carried on happily as
if she had not been widowed. A shocked Margaret, who was observing strict
mourning, wrote disapprovingly to Lady Grey of the succession of dinner
parties, trips to Edinburgh, a tour of the Highlands and plans to travel in
France and Italy. However, there was no permament rift and they kept in
touch until Queeney died in 1857, though in the meantime, Georgy's extravagance was to cause Margaret many problems.

Just as Margaret's close relationship with her domineering father was affected by her marriage, so was that of Charles with his adoring mother. Since he was serving, as she said, "two terrible masters, business and marriage", the time was coming when she would have to depend on others for his news, for he seldom replied to her letters, regarding them as no more than "scraps of papers, once read, then forgotten." While recognizing that she now had to take second place to his wife, Adèle continued to show her feelings and was pleased that Margaret, whom she now addressed as "ma fille", kept her letters, unlike Charles. She amused them with Paris gossip, related what was said about them, and gloated over the annoyance caused by their marriage to "les ultras" or die-hard royalists. Her frequent declarations of love, "my Charles and my daughter I love you with my entire being", were interspersed with requests for every detail of their health and family life.

They were never out of her thoughts. So that they could offer their guests the best Bordeaux, champagne, sherry and port, she entrusted her husband, M. de Souza, with buying wine for them. For the comfort of Meikleour House she embroidered garlands of rose-coloured marguerites for the seats and backs of a set of six side chairs, and Margaret's initial M, with poppies, with hounds in pursuit of a stag and a cat and dog ("my view of marriage!"), for an armchair, cushions, a screen, and a footstool for Charles should he ever suffer from gout. Parcels arrived with the latest fashions from Paris: elegant bonnets; six pairs of shoes; a mousseline dress; embroidered handkerchiefs; and gloves. More well-chosen gifts: a bedside lamp for Margaret, a reading stand for the library, came to mark the New Year. Before the birth of Emily in 1819 she sent a layette, bought from the supplier to the duchesse de Berry, and promised more to follow. A delighted Margaret informed Lady Grey, who had just given birth to her son William:

> I wish I could show you a cargo of most quizzy baby caps which Mad[me] de Souza has sent me from Paris. They are the exact models of the *cornette du matin* of a Parisian coquette, covered with white puffs of lace and bows of brocade ribbon tying under the chin. I think I must send you one to put upon your baby, the day he receives his old fashioned name.[2]

In reply to Margaret's gift of a lock of her daughter Emily's hair, Adèle thanked her for the

> . . . jet black hair of my granddaughter, which makes me
> hope that she will also inherit the dark eyes of her father. I
> have only one desire which is to see them all and then I shall
> die happy.[3]

Having made her home in Scotland Margaret now had the time and opportunity to see more of her Elphinstone relations: Lord Keith's brothers, four sisters and their children. Although she had been brought up by her unmarried aunts, Primrose (d. 1802), and Mary (d. 1825), she was also close to Clementina, Lady Perth (d. 1822) , to Eleonor (d. 1808) and her husband, the courtier William Adam, and their son, Frederick, whose sudden death at Greenwich in 1853 she much regretted. Just as Lord Keith had done, the two uncles both succeeded in life through brains and tenacity. William Fullerton Elphinstone, who became a director of the East India Company, had three children who shared Margaret's admiration for Napoleon. The eldest, James Drummond Fullerton Elphinstone (1788–1857), became a cavalry officer who was wounded in the arm at Waterloo, taken prisoner and brought before Napoleon, who sent his surgeon to look after him. In gratitude, the Elphinstones sent from Canton various expensive objects each with shield and crowned N: an ivory game of chess, two ivory openwork globes and a box of mother-of-pearl counters, which were used by Napoleon at Saint Helena.[4] There, one of James's sisters, Clementina, who married Admiral Sir Pulteney Malcolm, wrote a very sympathetic account of the interesting conversations they had with him,[5] and the other, Anne, had rushed down to Plymouth in the hope of catching a glimpse before he sailed into exile. She and Margaret became close friends.

The eldest uncle, John, 11th Lord Elphinstone, was the father of the 12th Lord Elphinstone (d. 1813) and of Charles, an admiral who assumed the additional name of Fleeming and inherited in 1799 his grandmother's estates at Cumbernauld House in Dumbartonshire. With his Spanish wife, Donna Catalina Paulina Alessandro, he had four children, including a son John, who became the 14th Lord Elphinstone but never married. On his death, the estate passed to his three sisters: Clementina, who married Viscount Hawarden in 1845, and achieved fame as a pioneer of the art of photography;

Mary, the "very pleasing, quiet and ladylike Missy"; and Anne Elizabeth, who married William Bontine in 1851. Their uncle, Charles Fleeming's brother Mountstuart Elphinstone (1779–1859), made a great reputation for himself as an administrator of British India. Similarly, John, third son of the 11th Lord Elphinstone (1807–1860), who became the 13th Lord in 1813, had a very distinguished career in India as Governor of Madras and Bombay, and handled the problems of the Mutiny with great competence. Margaret and he conducted a very lively correspondence, she relating all the latest news and gossip and undertaking to buy him what he needed from Europe to furnish his Indian residences. On his death she observed, "What a bad tomb India has been for our relations: I think I have lost 10 from the effects of that dreadful climate". This large clan was always welcomed at her houses at home and abroad, and she used her political influence to obtain pensions and appointments for children and widows.

Margaret was very close to another aunt, Clementina (1749–1822), wife of Lord Perth of Drummond Castle, who did her best to persuade Lord Keith to accept the marriage with Charles. The couple had met at the London house of Lady Perth's daughter, the heiress Clementina Sarah Drummond, who married Peter Robert Burrell in 1808. The Burrells changed names when they inherited the title of Gwydyr in 1820, and again in 1827 when they became Lord and Lady Willoughby de Eresby. Of their four surviving children (Frederick died in infancy), their son, Alberic (1821–1870) was described by Margaret as "an aimable and agreeable young man, perfectly gentlemanlike, which is not extraordinary having such an example before him as his father who is that par excellence". The eldest of the three "Burrell girls" was Clementina Elizabeth (1809–1888), later (1827) Lady Heathcote and then Lady Aveland, and the youngest, a friend of Emily, was Augusta, who in 1840 married the 2nd Lord Carrington. When the second daughter, Elizabeth Susan (1810–1853), died after seven years' illness, Margaret wrote, "I lived so much with the Willoughbys in my early days that I considered her children almost as my own and I am much pained by the loss which causes many other chords to vibrate mournfully."

After Margaret's marriage the two couples remained close friends, staying often in each other's houses, both in Scotland and England. Charles never missed the grouse shooting at Drummond Castle for the week of the twelfth of August and returned in early September for the first days of the partridge

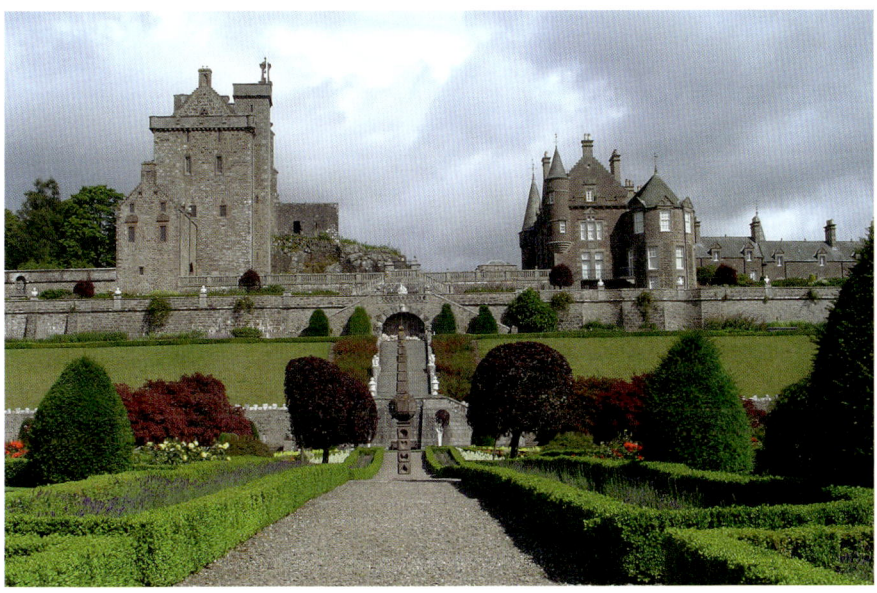

14 **Drummond Castle, Perthshire**

season. With their children the Flahauts were often in Lincolnshire at Grimsthorpe, the Willoughby mansion with its north front designed by John Vanbrugh. In 1839 they spent six weeks there after their plan to winter in Scotland had to be abandoned when the chef, after sixteen years' service, gave his notice so as to open a restaurant in November and the other French servants all refused to go north. The family were immediately rescued by the Willoughbys, who invited them to stay until the London season began. This long visit was a happy one, and as field sports were the great attraction of Grimsthorpe, Charles went out shooting every day. In later years the two couples and their children also stayed together in Dover and Torquay, where they went sea-fishing on Lord Willoughby's boat *The Leopard*. As he acted as one of her trustees Margaret relied on him to support her claims on the estate, though she was careful to get her timing right and not disturb his favourite pursuits: "Lord Willoughby dislikes reading a letter and answering it so much, I will not write to him at Torquay." In her will of 1859 Margaret acknowledged her affection for them both: "I bequeath to my dear cousin

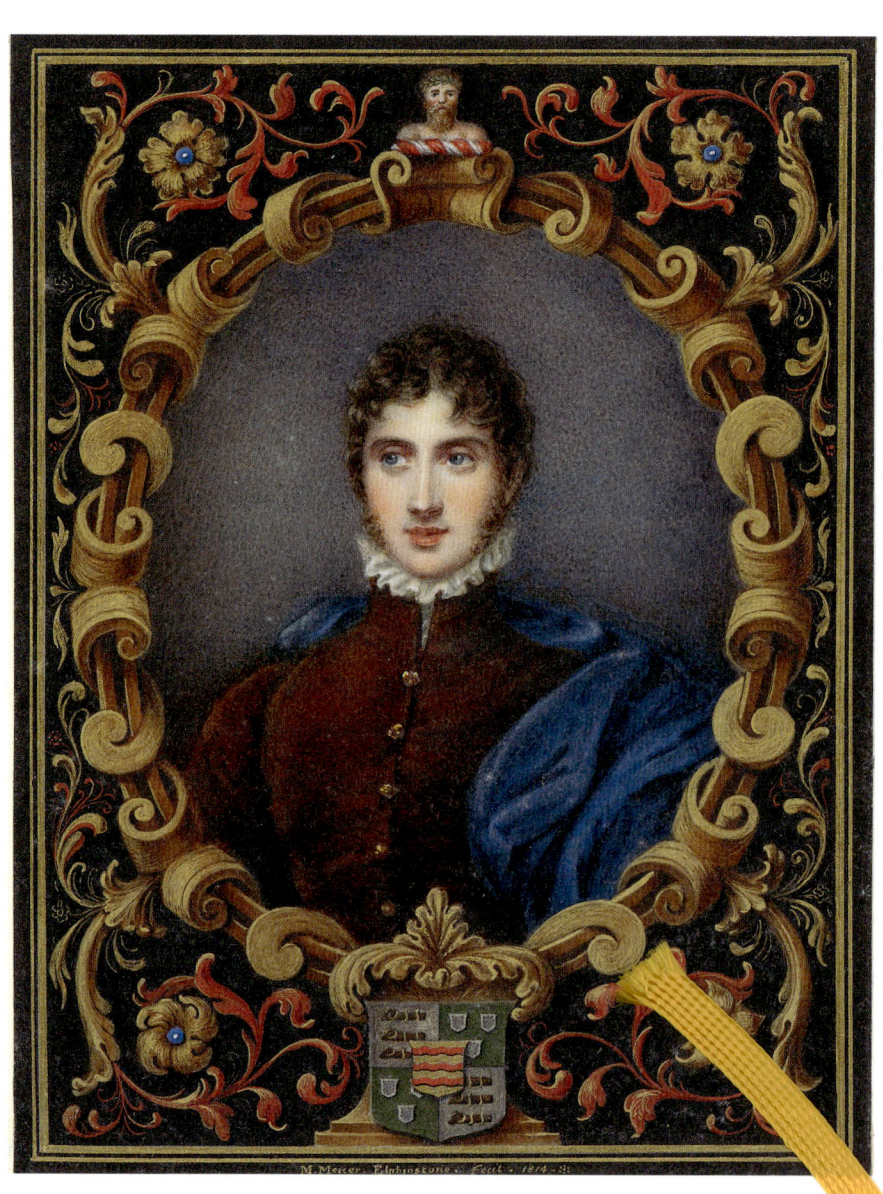

15 Miniature of Peter Robert Drummond-Burrell,
22nd Baron Willoughby de Eresby by Margaret

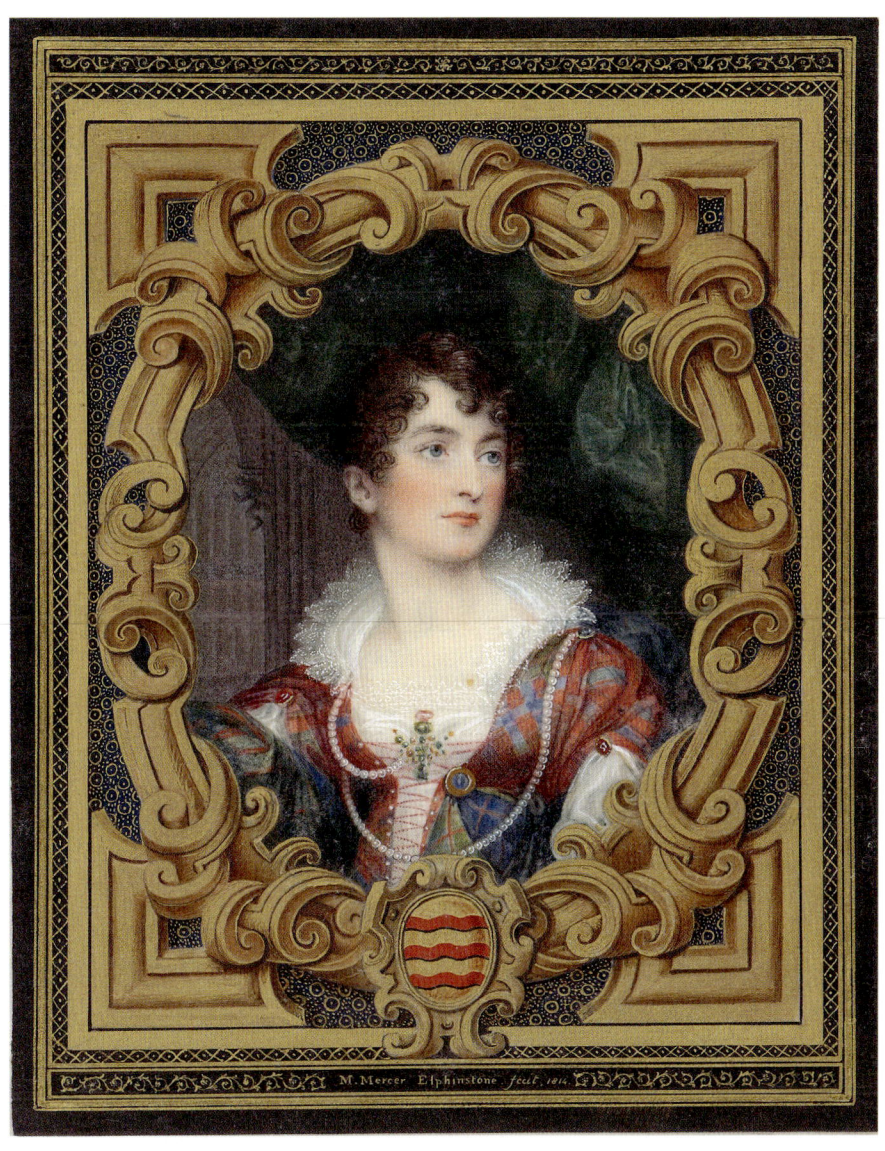

16 Miniature of Clementina Sarah Drummond-Burrell,
Baroness Willoughby de Eresby by Margaret

Lady W d'E whom I have always considered as a sister the gold chain bracelet with emerald clasp my gift from Princess Charlotte and miniature picture of Princess Charlotte painted by Mrs. Mee", and "To Lord W d'E who has always been more of a relation to me I leave the pair of vases now in the corridor of Tulliallan and two small columns in lapis with gilt figures now on the chimney piece of small drawing room at Tulliallan."

Every so often they were obliged to leave Meikleour and stay in Edinburgh. There the French traveller, the marquis de Custine, was struck by the strange mixture of people: "If you can imagine a scene where men dressed like savages walk in the streets crowded with the sort of people you meet in the rue de la Paix every morning, then you will have some idea of the capital of Scotland."[6]

Picturesque as this scene may have seemed to Custine, it did not appeal to Margaret, who came to Edinburgh for her confinements, having little confidence in the local Meikleour doctor. Her dislike of "this odious town" could have been because she was so often ill there, considered the hotels noisy and dirty and found it almost impossible to rent a comfortable house. Once settled, she and Charles kept open house for the cleverest men in the city: William Playfair, the architect, and the eminent Judge Jeffrey, much liked by her for "his very frank and communicative disposition, and the readiness and good humour with which he seems to deliver his opinion and information upon all subjects". In his company they discussed *Mandeville: A Tale of the Seventeenth Century in England* (1817), "a disgusting Rhapsody, the most odious book" by William Godwin (1756–1836), *Lalla Rookh*, an Eastern Romance by Thomas Moore, and the latest volume of Walter Scott's *Rob Roy*, which greatly entertained Margaret.

Another visitor was the American George Ticknor, who was impressed by both husband and wife:

> He is a Frenchman, an elegant man, bred in England and
> with English habits and feelings; and now married to a
> daughter of Lord Keith, a woman of a great deal of spirit,
> talent and culture, who was the most intimate of the personal
> friends of the Princess Charlotte, and had more influence
> over her than anybody else. Her health was not good, so they
> were always at home, and had more or less informal society

every evening. Among the persons who came there, besides
Lord Belhaven and Lord Elcho . . .were [the lawyers]
Cranston . . . Clerk, Thomson, and Murray . . . The society
[in Edinburgh] is certainly excellent . . . It is a great thing . . .
to have so much influence granted to talent as there is in
Edinburgh, for it breaks down artificial distinctions in
society, and makes its terms easy to all who ought to enter
into it, and have any right to be there.[7]

As well as good talk there were musical evenings, and in 1819 Charles and
Signor Pazzi sang with the two Liddle sisters, who went on to great acclaim
before large audiences in Edinburgh and Glasgow.

While Margaret was confined indoors, Charles got out and about.
Margaret told Lady Grey how he spent his time in July 1818: "This is the
first day of Edin[r] Races, and Mr. de Flahaut. is gone to them . . . it is a week
of *great gentry* for him, tomorrow he anticipates the pleasure of hearing 18
Bagpipes playing at the same time, and seeing 100 Highlanders dance Scotch
reels, in their national garb, and the next day, he is to attend the election of
Scotch peers and witness the triumph of Lord Rosebery and Lord Tweeddale
who are to be brought in without opposition at the recommendation of ministers . . ." Then on 15 April 1819 . . . "I cannot give you a better account of
Mr. de Flahault than that he is out every night dancing and flirting with all
the young Misses in Edin[r], and it agrees with him so well, and he looks so
much better than he did, that I almost regret that the gay season is coming
to a close . . . Nov. 1st 1822 Mr. de Flahault is gadding and this day meets the
Fergusons, Balfours &c at Lord Gillies!" He often dined with his close friend
the lawyer John Murray, who had attended the Flahaut wedding in 1817,
and made short journeys to visit friends such as the Peninsular War hero
Lord Lyndoch (1748–1843) and Lord Fife (1776–1857) of Duff House, co.
Banff. Everyone liked him and he was only criticized for not drinking
enough, though on his part the one aspect of Scottish hospitality to which he
objected was the custom of remaining for hours at the dining-table after the
departure of the ladies.[8] In recognition of his contribution to Scottish life,
Charles was elected in 1821 to the Edinburgh Highland Society, whose aim
was the "preservation of the martial spirit, language, dress, music and antiq-
uities of the Caledonians and rescuing from oblivion the remains of Celtic

literature", an honour which pleased him greatly. Their cultural and social interests ranged wide and in 1836 Margaret attended a great assembly of scientific men, "an exhibition of Lions!"[9]

After attending the coronation of George IV with Casimir de Montrond,[10] in London in 1821, Charles was also present when that monarch visited Scotland the following year to emphasize the historic union between England and Scotland. There, thanks to Mr Peel, the king gave him letters of denization regularizing his legal position in Britain, previously obtained through his purchase of shares in the Bank of Scotland at the time of his marriage.[11] Margaret remained at Meikleour House while Charles enjoyed the Highland pageantry organized by Sir Walter Scott, but she joined him in Edinburgh for the birth of Georgina, after the king had left. For her next confinement in 1824 she rented no. 22, Charlotte Square, "a most comfortable well furnished House, which I much prefer to any other I have been [in] in this detestable Town," and continued, "I have been now in Edin[r] a week . . . today, however I am much relieved, and hope to have a little rest before my confinement takes place which may be in ten days or a fortnight. We have got a clean airy House in a quiet situation which will suit my present circumstances and tho' it is very scantily furnished I have made it tolerably comfortable and hope to get out of it before I find out its numerous wants and inconveniences. We have hardly any society and Edin[r] has so deserted an appearance that it looks like the City of the Plague; it is singular to see a town where splendid palaces are springing up like mushrooms every day with so little appearance of habitation or life. A carriage passing in the street is an event, and on an average I do not suppose that you meet two foot passengers on a mile of Houses."

The most lively and detailed, though critical, account of Charles and Margaret's Edinburgh salon 1818–19, was written by Elizabeth Grant of Rothiemurchus. She described how a Miss Maclean, "a real beauty", became famous during that season, explaining that

> [w]hat stamped her celebrity was the notice taken of her by
> the Count and Countess Flahault; they invited her to stay
> with them, and as they saw company in an easy way every
> evening, Miss Maclean was at once raised into our great
> world. The Countess, Miss Mercer Elphinstone by birth,

Baroness Keith in expectancy, had fallen in love with this most attractive foreigner and would marry him. An heir to her vast fortune was of consequence, and an heir did not come; all sorts of accidents preventing it. Little Dr Hamilton was consulted, and when the next occasion presented itself Madame de Flahault was condemned to her sofa; but as her mind was to be amused she was to pass her time cheerfully. There she lay, covered with a lace overlay lined with pink silk, her hair nicely arranged, chattering at a great rate to thirty or forty guests. She was a very ugly woman and not a clever one and very far from being generally agreeable. I do not think she would have continued to attract much company, men at least, whom she greatly preferred, without some such magnet as her new protégée. Miss Maclean's reign was short.

She returned to Berwick, married a lieutenant in a marching regiment, "went with him to Bombay and died".

As for Charles, she went on, he was "in manner perfection, a finished frenchman, than which one can go no further in describing a gentleman; very handsome too, of a lively conversation truly agreeable". At Mrs Munro's small party there were young people, but no music for dancing. Who would play? After an awkward moment Charles volunteered to do so.

He played particularly well, so that it was a treat to dance to him . . . his intention was to assist the amusement of evening, make every body happy, and pay a neat compliment the while. It was all so high bred, so very un British. He behaved very well to his somewhat haughty wife, and she got on very well with him always.[12]

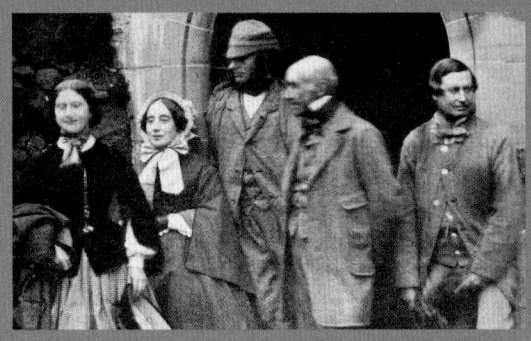

CHAPTER 9

Country Life in Scotland: Meikleour and Tulliallan

*Il me semble que je retrouve ma patrie en mettant le pied
sur une terre, dont, grâce à Walter Scott, je connais si bien
l'histoire et les habitans*

Astolphe de Custine

Queency and Lord Keith had predicted that Margaret and Charles would soon tire of life in Scotland, and that the marriage would end "in Mutual disgust and joy at Separation", but they were proved wrong. For Charles, Scotland was not, as Lord Byron saw it, proud though he was to be a Scot, "a land of meanness, sophistry and mist", but one of great attractions. Whereas the French vicomte in C. J. Lever's *Confessions of Harry Lorrequer* (1845), who had also married a Scottish heiress with an ancestral home in the Highlands, "pined for Paris, its cafés, its boulevards, its maisons de jeu, and its soirées" and passed his days bored to death, "looking from the deep and narrow windows of some oak-framed room upon the bare and heath-clad moors, or watching the clouds' shadows as they passed across the dark pine trees that closed the distance", Charles took to the laird's way of life. As early as October 1817, he made a good impression on Mr Loch, Lord Keith's agent, who told Lady Granville that he "seems perfectly happy cutting down trees, planting, shooting, fishing and is only blamed for not drinking enough," and that Margaret would be the first to be tired of retirement to Scotland.

In 1818 Captain Basil Hall, RN, who visited them, sent an enthusiastic report to Miss Elliot in Madras: "She is affable, gentle, temperate in discussion and in politics, obliging, considerate, in short a most amiable and well informed person."

As for Charles:

> . . . a man of the highest possible cultivation devoid of
> prejudice, liberal beyond anything on questions of national

advantage and superiority, most minutely and accurately informed on all kinds of topics particularly in anything relating to this country. Knowledge extensive, unbiased mind, conversation rich and instructive, obliging gentleness, comforts of those about him occasional sort of feminine delicacy unusual in that he has spent so much of his life in camps. Talks with all the country gentlemen on their own subjects as if he had been living among them all his life and does the same with farmers and countrymen all without ostentation or any effort. By these means he has melted away the prejudices which at first pressed so cruelly around him and his circle of friends and admirers is rapidly extending. Likes the country, has no wish to go into society or dash into any gaiety. She is naturally disposed to look to society again. Seems very happy: I never in my life met 2 people who agreed better.[1]

Meikleour House, named after the Gaelic term for a large place, was built in 1730 by Robert and Jean Mercer. In August 1817 Margaret sent Lady Grey an account of life there. She described the difficulties of settling in in "this long neglected mansion" in a miserable state of dirt and rubbish, "incessantly driven from room to room followed by mops and brooms and still scarcely having a clean corner to sit down in". The weather was always a problem: in one tremendous storm the hailstones broke the windowpanes of the house. Heating was difficult, and on 7 March 1821 she reported to her father:

> . . . in middle of heavy fall of snow . . . we have arrived safely . . . no chance of keeping warm. A gale of wind blows in at every window and door, smoke comes from the fires in the few rooms left to inhabit, so we are in a very uncomfortable confused state but I'm busy papering up windows and doors in hope of improving it".

She soon had had enough, and the following year engaged the architect Ignatius Bonomi to provide protection and comfort against the cold.

Guests, who came frequently, often staying for several weeks, were warned to bring furs, heavy coats and woollen clothes. They begged Lord and Lady Grey to visit and happily received Margaret's relations, including Colonel and Mrs Tarleton, as well as Charles's Italian friends Baron Sigismondo Trechi and the Napoleonist Ugo Foscolo. In 1822 while her father and Queeney went to Edinburgh, she was left in charge of her sister Georgy, "a plain child with few advantages, but on the whole well disposed and kind and affectionate to me and her nieces", and at the same time she entertained Clementina Elizabeth and Elizabeth Susan, the two young daughters of her cousin Clementina Sarah of Drummond Castle, "making a very gay young party".

Meikleour House was pretty, with the river running beneath the drawing-room windows. While Margaret organized her household, supervised repairs and improvements and planted a rose garden, Charles enjoyed the excellent sport on the estate, setting off for the grouse moors at 4 a.m. and fishing salmon on the river Tay. He loved the landscape and took as much interest in the Meikleour trees and his farm as if he had never had any other society or occupation. He managed it well, giving very specific instructions to the agent Menzies, negotiating the purchase of livestock – colts, fillies and a bull – and by employing an engineer was able to improve the water supply due to the discovery of a magnificent spring in a quarry. Anxious to improve their finances, and foreseeing the investment potential of the railways he made enquiries about the locomotives being made in Newcastle while staying with Lord Morpeth at Castle Howard in 1825. Their family life was happy, and while Margaret drove out in a gig for two hours every day, enjoying the beauty of the drives around the house, the children rode in baskets on a donkey. In June 1822, after five years of marriage she acknowledged, "I am in the most extraordinary state of prosperity considering all circumstances, and am able to walk about like other people. The white pony is in the greatest beauty and as usual is the comfort of my life." As for Charles, when the time came for them to leave, he was full of regret and wrote to John Murray in July 1823 "Alas, poor Meikleour, I know I shall never inhabit more and I shall not be as happy as here but so it must be."

In July 1823, persuaded by the financial advantages, they moved from Meikleour House to Tulliallan, a better house, recently built by Lord Keith in neo-Gothic style, but "in an odious place" which remained their Scottish home until they died, when it was inherited by the eldest daughter, Emily. The decision to do so meant that they were now governed by trustees, who

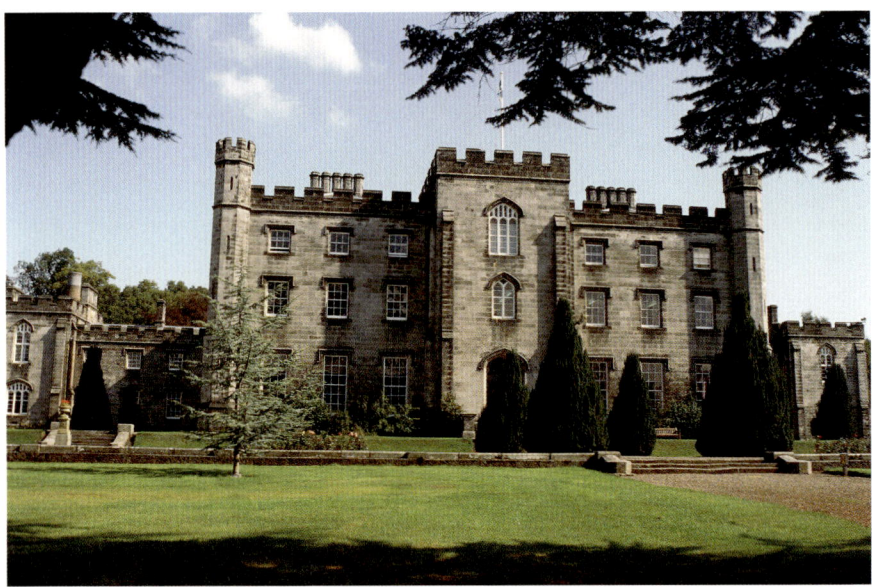

17 Tulliallan Castle, Fife

at first Margaret hoped would defray every expense of the place and establishment, except personal ones. Unfortunately, there were problems right from the start as Margaret complained:

> I have been teased to death with a great deal of disagreeable business with the Trustees, who tho' very well inclined to me personally were desirous of keeping more power of interference in their hands than could have been consistent with our comfort residing there, and our negotiations were very nearly coming to an end. However the *law* in this case has been more *friendly* than *my friends*, and fully authorized all my claims to a much greater extent than the Trustees proposed, so I hope all our affairs will soon be concluded to our satisfaction . . .

The trustees – lords Willoughby de Eresby, Elphinstone, Rosslyn, Rutherfurd and Edward Ellice, "natural friends in Trust activity, zeal and friendship equal", were nominated from her family, for she insisted that "it was never the wish of my father that the interests of myself and my children should fall into the hands of strangers and lawyers". She also claimed that in return for taking such pains and trouble over Tulliallan, and the sacrifice of Meikleour House she should be paid as any other servant employed on a property. She argued constantly with the agent Mr Loch, nephew of William Adam. She considered his management fee preposterous, while he accused her of overspending, and subjected her to long delays in getting the money for building cottages, and a lodge by the new approach to the house, claiming a "want of funds". In 1841 the house was closed until agreement was reached on the conditions which had induced her to accept it as a residence, though she was still kept in suspense over the money available year after year. Always practical, since the cooks could not work in winter with the windows and doors open, Margaret asked her friend William Playfair (1789–1857), the Edinburgh architect, to alter the kitchens, so that the smoke and smell did not fill the house and for some years the house was overrun with builders and painters.

Many problems were caused by Margaret's half-sister, Georgina. Small of stature, light in weight, a keen rider, she grew up to become one of first women to invade the hunting field, previously restricted to men, and as a steeplechase rider she rode harder than anyone. Charles tried unsuccessfully to persuade Georgina's cousin, the 13th Lord Elphinstone to marry her, but in 1831 she accepted the Hon. Augustus John Villiers (d. 1847), with whom she shared a passion for racing. In 1838 the Villiers stayed at Tulliallan, leaving the house party to attend race meetings south of the border, and Margaret told Lady Grey her misgivings: "They are elated by his success at Doncaster, but he has played more than usual this year, is not disposed to reform his establishment, a crash is inevitable but meantime they are UP IN THE WORLD". Their extravagance and Queeney's negligence led the couple to take legal advice so as to upset Lord Keith's settlements, and they asked Margaret to assist in obtaining an Act of Parliament to set them aside. Margaret, who did not believe it could succeed and would be very expensive, declined taking part, remarking that as Georgina was the next heir to the property which, should she have no son, reverted to the Flahaut children, it was in everybody's interest to preserve it. She regretted that the Villiers were "guided by the opinion of an intriguing lawyer of house of Tennant, with a bad reputation". On her side, Margaret relied on the advice of the eminent judge Lord Rutherfurd, who became a close friend, and encouraged her to stand firm and not initiate legal proceedings. Charles did not interfere but pointed out the irony of the situation: that the Flahauts should be respecting Lord Keith's settlements so that his widow and younger daughter could attack them.

Besides the children and their nurses, there was Margaret's Aunt Mary who moved in with them until her death in 1825. Intellectually alert almost to the end, she enjoyed conversation, discussed the Burmese War disputes between Lord Amherst and Sir Edward Paget and spent hours poring over the map of India, "hunting out stations of native troops as if she were Governor General". Another addition was Emily's governess Miss Powell, daughter of a china painter (an interest of Margaret's), who had been sent for training in Paris by Margaret. Since French servants could not stand the winter in Scotland and English habits and prejudices made long residence there difficult, they finally solved the problem of finding suitable domestic staff by engaging a good Scottish housekeeper, Margaret Husson, who could be entrusted with the house during their absence.

Notwithstanding the weather, which was always unreliable, their life in Scotland suited them, and they considered that being "drowned by rain, blown away by heavy gales was better than being boiled by the London and Paris heat waves". Although she enjoyed fishing perch, riding, visiting, and arranging the furniture in the house, Margaret's greatest pleasure was the garden. In a letter to Emily in 1836 she wrote:

> I am very busy in the Garden here finishing a piece of rock work which I am sure you will think very pretty when you see it, and today we are pulling up some granite pillars my Father brought from Egypt in the small Island in the pond, which I expect will have a *marvellous* effect. You see I continue to amuse myself and pull about stones and trees.

In the evening the family played games, and Margaret explained that

> Graselbags has been the rage, the natural consequence is to quarrel with your best friend, like a double patience where

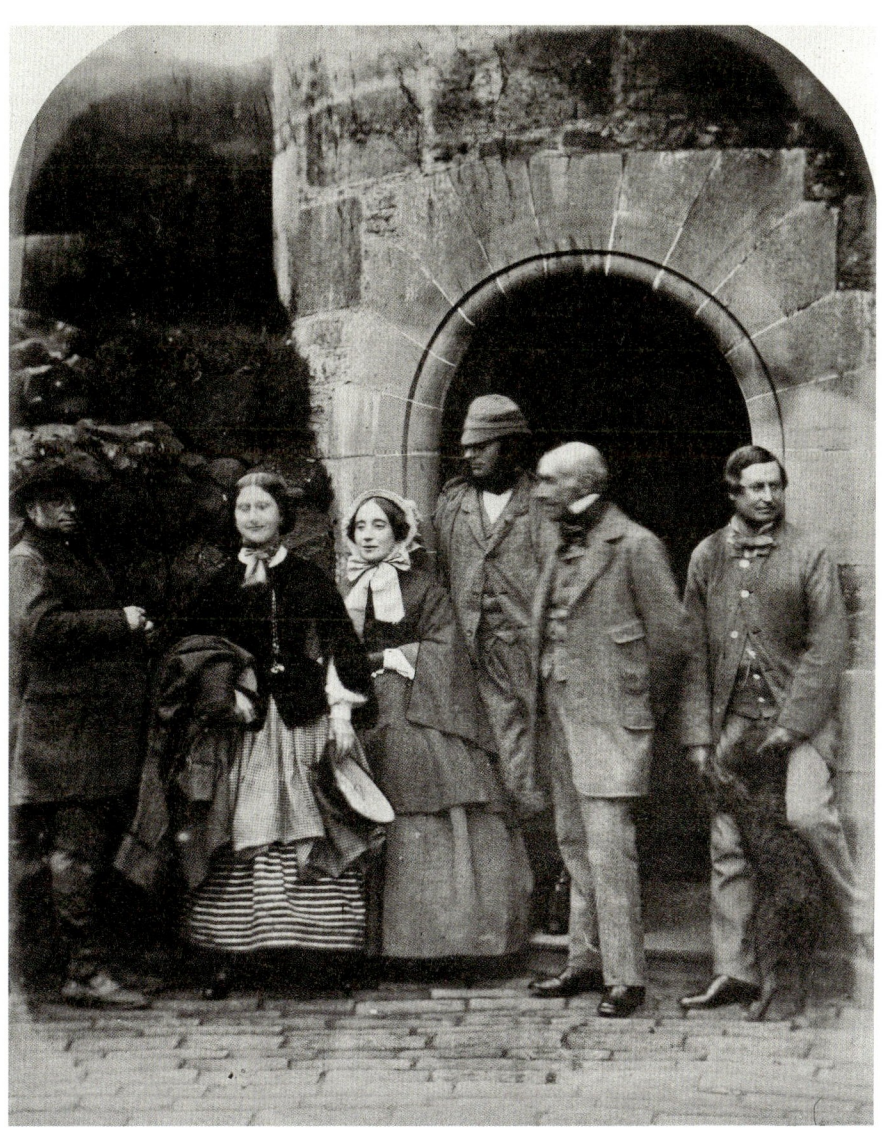

18 Photograph of the Flahauts at Drummond Castle in the 1840s: Charles is second from the right, Emily next to him and Félix de Lavalette on the far left

> you and your adversary scramble and fight for who is to
> make up their pack from Ace to king first – quick eyes, light
> fingers are talents required – Adèle beats us all.

Charles was in his element; as William Cowper observed in 1838, "I think he succeeds better in his capacity of Laird than in any other" and his occupations "consist in farming, making walks, planting etc etc which make one's time pass pretty well". As a sportsman he was out shooting or fishing every day. Indoors his main preoccupation was organizing the very fine comprehensive library, for he was a keen reader. He had no regret for the bright lights of the city:

> . . . what people call our dull solitary life is 10.000 times more
> agreeable than this way of passing our time . . . I will say the
> same of Paris: it is a dull commerce of empty phrases and
> affected manners which appear the greatest absurdity when
> one has had the time to lose the habit of them.

In these circumstances the marriage continued happy, and in April 1825 he wrote to Margaret:

> I can well say that no recollection is more agreeable and
> happy than that of the last 8 years though I can tell you now
> and then that you are provoking. But a perfect reliance on the
> affection and kindness of one's dearest friend is a source of
> constant happiness.

In 1829 after visiting Hortense at Aix he brought their son Auguste Morny to Scotland, so that he should experience the pleasures of life there. They first stayed with Lord and Lady Murray outside Edinburgh, then went to Callander for the shooting, and on to Tulliallan. On 21 August he wrote from Drummond Castle that in spite of the unending rain he had "made Auguste ride from Callender [sic]. I am glad to profit by every opportunity to cure him of the habits of softness to which Mad. de Souza has accustomed him." During this visit Auguste seems to have pleased his father, learning to shoot game, behaving very well and in spite of not understanding much English did not appear uncomfortable or awkward at the dinner-table, and returned back to Scotland many times, so much so that he seemed to be "always there".

As at Meikleour, Tulliallan was almost always full of visitors, the number growing as ever more people discovered Scotland, attracted by a landscape evocative of Shakespeare's tragedies and the novels of Sir Walter Scott. The marquis de Custine was surprised to find so many in 1830: "Whereas you might believe that hardly anyone went there, the truth is that the roads are packed with elegant women and smart gentlemen and that even in the remotest villages the inns are full and rooms must be booked in advance. Scotland is the English Tivoli, the playground of these masters of the seas who go there every summer to dissipate the boredom of wealth".[2] Staying with the Flahauts was not without its dangers. In September 1823, barely three months after moving in, Margaret entertained two of Charles's oldest friends, Gabriel Delessert and Casimir de Montrond, who, after wandering over impassable mountains, full of bogs and without guides twelve miles from any human habitation, got lost on their way home.

Far less worrying was a visit in September 1824 of the singing Liddle sisters with

> some risk of Miss Anne singing herself to death in the meantime, for she and Mr. de Flahault are *at it* from morning till night, and every day they awake with an extinction de voix from fatigue, which only causes them to exert their lungs with increased zeal and energy and they scream the notes they ought to sing, so that with Mrs. Liddle's thumping in imitation of Rossini, and the assistance of the Miss Ardens [?] and Mr. Liddle (with an uninvited squeak of the Bagpipes occasionally) we produce choruses which would rival those of the Chaussée d'Antin in point of noise.

English and Scottish guests were more numerous, filling the house for the months of August, September and November, often arriving without much notice, following the Scotch fashion of writing to announce oneself. Some, like Lady Alvanley, wife of the Chief Justice of the Court of Common Pleas, fell ill (1824) and required nursing for two weeks.

Margaret not only entertained at Tulliallan but joined other house parties

19 Photograph of the Flahauts at
Drummond Castle in the early 1860s.
From the left: Charles; Georgina; Emily
seated; her daughter (also Emily)
standing close; with "Clan" (?);
Hon. Mrs Georgina Villiers and Lord
Edmond Fitzmaurice at the back; with
Margaret seated on the right and in the
foreground Henry Thomas Petty-
Fitzmaurice, Earl of Shelburne, later
the 4th Marquess of Lansdowne

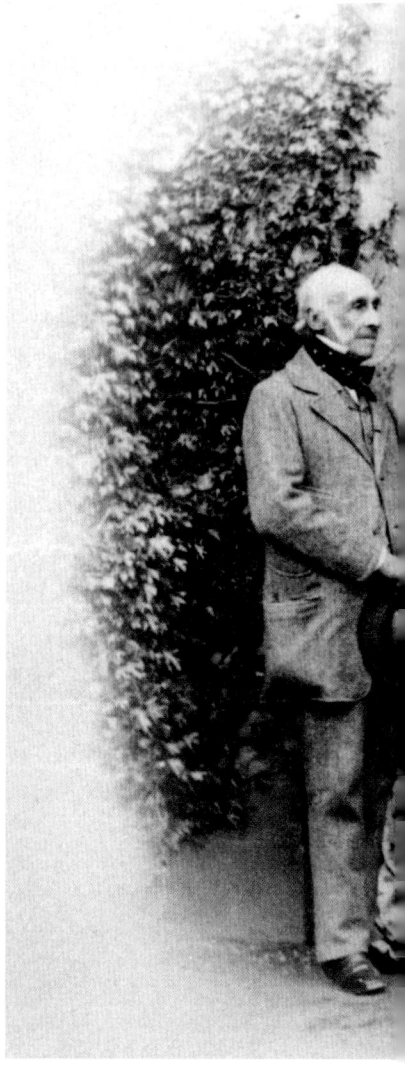

elsewhere in Scotland: at the Duke of Hamilton's; with the Mansfields at
Scone; the Roseberys at Dalmeny; and the Flemings at the family seat of
Cumbernauld.

In 1824 she related to Lady Grey a tour of visits in Fife in the previous
week:

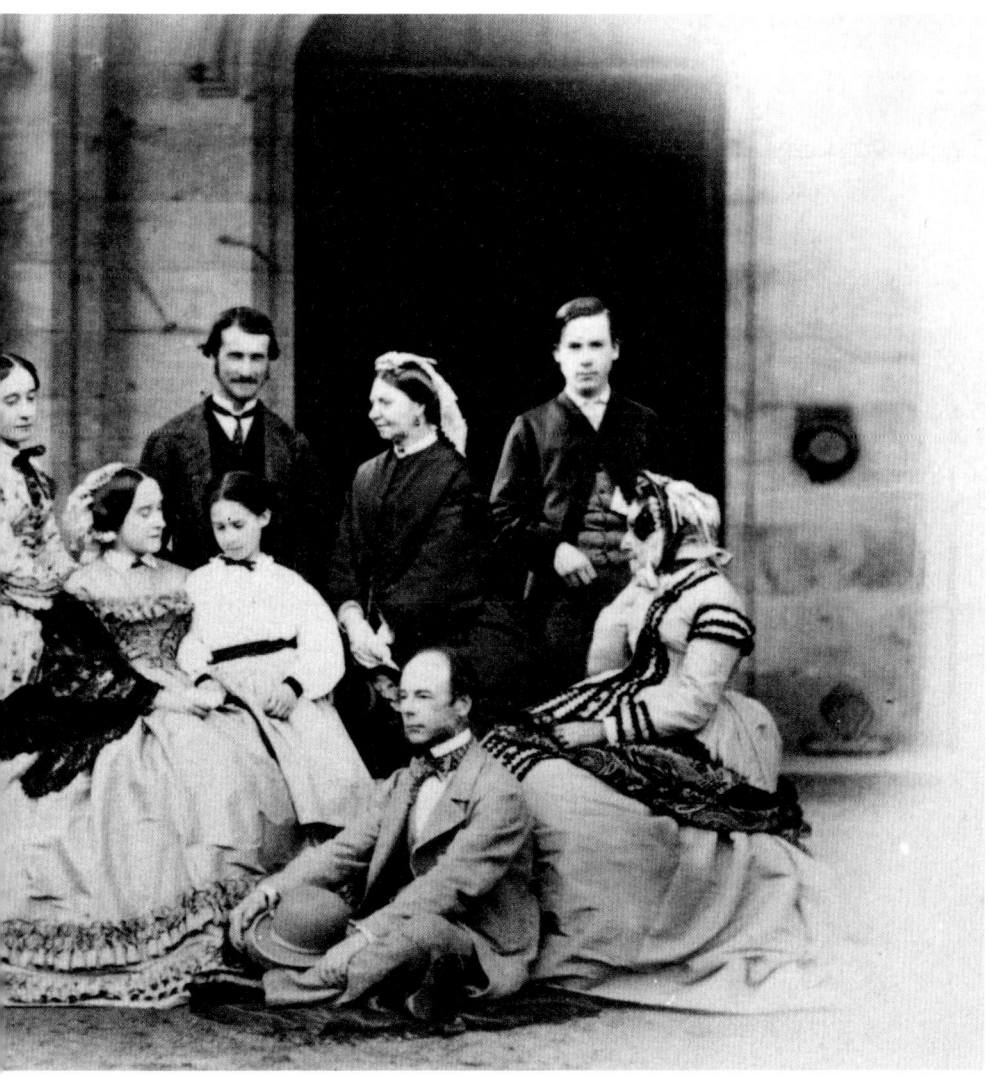

I began my peregrinations by committing a great sin and visiting Mrs. Ferguson at Raith, but I trust it has been redeemed since by the virtuous action of having passed two days with the Chief Commissioner and his daughter at Charlton, from whence we came here about an hour ago.

> Lady Janet [daughter] is as usual and Ld Rosslyn the most
> amiable and obliging of men . . . Raith is a beautiful place, and
> the men had excellent sport, killing pheasants all the
> mornings and playing cards all nights. It is not so lively for
> Ladies as I do not think Mrs. Ferguson particularly agreeable
> herself, and her society is rather circumscribed.[3]

A favourite expedition was to Lake Katrine, celebrated by Sir Walter Scott
in his poem *The Lady of the Lake*. From Lake Katrine her visitors could leave
by steamer to the Duke of Argyll at Inverary Castle, or north to the Duke of
Sutherland at Dunrobin. Guests came and went from Drummond Castle to
Meikleour House all the time, for the two homes were separated only by a
pretty drive of thirty miles, and Margaret was often there with Charles. He
enjoyed the shooting which was better than at Tulliallan, and Margaret
helped her cousin Clementina Sarah entertain the women guests. On one of
these frequent visits to Drummond Castle, Margaret had to act as hostess in
the absence of Clementina Sarah, who was suddenly called to London when
her mother, Lady Perth, was dying. That very evening two grand French
travellers, Madame de Noailles and Mr de Saluces arrived from visiting
Fingal's Cave, made famous through *Fingal, an Ancient Epic Poem, in Six
Books* (1761). This is a melancholy, sublime poem of Celtic Scotland alleged
to have been written by Ossian, son of King Fingal, but in reality by James
Macpherson. Charles was confined to bed with a cold and Margaret, "being
the only woman in the House was obliged," she wrote, "to exert myself to
make her séjour as agreeable as I could while she chose to remain, and that
of the party of guests invited to meet her, but between the fatigue of doing
the honours to her all day and being a sick nurse all night, I was very nearly
knocked up myself". Charles and Margaret also went on short visits to neighbours: Lord Abercromby, Mr Fox Maule, Mrs Colville, sister of Lord
Auckland, for "in this country we may consider ourselves as neighbours
within five and twenty miles".

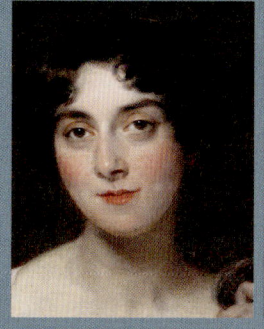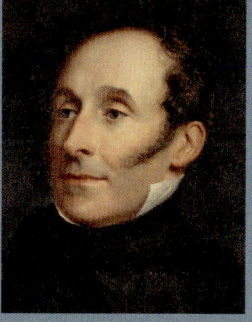

CHAPTER 10

The Great World:
Paris I

*Paris, la métropole des arts, l'abbaye de Thélème de la
fantaisie, le grand bazar du luxe européen, la Mecque où se
rendent, de tous points de l'horizon, tous les croyants du plaisir*

*Paris est la mine inépuisable, le sujet toujours neuf, le thème
sur lequel l'antiquaire, le philosophe et le poète peuvent broder
des variations à l'infini*

Théophile Gautier, Introduction, *Paris et les Parisiens
au XIXe siècle* (1856)

Assured by General de La Tour-Maubourg, ambassador in London,
that they would be allowed to live in France "without molestation
from any party", the Flahauts decided to stay in Paris for some
months in 1819 with Adèle and M. de Souza. After enduring seasickness on
a stormy crossing, then the tedious sessions with customs officers, followed
by a long coach journey, on their arrival in Paris Margaret found most of
Perthshire already there. They were part of the British invasion which started
immediately after Waterloo: some were rich people on a visit, staying either
at hotels like the Le Bristol on the place Vendôme, Le Meurice, the Rhin –
or else in houses rented at exorbitant prices. Besides these grand visitors, there
were others, much less well off, such as Captain and Mrs Collier, who settled
in 1825 as permanent residents,[1] named "hardy adventurers" by the novelist
William Makepeace Thackeray. These émigrés hoped to find a better life,
free from the constraints of respectable English society, and perhaps also
respite from their creditors, because the English bankruptcy laws did not
apply on the other side of the Channel. Soon sherry and ale were on sale
everywhere, as were mutton pies, calf's foot jelly, apple dumplings, muffins,
and crumpets in shops and tea rooms. Also catering for the needs of expatri-
ates were English churches, chemists, bookshops, the *Messenger*, Librairie
Galignani's English-language newspaper, and a theatre where the plays of
Shakespeare were performed, just as in London. The Jockey Club, founded
by Lord Henry Seymour in 1833, introduced steeplechasing to France and
encouraged the improvement of French bloodstock by importing British
studs and mares. Other well-known residents were Lord Henry's brother,
the future 4th Marquess of Hertford, who from 1848 lived in the Château

de Bagatelle in the Bois de Boulogne, Lord Granard with his daughters, the ladies Adelaide and Caroline Forbes, Lord and Lady Munster with their three boys, and Lady Rancliffe and her sister. Their presence led to Anglo-French marriages such as the Polignac–Rancliffe match which took place in 1824 and that between Gustave de Coigny and Miss Dalrymple Hamilton, which was finally arranged in 1822, in spite of the opposition of her parents, who admitted that Gustave's only fault was being French.

In his journal for 9 March 1834, Thomas Raikes, the diarist wrote:

> The chief advantages of living here are, that the climate is better, the living is cheaper, and you may regulate your expenses on any scale without remark or reference to your neighbours.

In his journal for 30 April 1834, he remarked:

> Paris as a city and as a capital is certainly far superior to London. There is an air of ancient grandeur in the monuments, the palaces, the hotels of the nobility, the long avenues, and the spacious quays, the gardens, and the statues, which must strike every foreigner with admiration, and some with subject for reflection.[2]

Princess Lieven was even more succinct in her comparison of the two cities in 1840: ". . . along the Paris boulevards all is so bright and animated whereas London is grey and sad". English watercolourists were particularly drawn to Paris, rather than to Rome and Naples, as in the previous century. Among them were Richard Bonington, Thomas Girtin, Thomas Shotter Boys, as well as William Callow, who was engaged by the duc d'Orléans, future Louis-Philippe, King of the French, to give drawing lessons to his sons.

The English, who had sheltered the exiled Bourbons, were welcomed at the Tuileries but their expectations of similar hospitality from the British Embassy caused problems.[3] In 1836 Thomas Raikes complained that of the 40,000 English in Paris a great proportion

> . . . leave their names at the Embassy, and expect to be invited

to the assemblies: and of those who are naturally omitted on
such occasions, some have the vulgarity to write and inquire
the reason, others send pasquinades to the English
newspapers, and in a few instances have absolutely made
complaint at the Foreign office in Downing-street of the
neglect which they have experienced from their ambassador
in Paris.

This attitude, he concluded, was "one of the inconveniences of our new
levelling system at home", referring presumably to the movement for
Parliamentary Reform.[4] Like Raikes, Margaret was not impressed by the
company at an embassy party:

> I never saw such a Bear Garden in my life as the Embassy
> was last Thursday. 700 people, of whom half might have been
> drawn from the purlieus of St. Giles and Seven Dials.

She elaborated on the subject in a letter to Lady Grey:

> The gaieties of Paris are now at their height, and there are two
> or three balls every night besides the usual soirées. The grande
> mode here is to remain at home one night every week to
> receive visits from those to whom you pay them the other six. I
> have my day like the rest, but you would laugh if you knew
> the persecution it is to me, for swarms of English people who
> would not come near me in London, take advantage of this
> French habit of evening visits, and walk in uninvited
> wherever they see a few candles lighted. I really do not
> wonder that our compatriots are hated and laughed at abroad,
> for you have no idea what a vulgar set there are here at present
> and how ridiculous they make themselves in all ways; even
> those who are among the most fashionable do outrageous
> things; for instance all Paris turned out during the frost to see
> Lady Glengall skate, and were much edified by a chute she
> made on the ice, tho' not a little disappointed at finding her
> Ladyship so well dressed in anticipation of the accident.

The French also disapproved of the free and easy manners, shrill voices and unrestrained laughter of English women, so contrary to their ideas of good taste.[5]

The number of her countrymen and women in France rose in the following years as a result of the development of the railway network across England and continental Europe and the introduction of a steamboat service for crossing the Channel. Not everyone appreciated the benefits of faster communications. Raikes complained that "These railroads have spoiled all the pleasure of travelling, and though they have wonderfully increased the rapidity of one's movements, there is a constant anxiety to be in time for the train". Journeys, he continued, now reminded him of the Biblical prophecy – "People shall run to and fro and knowledge shall abound" – which was to announce the imminent end of world.[6]

During their first visit, the Flahauts, with their daughter Emily, spent several months in an apartment on the first floor of the house in the Grande-Rue-Verte, home of Charles's mother Adèle and his stepfather M. de Souza, formerly Portuguese ambassador to France. Margaret, who appreciated the privacy of this arrangement, told Lady Grey that

> excepting at the hour of dinner we have no connexion with the ménage au rez de chausée [sic]. I mention this as I know you have a real English horror of such family arrangements but here they are much better understood than with us and I enjoy perfect liberty and feel no inconvenience whatever from it.

However, it took time to adapt to other French ways and after a week she wrote:

> I am something like a dog who turns round three times before he can settle himself to sleep and I require to make at least as many circles round a room before I can find my own corner in it. Till this is accomplished nothing else can be done . . . and it is the more difficult discovery to make in a French house than in any other, for one marble table in the middle of each room and a secretaire in your bedroom (where all the

writing apparatus is concealed with the most mysterious ingenuity) are the only useful meubles which a Parisian lady conceives it possible to want in her apartment.

She therefore set about ordering carpets, putting up blinds and making the place more comfortable, and, after visiting the Exposition des produits de l'Industrie at the Louvre, compared the English and French ways of life.

> I look with a jealous eye at the superiority of some of the manufacturers over ours, especially at the carpets – too beautiful to be walked upon. Pictures call for rapturous ecstasies from a crowd of gazers every day but it requires fresh eyes to admire them, mine are almost put out by their brilliant colours and I think a gaudy bed of tulips has quite as much beauty and beaucoup plus de nature. There are four large and magnificent apartments filled with most splendid and beautiful specimens of French art and ingenuity en fait de meubles, porcelains, dentelles, soieries, tapisseries. . . . At the same time I must add that we get the better of them in all the comforts of life and nothing can be more striking than the mixture of finery and shabbiness which is to be observed in every French house for instance your apartment is hung with satin and glitters with gold and yet you have locks to the doors and windows which would disgrace a barn. The carriages are as gaudy as the Lord Mayor's and the horses and coachmen like those of . . . in short there is no proportion in all these matters and I much prefer the general neatness of an English establishment.

Charles saw his great friend Casimir de Montrond, as well as Madame de Girardin and her sister Madame Greffulhe, whom Margaret considered "the most illiberal ultras enragées I have yet met with, however, they have always shown a steady attachment to him and I make the best of their folly". The Flahauts met them often, not only in Paris and but also at Bois-Boudran, the Greffulhe country estate. It was at a masked ball given by the Greffulhes that they met a nephew of Louis XVIII, the duc de Berry – whom Margaret had known in England – and enjoyed talking to him. He was assassinated the following night, and, returning home in the small hours of the morning from another ball at Marshal Suchet's, they were shocked to encounter his corpse, a portent of the violence which was to plague future French politics. Every Sunday Margaret was "at home" to a "curious medley of all sorts, French and English. There was the author Benjamin Constant and the imperialist generals Sébastiani and Foy, with Madame de Lobau, wife one of the proscribed aides-de-camp to Bonaparte, "a very comfortable pleasant person. She is niece of the Comtesse d'Albany and certainly the prettiest woman in Paris though her beauty has been much impaired by her misfortune and her wanderings with her husband during his exile". Margaret also approved the duc de Broglie and his wife, Albertine, "who are both excellent people". Visitors from home included the Duke of Devonshire, whom she met every day during the fortnight he spent in the city, the Irish poet Thomas Moore, the Whig politician Edward Ellice and the writer Lady Morgan. Some people came to stay, and Margaret reported:

> For the last three weeks I have been employed doing the honors of Paris to our friend Mr. Loch [her Scottish agent] who has been so kind as to pay us a visit here, and I was happy to take the opportunity of seeing its environs which I had omitted doing last year. We have been to Versailles, Malmaison, St Cloud &c &c and tho' I am almost dead with fatigue, yet I must allow our time was passed agreeably and my expectations fully answered. You have no idea of the *perfection* of the weather here, such fine evenings that all the people are sitting upon the Boulevards or driving up and down in open carriages till 12 o'clock at night.

Back on one of her brief visits to England in 1820, Margaret missed the animation of Paris, writing to Lady Grey:

> There is not a soul in London, and nothing can be more dreary or deserted than its appearance. It is such a change from the gaiety of Paris, where the streets are full of flowers and well dressed people equally gaudy in their colours, and

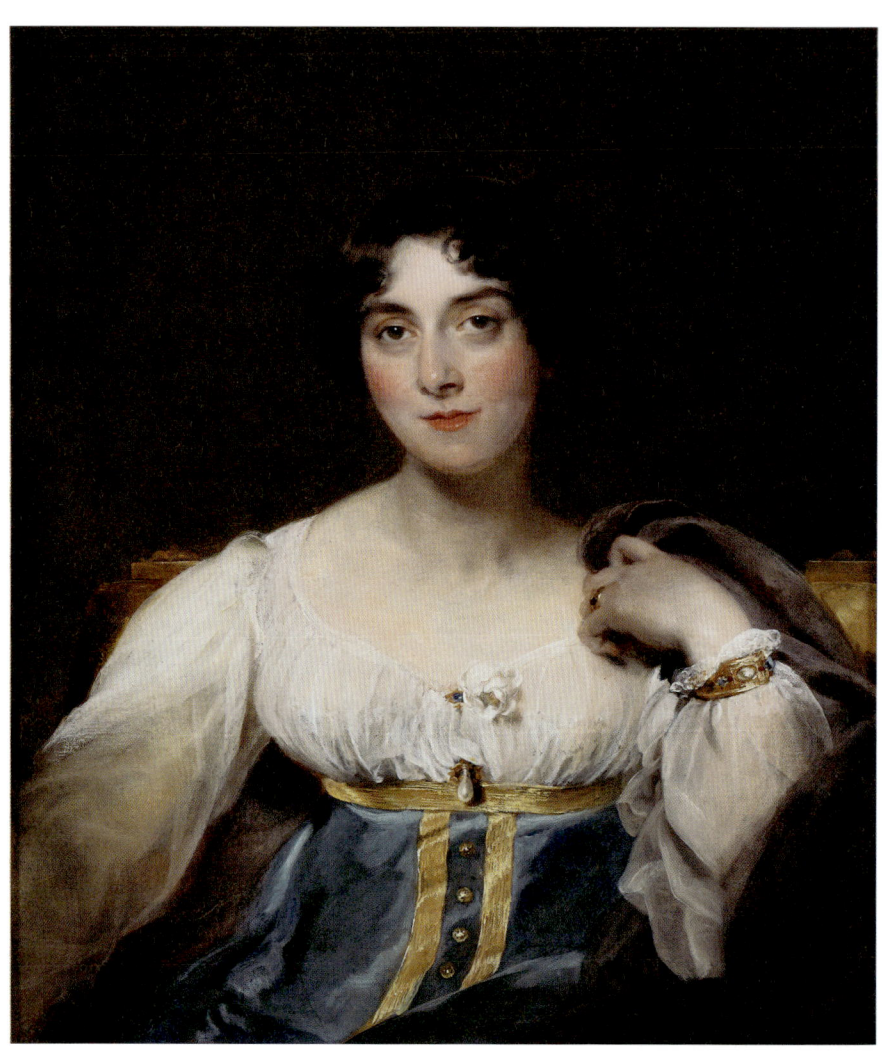

20 Thomas Lawrence (1769–1830): Margaret in her Russian-style dress

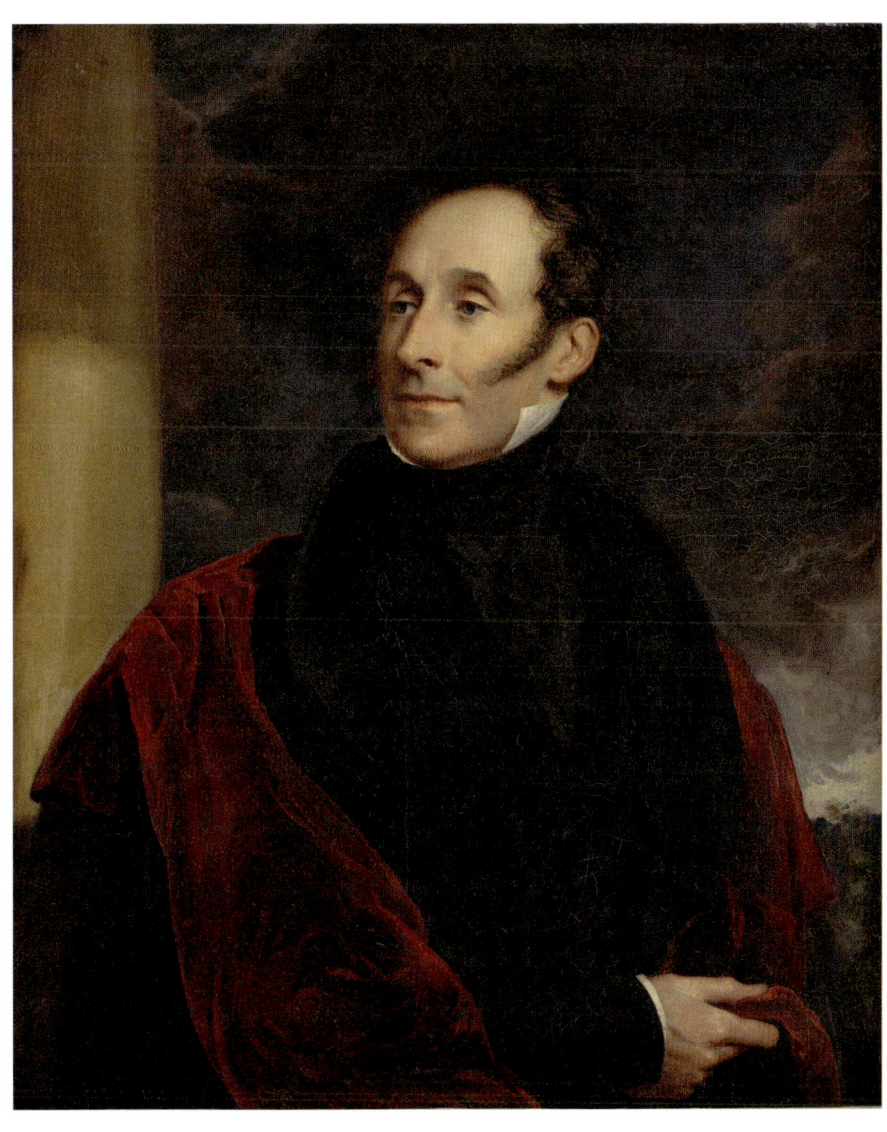

21 George Hayter (1792–1871): Charles de Flahaut

all loitering about the Boulevards chattering in groups and
eating Ice and Cakes.

During the following years, the Flahauts returned to their life in Scotland
interspersed with visits to Brighton, London and country houses, and Charles
only went back to Paris intermittently. However, in 1827 they decided to settle for the next two years in a house at 55 rue du Faubourg Saint-Honoré,
where they lived until driven away to Brighton by the summer heat of 1830.
As Margaret quickly made her mark as a patroness of the Opéra, an organ-
izer of charity balls and hostess, they decided the time had come to acquire
a permanent Paris residence, the house eventually known as the Hôtel de
Massa on the Champs-Élysées. After the July Revolution of 1830 brought
Louis-Philippe to power and with it the possibility of employment for
Charles, they became even more deeply involved in many aspects of French
political, social and cultural life until 1841, when Charles was appointed
ambassador in Vienna.

Health continued to be a major preoccupation. Expressing a preference
for the delicious, softer air of Paris over British damp, Margaret made up
her mind about the French medical profession as soon as she arrived in 1819:

> I have little faith in the skill of French physicians but their
> surgeons are most skilful and the medicinal baths and waters
> in various parts of France have such powerful effects that
> when taken under the direction of those who understand
> them I believe great cures have been performed by the use
> of them.

Impressed by "the eminent surgeon here in Paris, Guillaume Dupuytren,[7]
well acquainted with these various waters", she enthused about those at
Tivoli in Paris where, she took twenty baths, and afterwards smothered
herself "in clothes and came back in a close carriage, and made a point of
never going out of a warm room for the rest of the day . . ." She spent some
of the summers at Spa and Aix – her favourite – but still complained of
tortures from "nervous infections", violent headaches, inflammation of the
eyes, toothache and haemorrhages which obliged her to spend days on
her sofa, hardly ever going out.

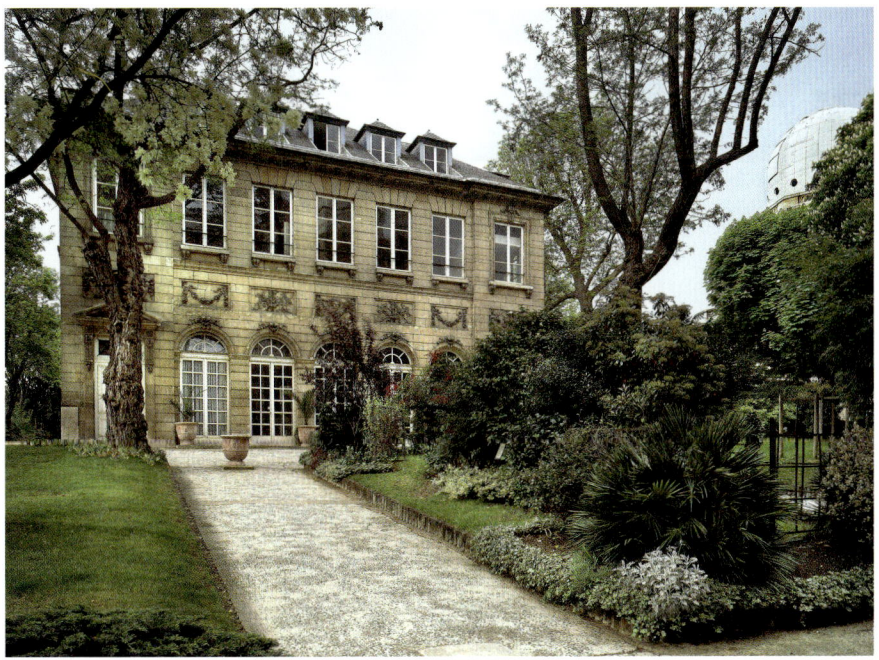

22 **Hôtel de Massa, Paris**

Always hoping to find a cure, ready to try anything new, in 1839 she and Emily spent three weeks in Leamington, according to Charles:

> . . . to consult Mr. Jefferson the great oracle who is perhaps a quack like most of his tribe. She has great faith in these sorts of people and the failure of all the college of physicians of Paris, London and Edinburgh to do any good instead of shaking her confidence in them makes her all the more anxious to consult any new performer of miracles that she hears of.

Ill again in February the next year, she wrote from Rome:

> . . . in addition to my other infirmities I have suffered so

> much from horrible pains in the back part of my head that it
> has been a great effort for me to write even a few lines – a
> melancholy time obliging me to make long journey on a bed
> in the carriage and for two months after my arrival here was
> confined to a sofa – now better, I am able to walk about,
> thanks to a new doctor treating me with bark.

Although one suspects a tendency to hypochondria, in fairness it must be remembered that she was also victim of the limitations of nineteenth-century medical expertise.

At first the health of the daughters seemed good, and in 1827 Margaret received compliments on the eldest, Emily: "her complexion would turn her head at 16 but I am not surprised when I look at the children here, for they are so ill managed and so ill dressed that they look like crumpled up old women as black as crows and Emily, with her fair face and the free use of her limbs, it must be confessed appears to great advantage". In accordance with English habits, the children played all day long in the garden of their Paris home, recalled by Margaret in July 1844 when she sent Emily sheets of paper ornamented with wild flowers of Bad Ischl, "as a souvenir and to put you in mind of a happy time when you were little girls in the garden at Paris".

Following the advice of Dr Hamilton of Edinburgh, there were frequent visits to Brighton for the air and for sea bathing. However, a shadow hung over Clementina, the prettiest and Charles's favourite, who at the age of 16 died of typhoid in January 1836, to their huge sorrow. Another family tragedy was the death of Adelaide from consumption (tuberculosis) in March 1841 after years of false hopes of a cure and as Prosper Mérimée, writer and friend, commented "a masterpiece of homeopathy". These deaths affected Charles more than Margaret, "who in all things seems to have the courage of a man", according to Princess Lieven. Lady Granville described them:

> Flahaut is scarcely in his senses, refuses all things and she, as
> in all things, the very reverse of him, wretched and alarmed
> but feeling what is true, that his giving way so entirely is
> terrible for the other girls. He never goes to bed but remains
> outside her door all night.

His mother, Madame de Souza, had died in April 1836 after many years of suffering, leading an almost recluse-like existence. Much affected, Charles wrote:

> When one looks back at the many painful experiences of her life and one knows the fatal effects they produced upon her happiness and comforts added to the bad health she suffered for years there is little to regret on seeing her released from such worldly misery.

Staying with the de Souzas during her first Paris visit, Margaret got to know Auguste Morny, son of Charles and Queen Hortense, who lived with his grandmother, Adèle, until 1829 when he joined the Flahaut household. While in Paris, she painted his portrait. From 1830 to 1832 Auguste was at the École d'état-major – he became a sub-lieutenant and then began a military career at Clermont-Ferrand. As he grew older he found it difficult to accept his situation and Charles did all he could to help him come to terms with it. When on leave, removed from Adèle's care and installed at home with the Flahauts, he suffered moments of depression. Worried by his son's unhappiness, Charles appealed to Margaret in 1832:

> . . . what I ask is that you should show him some kindness & interest. Far from complaining, he has in a letter which I received from him some days ago, expressed great gratitude for your friendly manners towards him. What you say about his relationship not being avowed is unfortunately too much known & well explains sufficiently anything you will be so good as to do for him.

Given a home by Margaret, however reluctantly, but much loved by Charles and the girls, Auguste returned their affection in full measure, and almost became the son and brother they had never had. He grew particularly close to Emily, wrote amusing letters when the younger girls were away from Paris and sent them well-chosen presents – pretty brooches and dolls with lots of changes of dress.

Margaret took great trouble over the education of her children. She

engaged a succession of governesses who were required to have "good principles, good manners, good sense, and a degree of useful knowledge usually
expected and not usually found", and outside tutors were also engaged. They
were taught languages by Alexandre-Pierre-Edmé Klor,[8] drawing by
M. Harmand,[9] and their lessons for the piano and singing were supplemented
by frequent visits to theatre and opera. Their reading ranged from the
novels of Walter Scott to G. B. Belzoni's account of his discoveries of the
tombs of ancient Egypt. Charles was by no means an absent parent but
enjoyed the company of the girls and arranged excursions for them not only
in France but to see Alexander Pope's villa at Twickenham and Horace
Walpole's Strawberry Hill, where he introduced them to Miss Berry,
Walpole's close friend.

Paradoxically, the defeat of France and the collapse of the First Empire
was followed by a great cultural renaissance. All the arts flourished in the
Restoration and the July Monarchy, making Paris the world's intellectual
and artistic capital. Keen theatre-goers, Margaret and Charles were present
at the first performance in February 1830 of Victor Hugo's highly charged
romantic drama *Hernani* and noted the influence of the author's vivid style
on political speeches and ordinary conversation. From out of the huge number of books published the great French novel emerged, though Margaret,
an assiduous reader was not impressed, not even by the novels of Balzac,
Eugénie Grandet, Les Célibataires, Le Père Goriot, "all much admired, but I
do not like the style which is vulgar and entortillé!" Her preference was for
history, and she read Tallement des Réaux, *Historiettes* (1834–5), William
Bray, *Memoirs Illustrative of the Life and Writings of John Evelyn* (1818), and
William Coxe's biography of the Duke of Marlborough (1818–19) as soon as
they were published.

Most of all, Charles and Margaret enjoyed the delights of the Paris musical scene, which was dominated by the influence of the "Pesaro Orpheus"
Gioachino Rossini (1792–1868), appointed director of the Théâtre des Italiens
in 1818. It was another shared interest, so when Margaret was away, Charles
kept her informed, criticizing or praising the various performances, especially
those at the Italiens, where they rented a box every season, though they also
attended the less prestigious Théâtre de l'Opéra, where the behaviour of the
audience often left much to be desired. Charles complained in a letter of
March 1821 that there were not enough Rossini operas, but by 1824 this had

changed and *Rossinisme* was in full swing. Large, fashionable, music-loving audiences were attracted to the repertoire of the Théâtre des Italiens which was almost entirely Italian, wonderfully sung, spectacularly staged and supported by a group of sixty influential dilettanti led by Marie-Henri Beyle, the writer who wrote under the pen name of Stendhal.

Margaret enthusiastically reported in 1828:

> My greatest dissipation here is the Opéra, both French and Italian. Mad^elle Sontag has just made her appearance at the latter, and nothing can be more delightful than the way in which La Donna del Lago [opera by Rossini] is got up – with Mad^elle Sontag Mad^me Pisaroni, Donzelli &c it really is the greatest musical treat I ever heard. At the same time I must add that I think Mad^elle Sontag's talents have been both overrated and that she is by no means comparable either to Mad^me Pasta or to Mad^me Fodor [Joséphine Fodor, wife of Mainville, singer, 1789–1870] who [*sic*] she more resembles.[10]

On October 14th:

> Yesterday I went to the Italiens with Madame Suchet and Madame de La Redorte who asked after you. We heard Sémiramis [the opera *Semiramide* by Rossini] with Mlle Grisi in the leading role. Not only is she beautiful, but she sings very well, and although her voice is still rather feeble, as she is only 20 years old, she is sure to be an excellent acquisition for that theatre.[11]

Another pleasure for Charles in 1832 was hearing the bass Antonio Tamburini (1800–1876) and Fanny Eckerlin sing in Rossini's *La Cenerentola* "which is very well got up", though he later had reservations about Madame Eckerlin, who was "no good as Ardsace" in *Semiramide*; but "no one can replace Madame Pisaroni in that role". He seems to have approved the introduction of ballet in the opera *William Tell*, first performed in Paris in 1829. Accompanied by a large chorus, Maria Taglioni (1804–1884) danced Tyrolean ballets, floating across the stage like a sylph. In 1834 Charles took Lord Minto to see her in the *Révolte* [*La Révolte des femmes* or *La Révolte au sérail*, first performed at the Paris Opéra in 1833]. "Nothing can equal the beauty of her dancing it with Perrot, you would have been delighted." He then went on to complain that "that beast Véron", director of the Paris Opéra, favoured the Elssler sisters, Fanny and Theresa, who "danced but not at all to my taste. One of them would do for a Grenadier, their style is nearly grotesque. The little one Fanny is pretty; here they call her the tomb of the Duke of Reichstadt."[12]

Their enjoyment of music was not confined to performances at the theatre. Instead of taking their guests to the opera, after dinner many hostesses, such as Lady Granville and the Austrian Countess Apponyi, organized concerts at their embassies. The standard was extremely high. On one of these occasions Countess Samoyloff invited Charles with the Italian composer Giovanni Pacini, "with whom & Schwarzenberg we sang till 11 o'clock. He accompanies beautifully & has that manner of singing of the composer which has so much effect". Charles, sometimes with Prince Belgiojoso, who had a fine voice, also sang with the professionals at his own private soirées, and reported to Margaret:

> We are now hearing every day the most charming music in
> the world Henriette Sontag here comes two or three times a
> week with Bellini and a few amateurs and sings for hours she
> is most aimable person in the world and so good humoured
> and unaffected that we are all delighted with her. Giovanni-
> Battista Rubini [1794-1854] 'roi des tenors' in Paris and
> Antonio Tambourini came to hear her, all sang duets and
> trios together divinely wish you and Lord Grey could have
> been in a little corner.

The Flahauts were on excellent terms with these men and women singers, the Italian composers Rossini, Vincenzo Bellini and Gaetano Donizetti, and also with the French romantic Daniel-François-Esprit Auber (1782–1871), who in 1837 sent Margaret the score of a march he composed for the duc d'Orléans at Compiègne. They transmitted their passion to all their children, sending them to the Opéra-Comique to enjoy the light-hearted works of Ferdinand Hérold and Adolphe Adam, and engaging the best music teachers. After hearing Frédéric Chopin play the piano, "I must say admirably", for Lady Granville at the British Embassy soon after his arrival in Paris in September 1831, by December Margaret had engaged him to teach Emily, though Charles thought "an accompagnateur would have been better for time, though M. Chopin is an excellent master". He must have had to change his mind very soon, for according to Liszt, Chopin was not only a born pianist but "strict on questions such as time and always used a metronome himself, telling his pupils to do likewise". Chopin would have appeared to the Flahauts exactly as Liszt described: ". . . his bearing had so much distinction and his manners such a cachet of good breeding that one naturally treated him as a prince".

His combination of musical and social gifts soon made him the most sought after and highly paid teacher in Paris, giving up to five lessons daily. He dressed at the best tailors, drove everywhere in hired cabriolets instead of a normal cab and wore white gloves, believing that he would have no *ton* without them. A born teacher, he advised his pupils: "One should sing with the fingers!" in the style of the Italian *bel canto*. He urged them to go to the Italian opera and listen to the Italians singing. His ultimate model was Giuditta Pasta (1798–1865), the incarnation of romantic soprano, and he insisted, "You must sing if you wish to play the piano". As he said to one pupil, "Forget that anyone is listening to you and always listen to yourself."[13] The lessons with Emily continued and early in 1833 she wrote, "Chopin and I are great friends this year, I don't know whether he is less grognon or whether I practise better than last year". He must have approved, for in 1834 when he published his Boléro opus 19 it was dedicated to her.

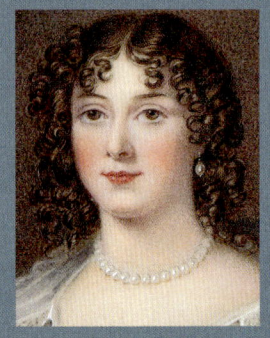

CHAPTER 11

Home and Garden: Paris II

Nous respectons l'obscurité des femmes qui se contentent des plaisirs de la famille et des querelles de ménage ; mais vous [Madame de Flahaut et la princesse Lieven], qui vous mêlez des querelles de l'Europe, vous sortez des lois ordinaires. En faisant tout ce qu'il faut pour acquérir une grande influence, vous nous avez donné le droit de la constater

Madame de Girardin, *Lettres parisiennes*, VII,
15 December 1836 (Les Salons politiques)

While living in Paris, Margaret continued to follow political events in England, applauding the first important step towards reform, the passing of the Catholic Emancipation Bill in 1829. She commented on every twist and turn of the long drawn out battle to pass the Reform Bill, which extended the franchise, redistributed seats and added 217,000 voters to the electorate of 435,000 in England and Wales. After the huge excitement generated by the passing of these two bills, Margaret continued to involve herself in politics, watching developments in England, never missing a chance of attacking the Duke of Wellington, "standing alone on his pedestal, the model of ambition, vanity, fortune and power", the bully, "who does not show himself to be an able General in politics whatever he may be in war". Nor did she spare his colleagues, even the moderate Robert Peel, who headed the Tory Coalition. Although she had never admired another statesman as much as Lord Grey, after his retirement she gave her wholehearted loyalty to Lord John Russell, whose task in the second half of the century was to widen the franchise.

Margaret was not only interested in English politics but her *politicomanie* extended to France, and from 1827 she sent Lord and Lady Grey admirably written detailed accounts of the current situation.[1] Exceedingly well informed, she was an avid reader of the newspapers such as *Le Constitutionnel, Le National,* the *Journal des Débats, La Presse* and *Le Moniteur,* and attended debates in the two Chambers, considered "one of the best spectacles in Paris". During her first stay in France she had made the pilgrimage to the country house of the marquis de Lafayette,

> the most consistent and devoted supporter of all great
> principles of liberty, philanthropy and tolerance . . . a life pure
> honourable and glorious if not greatest man of his age the
> most virtuous sans tache et sans reproach [sic].

She further demonstrated her support for the French Revolution by holding a small ball on 21 January 1830, the anniversary of the execution of Louis XVI. As the Polish diplomat André-Édouard Kozmian noted, "all the other French houses were closed that night and for that reason Margaret decided that she would celebrate with dancing mazurkas and music". Her house was a centre for the liberal opposition and Henry Greville noted how she expressed her opinions more violently than her husband. Invited to dinner in March that year, he wrote that the company, which included Talleyrand, Madame de Dino, General Sébastiani and the duc de Broglie, talked politics all the time and agreed that the Polignac government could not stand, and in July 1830 they were proved right.

Relations between husband and wife were stable in spite of complaints from Margaret about possible infidelities on his part. He continued to attract women, and was challenged to a duel by the banker M. Perregaux, who suspected he was having an affair with his wife.[2] The comtesse d'Armaillé remembered how the presence of Charles in a salon "caused a stir among all the elderly ladies" and that the vicomtesse de Noailles loved him "madly, not being in the least discouraged by his many infidelities".[3] André-Édouard Kozmian thought the secret of his success was

> an overall friendliness, a charm, easy manners and talk, all
> bearing the stamp of a well bred man. More than anyone he
> was master of the art of agreeable salon conversation. He had
> been very good looking and women, including queens, were
> very attracted to him. If I had a son or a brother about to take
> their place in society I would advise them to be 'just like M.
> de Flahaut'.[4]

He seems to have done his best to avoid upsetting Margaret. The shrewd Lady Granville, wife of the British ambassador, noticed during an evening with them in October 1827 how

> . . . every French woman, and a few Poles and Russians are in
> love with said Comte and all detest poor Lady Keith who lies
> on her couch and returns the compliment. I like her very
> much. She says Flahaut is become more English in his
> domestic habits but that here all is *calqué* upon a footing
> calculated to destroy them. He behaves perfectly to her which
> makes all the little things indignant . . .[5]

and continued:

> I wish I could describe the court paid to Flahaut while Meg
> lies on her couch. He pays her the greatest attention and left
> many an anxious sufferer after dinner yesterday to go and sit
> two hours with her and the sufferers awaited his return with
> the most patient devotion.

This opinion was shared by the Marshal de Castellane who wrote in his journal after dining with the Rothschilds in November 1827 that

> the comte de Flahaut is much sought after on account of his
> good looks and noble manners. Made a general when young
> by the emperor, he married a rich English woman who both
> looks and behaves like a great lady. After having had many
> love affairs Charles de Flahaut has become a good husband.[6]

When away from home, Charles affirmed his dependence on his wife.
After only three years of marriage, left in Paris on his own, he wrote,

> . . . my dearest Margaret, think of me a little in the middle of
> your busy life and believe that you are the object of my
> constant thoughts and most sincere and tender affection.
> How strongly I desire you again with me.

A few days later he declared that

> as long as our happiness depends on us alone, as I hope it

always will, all other points are of secondary nature.

Away on a diplomatic mission to Berlin in 1831, he assured her:

> . . . my dearest Margaret, I regret every day more and more
> our separation and think myself the greatest ass in the world
> for having consented to it.

He went on:

> I shall however be perfectly satisfied with our fireside & a few
> friends & the Italian Opera will be excellent. A quiet,
> comfortable & independent life is worth any official situation
> even the highest, especially with a home in which one finds
> one's happiness. I long to have you & the children back.[7]

During 1834 relations between them were less happy, as Margaret con-
tinually reproached him for his involvement with another woman. On his
way to France at the end of the summer he wrote from Dover,

> I can assure you with all truth that you have no reason to
> complain of me but I hope that all that will cease and that a
> more confidential manner will be restored between us.

This was not sufficient to allay her suspicions, for on 13 October he replied:

> I have just received this moment yours of the 10th my dearest
> Marg[t] & what you say of your melancholy & solitary situation
> when Anne [her cousin Anne Elphinstone] leaves you makes
> me feel very much disposed to join you. In fact, as I told you
> before I am determined to do all I can to contribute to your
> happiness which I feel to be my duty & will be my pleasure &
> when I recollect the sad moments we have passed I cannot
> conceive how even your injustice could make me angry
> enough to bear your grief. I hope we shall in future have no
> more troubles.

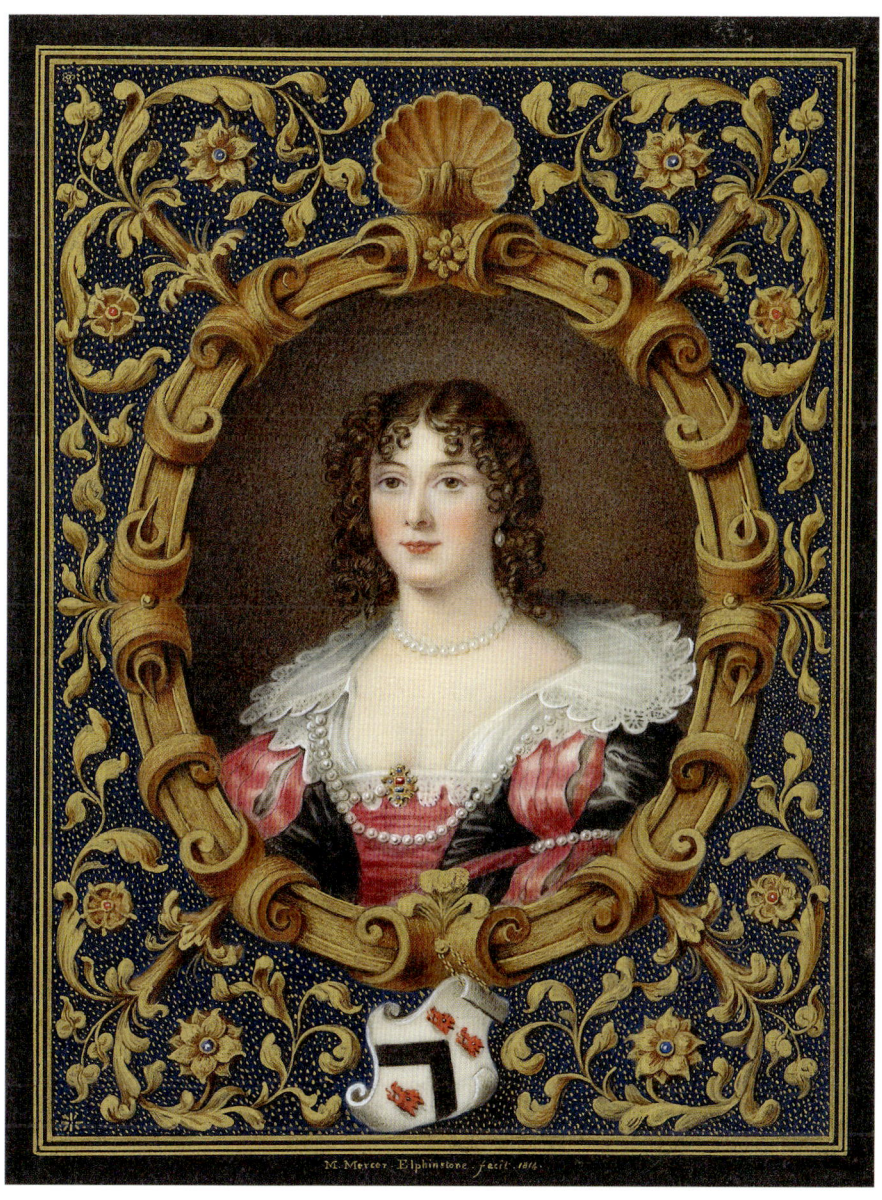

23 Miniature of Anne Elphinstone by Margaret

It seems that Margaret blamed the comtesse Delphine Potocka, as a few weeks later he admitted:

> The day before yesterday I went to see M^ad^. P[otocka]. What I wish is to please you but . . . pray do not ask me to act unkindly to a person who has always been kind & friendly to me & who has done me no wrong. It would be contrary to my nature, but depend on it that my souvenirs, my affection & my duty will always dispose me to do everything that can make you happy.

He welcomed any softening on her part:

> I have just received your letter . . . which is a joy as it proves that we are so much nearer one another. I wish very much for your return & this life of garçon which you sometimes say suits me so well does quite the reverse.

Peace was eventually restored, for their marriage was strong enough to weather this – and indeed other storms – because husband and wife knew that they could not do without each other. When faced with an important decision he always relied on her judgment, as is clear from the long letter he wrote to Margaret on 14 August 1830. After setting out in detail the various options for the diplomatic post he had been offered under the Orléans dynasty he concluded, "Weigh all as I have said here and give me your opinion."[8]

Their joint achievement, much admired by their friends, was their installation at the house later known as the Hôtel de Massa, at the corner of the rue d'Angoulême and the Champs-Elysées, acquired by the duc de Richelieu in 1788. This elegant neo-classic "folie" had a large terrace looking over the Champs-Elysées and a fine garden, where the duke placed the two marble *Slaves* of Michelangelo, now in the Louvre. During the Empire Charles may have been invited to the sumptuous receptions given there by the Italian ambassador Marescalchi. Having friends, as well as Adèle, already living in the Faubourg Saint-Honoré, and liking the smart but politically liberal tone of the quarter, the Flahauts decided to acquire the house from the next owner, the marquis de Juigné. A dissenting voice came from Talleyrand, who thought it definitely not a *trouvaille* but "damp, sad", adding that "a better house might be built on the other side of the Champs-Elysées"; others complained about the location "fort loin".

They engaged the architect Louis Visconti (1791–1853), who produced plans for the entrance hall, the ground floor, the staircase and Margaret's sumptuous bedroom. Charles, away on his diplomatic missions, had every confidence in Margaret's talent for homemaking. From London early 1831 he gave her a free hand:

> I have your budget today & must leave entirely to you what relates to the house. The difference of expense is nothing, therefore choose what is best, but consider well if the communication left with the first floor will be such as an apartment of that description is entitled to. However without any restriction I leave all that to your taste which I think much better than mine.

He urged her to buy tables, wallpapers, and a new open carriage and pointed out that he kept his own expenses in check, for, unlike most men, he spent no money on port, horses, staying at inns and all foolish fancies, so they would not run into debt. However, by 1837, as they continued making new purchases and more alterations to the house he warned that they were in danger of overspending, and that he might find himself in the debtors' prison of Sainte-Pélagie.

In tune with the prevailing nostalgia for the past, Margaret decorated the house in the style of the *ancien régime*, so much at variance with her political views, as Rudolf Apponyi noted:

> It is rare to find a person with her taste and talents for interior decoration. Inside her apartment is just like living in the reign of Louis XIV. It is really extraordinary to see how the very people who claim to detest that period are those who choose to surround themselves with objects recalling it.[9]

Thomas Raikes also observed how

> Everything now tends to old recollections; revolution is a
> bugbear and *mauvais ton*. Old names, old furniture, old
> châteaux, old forms and ceremonies, old tapestry, old china,
> old plate are now the rage even with the *nouveaux riches*.

He went on to claim that

> . . . it is English society that has brought about this wonderful
> change here. Sixteen years ago, when we were buying up
> with eagerness the buhl [inlaid furniture in the late
> seventeenth-century style of André-Charles Boulle], the
> Sèvres, the bronzes and other objects of taste, the French
> would ridicule our fancy for *vieilleries* and *rococo*, now they
> are collecting them with the greatest eagerness, and the prices
> are more than doubled.[10]

H. de Balzac in his novel *Le Cousin Pons* describes how contemporary, knowledgeable buyers such as Alexandre du Sommerard (1749–1842), Alexandre-Charles Sauvageot, Lord Hertford, and the fictional Pons could acquire masterpieces by the celebrated *ébéniste* J. H. Riesener (1734–1806); "furniture inlaid with Sèvres plaques decorated with bunches of flowers . . . wonders from the France of Madame de Pompadour", "from marchands de curiosités such as the Auvergnat dealer Remonencq." Margaret, however, was more likely to have bought her furniture, porcelain and objets d'art from the shops on the boulevard de la Madeleine rather than from scrap merchants like Remonencq. There was plenty to choose from, and as Balzac observed, ". . . here in Paris, the city where the greatest quantity of antiques are to be found, the number of dealers has greatly increased over the past twenty years, and as for Old Master paintings, these are sold in three cities only – London, Paris and Rome".

Margaret had started buying Boulle furniture and ebony furniture inlaid with Florentine hardstones in the 1820s, but now for her new house concentrated on the great eighteenth-century makers. Her first purchase was a marquetry writing-table inlaid with a Sèvres plaque of a pheasant, and this was followed by a magnificent *bureau plat* signed by J. F. Leleu, c. 1770, and examples, in Balzac's words, of "véritables tableaux en bois" by both German and

French craftsmen. Five gilt-wood armchairs with shaped rectangular backs were signed by J. B. Boulard, who supplied a similar set for the Cabinet intérieur du Roi at Saint-Cloud in 1788. Unusual but wonderfully decorative was a marriage coffer, or jewel cabinet, on a stand veneered in green horn with red and green foliage and flowers. As well as this fine collection of furniture signed by the best eighteenth-century makers, no longer available in the original sets or pairs, copies were ordered from Jean-Baptiste Béfort and from Alexandre-Louis Bellangé. As both these cabinet-makers were trained to the exacting standards of the period before 1789, Charles could see no difference between their commodes, tables and chairs and the original models. An ormolu-mounted marquetry centre table inlaid with trophies of Science, the Arts, Gardening and Navigation, supported by a column on which ormolu winged Victories were applied, made by L.-F.-L. Puteaux had a royal provenance. Given by the Ville de Paris on the Feast of Saint Louis to Louis XVIII in August 1814, the table was placed in the Salon de famille du Roi in the palais des Tuileries until sold in 1831. When Empire styles suited, they were also mixed with the earlier furniture, and this combination set a fashion adopted by others during the 1830s.

Pons himself bought soft-paste Vincennes and Sèvres porcelain from the barrows of the Auvergnat scrap dealers and his passion for the fine shapes and delicate decoration accorded this beautiful material was shared by both Flahauts. Margaret had mastered the art of painting it, and their exquisite collection, created for princely patrons was displayed in cabinets. In addition, they acquired more eighteenth-century porcelain from Mennecy, Tournai, from the German factories – Meissen (figures), Frankenthal, Höchst – as well as from Vienna and from England. For the table there were contemporary porcelaine de Paris and other elegant services, and a large collection of plate. When, in spite of the reluctance of the trustees, they managed to obtain Admiral Keith's silver from Tulliallan, they found that this was not extensive enough for their dinners of forty guests. They therefore went to the best Parisian *orfèvres*, discussing the purchase of a silver-gilt dessert service from Jean-Baptiste Fossin of the rue Richelieu, and of a grand *surtout de table* and candelabra with many candles from Odiot.

Contributing to the individual atmosphere of the house was Margaret's collection of objets d'art. There were ormolu-mounted vases of Chinese monochrome – celadon, *sang de bœuf* – as well as Kangxi porcelain painted with figures and a pair of multicoloured parrots. Inkstands and caskets made of Japanese lacquer echoed the taste of Madame de Pompadour; and in December 1832, Charles was tempted by "a magnificent lacquer screen at Brussels. It belonged to the Prince Charles of Lorraine & represents on one side the palace of the Emp. of China."

From Italy came gilt-bronze figures of Apollo and Diana on lapis lazuli columns. Of the elegant clocks – both mantel and freestanding – the most striking was a sculptural composition illustrating History's Dominance over Time, she holding an open book, he wielding his scythe, by the clockmaker C. G. Hautemanière, who signed his work Manière. Candelabra and lamps designed in similar sculptural style bought from Gilbert-Honoré Chaumont and Armand Feuchère were hung and placed where needed. Below one of the many chimneypieces and guarding the hearth was a fender flanked by fire dogs of a Persian cat and a poodle seated on tasselled cushions, representing the great master Jacques Caffieri. Yet with all their charm and artistry these objects were eclipsed by the magnificent pair of honey-coloured Egyptian alabaster vases designed by F.-J. Bélanger 1770–5 with naturalistic ormolu mounts of laurel, oak and sunflowers by Pierre Gouthière. Executed for the aesthete duc d'Aumont at the workshop in the Hôtel des Menus Plaisirs, they had been acquired in 1782 by Louis XVI at the auction held after his death.

Their paintings by Old Masters, acquired mainly by Margaret, were far outnumbered by contemporary portraits of the Orléans royal family, of the couple and of their children by François Gérard, John Hoppner, Thomas Lawrence, George Hayter, Ary Scheffer, Franz Xaver Winterhalter and Alfred de Dreux. Charles's Empire career was evoked by a portrait of Napoleon and Horace Vernet's paintings of the Battle of Hanau and of the death of his valet David from the cold at Beresina, during the retreat from Moscow, commissioned as a wedding present by Gabriel Delessert.[11] Besides these pictures on the walls there were miniatures of Napoleonic, royal and famous friends and relations, each with a story to tell.

From their correspondence it seems clear that they set great store by the beautiful textures and colours of curtains, cushions, carpets, and upholstery made up from Persian, Indian and European damasks, brocades, velvets, embroideries and cashmeres. As Margaret was an accomplished needle-woman Charles sent her from Berlin "beautiful patterns & the things necessary to work them which you will keep or give at St Cloud", and "I have sent by M. de W. 9 drawings one of which is beautiful. 6 are for chairs. I have sent also the materials. The work must be done what is called grand point that is taking two threads of the canvas at each stitch. The blue of the bird's tail is to be done in silk . . ." Since "M. de Talleyrand says that we ought to furnish our house with English chintz & not silk that the dust will spoil everything that does not wash", he suggested that if Margaret agreed then "there is a bird pattern the most beautiful thing possible . . ." He also gave much time and thought to the best means of covering the polished parquet floors, frequently changing his mind:

> My carpet arrangements are off again. We brought the
> moquette to the house & instead of going with all the rooms it
> made the gold look like silver & killed the cerise. I think that
> I shall have Rogier's who has shown me a new green one
> which I think will do for the great drawing room . . .

He liked the effect of a red carpet in her bedroom which "looks very well with the tenture, the only fault is the excess of gilding. It looks like the folly of a fermier general. I am going to get Turkey carpets from Sengreva through the kindness of two Dip[lomats] & the fun is that one of them is Dutch & the other Belgian, one for the dining room & the other for the drawing room . . ."

The large garden was not forgotten. He placed busts in it and wrote from Berlin on 9 July: "I see by the papers that the Archevêché is to be pulled down.[12] If so, buy the grille that stood along the quai; it will secure our garden against any marauders. From what you say of its beauty, it would be a pity that it should not be guarded". He reminded her that as they have been promised plants from the royal nurseries, she must ask for them in time for planting. A year or so later he told Emily, "our camellias are splendid & are the admiration of all who pass in the Champs Elysées". Inside the house, flowers freshly picked from the garden were arranged in *jardinières* and vases, their colours harmonizing with the upholstery, curtains and carpets.

When all was ready in 1832, their guests were immediately struck by their success in combining the best of French taste with English ease and standards of comfort including water closets. This new trend for living with French eighteenth-century art was soon followed by the wife of the first Belgian

ambassador to France, comtesse Le Hon, and by the young duc d'Orléans
for his apartments in the Tuileries, "beautifully furnished with magnificent
Lacquer, marquetry and Boulle rescued from the dust and cobwebs of the
Garde Meuble where they have remained unheeded since the days of Louis
XV", according to Margaret, a guest at his first party, celebrating the queen's
birthday.[13] His aunt, Madame Adélaïde, similarly impressed by her perfect
taste, consulted Margaret over the lighting of the grand rooms in the Château
de Pau.

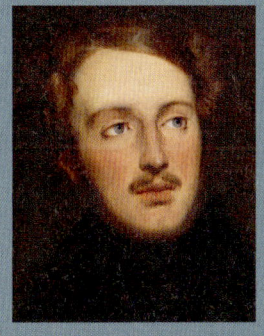

CHAPTER 12

The Orléans Monarchy: Paris III

The crown . . . is too perilous today to be an object of
ambition

Adolphe Thiers to Madame Adélaïde, July 1830

C harles and Margaret were staying in Brighton with their children during the July Revolution (July 27–30). They welcomed the news, which brought the liberal-minded Louis-Philippe of the junior Bourbon branch to power and raised hopes of diplomatic or military office for Charles, who as an ardent Bonapartist had been ineligible during the reigns of Louis XVIII and Charles X. The Flahauts and the Orléans were already aware of each other. In December 1816 Charles had met them at Twickenham, and although Louis-Philippe, then duc d'Orléans, affirmed his regard, his sister Adélaïde was more reserved[1] and his wife, Marie-Amélie, thought him "tall, elegant, good-looking though rather worn, very smartly turned out, and socially agreeable, but rather too pleased with himself, being so attractive to the ladies".[2]

When the Orléans family and the Flahauts were both living in Paris a closer connection had been established with the eldest son, then duc de Chartres, who subscribed generously to Margaret's charitable events, such as the ball for Portuguese refugees held in 1829. She told Lady Holland that there was

> nothing more amiable than this young prince and on this occasion he has been really perfect. He came to me for his ticket and said that on account of his studies and the courses which he regularly attends could not be one of the

24 **Ary Scheffer (1795–1858):**
Ferdinand Philippe, duc d'Orléans

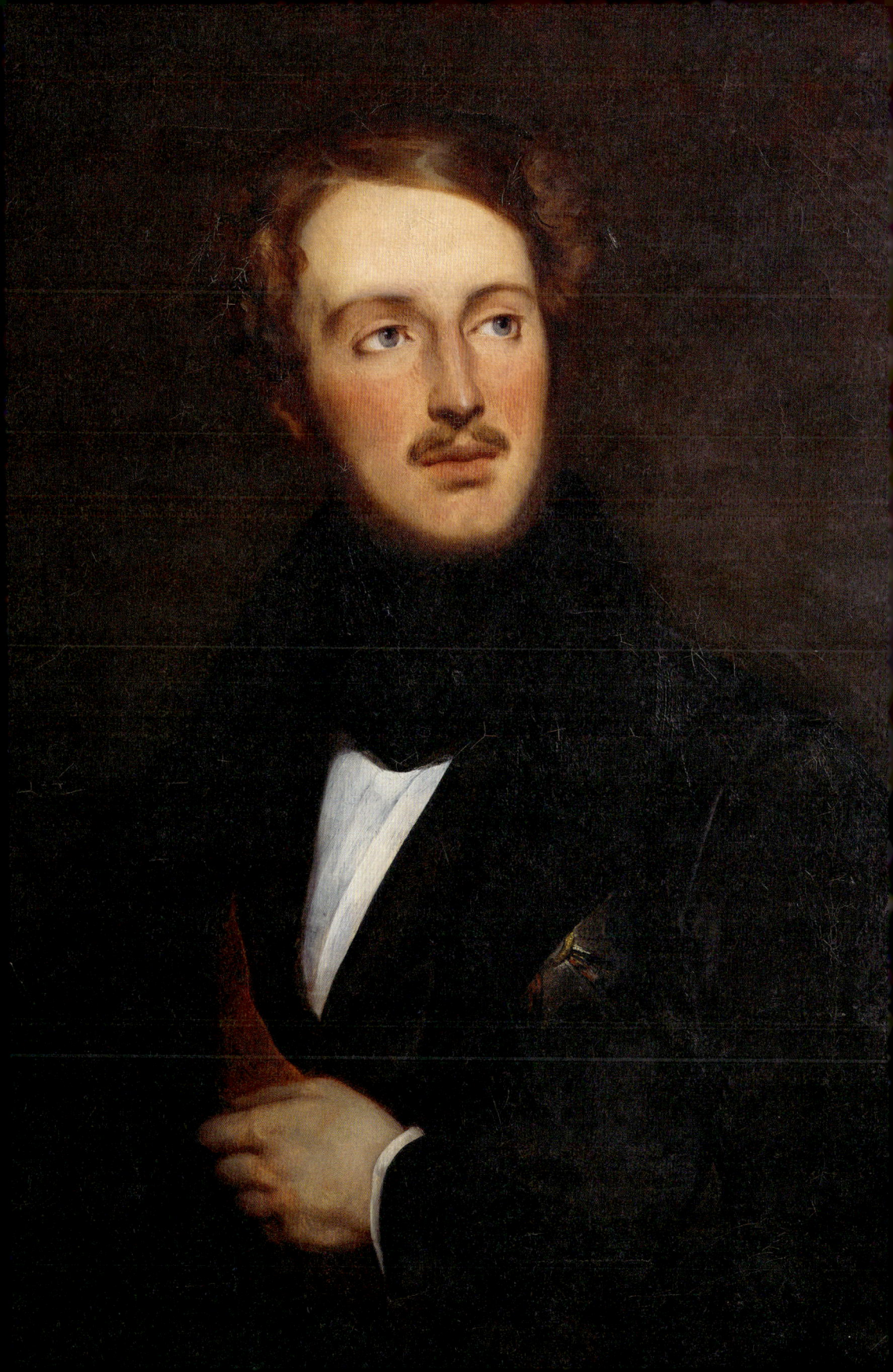

compatronnes for the arrangement of the ball, but named Mr.
de Benningsay as his remplacement and to propose the
Service de Comptrolles of the Palais Royal to superintend the
decoration of the Salle, – all good offers gratefully received.
He stayed from 8.30 sans quitter la place until 2 which
pleased everybody and those who never dreamt of a chance of
dancing with a Prince.

The following January he excelled himself again at the Charity Ball organized for the relief of the poor. By now well integrated into Parisian society,
Margaret, who was one of the organizing committee, considered it

the most pleasant fête that ever was and raised 120,000 after
paying all expenses. Chartres, with whom the idea originated,
presided at our council with all the zeal and bonne grâce
possible and the Orléans family had all the honours of the
evening as our fête was disdained by the Tuileries [Charles X,
his son and daughters-in-law] since the patronesses were not
received in court.

At this point the stage was set for the development of a friendship, similar to
that which Margaret had enjoyed with Princess Charlotte.
  Urged on by Margaret, who according to Count Apponyi, jumped for joy
at the news of the revolution,[3] Charles hastened back to Paris. On arrival he
went immediately to the Palais-Royal where the

Beautiful hall and stairs were full of a motley assembly of
National Guards from all parts of France dressed in all sorts
of ways and every colour recalling first revolution . . . In the
Drawing Room he found the Duchess of Orléans with her
family, Madame de Vaudémont, Madame Gérard and
Madame de Toncy, Generals Gérard and Sébastiani, Count
Lagrange, and a tribe of colonels and officers of all armies
and régimes. Then a Deputation arrived bringing an address
for Pasquier to read the offering of the Crown to the Duke of
Orléans who made an excellent reply. After that, numerous

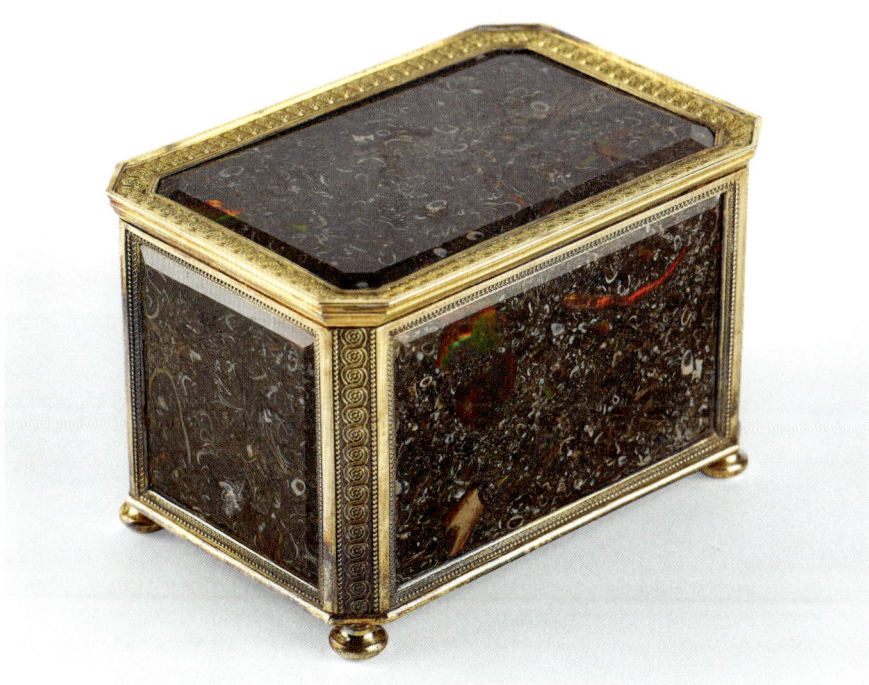

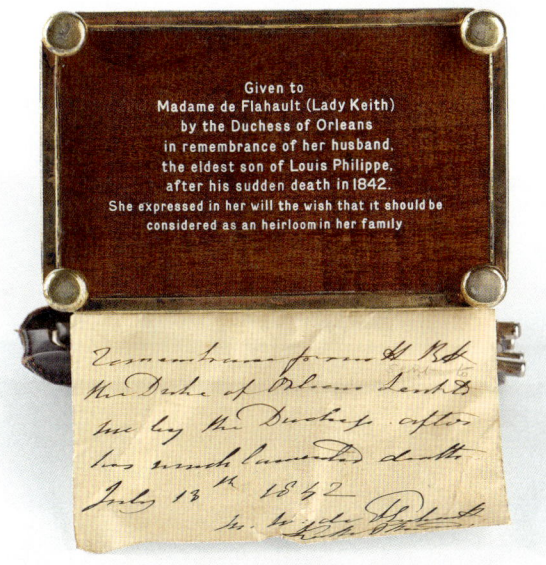

Given to
Madame de Flahault (Lady Keith)
by the Duchess of Orleans
in remembrance of her husband,
the eldest son of Louis Philippe,
after his sudden death in 1842.
She expressed in her will the wish that it should be
considered as an heirloom in her family

25 Labradorite/opal
matrix box bequeathed by
Ferdinand Philippe, duc
d'Orléans to Margaret

26 Detail of the box
inscription

145

Peers, who included Talleyrand, Montmorency, Mortemart, d'Aligre, Molé, Barante, Rigny, Marbois, Mortier, MacDonald, made a shout of VIVE LE ROI, VIVE LA REINE. Out of doors bands of music played the Marseillaise to loud huzzas of people crying VIVE LE ROI, LA REINE, EGALITE, all in same breath and Louis Philippe took the oath.[4]

and a few days later: "Everything is returning to order. Everybody wears the national colours, and M. de Duras & St Chamans wear bows of ribbons in their button holes."

Yet, even at this early stage Charles had reservations about the July Monarchy and was shocked by

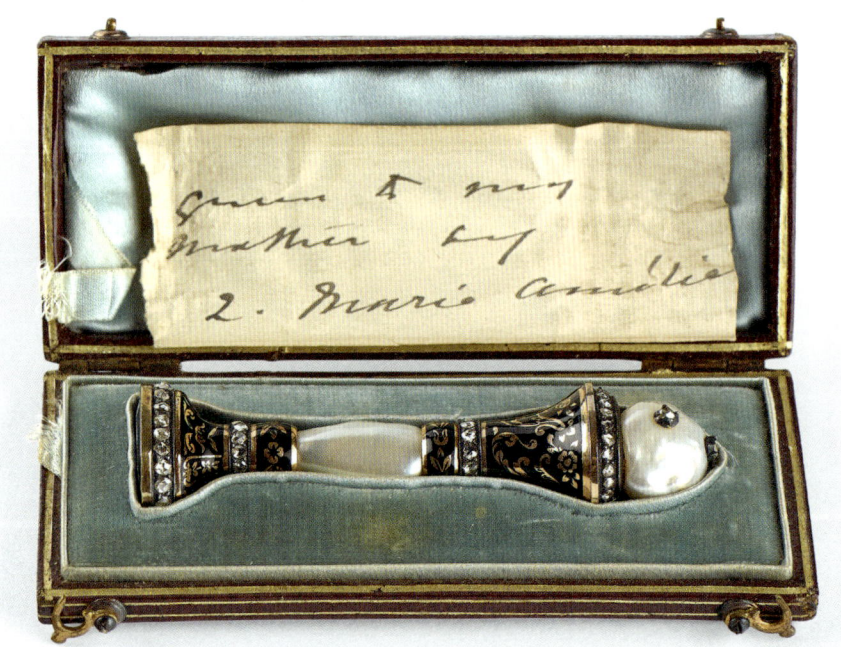

27 **Baroque pearl seal given to Margaret by Queen Marie-Amélie**

... the horrid bad company one meets at the Palais Royal –
all intrigants of all régimes flock there, they are so bad that
La Grange and Forbin Janson might be reckoned pure and
immaculate. It has so disgusted me that I have only been
there once and have not been asked to dinner. The King
lowers himself a great deal by his shakings of hands with
everyone and his embrassades – it does not add to his
popularity, and it takes away from the respect so necessary to
a crowned head or even to the President of a Republic. He
must not forget that he does not owe his throne to popular
enthusiasm and has not got the qualities that excite it. There
arc 100 times more people who would have been for
Napoleon II,[5] but all reasonable men have given up their

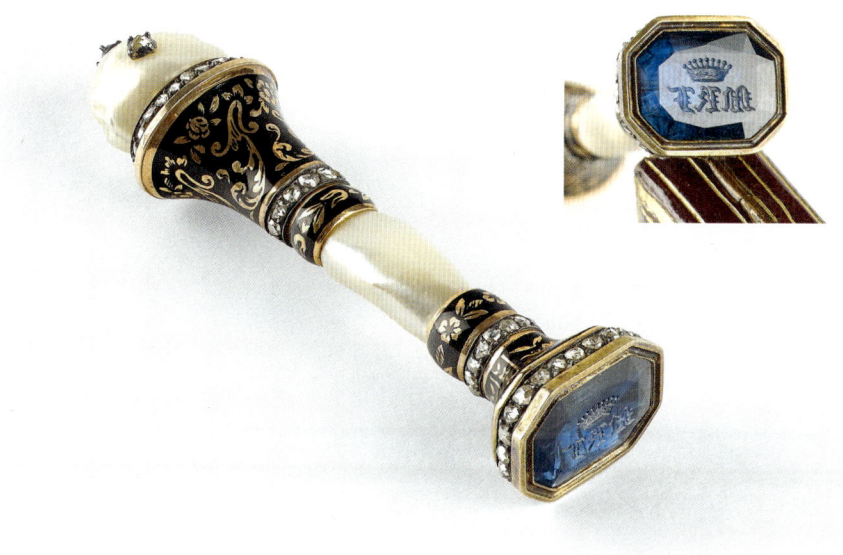

28 **Pearl seal, the sapphire intaglio engraved with Margaret's initials**

sentiment and affection to secure a wise and liberal
government under a tried prince. He is a king crowned by
reason, and should act his part accordingly and be very
simple, very economical with his subjects' money and show
no partiality to anyone and be gracious and dignified to
everybody. M. Maugin takes him by the button to lead him to
the embrasure of a window. He embraces Lafitte on the
balcony, presses Lafayette to his heart and even the common
people laugh at it. The truth is that his support comes from
Bonapartists, Republicans, moderate Royalists, in short the
whole of France except a few Ultras."

He added that it was "not a good idea to put his heir on the Council because
he will incur odium when unpopular measures are proposed".[6]

However, by September he was rather more optimistic:

The tranquillity is not to be believed after such a
bouleversement – however the meetings of workmen give
hope to the mischievous, uneasiness to the timid and trouble
to the National Guard but are of no serious consequence and
will subside – Yesterday bakers, today the smiths, tomorrow
ironmongers are expected to come forward with opinions
and wishes.

He did not keep his thoughts to Margaret and himself and told Count
Apponyi that in spite of his liberal reputation and friendship with the
Orléans, events had gone too far and that it would have been better to try
and restrain Charles X rather than to make Louis-Philippe king.[7]

Charles told Margaret that Louis-Philippe had promised to restore his
peerage and military rank, but although there were rumours in the press of
his appointment to the London embassy, no one could confirm it, and he
sensed it had already been promised to another. In any case, he was sure that
his close relations with the Whig party, then in opposition, might not be
acceptable to the British government, and especially not to the Duke of
Wellington, and his "honesty and independence would not be considered a
sufficient safeguard". Rather than face failure in England, and with it the

end of his hopes of a career in diplomacy, he thought the Russian embassy – which had been offered to him – might give the chance of success.[8] However, Margaret – to his surprise – rejected the Saint Petersburg post on grounds of the bad climate and the tyranny of the Emperor Nicholas. Outspoken and opinionated, she might well have been a liability rather than an asset to him, and he warned that if he accepted, then her "liberty of speech must be confined to bedroom conversation".

Charles therefore reconciled himself to the improvement in his situation through the restoration of his military rank and the peerage, which would give him a political stake in the affairs of his country, and agreed to wait for a more acceptable offer. In January 1831 he accepted a brief semi-official mission to London to sound British ministers about Belgian independence and neutrality but felt that Talleyrand, as ambassador, resented his close rapport with the Greys, and was not happy about being used to execute Louis-Philippe's secret plan of obtaining the throne of Belgium for his younger son, the duc de Nemours.[9] Sent to Berlin from June to September 1831 to represent French interests on Belgian and Polish issues, he regretted his acceptance almost as soon as he set out. He hated the climate which brought on frequent fevers and attacks of rheumatism, found Berlin dull and insanitary, and although well received by the king, felt "this residence is where my few talents could be of the least use".[10] Towards the end of his mission he admitted to Margaret that, like her, he was not tempted by any diplomatic post except London or possibly Naples, and was quite content to return to private life.

He seemed fated to stay there, for as he failed to succeed Talleyrand even when his friend General Sébastiani was foreign secretary, the London post continued to elude him. Reluctant at first, because he was not impressed by the list of peers which "belongs to the government to lower everybody and everything", he involved himself in politics so wholeheartedly that Margaret complained, "As for Mr. de Flahaut I never see him at all, for he goes to the Chamber of Peers every morning at eleven and only returns in time to dress for dinner." Yet it must have been through Charles that Margaret became so well informed about the French political scene, through his letters when she was away in England.

In 1837, recognizing his qualities, his *savoir-vivre*, perfect manners, elegance and animation, Louis-Philippe appointed Charles as *premier écuyer* to the young heir, formerly Chartres, now the duc d'Orléans. Having had all

Europe at his feet as aide-de-camp to Napoleon, Charles might well have felt that he deserved better than a place in the household of a prince with a limited sphere of influence and whose abilities were still unproven. However, over several years' friendship he had grown to like the prince and admired him for accepting the responsibility of visiting the victims of the cholera epidemic in hospital, and for his courage. This was put to the test when, enduring terrible weather and a swampy terrain, they participated in the siege of Antwerp on behalf of Belgium from 19 November until the city capitulated on 23 December. Charles took his turn in the trenches, causing Margaret much anxiety.

Back from the siege, he claimed that it had completed his military education and made him regret that he had ever left a career where his advancement had always been won by his own service on the field of battle, instead of depending on the intrigues and expediency of politicians. The prince acknowledged his support by handsome gifts: his portrait by Ary Scheffer (see page 143), and, as a memento of the Antwerp military cavalcades, a charger fully caparisoned. From his former adversary Leopold I, King of the Belgians, he received the great cross of his military Order, accompanied by a flattering letter written by the royal hand – causing Margaret to exclaim, "How times have changed!"

In the following years he accompanied the prince to Compiègne for the military training *camps de manœuvre* and noticed how popular he was with the troops, inviting 30 to 60 to dine with him every night and lodging 700 in the château, then organizing stag-hunting or shooting, promenades in forest by day and whist, music dancing, and – once weekly – theatre from Paris in the evenings. There was another side to the Orléans coin, for as they were also "living in terrible times in which every day and every hour produced new dangers", together he and the prince courageously faced insurgents in the narrow streets of Saint-Denis, narrowly escaping death from a huge paving stone thrown from a window. On a lighter note they enjoyed shooting game together on the Chantilly estate of the duc d'Aumale and with the Rothschilds in the forest of Saint-Germain-en-Laye.

Although the festivities at Fontainebleau for marriage of the duke with the German duchess Helen of Mecklenburg-Schwerin in 1837 went well, and both Flahauts approved of the bride, it soon seemed that they had come to the parting of the ways. Charles suspected that he was being edged out by the duc de Coigny, but the first sign of real trouble came over a question of precedence, obliging the prince to choose between him and his governor General Baudrand, to whom he showed a preference.[11] Princess Lieven believed that Queen Marie-Amélie was

> entirely on his side, and, according to what is said, the King also was only too glad to rid himself of Flahault. You would hardly conceive how tenacious Margaret was of her position at Court, and really, as between 'gentlemen,' the matter was pushed rather too far. She must have a perfect rage for domestic service, since, after all, one has to wear livery when one accepts a position at Court, and for my part, I cannot understand being fond of this slavery, when one has the means of freeing one's self.[12]

Louis-Philippe sent General Baudrand and Marshal Soult respectively to congratulate Queen Victoria on her accession and to attend her coronation, much to the disappointment of Charles, who had been rejected previously by William IV in 1831. He resigned from the household of the prince in January 1838, and thereafter, being regarded as suspect by the king, it was only their friendship with his sister Madame Adélaïde and the duc d'Orléans which kept the Flahauts loyal to the throne. Years later Charles explained this to Emily (see Chapter 19) and when asked by Napoleon III for his opinion of the young duke he replied, "Charmant, surtout charmant, and had he been alive the Revolution of 1848 might never have happened". He added that as early as 1834 riding through the streets beside the king he was convinced that he would lose his head in an uprising, exactly as occurred when he fled Paris ignominiously, wearing a wig.[13]

On her side, Margaret, in her Whiggish desire for involvement in political life, lost little time in ingratiating herself with the new régime, as Madame Adélaïde acknowledged to General Sébastiani: "Madame de Flahaut declared for us in 1830 right from the start and broke with all her former circle for our sake. I am grateful to her and as I have often told you I do not forget these things."[14] This was the beginning of their friendship. Thereafter Margaret made frequent visits to the Palais-Royal where the family cross-questioned her on the political situation in England, acknowledging her as the authority she certainly was, albeit strongly biased. In October, asking Lady Grey to continue keeping her informed, she compared dinner with all the Orléans children on the birthday of the prince de Joinville "to an evening at Howick rather than a royal feast. They really are the most comfortable people I ever saw, and feel quite in heart about the state of affairs here".

While keeping on good terms with the family, Margaret continued to gain the confidence of the heir, now duc d'Orléans, by entertaining for him and defending him "like an enraged she-wolf" from the attacks of the Carlistes, the Legitimist supporters of Charles X, who regarded Louis-Philippe as a treacherous usurper. Groups of young Carlistes did their best to embarrass the duke socially, going about in bands, taking possession of the salons, insulting him to his face at balls and receptions, and making sure that when he danced "no vis à vis could be found, nor ladies to waltz with him in the Cotillon", thus ensuring his hasty departure. In contrast, Margaret and some Dames du Juste Milieu, that is those loyal to the principles of the July Monarchy, invited him to smaller parties, attended only by the most elegant diplomats, foreigners and by pretty, aristocratic women who had been received at court. She insisted that he spoke to everyone, reproved him for preferring a tête-à-tête rather than general conversation and encouraged him to speak more loudly so that all could hear what he said. Margaret also persuaded Madame Apponyi and Lady Granville to invite only those guests accepted at the Tuileries to parties at which he was present and smoothed his way so successfully that not only was he pleased but so was the royal family. In April 1833, they showed their appreciation when Margaret was confined to her sofa after an accident to her back, for Madame Adélaïde paid her several visits and the prince called every day after his ride, spending his last hour with her before dinner. Knowing him so well, she told Lady Grey that she could tease and

> say many things to him in a light gossiping way that I could not normally touch upon seriously to a royal duke. He really is so kind to me and talks to me so confidentially upon his most intimate concerns that it would be wrong to withhold the truth from him.

She helped plan his visit to England in May, warning her friends there to expect a certain social diffidence due to his short sight[15] and hastened to give his parents glowing reports of his reception from Lord Holland and Lord Grey. Possessive as she was, she was obliged to put a brave face on this visit since Charles, who could have made himself very useful, was not invited to join the party. His influence was criticized by people such as the comte Alexis de Saint-Priest – a friend of Talleyrand – who observed that in London, the prince behaved perfectly, without a trace of the "dandyisme vulgaire" recommended by M. de Flahaut.[16] Margaret and the prince continued to get along well and after dinner with him in 1835 she declared:

> [H]e is really admirable in feelings, in language, so calm, so just, so moderate, with all the courage and energy of youth but without passion or violence. . . . I wish to God that these good and wise feelings were more generally appreciated instead of the provocation and persecution pursued by the Ministers.

Margaret was invited to social events held by Louis-Philippe and Queen Marie-Amélie – dinners at the Tuileries, concerts and fireworks in the gardens, and Naval battles on the Seine – and regretted that while the decoration was superb, the company was far from select. A visit to Fontainebleau was more enjoyable.

> The weather prospered the party, and enabled us to take beautiful drives each day in the Forest, which is really magnificent in all its details, and abounds with fine trees, grand masses of rock, and picturesque points of view. In short, it possesses everything but water, and good roads. All these Promenades were performed in charabancs for twelve people drawn by six horses, which with the gentlemen on horseback in gay uniforms, detachments of Lancers preceding the Royal carriages, and innumerable Picqueurs in red livery scampering about, among the trees, made the gayest, most animated scene imaginable. On the first night there was a concert with all the best singers from the Opera, on the second a spectacle with the actors from Paris, and on

the third a Ball to which all the *natives* of Town and neighbourhood were invited. The whole affair ended with a great review, and the usual enthusiasm, hats off, handkerchiefs waving, Vive le Roi, &c &c. All the Ministers came in succession for a day and the Marshall [*sic*} Soult was *en permanence* during the whole visit, with his wife.

In similar detail she described a day at Versailles in 1836:

[A]fter going to the Tuileries at 11 o'clock we did not leave Versailles till ½ past 8 and it was 11 o'clock at night before I was housed again more dead than alive and I am sure I should have been left among the *reliques* if it had not been for delightful little carriages in which all the ladies were rolled about a great part of the time. The party consisted of the King, Queen, Madame, the two Princesses, Prince Joinville and the Duke de Montpensier, to which there was only added the Landgrave of Hesse-Homburg and Madame de Bondy. We went in the large omnibus, which is very comfortable and an excellent family caravan. No word, much less a pen, can give you a description of all the riches in historic lore which we saw yesterday, and certainly a month passed in the Palace would be equal to many of old Klor's [history tutor to the Flahaut girls] lessons, for every century is so distinctly classed and every point of history so well illustrated and placed in chronological order that much useful information is easily as well as agreeably acquired, especially when explained by cicerone as able as the King, who is really an ambulating library . . . What pleased me most was the collection of old portraits which are placed in the attics, an unique collection of royalties and celebrities of every age; they were all found in attics and have been brought to light and restored by the King. I wish they could have occupied the best places below, which are invaded by ugly old Marshalls [*sic*} and portraits of the present time, but I must admit that the King has acted more wisely in ordering it otherwise.

After reflecting on Versailles of the past and the present she concluded that even if Louis-Philippe did succeed in his object of occupying the seat of Louis XIV, he would not find

> the brilliant court, the splendid fortunes, the high bred
> nobility which reflected so much lustre on the monarch of
> that era in the parsimonious, money loving, self opinionated
> plebeian ranks of lawyers and editors by whom he is
> surrounded. The days of courtly magnificence are gone
> for ever.[17]

At first supportive of Louis-Philippe, in 1831 she was pleased by the behaviour of the crowd on the annual celebrations of the Three Great Days of July 29–31, which passed off

> very tranquilly, no soldiers or police seen, the whole
> population in streets happy and joyous King and family
> received everywhere with enthusiasm illuminations of houses
> 3/4 stories high, on the Champs Elysées beautiful festoons
> from every tree, with millions of people walking, singing,
> dancing, carousing, no drunkenness, no fighting.

On another such occasion, always wishing to bring the two countries together, she regretted that Lord Granville, the British ambassador, did not show up at a Pantheon anniversary ceremony, "which would have been a compliment to our own revolution of glorious memory [1688, which brought the accession of William III] as well as the one which placed Louis Philippe on the throne of France". She also wondered if a monarchy born of a revolution could survive, particularly in France, where those who wanted a king were divided between the Orleanists and the Legitimists, who continued to resent the overthrow of Charles X, and supported the return of his heir, "Henry V", comte de Chambord. Republicans, who disagreed with both, were also divided into extreme and moderate groups, both constituting a serious threat to royal authority. So many conflicting opinions meant that it was always difficult for the successive ministries – seventeen of them from 1830 to 1848 – to obtain the majority of votes in the Chambers. Public discontent manifested itself in insurrections in Lyons and in Paris and by a series of attempts to assassinate the king, of which the worst was perpetrated by Fieschi in 1835.

Always outspoken, she hardly ever had a good word to say about the leading politicians, though at first disliking him, she came to support Adolphe Thiers, and remained firmly antagonistic to the doctrinaire François Guizot, not only in politics but even refusing to read his well-received biography of Oliver Cromwell. Aware of her attitude, he told Princess Lieven in a letter of September 1840 that he was not all surprised to hear of the lying and hostile reports she was spreading about him.[18] Her views were so well-known that in 1836 when the king was unable to form a ministry a journalist proposed an alternative composed of six women, putting Margaret in charge of the War Office. She quickly pointed out that as most of the ladies named belonged to different parties, "there would not be much accord in our Cabinet". Yet the joke was not so wide of the mark, for Princess Lieven thought that she seemed to be studying the profession of a minister of the Crown in her Whiggish determination to influence the course of events. Her endless criticisms of the current government led to a row in her house one evening in September 1840 when the princess, not wishing to be quoted, refused to join in a very heated discussion about the Eastern Question, arising from the decline of the Ottoman Empire. Margaret was furious that her friend, so influential, so knowledgeable, kept silent and after making a violent scene next day burst into tears, eventually calmed down, and after peace was restored their friendship continued. Determined to secure an appointment for Charles where his talents and experience could be put to good use, she laboured and intrigued sometimes counterproductively. Finally, after many slights – real and imagined – false hopes and disappointments, in 1841 Guizot gave him the post of ambassador in Vienna, taking them away from France and opening up new horizons.

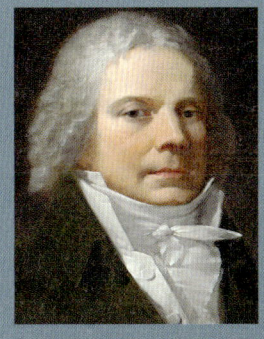

CHAPTER 13

Margaret and Talleyrand

. . . le plus impénétrable et le plus indéfinissable des hommes

Madame de Staël, *Mémoires*

For some years, Margaret, never intimidated by persons of power and influence, blamed Talleyrand for placing obstacles in the way of Charles's diplomatic career during the reign of Louis-Philippe. Celebrated for his wit and diplomatic skills and for successfully serving so many different regimes, Talleyrand, as his reputed father, had a special, albeit ambiguous, place in the life of Charles de Flahaut and that of his family. After the Flahauts moved to Paris in 1827 the three got on well, dining in each other's houses, and going to the theatre. Talleyrand took an interest in Emily and her sisters, and also in Auguste, predicting he would one day be a minister.[1] From his country estate Valençay, he urged Charles to bring them all to stay, and said how much he wished to see more of Margaret, "for although I hardly know her she already has won an important place in my heart by making you so happy".[2]

At Valençay Talleyrand lived the life of a very grand seigneur, surrounded by sculpture, paintings, fine furniture and a library containing 10,000 books. His hospitality impressed Margaret, who, at the end of a fortnight in October 1828, wrote that she would leave Valençay with the "greatest regret for it is impossible for anybody to do the honours of his house with more friendship, simplicity and esprit". According to her, the large and handsome house with its tiers of orange trees, terraces and balustrades, built in the picturesque François I style of architecture was only surpassed by the palaces of Versailles and the Tuileries, "but the real magnificence of the place consists in the numerous forests attached to it – 16,000 acres of oak woods opened up in the

29 **Pierre-Paul Prud'hon (1758–1823): Talleyrand**

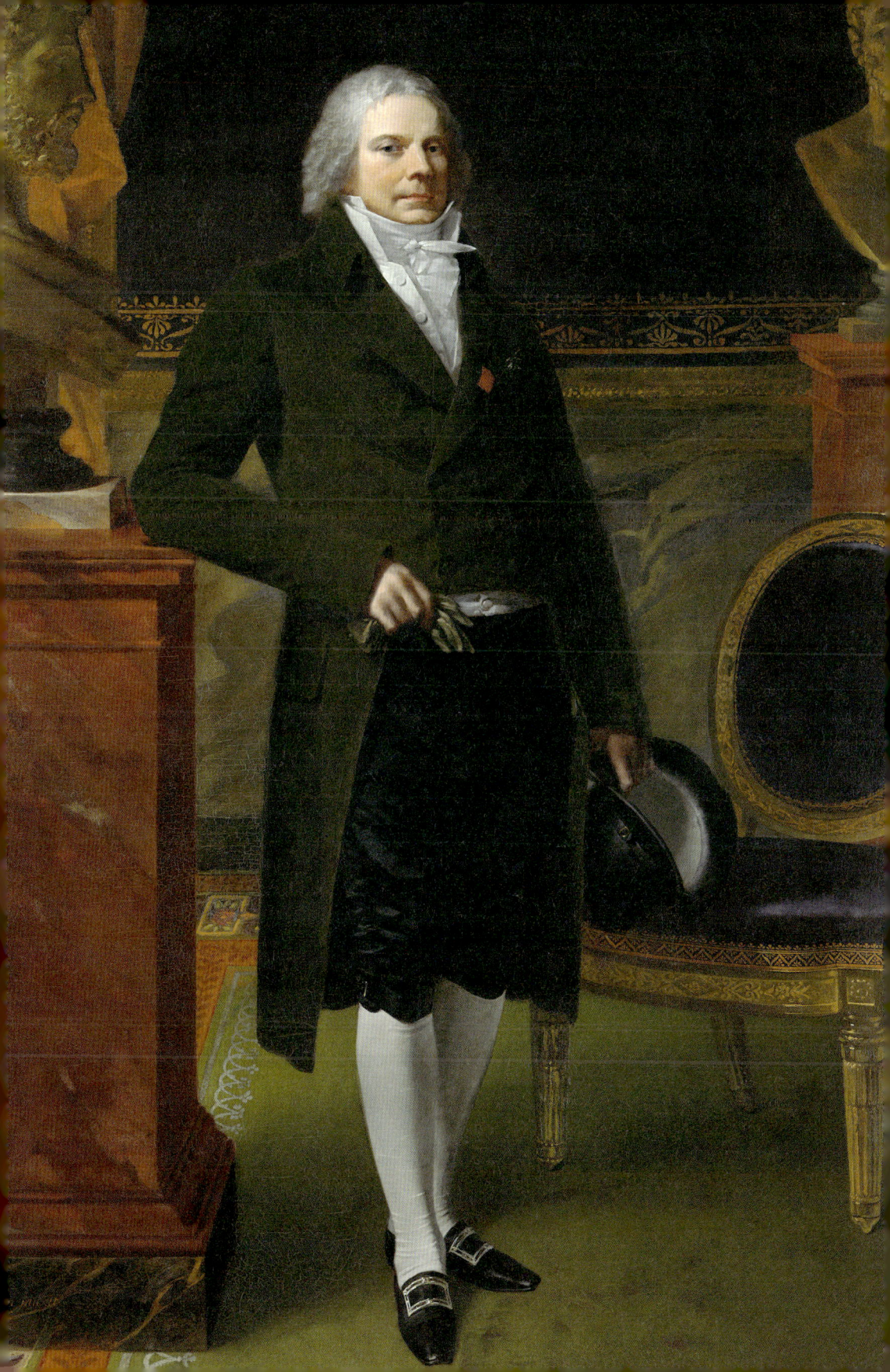

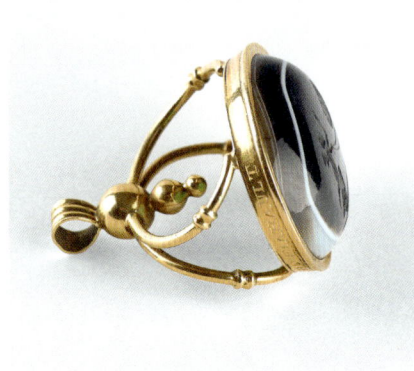

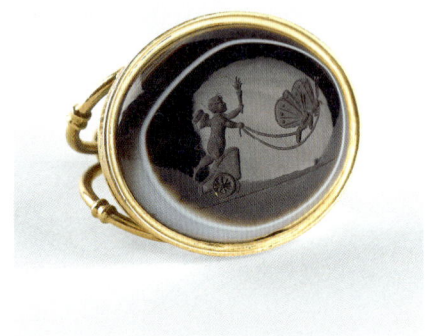

30 Seal representing the Triumph of Love given by Talleyrand to Emily de Flahaut

31 Detail of the Triumph of Love

French manner by carrefours and étoiles from which alleys radiate in every direction opening up charming vistas". She went on to describe the daily routine: "[W]e all assemble at 11 for breakfast, dine at 5 and pass the evening working and talking around a large table until the post arrives which furnishes conversation for an hour or two more". Besides the permanent entourage of Talleyrand's brilliant mistress Madame de Dino and her children, the Portuguese diplomat M. de Sampayo, and the devoted Polish Countess Tyszkiewicz, she noted that there were at least twenty others at table. These included the doctor, chaplain, tutors, musicians, agents managing the estate, and the occasional *préfet*, but who, except for commenting on the entrées, contributed nothing to the conversation. Most of all Margaret enjoyed Talleyrand's witty company and recollections of people he had known. She drove out with him every day for two to three hours, and in the evening listened as he read out his Memoirs. These she approved: "[N]othing can be written with more grace or naïveté than the domestic scenes of his childish years".[3] In spite of the anxiety caused when Charles accidently shot another guest, the old man enjoyed their visit: "Ils sont excellents, aimables, et parfaitement commodes à la campagne",[4] and was very disappointed when the Flahauts, with their *tribu*, could not return to Valençay every year. Instead, they continued to meet at the theatre, at balls and dinners in Paris, and stayed for three days with him at his estate at Pont de Saint, where he took the waters. Anxious to please, he offered Margaret the use of his boxes at the theatre and sent fond messages at the beginning of the New Year, when they exchanged presents, as in 1830 when he wrote to Margaret:

> [T]hose cups you gave me are charming, the Chinese could not make them in better taste – thank you so much. No-one admires you more than I.

In July that year, seemingly disillusioned with events in France, he told Charles how much he appreciated the

> blessings of vie casanière, lots of reading of old books – St Simon – the thoughts which come to mind after reading are like a dream which is so much more agreeable than worrying about the sad realities of politics.[5]

However, he never gave up, and in spite of poor health and the infirmities of age, accepted his last great assignment as Louis-Philippe's ambassador to England, to negotiate the terms of Belgian independence and strengthen Anglo-French relations with the Duke of Wellington and the Tory government. This was to cause a rift with the Flahauts, who thought he had supplanted Charles. Always the showman, accustomed to the stage of public life, Talleyrand arrived in London with a huge tricolour cockade in his hat, indicating his solidarity with the July Revolution.[6] He shared the embassy with Madame de Dino, his mistress, the wife of his nephew, a good-looking, clever, worldly "femme politique". She justified her presence in his house in a letter to the baron de Barante, explaining that Talleyrand needed to talk over the never-ending flow of strategic setbacks, hopes and duties which crowded into his always busy, reasonable and practical mind. "Although he is highly respected for his wisdom he can only open his heart to me, which is why I'm here."[7]

Soon after his arrival the Wellington government fell and was replaced by Lord Grey and the Whigs as the battle for Reform began, and with it a diplomatic duel. Talleyrand, with his huge experience and personal authority was pitted against Lord Palmerston who, as head of the Foreign Office, was obliged to act in accordance with the wishes of Parliament and defend British interests. He showed the French no favours, obliging Talleyrand to go to him in Downing Street, and after making him wait his turn accorded him the briefest of interviews. However, in his New Year greetings to Charles, after declaring that "I have loved you for the past forty years and am happy to tell you so on January 1st", Talleyrand praised Palmerston, "who runs his department wonderfully well, works hard, has a clear mind and makes dealing with him easy and agreeable", and then he turned to foreign affairs, discussing Belgium, Poland and finance.[8] In spite of such apparent goodwill, Charles, sent to London on a brief diplomatic mission by Louis-Philippe, sensed a certain awkwardness, As he wrote to Margaret in February,

> M. de T. has received me with great kindness & has I believe full confidence that all my conduct is open & fair to him, but yet I do not believe that my position here makes him desire that I should stay too long. My habits of great intimacy with Ld Grey & others of the ministers do not, I believe, inspire him with jealousy but create now & then a little embarrassment. In a moment of difficulty like the present he often sends for me & acts with me in concert & full confidence & we settle together what is to be said & done but once the important point settled I think he will see me return to Paris with pleasure & I shall be glad to spare him the little *ennui* of my presence.[9]

Not surprisingly, given his good relations with Lord Grey and the Whig party, Charles continued to hope for the London embassy, telling Margaret from Berlin later that year that he "will wait for a situation that suits me, and Mr. T cannot stay where he is for ever".

From this point relations deteriorated, probably because Margaret, driven by her Whig principles and desire to see her husband succeed, could not restrain herself from criticizing Talleyrand's pro-Coalition stance on English politics, writing on 15 July 1831:

Some French would regard the fall of the Grey administration as a misfortune, others, more under the influence of Talleyrand's opinion and Madame de Dino's pen, seem to think that a moderate Tory administration with Sir Robert Peel at its head will settle everything amicably and that a more conservative Parliament will be obtained by a dissolution which will have a happy effect in England, while the name and authority of the Duke of Wellington will regain the necessary influence in foreign courts – this is the substance of the correspondence held by those entrusted to represent and advocate the interests of constitutional France.[10]

Two weeks later, on 29 July, she complained to Lady Grey that

M de Talleyrand hardly writes at all and never gives an opinion when he does, or holds out the least ray of hope in favour of the present administration. He seems quite subdued by the intrigues of Madame de Dino to obtain favour at Windsor and must either have no means of obtaining information upon English politics except from conservatives or is determined to withhold the communication of it.[11]

Confident in her own judgment, she told Lord Holland that since Talleyrand always drew the wrong conclusions from the state of politics in England, especially on the question of Reform, basing his views on no more than gleanings from society gossip, she now felt obliged to present her own views on the true state of affairs directly to Louis-Philippe. Not surprisingly, by 16 November in that year Talleyrand had turned against her:

I am certainly not thinking of retiring to Paris . . . that is a story told by Madame de Flahaut who wants to return to England, but can't because no one likes her and her husband is not important enough for the London embassy: in all other respects he would be suitable: he is charming, knows everybody and his English is excellent, but that is not enough for the job.[12]

The following June and July Margaret blamed the "diableries" of Madame de Dino for spreading calumnies as a pretext for blocking the appointment of Charles as Talleyrand's eventual successor in London, which she thought "an ungenerous return from an old friend to whom he has shown a constancy of attachment through many trying times and circumstances which political life of Talleyrand rendered scarcely justifiable to friends and party". The rift between the two couples widened and on 16 October 1832 Talleyrand confided to the princesse de Vaudémont, "I am embroiled with the continual intrigues of Madame de Flahaut". He explained that Margaret, when in London, was always with Lady Grey or holding forth at Holland House, running down the new French government and making his life impossible.[13]

In her turn, Margaret complained directly to Louis-Philippe, who, she said, was "much shocked by hearing how ill I had been received by his ambassador in London compared with those of Louis XVIII and Charles X who had always treated me and Charles with great politeness and attention", and expressed his total confidence in her. The battle continued throughout 1833 with Margaret accusing Talleyrand of misrepresenting English political affairs. She feared his bias towards the Tory Sir Robert Peel and the Duke of Wellington could threaten the Anglo-French alliance. Charles, who by now had joined in the attack, warned Louis-Philippe against him and set out his reasons for distrusting Talleyrand in a letter to Margaret:

> That man is really the greatest intrigant that was breathed, he has done nothing else all his life than trying to destroy what he had contributed to raise. A priest, he did more than anyone to destroy the clergy. A servant of the Directory he was active on the 18th Brumaire. A dignitary of the Empire he cooperated with the Allies in the destruction of the Emperor. Author of the Restoration he took an active part in the Revolution of July & now out of hatred to Palmerston he would willingly sacrifice the best interests of his country to a feeling of revenge & after having had the good fortune to sign the quadruple treaty being about a rapprochement with Russia & destroy the only real security of the cause of Liberty which can only be found in a good understanding & intimate connection with England. I do not doubt that if he was not,

thank God, so near the grave, he would some day be found implicated in some conspiracy against Louis-Philippe. However the idea of displeasing him & making him an enemy causes a sort of turn: it appears that he had said to the King himself that he is sorry to be upon those terms with us & *they* are very desirous to see that state of things terminate.

Another cause for dissent between Madame de Dino and Margaret followed the visit of the duc d'Orléans to Valençay in October 1834. Margaret, bursting with indignation, explained to Lady Grey:

> Her persecution of me continues unabated, and on my arrival here I found the whole Society occupied by a cancan which at last became so serious that it reached the ears of the Royal family, and obliged me to pay more attention to it than it deserved. It appears that Mme de Dino had made a formal complaint against the duc d'Orléans for ingratitude for Mr. de Talleyrand in having written a letter to me from Valençay, turning into ridicule the party there, which letter I was said to have read to Lady Holland from whom they received the information. There is *not a word of truth in the whole story*, which a full explanation with the duc d'Orléans, and a letter from Lady Holland has [*sic*] satisfactorily proved, therefore the shame must remain with those who have been base enough to invent so vile a calumny. The motive of it has been clearly to make a coldness between the Prince and me, for it seems that Mr. de Talleyrand is very much annoyed at the intimacy that exists between His Royal Highness and Mr. de Flahault and is doing all he can to thwart it. Fortunately, on this occasion their intrigues have been completely foiled and *mis au grand jour*. It is almost degrading to be obliged to justify oneself from the contemptible attacks of such an infamous slanderer, but in these days where falsehood and intrigues alone flourish, and honesty and integrity meet with no reward but what proceeds from a good conscience and pure conduct, it becomes necessary not only to hold one's

head high, but to defend oneself against such powerful and
secret enemies. I must add that the duc d'Orléans and indeed
all the Royal family have been perfect for me in this
circumstance.[14]

And so the antagonism between them intensified. Charles declared, "I don't
believe that there is in the world such a couple as the uncle and niece and so
disgraceful and criminal connection"; Talleyrand deserved hanging, Madame
de Dino was a "lying little devil" and "an odious mischief maker from whose
persecution it is impossible to escape". Margaret angered by the continual
stream of venomous correspondence, "vile tripotages" and deep intrigues
from London, said that her smile "in a way shows she would like to kill me
on the spot. I despise her from the bottom of my heart". Perhaps they were
too alike. Now battling on behalf of the men in their lives each was an ambitious, influential "femme politique", who from her earliest years had known
the leading figures of the day and lived in the corridors of power, accustomed
to getting her own way and quick to take offence.

Margaret, who never let up on her barrage of criticism, blamed
Talleyrand for the dismissal of the comte de Molé from the ministry of
foreign affairs, "sacrificed as everyone who crosses that old villain's path or
scorns to become the instrument of his intrigues".[15] She took advantage of
any encounter with Louis-Philippe and Madame Adélaïde to state her case.
Thus, after visiting the Tuileries in November 1834 she told Lady Grey that

> The King was extremely kind & promised to take me to
> Versailles the first day he goes. His manner was altogether
> more friendly than it has been for long. I touched upon the
> subject of politics & was happy to find that the English
> alliance had still the same place in his opinion. He said: 'it is
> essential, it is the cornerstone – everything else is mere
> decoration'. I told him how happy I was to hear him say so,
> for I had heard with grief that there were persons who were
> pushing in a different direction, upon which he looked at me
> & said Who? T.? I answered yes & he remained silent.[16]

The retirement of Talleyrand in 1834 raised the question of his replacement and once again Margaret hoped that Charles would be appointed, though she felt Madame de Dino would do everything to prevent it, representing him as a Jacobin. In his inimitable way Talleyrand discussed this possibility with the young duc d'Orléans during his visit to Valençay, as related by Prosper Mérimée in a letter of 1834: "When the duc d'Orléans, hoping to bring about a reconciliation mentioned M. de Flahaut, to his surprise M. de Talleyrand started singing his praises, declaring that no one else in France understood England so well, he had great influence there, everyone liked him as he could talk politics with the politicians and hunt the fox with the sportsmen", and concluded, "not only is he the best qualified to serve as French ambassador in London" (then, after a slight pause) "he might be equally suited to the post of British ambassador in Paris". According to Mérimée this was said in such a deadpan way that it took the prince at least fifteen minutes to get the point of the last phrase.[17]

Yet the real obstacle to the appointment of Charles was not the hatred of Talleyrand, bad though their relations were, but the attitude of William IV, who did not even want to receive him as the Representative of Louis-Philippe at his coronation in 1831. This was also the reason why he was excluded from the suite of the duc d'Orléans on his visit to London, for William IV had made it quite clear that he would not be pleased to see him. In a letter of 21 November 1834, marked "Confidential", Lord Palmerston explained:

> Flahaut in the passage in his letter which I have marked in pencil mentions a statement which is said to have been made by Talleyrand as to what was said to him by the King. That statement whether actually made by Talleyrand or not is in itself strictly true. The King did express to Talleyrand . . . a decided objection to Flahaut as the Representative of the French Gov^t at this Court; and the King told me afterwards that he had expressed this objection and desired me to communicate that to Granville. The King has also on different occasions repeated his objection alleging as the ground upon which he should found it, that Flahaut has become a British subject, and cannot therefore represent a Foreign Sovereign at the Court of St James's.[18]

Similarly, Queen Victoria told Lord Melbourne that although she would accept him as Ambassador Extraordinary at her coronation his presence would not be agreeable to her. In a letter to Lord Grey soon after the accession of Queen Victoria the Princess Lieven appraised their chances of office with her usual clear-sightedness:

> You will have the Flahaults with you before long. He wants
> to be made Ambassador Extraordinary for the Coronation. . . . it
> certainly surprises me that, being a peeress of England in her
> own right, his wife is willing to appear on such an occasion as
> this in the position of a foreign Ambassadress. Perhaps too,
> you in England will think France might send over someone
> rather more of a *grand seigneur* than Flahault. Be this as it
> may, the Flahaults have had worries enough over here in
> their Court quarrels, and they are both of them looking thin
> from it all.

She then reported that as Marshal Soult had got the appointment, the Flahauts, who had long been encouraged to hope for – and had almost been promised – an embassy, were greatly affronted.

> They have certainly been ill-used in this affair, and I hope it
> will cure them of their mania for Court appointments. They
> possess quite enough of themselves to be independent of it all,
> and it is far better never to have to count on the words of
> Princes.[19]

As it was obvious that Charles was not acceptable to the British monarchy Margaret was further angered by the newspapers:

> . . . we are provoked beyond measure at the renewal of
> reports about Charles replacing Talleyrand. They must be put
> in with the mischievous intention to produce jealousy and
> irritation here of which there is quite enough already
> produced by the active pen of Madame de Dino and her
> numerous agents dans le doctrine. You may depend on it

there is not a word of truth in T's intention of retiring
however he gives it out! Some people who believe it and
speculate on it accordingly – de Barante, Decazes, Molé, de
Broglie if g^{vt} fell – we would have no chance in any case we
may be victims of Talleyrand's hatred but will no longer be
dupes of his friendship.[20]

In fact, Talleyrand did soon retire, Sébastiani was appointed in his place and
Charles had to wait until 1860 before his and Margaret's ambition was finally
realized.[21]

Installed in his mansion in the rue Saint-Florentin, Talleyrand and
Madame de Dino were once again involved in Parisian social and political
life from 1836 to 1838. He now posed as a survivor of the *ancien régime*, with
a uniformed Swiss guarding the imposing staircase, lance in hand, and visitors had the impression of entering a privileged enclave or sanctuary. His
abiding interest in public affairs was now focused on Thiers, "so talented, so
superior, so clear minded and with all that, so very circumspect. What a
prodigy!" Margaret, always watchful, commented: "Talleyrand 'fait l'innocent' but underhand and directing intrigue expects to manage Thiers and
the destinies of Europe – both unmanageable! Thiers is disposed to free himself from the leading strings as soon as he can walk without them." She also
noted that Madame Dosne, the redoubtable mother-in-law of Thiers, was
jealous of Madame de Dino's influence and experience. However, she con-
ceded that Talleyrand's

activity of mind and malice is astounding . . . and will
prolong his life some years longer. He continues to go out
daily and receive people for dinner as usual, and quoted
Pozzo who said he would not die because 'le Diable protège
ceux qui le servent si bien'.[22]

Significantly, in a letter inviting Thiers to stay at Valençay during the visit
of the duc d'Orléans, Madame de Dino made it clear that no other members
of the government would be there "as we are not people like the Flahauts
trying to divide fathers from sons".[23] In these hostile circumstances Margaret
decided to keep out of the way and told Lady Grey,

> My quiet life keeps me en dehors of all these tracasseries
> which cannot fail to be consequences of Madame de Dino's
> presence in every place where she can have a mischievous
> action. I have only seen her once and keep on terms of cold
> civility.[24]

The couples were not reconciled until they were brought together by the death of Clementina Flahaut, aged 15, on 1 January 1836. A few days later Talleyrand sent his condolences, reminding them that

> You alone were responsible for disrupting the close
> relationship between us, for my feelings for you are still
> warm and always will be. I would have wished that the
> promptings of your heart would have brought us together
> again rather than the present cruel event.

Whereas Charles, in despair at the loss of his daughter, made peace immediately, and was with Talleyrand when he died in 1838.[25] It took longer for the two women to forget and forgive, but in that year Princess Lieven told Guizot that while Margaret was, as usual, the focus of much gossip and tittle-tattle, she and Madame de Dino were now on the most friendly terms, adding, "[H]ow times do change!" As for Margaret's views on Talleyrand, she came round to appreciate his wisdom once again, for in a letter to Lord Rutherfurd written from Rome in 1847, she regretted that the present-day statesmen and diplomats had not adopted Talleyrand's precept that "the faculty of speech had been given so as to disguise man's thoughts".

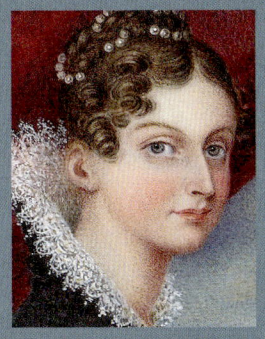

CHAPTER 14

Margaret's Friendships

To like and dislike the same things, that is indeed
true friendship

Sallust, *Catiline*, 20

Margaret's reputation as a hostess was soon recognized by Lady Granville when she wrote:

> . . . her house is delightful, talking, singing, whistling, and as he is acquainted with all sorts of people one meets the curious added to the pleasant and his popularity makes people too happy to go. She is more popular than she was and deserves to be so for she is very civil and very sensible always delighted to open her house, but her manner is hard.[1]

Notwithstanding this lack of charm her salon was a success, analyzed by the comte d'Haussonville:

> As a foreigner she was free to invite people one usually did not encounter elsewhere. Everyone wanted to attend the balls and concerts which, thanks to her large fortune, she could hold frequently. The Faubourg Saint-Germain was far from unfriendly, and Charles, in spite of his imperialist past and his present association with the Lafayette and Casimir Perier coterie was rightly regarded as a delightful host and a charming companion. He attracted the young of all parties, notably the duc de Chartres, and other favourites were Charles Lafitte, Achille Fould, Alexandre Walewski and Auguste Morny. Membership of this very exclusive club was restricted to the fashionable set only.[2]

They also kept open house for their English friends and for acquaintances from every corner of Europe. In his Journal, André-Édouard Kozmian described

> . . . an English woman, no longer young, never good looking but who fell in love with M. de Flahaut whom she married virtually in secret, without her father's consent. She has an income of 200,000 francs annually and should she produce a son, then she will have a further million. Her brusque manner puts people off, and she is inclined to say exactly what she thinks rather too loudly and too often, as well as being too inquisitive. She has a slight case of *politicomanie*, and her salon, which is a meeting place for liberals and the Faubourg St. Honoré is most agreeable. She receives every Sunday, and during the week she gives evening parties and excellent dinners.[3]

With five daughters there were also parties for children, including an

> . . . infants ball which grew in years towards the end for all the Mamas and Papas danced an eternal Grand Père which lasted till 3 in the morning, and Charles and José Maria [*sic*] Vila Real [son of his Portuguese stepfather, M. de Souza] were accused of having given ball entirely pour s'amuser.

Her dinners, both *intimes*, and *mondains* were perfect, thanks to an excellent cook who could produce the most interesting, varied menus, and on all counts Margaret won her laurels as an excellent hostess.

Inevitably, when other women had their salons, there was competition for the most sought-after evenings – preferably Sunday when there was no opera – and for amusing guests. In this respect Margaret had to remonstrate with the enormously rich Madame Delmar for taking her Sundays, but she never clashed with the Princess Lieven (1784–1857), an old friend whom she had known since the visit of Alexander I and the Allied sovereigns to London in 1814. Delphine de Girardin discussed the character of the two salons in an article in *La Presse* (15 December 1836). On the one hand she described

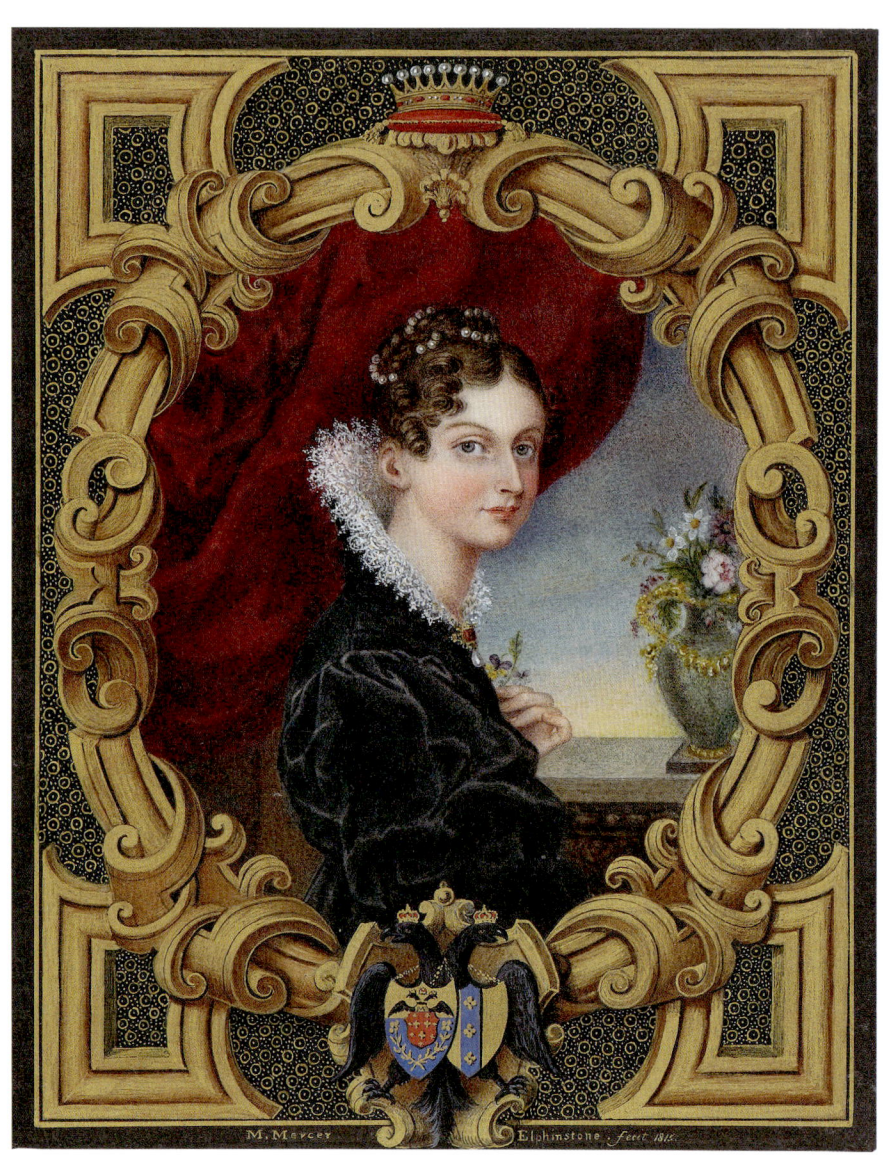

32 Miniature of Princess Lieven by Margaret

Margaret as "intelligent, capable and determined: her influence visible and vivacious", on the other, she compared Princess Lieven to

> . . . a planet with many satellites, with the calm of power, the patience of a will which knows its own strength. . . . she has chosen the only political role which suits a woman: she does not act she inspires those who act.[4]

Born Dorothea Benckendorff, married to Christopher Lieven, Russian ambassador to London (1812–34), through her talents as a hostess, her grasp of politics, her ruthless disregard of those not useful to her, with her imperious manner, the princess exercised such power in English society that she tended to eclipse her husband. Although they were very different, she and Margaret shared the same friends – Lord William Russell, Lady Palmerston, Edward Ellice, Lord Grey, Lord and Lady Holland – and exchanged gossip about people and politics in London and Brighton. She took a very realistic view of Margaret's ambitions for Charles, whom she had met in 1816 soon after his arrival in England. Thus, although she would have welcomed his appointment as French ambassador in 1830, she knew that the Duke of Wellington would never agree to it. Moreover, her friendship with the Flahauts was erratic. This was due not so much to personal, but to political differences, especially the cause of Polish independence, supported by the Flahauts through their friendship with Count Walewski. Ever loyal to the tsar, the princess used every means to prevent any intervention by England and France on behalf of Poles struggling to free themselves from Russia. She therefore warned Lord Grey: "Pray do not forget that every Frenchman of the present day is a born lover of revolutions and that Flahaut particularly, has a very tender corner in his heart for Poland when he speaks to you."[5]

When her husband was appointed governor to the tsarevich in 1834, she refused to live with him in Saint Petersburg on grounds of health and decided to settle in Paris. After so many years in London she was well qualified to compare life in the two cities, declaring that "Paris society is very different from anywhere else, quite unlike England. There is esprit without stint but there is also pretentiousness, much thoughtless chatter and much self sufficiency, much more than I used to notice in society in England". Now on her own, she became the mistress of François Guizot, ambassador to England in

1840, foreign minister 1840–7 and prime minister 1847–8. Her salon, in Talleyrand's former home in the rue Saint-Florentin, became Guizot's political headquarters and he could be found there every day, the first to arrive and the last to leave. Her relationship with Guizot accounts for the princess's significance in French politics during the July Monarchy and why Margaret, in spite of her dislike of Guizot, nonetheless continued to confide in her, discussing her hopes and disappointments. They went for daily drives together, each attended the other's salon, and in spite of the occasional row, or "grosse explosion", were close friends, and the princess was always sorry when the Flahauts were absent from Paris. When sending a daily letter to Guizot, she often referred to Margaret; for instance in March 1840, "She says something mischievous in every line but I'm still annoyed that she isn't here with me because anything, even Margaret de Flahaut, is preferable to solitude". Guizot, who bore no grudge against Margaret, advised, "In spite of all she says and does Margaret has great qualities. You should respect her friendship which is sincere".[6]

On a more personal level Margaret and Charles owed much to their friendship with Lord and Lady Grey, who had encouraged their courtship and marriage in spite of the intractable opposition of Lord Keith. Margaret never forgot the idyllic weeks in the summer of 1816 she and Charles spent with the Greys at Howick House in Northumberland, and in 1844 wrote to Lady Grey, "I always look back to my Howick days as the most joyous of my life and feel how much of my happiness I owe to the friendship and affection of you and Lord Grey".[7] These feelings were reciprocated, and on hearing that the Flahauts were moving to Paris, Lady Grey assured them that

> Lord Grey's extreme preference for Mr. de Flahault's society
> & the kind manner in which he has always appeared to return
> it contributed to the greatest degree to my happiness, and
> indeed it is not Ld Grey alone who preferred him, but all my
> children joined in this feeling & I assure you with the most
> perfect sincerity, that with the single exception of my eldest
> brother there is nobody we shall so much miss & regret.[8]

When Margaret told her in 1845 that the "news of death of Lord Grey grieves us as if we had lost one of our own family", Lady Grey replied that "he wrote

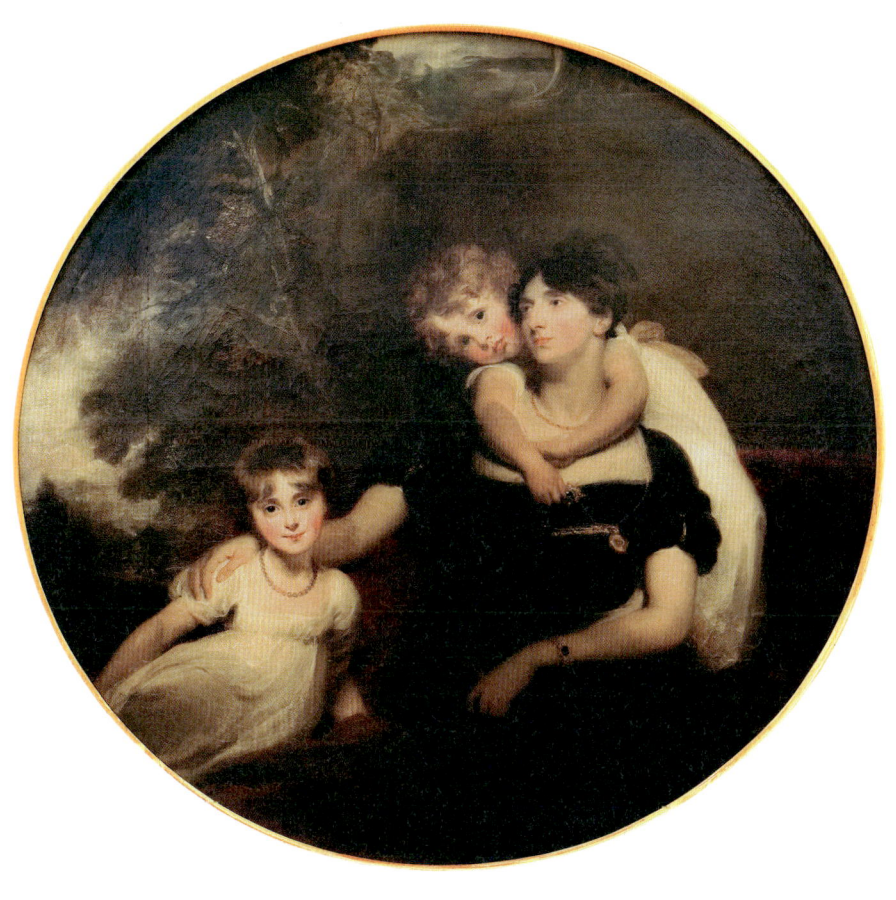

33 Thomas Lawrence (1769–1830): Lady Grey
with her children at Howick

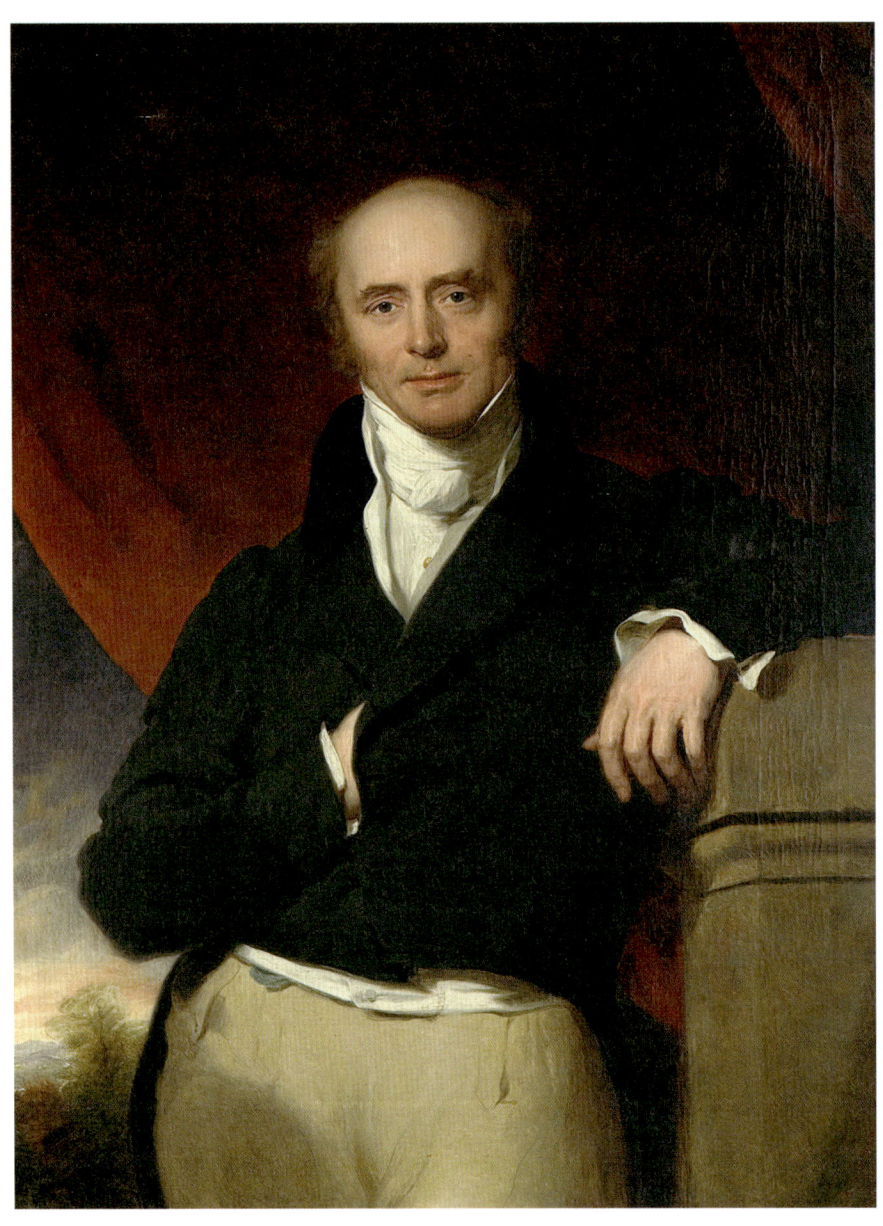

34 Thomas Lawrence (1769–1830): Charles, 2nd Earl Grey

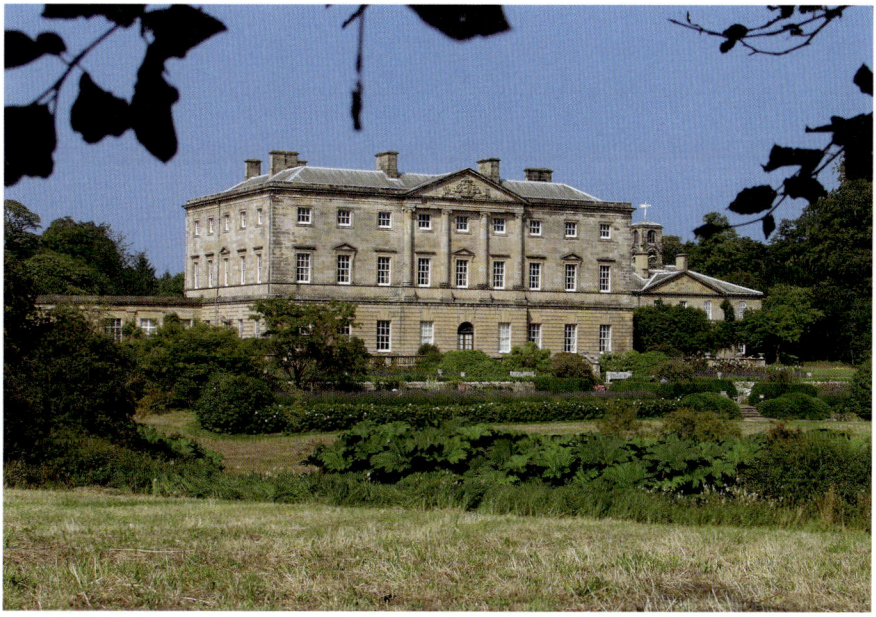

35 Howick Hall, Northumberland

most confidentially both to you and M. de Flahaut having few friends whom he valued so highly".[9]

Margaret took an interest in all the Grey children – seven boys and five girls – their health, their careers, their marriages and interests – and asked them to consider her house as "a home, as we always did Howick." She compared the comfortable family atmosphere of a birthday dinner at the Palais-Royal with Louis-Philippe and Queen Marie-Amélie to an evening at Howick, with the happy faces of the Grey sons and daughters clustered round the dining-table. Delighted that Lord Grey's services to the nation had been recognized by his appointment to the Order of the Garter in May 1831, Margaret, an excellent needlewoman, embroidered a Garter for him. Family matters are discussed in their extensive correspondence, which is often spiced with gossip, and when in 1818 Charles thanked Lady Grey for a letter to Margaret, who was ill, he added that "she was delighted with the news of the little scandal".

However, their overriding interest was in politics, as Margaret admitted in a letter to Lady Grey: "The only real interest I have had for years in politics has been Lord Grey and this first feeling was so associated with his friends and with every measure of liberal policy that it was impossible for me to separate them or imagine that any circumstance could." After recalling how she had first consulted Lord Grey over the projected marriage between Princess Charlotte and the Prince of Orange in 1814, she continued, "but for this circumstance I might never have had any opportunity of knowing either you or him and M de Flahaut and I should now be deprived of an interest in life which must ever have a great influence on our happiness and enjoyment".[10]

Thereafter Margaret followed every development in Lord Grey's political career, as the "Friend of the People "and the "Champion of Reform". Her letters to both husband and wife are running commentaries on the struggle for Catholic Emancipation, the passing of the Reform Bill and the abolition of slavery. She expressed her admiration for "his splendid talents and unpolluted character, his high mind and generosity", and declared that only his "skilful pilotage could steer the country away from the danger of revolution". She made no secret of her anti-Tory sentiments, castigated the "villainous House of Lords", and attacked both the Duke of Wellington and the moderate Robert Peel. Should the Greys think she was going too far she told them that she did not allow herself "to hold this language to others and am glad to disburden my mind to one who will accuse me of no evil intentions", though she always hoped that her opinions, so freely expressed, would coincide with theirs, for she would have been unhappy if they had differed. This was the case over Catholic Emancipation in 1829, when Lord Grey came to terms with the Tories, who took the credit for it, much to Margaret's annoyance. Accordingly, she wrote to Lady Grey:

> . . . it vexes me to think that there is *any* subject upon which you *cannot touch with* me in confidence, and especially *one* upon which *au fond* we must always think alike, perhaps I may have been too warm about it but be assured if I was, it was all in sorrow not anger. You must therefore forgive me if I was deeply grieved when I saw him [Lord Grey] sitting in a place surrounded by people so unworthy of him, and by

his talents and high character giving a triumph to their bad principles which they never could have obtained without him.[11]

Once established in France, Margaret appointed herself Lord Grey's agent, sending him thoughtful analyses of the current political situation, which supplemented the official reports to which he had access. It says much for her abilities that she was capable of corresponding at such a level with one of the eminent statesmen of the age, and she made her points with wit, spontaneity and sparkle. In a typically frank letter on the subject of Franco-British relations, she wrote, ". . . forgive me, dear Lord Grey, if I say that I think you are misinformed, if you suppose that any deep rooted national hatred exists between our two countries". In her opinion the problem was the Duke of Wellington, whose "name is so connected with the humiliations and misfortunes of France, that as long as he remains at head of our government nothing but bitter feelings will be generated between the two nations". She then explained that while "his military successes would have been generously pardoned long ago like those of other nations", the French blamed him for his part in the violation of the Treaty of Paris, the execution of Marshal Ney and the restitution of works of art to Italy. As the friend of Prince Metternich, the duke, according to Margaret, stood for the reactionary ideas of a powerful aristocracy and primogeniture. She defended this opinion, which she admitted would certainly differ from those from other sources and assured him that it was a résumé of those "collected from many of the chiefs of the liberal party here with whom I have conversed since I received your letter with the view of giving you the best information I could upon the state of the public mind."[12]

After the abdication of "that old idiot Charles X" and the establishment of the Orléans monarchy, the flow of letters continued, giving the Greys the most up-to-date reports on the confused, constantly shifting pattern of French politics, spiced with forthright comments on personalities: Thiers was "a little scamp", or "a profligate little man", the duchesse de Berry "a wretched little duchess", Molé a coward, and so on. In return, Margaret kept Madame Adélaïde informed of the contents of her letters from the Greys and acted as a go-between when the duc d'Orléans planned to visit London in May 1833. When the row with Talleyrand and Madame de Dino was at its height, she relied on Lady Grey for sympathy, and asked Lord Grey as her "best friend", for advice about Charles's future. It was then, feeling humiliated and disgraced, that they most appreciated the relationship and in 1833, after a series of setbacks, Margaret wrote to Lady Grey, "M de Flahaut and I have too much confidence in your friendship to require any profession of it, yet there are chords when struck which must always vibrate to the heart and we always feel deeply any new proof of your long tried affection for us".[13]

From their long correspondence it seems clear that Margaret regarded Lady Grey as a warm-hearted, generous friend, totally devoted to her handsome, clever husband and large, happy family. It is therefore difficult to see her through the eyes of Princess Lieven, who wrote, "Lady Grey is a horrible woman, passionate, bitter, Jacobin, everything that is most detestable."[14]

Equally controversial was another leading member of the Whig aristocracy to whom Margaret was attached, the formidable Lady Holland. She and Lord Holland – a Whig of the old school – who had befriended Charles's mother Adèle as an *émigrée*, welcomed him on his arrival in England, supported his marriage and lent the young couple their country house Ampthill Park in Bedfordshire for the winter of 1820. In London they held court at Holland House, an early seventeenth-century mansion set in 57 acres of beautiful grounds, remembered for their circle by Lord Macaulay as:

> . . . the favourite resort of wits and beauties, of painters and poets, of scholars, philosophers, and statesmen. They will then remember, with strange tenderness, many objects once familiar to them, the avenue and the terrace, the busts and the paintings, the carving, the grotesque gilding, and the enigmatical mottoes. With peculiar fondness they will recall that venerable chamber, in which all the antique gravity of a college library was so singularly blended with all that female grace and wit could devise to embellish a drawing-room. They will recollect, not unmoved, those shelves loaded with the varied learning of many lands and many ages, and those portraits in which were preserved the features of the best and wisest Englishmen of two generations. They will recollect how many men who have guided the politics of Europe, who have moved great assemblies by reason and eloquence, who

have put life into bronze and canvass, or who have left to
posterity things so written as it shall not willingly let them
die, were there mixed with all that was loveliest and gayest in
the society of the most splendid of capitals. They will
remember the peculiar character which belonged to that
circle, in which every talent and accomplishment, every art
and science, had its place. They will remember how the last
debate was discussed in one corner, and the last comedy of
Scribe in another; while Wilkie gazed with modest
admiration on Sir Joshua's Baretti; while Mackintosh turned
over Thomas Aquinas to verify a quotation; while Talleyrand
related his conversations with Barras at the Luxembourg, or
his ride with Lannes over the field of Austerlitz."[15]

Napoleon was one of the great interests of the Hollands, they campaigned
for better conditions for him at Saint Helena, and placed his bronze bust by
Canova in their Dutch garden.[16]

Margaret, who belonged to this world, stayed as a guest in the house, and
when not in London kept up a lively gossipy correspondence with Lady
Holland.[17] Very well read, much travelled, autocratic in manner, she was
described by Lord Macaulay in 1831 as "a large, bold looking woman with
the remains of a fine person and the air of Queen Elizabeth". Earlier, in her
novel *Glenarvon* (1816), Caroline Lamb presented Lady Holland in the character of the Princess of Madagascar of Barbary House, who "spoke of her
own country with contempt: and, even in her dress, which was magnificent,
attempted to prove the superiority of every other over it". Lord Macaulay
observed that she "shows in one respect great taste and sense. She does not
rouge at all: and her costume is not youthful so that she looks as well in the
morning as in the evening."[18] This wardrobe came from Paris, and Margaret,
who also loved clothes and was an experienced shopper, took over Lady
Holland's commissions for dress and accessories just as Adèle had done
in 1816.

It was not easy to buy clothes for such a demanding character, whose out-
size figure restricted her to few colours and shapes, and Margaret disliked
having to choose from "fashions which do not seem very pretty". She
explained that some requests came too early in the season before all the new

ranges were available, and that it was impossible to find previous models: "They never have the same silks two seasons following and in this country it is impossible to match anything 3 months after it is bought." However, she did her best, and from the correspondence emerges a fashionable wardrobe, influenced by the prevailing nostalgia for the past. Hence in 1836 she announced that the "Fashion is for rich brocades with large flowered patterns like those worn by our grandmothers" and predicted that hats would also return to similar long-forgotten fashions. She bought hats and bonnets for the dinner toilette from the famous M. Herbault, with whom she argued about which feathers – white or bird of paradise – would look best. In January 1831 she reported that "patterns for dresses, all shades of ruby, are beautiful, and Chinese satins rich and handsome are made in all colours and in changing colours black/red, black/green", In August 1832 she recommended a "Huge dress in tulle from Mlle. Marcelle – exactly as for Princess Amelia of Naples".

As a Scotswoman, she was not impressed by the fashion for Scotch mantles, "[M]ost of those are horrible tartans and put me in mind of old wives of Glasgow on breaking up of a market day", and preferred plain-coloured pelerines, worn wide and full. She looked out for *nouveautés* in triangular shaped fichus "casually thrown" over the throat, shoulders and bosom, and sent one she had embroidered herself to be worn "as a souvenir of me". As an alternative to the fichu she bought rectangular écharpes in grenadine silk, much liked by Lady Holland. Shawls, or "schalls" borrowed from Indian dress, seem to have been easily available, for she reports in October 1831 that "Shawls are to be had in all colours/patterns pretty in lilac/pale green with white ground coloured stripes: Lady Durham will bring you a schall of the new fabrique light and warm for a morning undress by the fire in darkest pattern I could find", and in 1836 : "La grande mode at present is large half square shawls in very soft silk trimmed with black lace very pretty and comfortable." With the taste of a Parisienne she chose a variety of elegant accessories: garnitures de jabot, peignoirs, muffs, gauze ribbons, shoes, gloves from Privat and perfumed sachets from Houbigant. Since handbags were scarcely in use, handkerchiefs were essential, and being for show, were trimmed with lace, individualized by crowned initials, embroidered with Gothic motifs, and finished with hems of varying widths. Only the quest for fans seems to have defeated her, for she wrote that they were very scarce, and

that it was impossible to find "large ones that give any air". Lord Holland
was not forgotten either, for she sent him waistcoats, mittens which she made
herself and quantities of pocket handkerchiefs, remarking that since none
with narrow borders were available he must accustom himself to those with
broad hems. The most difficult task was not the buying, which she enjoyed,
but getting even the smallest purchases through customs – and she wished
for a Traité de Commerce à l'Usage de Dames to make this easier.

Fashion and shopping were not the only subjects discussed in the long
correspondence between the two women, for Lady Holland wanted to be
informed about French politics and books as well. Nobody was better qualified to do so than Margaret, who shared her interests, and as a born writer
herself, always welcomed letters from Lady Holland which made "the days
of the post jours de fête pour nous". Margaret knew, too, that if she asked
Lady Holland to receive a young protégé such as Alexandre Walewski or
Henri de Castellane she could be sure that he would be welcomed at Holland
House. When Lord Holland died in 1840 she did everything possible to comfort his widow, including finding a suitable house in Brighton. It was through
this task that she discovered the railway; and was delighted with the "pro-
gressive" journey of no more than four hours from London.

Their friendship continued without interruption until Lady Holland died
in 1846 when Margaret wrote to Lord Rutherfurd from Rome:

> She makes a wide chasm in society and long years of
> uninterrupted kindness render it a matter of deep concern to
> me. To her I owed my greatest social enjoyments and tho' one
> sometimes laughed at her caprices and exigencies yet who so
> cleverly brought together the best elements of society and
> drew from every member of it its fullest value? It is an art
> little understood and seldom practised and we shall never see
> another Holland House or even its shadow such was at her
> salon in Stanhope St.[19]

She told Emily that she would never forget Lady Holland's kindness at the
time of her marriage when she received "little from those from whom I had
cause to expect it". Although Margaret was very touched that Lady Holland
had left her a diamond and emerald snake bracelet as a memento, Charles

was shocked, since he felt it should have been kept in the family. He complained to their daughter Emily: "I never knew her having any and next I didn't suppose your mamma would like to take anything of value from a succession where there are so many rightful heirs; and how can the mother of so many children trouble her head to leave her property to strangers?"[20] The Flahaut friendship with the Hollands was now transferred to the next generation. At first reluctant to stay at the "dear old Holland house without its former inmates", when she was invited there by Henry, 4th Baron Holland and his wife, Augusta, "although it brought back many painful recollections", she was charmed by everything they had done, adding to the comfort without destroying the old character.[21]

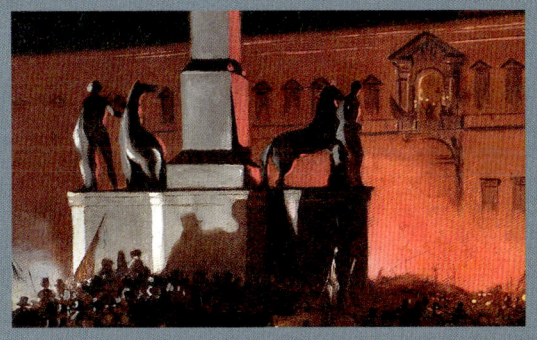

CHAPTER 15

Margaret's Travels

... there are peculiar powers inherent in ladies' eyes ...
but one in particular ... that power of observation which
... once removed from the familiar scene, and returned to us
in the shape of letters or books, seldom fails to prove its
superiority ... all ease, animation, vivacity

Lady Eastlake, "Lady Travellers", *Quarterly Review*,
June 1845

After her first experience of taking a train to Brighton in 1840 Margaret adopted railway travel and steamships for rivers, lakes and sea crossings. During the following twenty years she journeyed frequently across France to England and Scotland, to watering places, to Vienna and to Italy. Her primary purpose was not pleasure, but to discover a cure and a better climate for her daughter Louise, now an invalid. Unlike the artist Eugène Delacroix, who detested "those fiendish contraptions, railway trains", she preferred them to travel by road, though she complained about the delays caused by engine breakdowns, the disagreeable company of "vulgar boors, smoking bad tobacco and spitting à plaisir", and the horrors of "those dreadful receptacles für herren & für frauen which are built up with planks in sight of the whole train and no decent woman can attend". On these travels she found time to send lively accounts of events, people and places in her letters to Charles, to Emily and her friends.

Her description in a letter to Emily of a visit to Venice on her way from Vienna to Rome in November 1846 is typical:

Went about with Captain Cheney and Mr. Brown 'en contrabande' to see the duchesse de Berry's palace which is one of the first in Venice. With some remains of its antient furnishings and decoration forming a strange contrast to the quantity of modern knickknacks with which it is filled and portraits of all the most hideous race of Bourbons who were deprived of the Montespan blood to embellish it. The most ridiculous full length of Gérard's of the illustre veuve is there

in black with short sleeves and still shorter petticoat with a
pocket handkerchief in her hand perched on a high chair
squinting at the bust of her husband and the gown tight
according to fashion of the day and stretched over a gros
ventre which promised at least one more than came from it.
The most curious thing I saw in the collection was a high
shoe of Louis XIV upon the heel of which was a charming
painting by Watteau.[1]

Since she spent more time in Rome than anywhere else in Italy Margaret's
letters provide a detailed picture of the pleasures of life in the years 1820–60
before the picturesque city was transformed into the capital of the united,
modern Italy. It was then

> . . . like a small village within a great metropolis. The Pope,
> like a sovereign, ruled over a people tied to tradition, attached
> to their old ways, hostile to anything new, and xenophobic,
> even though foreigners were their only source of revenue. It
> was the centre of a past but great world which continued to
> attract men from every country and of all beliefs to study its
> ruins, which still retained their vitality . . .

In the salons of the Caetani, Wolkonsky, Torlonia, and Doria palaces visitors
might meet the elite of Europe. Then there was the beauty of everything
under the sky – ruins, landscape, people – the religious processions, and
moonlit visits to the ruins of the Colosseum.[2]

Writing to Lady Grey from their lodgings in Palazzo Poli, on 8 February
1840, Margaret said that the wholesome routine and the early hours suited
her, Charles and the girls. He dined out with the English "bulls" and her
salon was the meeting place for everybody of note. She was intrigued by the
reception given to the Pretender to the French throne, "Henry V", known
as the comte de Chambord, son of the duchesse de Berry. Forbidden by their
ambassador, the French did not attend, but all the English and Russians who
flocked to receptions tried to outvie each other in respect and attention
to him. There were dinners, plays, fêtes, a scarlet cloth was spread out, two
candles met him at door with all the etiquette of kingly state, and as he

proceeded to the salons decorated with lilies, loyal effusions in form of can-
tatas were sung and couplets recited, the mysteries of which were unravelled
according to the sentiments and wishes of the intelligent public. Finally, a
cavalcade of sixty horsemen, young Carlistes from all over France, escorted
him on his departure.[3]

In 1845, another visitor, Nicholas I, whose miniature she had painted in
1814, was less well received, as Margaret described:

> The Emperor of Russia leaves Rome after four or five days as
> little pleased with Rome as Rome is with him. No Gerandola!
> No visit from the Pope! Or from the body of Cardinals.
> Advent was the pretext for the first omission and his
> incognito for the second. No person has written name down
> for him (except that tuft-hunter Mr. Bosanquet) and he has
> seen the inside of no Palace not having been invited to look at
> the galleries and I suppose not choosing to go without some
> civil notification that they were at his orders. He has spent all
> his evenings au 3ème chez la femme du First secretaire à
> Rome who was a Troubetskoi and has a pretty sister whom
> he is supposed to rather admire. However la grande passion is
> at Palermo, demoiselle d'honneur to the Empress and she is
> supposed to be real cause of his traversing Europe. As he so
> dislikes his lodgings which are like a prison he will not allow
> Empress to stay there – presumably he will book Mellon's
> Hotel for her. Has done some popular acts dans le grand
> genre, redeeming all the pauper's effects at the Mont de Piété,
> commissioned 40 statues and bought high priced pictures but
> has shown little artistic taste or judgment. He hardly looks at
> works of art, and seems quite indifferent to them.

She watched him go round St Peter's:

> . . . this was accomplished in less than 10 minutes, I never saw
> a more irreverent scene for although Mass was going on,
> people were running after him as hard as they could, dodging
> and trying to meet him at every turn without the slightest

regard for the sacredness of the place. No one was present at
his interview with Pope Gregory XV1 except Cardinal Acton
and Mr. Bosanquet [. . . ?], so nothing to be depended on is
known, but as it lasted 1 hour 17 minutes, some conversation
MUST have taken place. When the Pope raised the question
of the Protection of Poles the Emperor denied all knowledge
of the scandalous persecution of a Roman Catholic Abbess
and her nuns and when asked if a legate could be sent to
look after interests of Catholic Church he turned it by saying
he could not agree to receiving a legate without consulting
his Ministers.[4]

In the winters 1845–6, and 1846–7, Margaret returned to Rome leasing
houses in Via del Babuino and the Piazza di Spagna. The latter, she
said was clean and comfortable enough, perhaps more than any other in
Rome, but low lying and therefore damp, getting no more than two hours'
daily sun, and so in case Louise caught a cold, constant fires were lit,
"which frighten the Roman visitors". Besides always worrying about Louise,
Margaret was preoccupied with the health of Augustus Villiers, husband of
her half-sister, who died in Rome in 1847.[5]

Whenever possible she was out of doors walking on the Pincio, painting
watercolours of the city, and making copies of the paintings in the churches
and galleries, later bound in an album.[6] Employing a good cook she gave
dinner parties, though she later said that even a small one in Rome was more
worrying than a grand dinner of thirty at the Vienna embassy. According to
Lord Malmesbury, who was in Rome in 1846, nothing could have been more
agreeable than the company at Margaret's house, when her daughter Emily
and her husband, Lord Shelburne, were there with Lord and Lady Canning,
the young Greys and others. She made it a real pleasure for her friends to see
the wonders of Rome, and not only for sightseeing but other events. For them
she hired a balcony on the Corso to watch the Carnival, and took tickets for
a Masquerade at the Apollo Theatre. In her element, Margaret received every
night and, according to Lady Canning, was "by way of collecting more society than anyone else". Besides meeting with English visitors to Rome
Margaret was soon on excellent terms with Roman society, though she disliked having to climb up three flights of stairs to encounter her friends in the

private apartments when she could receive them more conveniently on the first floor of her own rented house. An exception was the splendid dinner at Palazzo Doria: "I never saw anything handsomer than the house and the establishment, all Roman magnificence and English tidiness."

An obliging Monsignor Spada provided permits for museums, gardens and palaces, lent books, "to which he promises to add furnishing camellias to Georgina's balls during all the carnival". Through the Monsignor she and Georgina visited the important Etruscan collection of the Marchese Campana, "which is excessively augmented and very rich in bijouterie" and which was acquired by Napoleon III in 1861 for the Louvre. She shopped for Emily:

> By the first opportunity I shall send you a little bracelet composed of lapis and malaquite [*sic*] which I think a pretty combination but its greatest merit is being easily transported. I see very little new in the way of bronzes, but if you or Shelburne like the *genre*, or think of anything else here that would please you for your tables, let me know . . . there are some pretty varieties of antique lamp, which I admire very much, but they are not new.

Yet, much as she enjoyed the amenities of Rome her *politicomanie* continued unabated and she confessed to Emily that she longed to know how the visit of Adolphe Thiers to Lord Lansdowne at Bowood had passed off and "if it seemed to give mutual satisfaction".

The Duke of Devonshire and Margaret renewed their friendship during this visit. Together they watched the people of Rome congratulate the newly elected Pope Pius IX, and later she sent details of his reforms, "hopefully to roads and inns too, already pursued in Rome by attacking the gutters and spouts on tops of houses, always a hazard for those walking below. Now all have all disappeared as if by enchantment and leaden pipes are being placed to carry off water as in other civilized places. An announcement of a municipal institution is to be made soon." She mentions that Massimo d'Azeglio, the liberal future Piedmontese statesman, had great hopes of the new pope, and had been welcomed by him.

In April 1847 she reported on Holy Week writing that

... the Semaine Sainte was very laborious to those who went through it all, for there were such crowds seen at all the ceremonies, the sun smiled on the Pope whenever he appeared and the populace testified their affection by the most moving demonstrations. When he returned to the Quirinale there was a spontaneous illumination of all the streets he passed through and he has been accompanied by thousands with lighted torches. I am glad to see this for it was thought that his recent edict for regulating the Press had disappointed the people and might have affected his popularity. However it does not seem to have done so and the newspapers are as liberal as before and d'Azeglio has published a letter explaining and justifying this measure.

Then in May she wrote:

Pius IX continues to be the idol of his people and every now and then animates their ardour by some new popular act. His invitation to the provinces to send deputies to reside at Rome and form a representative Council brought forth a burst of enthusiasm such as I never before saw – in three hours after it became known a meeting was held in the Piazza del Popolo and a procession of 20,000 people divided into sections who all marched in regular order with lighted torches to Monte Cavallo to thank the Pope who appeared on the balcony and gave them his benediction surrounded by a glory of feux de Bengale which were exhibited the moment he appeared and as soon as he retired all was darkness, every torch was extinguished and the people separated in silence and returned home quietly – the whole scene was striking and very thought provoking. Now he has ordered the Dissolution of Accademia Ecclesiastica Nobile – a nursery of aristocratic monsignore neither remarkable for morality or acquirements.

36 **Ippolito Caffi (1809–1866): Pio Nono giving a torchlight blessing from the Quirinal Palace, Rome (overleaf)**

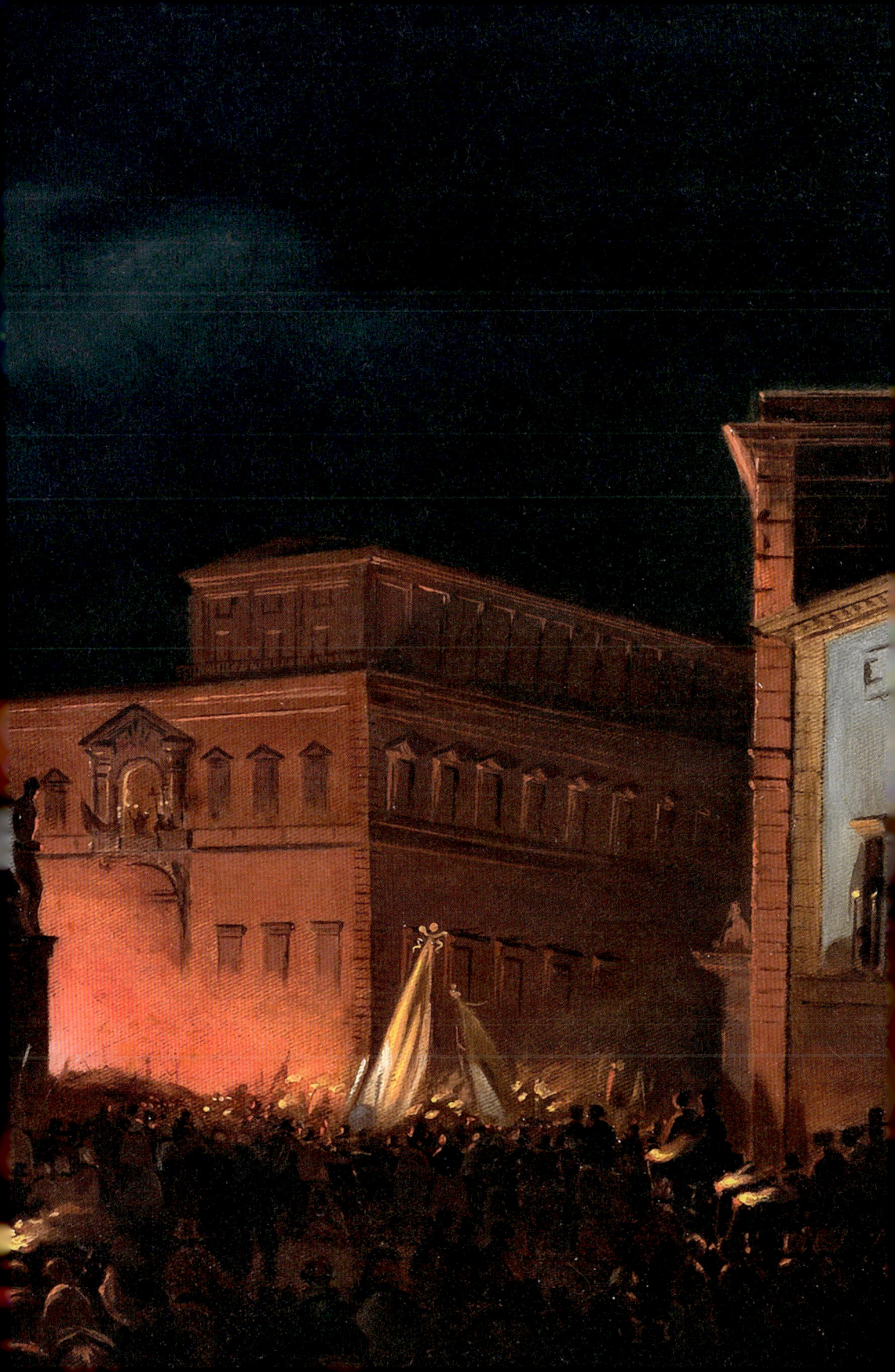

These initiatives were welcomed and at one of the patriotic dinners which were now held in Rome and Tuscany a toast was proposed to Pio IX who has told Italy, as Jesus ordered Lazarus, 'to Rise up and Walk'.[7]

She and the duke exchanged information about travelling – which inns were to be avoided, and which had the best food – and agreed to ignore the recommendations of Murray's *Handbook*. She lent him the latest novel of Alexandre Dumas, together they attended "the Cardinal's ceremony", or investiture in St Peter's, processions at the Gesù, opera performances, receptions at the princesses Lancellotti, Rospigliosi, del Drago, and Doria, and then, after he had left, she entertained him with reports of the expatriate life they had enjoyed together. In January 1847, for instance, she describes a

> Reception at the French embassy which was very brilliant
> attended by all the cardinals, and all the diamonds in Rome.
> Princess Piombino and Princess Torlonia were two
> constellations which obscured brilliancy of all the minor
> stars! The first had four rows of enormous chatons round her
> neck with large brooches of single diamonds like nuts, the
> fair Colonna appeared as if in a cuirass of diamonds for head,
> neck and gown were equally covered and upon each arm she
> had nine rows of large brilliants which filled up all the space
> between glove and elbow. Carlotta Grisi appears tomorrow.[8]

As the duke, now a close friend, took an interest in Margaret's children she sent him reports about their health, the various remedies prescribed by the Roman doctors, and the problems of her journey home with an invalid, without the services of the indispensable courier Kelbach. From Civitavecchia in May 1847 she wrote that

> because of delays in Rome due to the weather they missed the
> boat Capri – Genoa, and that as there was no room for them
> on the Marie Antoinette which had arrived from Naples, they
> would have to wait. However, the Captain of Marie
> Antoinette gave up his cabin to Louisa and her governess so

Georgina and Margaret proceeded on their own by vetturino and horses to Leghorn then on to Genoa and joined up with Louisa last night.

In return, his letters gossiped about the world they both knew so well – how the Prince of Lucca squabbled with the Grand Duke Constantine while staying at Windsor with Queen Victoria, and his agonies about the breakfast he was organizing for the Grand Duke, "all the plague of the one for his father [Emperor Nicholas I] without the satisfaction". He described the benefit performance for Fanny Elssler in Florence, how the stage was completely carpeted with magnificent bouquets, some crowned with pineapples and said to contain jewels, and deplored the fashionable disdain for the "astonishingly clear, true and intelligent" Jenny Lind. Back in England their friendship flourished, having so many interests in common. Margaret and Georgina, with Emily and her husband, visited his villa at Chiswick, and dined at Devonshire House, where she compared the refurbished great rooms with those of the palaces of Genoa and Venice. In reply to a letter she wrote to him when he was ill in April 1852, he assured her of his regard:

> My dearest Mme de Flahaut,
> It gave me immense pleasure to see your handwriting, notwithstanding our long absences and intervals I feel always the same affection towards you, and the same value for your friendship.

Unable to stay in Rome with Louise because of the heat, Margaret, now condemned to the life of a perpetual wanderer, was obliged to travel north in search of a cure. Arriving in Genoa they made their way across the south of France until they reached the thermal station of Eaux-Bonnes in the Pyrenees, where Dr Prosper Darralde was in charge. After weeks there, to no purpose, the decision was made to return to England in the autumn of 1846.

In July the following year, after another visit to Rome, Margaret passed through Paris where she attended one of the most important social events of the reign of Louis-Philippe, the ball given by the duc de Montpensier. As she described it to Emily: "This 'fabulously beautiful' Fête à Vincennes . . . in the

Parc des Minimes could only have been surpassed by dreams of the tales of the Arabian Nights." On arrival at the entrance she was greeted by immense military trophies composed of huge cannons, piles of cannon balls, pyramids of drums mixed up with tricolour flags and coloured lamps all very fantastically arranged, and the forest also was illuminated with coloured lanterns.

> You entered a long covered alley (like the Allée des Feuillants) brilliantly lighted with festoons of coloured lamps and on each side between the trees there were splendid suits of armour, horse and foot alternately, with groups of flags and musquets and at the end of this long walk was a large star of the Legion of Honour made with bright swords of bayonets upon a cloth of gold and Corinthian columns on both sides made with musquets and pistols arranged with wonderful taste and ingenuity. I am sure there must have been 500 coats of mail mounting guard and as both sides of this walk were open to the illuminated forest it was very pretty to see the groups of real soldiers, firemen etc. under the trees and all the well dressed ladies and brilliant uniforms walking up and down among them.
>
> They went towards a little town of scattered marquees and tents furnished and well lighted with servants and refreshments where parties might find their own drawing room and establish themselves with their friends. On the left of the long walk you entered a very large oval temporary room where the dancing was and where the queen of Spain and the four Princesses were. The little Duchess [Spanish wife of the duc de Montpensier] very gay, very happy and very civil for she jumped down from her bench and welcomed me as if we had been old acquaintances. This room was lined with flowered chintz and at one end there was a large recess for the band and a chorus of 50 voices to accompany it making a very good effect. You may remember in William Tell there was a ballet in which Mademoiselle Taglioni danced with the accompaniment of a chorus.
>
> At 11 supper was announced and the Princesses and 200

ladies went into another large tent lined with chintz in which a magnificent hot supper was served and as soon as we were placed the curtains were withdrawn and showed us the forest illuminated with coloured lamps, Chinese lanterns with bands of music playing and all the hungry gentlemen walking about and envying the more fortunate ladies. In a moment after lights of various colours from a feu d'artifice made all the trees look as if transformed into emerald and then changed to red as if the whole forest was on fire. . . . all these changes went on during the repast. I really never saw anything so pretty as the green light and all the leaves of the forest trees looked like jewels with their dark stems in relief upon the clearest and brightest tint of aquamarine. After supper I was lucky enough to get my carriage immediately and came home with General Carbonel at one. 1200 people were invited to this fête which is said to cost a 100,000 francs.

It will make the duc de Montpensier very popular for everybody was invited Position and Opposition, Victor Hugo, Jules Janin, artists of all description, élèves from St. Cyr, the Ecole Polytechnique. The first person who almost rushed at my person when I arrived was my little Professor Renaud, and the painter Gudin. . . . all the princesses danced every dance except the little duchesse d'Aumâle [sic] who is grosse à plein ventre. . . . the Queen of Spain has still a charming face, all smiles but too fat. The Duke de Rianzares is dark with an aquiline nose and is certainly handsome but her Gentilhomme de la Chambre the Duke de San Carlos is much more so and exceptionally distingué whereas the other looks vulgar. The Normanbys [British ambassador and his wife] were there and I believe I was a godsend to her for she gave me a place by her and we talked all the evening but I did not observe that any French people came up to her and I am afraid that they have a very bad position here – He seemed equally désœuvré and got so bored that he was on the point of going away, but I implored them not to before supper, which was lucky as she was designed to sit by one of the princesses and if she had not appeared in her place it would surely have been said that she had not been invited and had gone away on that account. I do not think that they are adroit.[9]

Margaret, who believed in the benefits of watering places never gave up on them. She went frequently to Aix-la-Chapelle and in August 1828 sent an account of her stay to Lady Grey. She complained that continual rain prevented her from enjoying the drives and beautiful walks in the neighbourhood and that

> the town itself is detestable being composed of narrow ill-paved streets and as all the water drinkers live in two or three hotels in the heart of it for the sake of being near the fountain and baths they must be crossed every time one puts a foot out which is a great nuisance. The waters are hot and sulphurous and seem extremely efficacious in all cases of rheumatism, contracted limbs, debility etc.

The routine was certainly wholesome: up at 7, dine at 2–3, bed at 9, whist in the evening, seeing native dance Gallops once a week at the Redoubt. One cure was not enough and within ten days she proceeded to Spa to drink the waters "much recommended for their tonic effects".[10]

During the years in Vienna, since the city was empty during July and August, Charles followed his friends to watering places, sometimes joined by Margaret and the girls. His health was not what it was; he suffered from rheumatism, and his stomach was frequently upset. This could be attributed to the Vienna water, which remained polluted until 1873 when a new supply was brought to the city. He described the routine he followed at Marienbad: wake at 6, drink three glasses of Kreuzbrunn, walking at least one hour after last glass, home for breakfast coffee or tea, then walking a little more, at 12 bathing half an hour, dinner at 1, walking again in the evening and drinking two to three glasses of the Waldbrunn and before going to bed a couple of glasses of the Kreuzbrunn again. While visitors hoped to benefit from this regime and the good air, the social life continued. As the atmosphere was less formal than in the capitals of Europe, it was more conducive to discussions between politicians, statesmen and diplomats; he saw friends as well as colleagues. such as the Russian envoy Medem, the Esterházys, and the British ambassador Sir Robert Gordon during the day. His evenings were spent with the Metternichs at nearby Königswart, where a room was always ready for him and a place at the dining-table. They usually read when the newspapers arrived but if particularly fine, might walk to the Schwarzensee, a local beauty spot. Music was another entertainment and on one occasion Princess Metternich hired a magician who amused them with card tricks.

As for Margaret, she hoped that taking the waters would do her good too, since she continued to suffer from headaches, liver problems and back pains, retiring to bed whenever they occurred. During their first summer in Austria, in 1843 at Bad Ischl, near Salzburg she and the girls tried the primitive life, the drinking of *petit-lait* [whey], "the nastiest stuff I ever tasted". On 30 August she enthused in a letter to Lady Grey:

> Ischl is the most enjoyable place I ever was at and every day
> we make an expedition to see some new lake mountain or
> waterfall in the most picturesque country imaginable. Roads
> excellent, fields all open and laid down like finest lawns paths
> cut in rocks by which you reach tops of highest mountains
> carried by Tyrolians [*sic*] in chairs without risk or fatigue – up
> an Alp I found green prairies well-wooded, cattle grazing,
> peopled with young girls in pretty costumes who pass
> summer there in picturesque Chalets to take care of their
> cows. They brought us strawberries and cream and sang.
> Tyrolian airs in parts sung harmoniously – nothing described
> by Florian could be more pastoral or pretty – the pretty
> cottages might be made similar in England.

It was such a success that the following summer, she was back, having rented Prince Kinsky's house for the season. The cost of staying in such a fashionable resort was so high that Charles complained that Bad Ischl was "a very expensive fancy". Although she left the Palais Starhemberg in June, taking the steamboat up the Danube to stay with the Esterházys at Landschütz, now known as Bernolákovo, and returned via the wonderful castle of Emmanuel Zichy at Rusovce, she had to delay her departure for Bad Ischl until July, being obliged to welcome Princess Clémentine, daughter of Louis-Philippe, to Vienna. In 1844 Charles tried the waters at the Bohemian spa town of Carlsbad, where Polish was almost the only language spoken, but decided that Marienbad suited him better, and, as was customary, went from one spa to another, finally joining Margaret at Bad Ischl. Although in July 1846 he told Margaret, then at Eaux-Bonnes in the Pyrenees, that "feeling the want of those waters", he was about to set off for Marienbad again; in September he admitted that he was "disappointed with the effects of the water this year . . . the fact is that all doctoring is to no purpose, old age will come on and is not to be resisted".

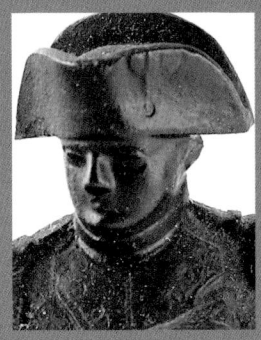

CHAPTER 16

Margaret's Cult
of Napoleon

Vivant il a manqué le monde, mort il le possède
[During his life the world slipped from his grasp, but in
death he possesses it]

Chateaubriand, *Mémoires d'outre-tombe,*
Book 24, Chapter 8

Margaret was not only a dedicated Whig in politics, but she was also a firm Napoleonist, one of a surprising number of British citizens who regarded their national enemy as an enlightened statesman and reformer rather than a brutal tyrant and plunderer. These Napoleonists were already active well before the victory of Waterloo, but there were many more of them in the following years. In 1828 Custine observed that the ogre of 1810 had become the hero of melodramas and his portrait – in bronze or alabaster busts, drawings and prints – was on sale everywhere in England.[1] That same year in Paris the duchesse de Maillé noticed that "English women mad with admiration for Napoleon" hung on every word uttered by Baron Vivant-Denon, formerly the emperor's director of museums.[2] Closely allied with Lord and Lady Holland, leaders of the Whig Napoleonists, Margaret, like Byron, joined their ranks early, certainly by the time Napoleon was exiled to the island of Saint Helena. It was the first sign of independence from her father, Admiral Lord Keith, inveterate enemy of the "Bonapartist crew", and she expressed her admiration for her hero by painting his miniature (Signed M. Mercer Elphinstone fecit 1815).[3] This portrait might have been meant as a gift to Lady Holland, who commissioned a fine bronze bust from Antonio Canova in 1814, which she placed high on a column in the Dutch garden at Holland House, with an inscription from Homer's *Odyssey*, here translated:

He is not dead, he breathes the air
In lands beyond the deep,
Some distant sea-girt island, where
Harsh men the hero keep.[4]

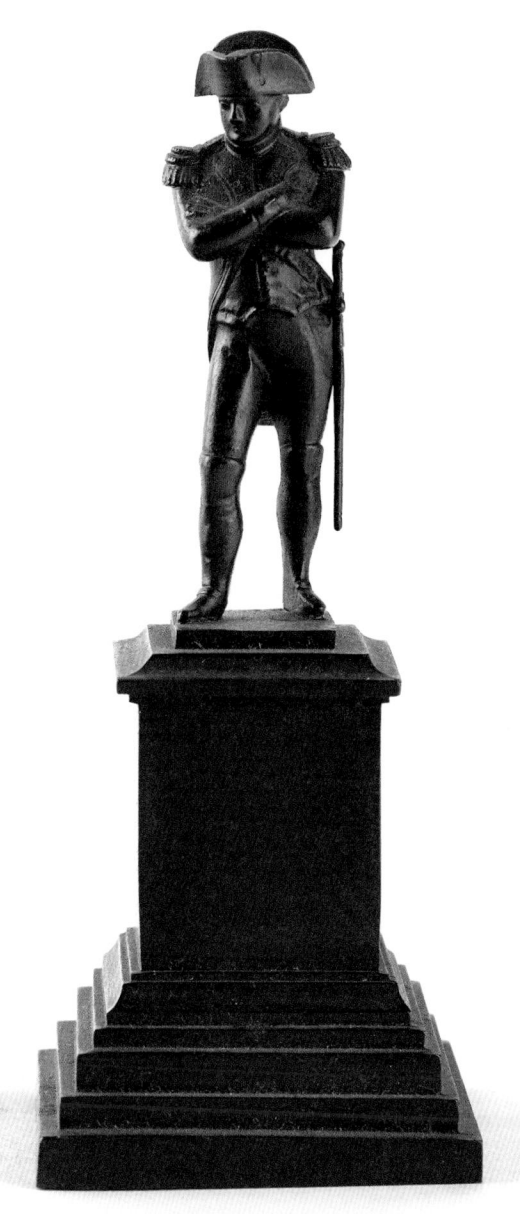

37 Margaret's Napoleonic paperweight

Margaret, who supported the efforts made by the Hollands to secure better conditions for Napoleon, criticized the severity of the governor Sir Hudson Lowe, approved the refusal of General Bertrand to take leave, and read every account of life at Longwood from travellers returning from Saint Helena. Drawn towards Charles de Flahaut by his close association with Napoleon, their marriage in 1817 put the seal on her devotion and throughout their long life together neither husband or wife swerved from a position of total loyalty to the fallen hero. Between them they assembled an impressive collection of Napoleonic memorabilia, acquired from various sources. In 1836, for instance, she bought from Fossin, her Parisian jeweller, a silver-gilt figure of Napoleon enshrined within a Gothic style canopy supported by lapis lazuli columns,[5] and in August 1860 at the Samuel Woodburn auction, a copy of the full-length portrait of the duc de Reichstadt by Thomas Lawrence. It was a reminder of the son of Napoleon, who, "born with such brilliant hopes and showed so much promise", was fated never to rule as Napoleon II and died young in 1832. Although these were mostly shown in a room in the round tower of Tulliallan, Margaret liked to keep some of her own mementoes: miniatures, medals, and a monogrammed crowned N handkerchief (a souvenir from her father) always with her. She used a bronze statuette of the emperor in military dress as a letter press on her desk, and displayed two biscuit-porcelain portrait busts in her London bedroom.

Regarding the victory of Waterloo in 1815 as "an unfortunate battle", Margaret resented the Duke of Wellington for his part in it, and never ceased to attack his political activities. For this reason, she refused an invitation to the Waterloo anniversary banquet, and made her position clear to Queen Victoria's lord chamberlain, Lord Francis Nathaniel Conyngham, in 1838:

> Monsr. de Flahaut who was aide-de-camp to the Emp[r]
> Napoléon at the Battle of Waterloo must always consider this
> as a day of mourning for his country and tho' as an English
> woman, I should assist with heart and soul at any
> commemoration of the glorious achievements of my
> countrymen, yet on this anniversary I hope that her Majesty
> will not disapprove of my making a sacrifice of my own
> feeling to those of my husband and abstaining from

appearing at the brilliant fête which otherwise would have
been so gratifying to me.[6]

While living in Scotland she heard from a naval officer that the British
Government had offered Dr O'Meara a yearly pension £200 in return for
keeping silent about conditions in Saint Helena and asked Lord Grey if this
was true.[7] Later, in Paris, 1819–20, and then during the years 1827–41, she
watched out for any event or publication concerning Napoleon. From Aix
in 1829 she told Lady Holland that she had witnessed in the theatre

> . . . a curious manifestation of the attachment of the whole
> population, French at heart, to the souvenir of the petit
> homme took place at the theatre. At the end of the play, a
> new piece about the Polish hero, General Kosciuszko, when
> the Emperor arrived to review his troops, and stood for a few
> minutes looking through a telescope in his usual military
> costume and attitude, the house rang with applause. Every
> performance was sold out.[8]

Present in 1833 at the unveiling of the statue surmounting the column in the
place Vendôme, she was "much pleased with it. The attitude is simple and
imposing, the great coat so well arranged that aided by an imaginary breeze
it assumes folds that give it effect of a graceful drapery." Yet she did not
entirely approve: "I cannot however help regretting that the Emperor of the
French was not replaced on the column instead of General Bonaparte – this
seems to me a fault." However, she was pleased to note that the unveiling, in
the presence of Louis-Philippe, his sons, marshals and ministers was "accompanied by shouts of triumph from the surrounding multitude". Nothing
escaped her, and she observed that while the king and the princes saluted the
statue and waved their hats, the disdainful attitude of the duc de Broglie and
Guizot made "a strange contrast to the exaltation of all the other assistants
at the ceremony".[9] An even greater moment came in 1840 when the remains
of Napoleon were returned to France. To mark the event, she held a reception at her house, which overlooked the procession as it passed under the Arc
de Triomphe down the Champs-Élysées on the way to the final resting place
in the chapel of Les Invalides. In spite of the cold, which evoked the retreat

from Moscow, a crowd of one million people lined the route. More like a triumphant military review than a funeral, the cortège consisted of trumpeters, eighty-six representatives from the different cavalry regiments, each carrying an eagle standard, eighty thousand troops, and five hundred sailors from the frigate *Belle Poule*, the ship which had repatriated the emperor's remains. The funeral car, designed as a tomb surrounded by six allegorical figures of women holding up a crown, was drawn by sixteen horses. These, draped in black crape embroidered with bees, were led by grooms in the imperial livery of green and gold. The car was followed by former officers of Napoleon, including Charles, bare-headed, but in uniform. Margaret who invited the widows of the Bonapartist regime – the duchesses d'Albuféra, and de Rovigo, Maréchale Ney, General Bertrand's daughter Madame Thayer and her son – insisted that all present were dressed in strict mourning, "grande toilette de deuil". As the funeral car went by there was silence, broken by the sobs of the pale, weeping women, moved by the restoration of the corpse of the extraordinary man who had risen to the heights of glory and fame and then ended his days as an unhappy exile. Thereafter, when in Paris, the Flahauts attended a memorial mass for Napoleon on the anniversary of his death, 5 May, in the chapel of Les Invalides.[10]

Living in Paris, Margaret made friends with the imperialist families, notably General Sébastiani and his daughter Fanny, duchesse de Praslin, murdered by her husband in 1847.[11] After the July Revolution of 1830 she and Charles with the leading Bonapartists – Gourgaud, Las Cases, and the marshals Lobau, Soult, Mortier, Marmont, Bugeaud with the duc de Pasquier – were made welcome at court by Louis-Philippe and some were given appointments. However, Charles always felt that as a Bourbon, the king held his strong Bonapartist loyalty against him and would therefore never seriously consider him for the London embassy. At home in England, Margaret enjoyed the company of other Napoleonists such as Andrew Rutherfurd, the eminent Scottish judge who, as a great admirer of Napoleon, compared him to Julius Caesar, because "all other greatness pales before his!" Concern for a gallant Polish officer who attempted to join the exile in Saint Helena brought her in touch again with the Duke of Devonshire, "out of sight and thoughts for years", to whom she wrote in 1827 from Brighton:

> ... the remembrance of past times has been strongly recalled

to my mind by the kindness you have lately shown to the
unfortunate Count Piontkowski and M de Flahaut is so
anxious to express to you his thankfulness for your generosity
to this faithful follower of his old master and at the same time
to add the sense he entertains of his worthiness that I cannot
resist writing a few lines to this effect. His devotion to the
Emperor is the more remarkable and praiseworthy as all the
proofs of it were given during his exile when he was
abandoned by all the world and even among the few friends
of his adversity none showed him more zeal or attachment
than this unfortunate Pole.[12]

She and Charles followed Count Piontkowski's career for many years after
this, and he is mentioned during their years in Vienna 1841–8. Soon after she
arrived there in 1843, Margaret, most reluctantly, was obliged, as wife of an
ambassador to meet the Vienna-born ex-empress Marie-Louise. Although
this was an official presentation, she showed, by her distinctly cold manner,
how much she disapproved of the way the ex-empress had abandoned
Napoleon after his abdication of 1814, and of the dereliction of her duties as
a wife and mother.[13] At Baden she made no secret of her loyalties when she
met Princess Mathilde Bonaparte, newly married to Anatole Demidoff, who
described her as a "farouche bonapartiste".[14]

While the emperor was alive the Flahauts tried to alleviate the hardships
of exile by sending papers and books, including a copy of Adèle's latest novel,
with an inscription on the title-page expressing Charles's "attachement et son
dévouement à l'illustre prisonnier". Travellers from Saint Helena always
found a welcome from them. On 14 March 1818 Captain Basil Hall, who
spent three days at Meikleour, related his conversations with the emperor,
and painted a very different picture from the reports published in the
Courrier. Margaret not only read newspaper accounts but also every book
about the emperor, both those such as Dr O'Meara's *Voice from St. Helena*
(1822) and historical accounts. In 1825 she told Lady Grey:

I have been very busy reading Gourgaud's critique upon Mr.
de Ségur's narration of the Russian Campaign, which
certainly damages it very considerably and detects many

inaccuracies contained in it. I regret it is written in such an
offensive insulting stile, but I rejoice at the publication of it,
as I could not bear the esprit in which the other was written,
tho' the subject and the stile made it both interesting and
seducing and blended awe to so *manifold sins and wickedness.*

She then added:

> I look at Mr. de Flahaut with wonder, when I think of his
> having passed thro' all the hardships and dangers described
> in that book, and which are by no means exaggerated.[15]

In a letter to Edward Ellice, politician and neighbour dated 11 August,
she asked:

> Have you read Mr. de Ségur's campaigns in Russia? He *ought*
> never to have written it, but yet it is a most interesting work
> and written with great force and effect, and the descriptions
> of some of the most remarkable scenes are very faithfully
> given. There are parts of the book however which I think,
> even if true ought never to have been published by a
> French man who professes the opinions and sentiments
> of M. de Ségur.

Both she and Charles felt that the book would lower Napoleon in his military
character, hitherto considered as invulnerable; as she explained: "[N]o great
man ought to be looked at through a telescope, and the heroes of old times
were fortunate in not being surrounded with idle equerries and chamberlains
armed like porcupines, ready to note down every trifling word and action".[16]
From Rome in November 1845, impressed by the masterly *Histoire du
Consulat et de l'Empire* by Adolphe Thiers, she enthused to Emily: "I hope
you have read his *5 volumes*. I have just finished them, and really never was
so *entraîné* by any novel as I have been by that most commented history of
the wonderful events of our own time!" Later she commented again to
Emily, that

> Every Lady must make the same remarks you do about the
> battles except military people, who are all amazed at the truth
> and lucidity of his descriptions and remarks – it is more easily
> to be accounted for if one recollects that he wrote with all the
> official dispatches of the Generals lying on his table, as well as
> having free access to all Napoleon's private correspondence
> with his Generals. No historian ever had such advantages
> before.[17]

Margaret transferred her admiration for Napoleon to Alexandre
Walewski (1810–1868), his natural son by the Polish countess Marie
Walewska. At 17, the young man had the advantage, according to the
maréchal de Castellane, of resembling his father: "the same eyes, the same
voice as his father, though taller and with better features".[18] His presence
evoked not only the victory of Wagram, which was followed by his birth,
but the devotion shown by Marie Walewska in offering to share the exile of
the defeated Napoleon in 1815. André-Édouard Kozmian, who thought
Walewski had taken the place formerly occupied by Lord Byron in
Margaret's mind, described how she "adored him, with a love bordering on
jealousy, gave him good advice and frequently told him off".[19] In December
1827 she recommended him to Lady Holland.

> We have a young Count Marlewsky [*sic*] here who is much in
> fashion and rightly so for he is a very remarkable young
> person in all respects and I'm sure you will be pleased with
> him when he goes to England. All the Emperor's friends are
> struck with the resemblance in voice, manners and
> appearance and his abilities are certainly above par. He is only
> 17 and his conversation is that of a person double his age
> though without pedantry or affectation.[20]

Walewski, who was proud of his Polish blood, joined the patriotic movement for independence from Russia, and, after the battle near Grochów in
February 1831, was awarded the Polish Virtuti Militari Cross. He was sent
by Prince Czartoryski in March 1831 to win over Paris and London to the
idea of restoring the Polish crown, but failed to enlist any support, although

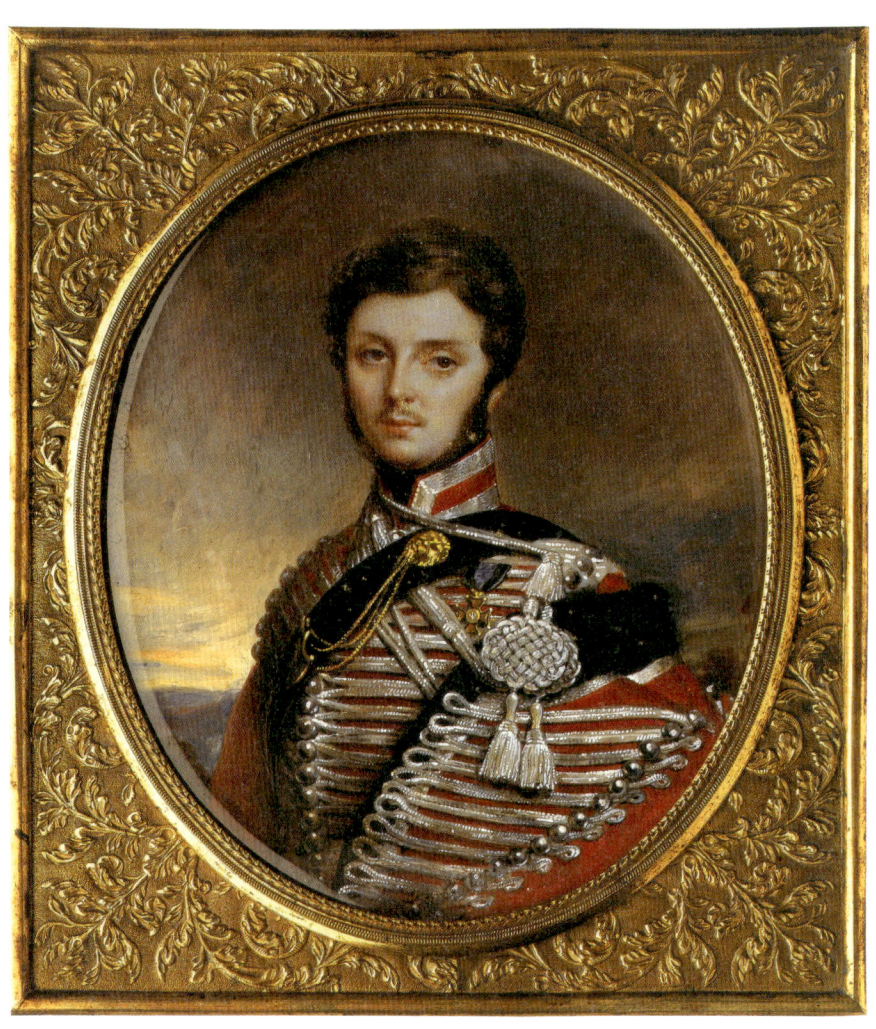

38 Portrait miniature of Alexandre Walewski

his looks and manners made a good impression. Margaret, who had other Polish friends as well as Walewski, followed events of the next months carefully and suggested to Lady Holland that this cold reception might be attributed to the influence of Princess Lieven upon Lord Grey and Lord Palmerston. She added, optimistically, that

> Every Frenchman considers the Poles as his brothers and the feeling is hourly increasing that they must be saved and Poland re-established as a frontier to repel the growing power of Russia. The Austrians here hold the most sensible language, and invite all Poles to return to their country by way of Galicia and answer for their safety.[21]

Her hopes were doomed to disappointment, for England refused to ally with France, and save the "heroic victims from barbarous conquerors". Depressed after the capitulation of Warsaw in September, she declared

> that it was a disgrace to civilised Europe that this gallant people should have found so little aid and protection to avert their sad destiny. It will be a very ugly page in history for our children's children to comment upon.

Margaret was right about the fate of Poland, for Nicholas I embarked on a savage programme of repression aimed at exterminating the national identity with its language and religion. It was not until 1863 that the Poles tried again to overthrow Russian rule, but by then the friendship between Walewski and the Flahauts had come to an end, and Margaret had come to believe that his obsession with the resurrection of Poland was so dangerous that it could lead to war.

However, that lay in the future and back in November 1831 Margaret, anxious to keep his friendship, was concerned about the marriage of her young protégé with Lady Caroline Montagu, daughter of the Earl of Sandwich. Neither Caroline nor her sister Harriet were popular with French ladies, who were "jealous of way they take possession of the duc d'Orléans", who is much amused "by their mirth and familiarity and calls them 'Les Anglaises Pour Rire'". After asking Lady Holland what was said about the match in England she commented:

> It seems an improvident affair on both sides for his fortune is
> now much reduced and this high dame will find herself in a
> position not suitable to the blood of the Montagus of which
> she is so proud. He, I fear, will stifle the natural serenity of his
> beautiful temper which cannot be too much praised. But
> what can have induced Lady Sandwich to have run after this
> marriage in the way she has done? Inexplicable. Please let me
> have the on dits.[22]

This marriage of inclination on both sides turned out so happy that Walewski
was in despair when Lady Caroline died in 1834, leaving no surviving children. She was also much regretted by Margaret, who had become a close
friend. After this, various candidates including Georgina de Flahaut were
suggested as her successor, but instead, Walewski opted for living with the
great actress Mlle Rachel as his mistress. Years later when he broke free from
her "seduction and tyranny", he told Margaret that although he "loved her
devotedly, he could not support her temper: she was an angel for three weeks
but a demon for the next".[23]

During the years with Rachel, Walewski joined the army and participated
in the North African campaign before involving himself in politics. His per-
spicacious essay reflecting on the prospects of the French conquest of Algeria
in 1837 was followed by the publication of another, entitled *L'Alliance
anglaise,* urging the importance of a Franco-British entente. In this brochure
he not only echoes the opinions of the Flahauts but makes the point that
Napoleon never wished to make war against the English people, but rather
against the Tory government then in power. Walewski's intelligence, open
mind and understanding of the complexities of the European diplomatic
scene not only impressed Margaret but also the politician Adolphe Thiers,
who guided him towards a diplomatic career. They were close friends, and
sharing an interest in the history of the Consulate and Empire, the two visited
the sites of the battles fought by Napoleon.

In 1846 Walewski decided to marry a Florentine, Marianne de Ricci, who
reinforced his links with Poland through her mother, *née* Poniatowska. Well
dressed and vivacious, she was the perfect wife for the diplomat Walewski

was to become as soon as Louis Napoleon was elected president of France in 1849. He was sent on missions to Florence and Naples and in 1851 was appointed ambassador to London, thus fulfilling Napoleon's instructions to the executors of his will: "My desire is that Alexandre Walewski should serve France". As a dedicated Bonapartist, Charles saw him often and regretted his departure from London on his nomination as minister of foreign affairs in 1855. This was the apex of his career, and he and his wife enjoyed the grandeur of his position in the Empire. The Flahauts and the Walewskis remained on very friendly terms until they quarrelled in the 1860s. Ironically, while it was the relationship of Alexandre Walewski with Napoleon which had brought them together, it was bitter disagreement on issues connected with the publication of Napoleon's *Correspondence* which caused the break.

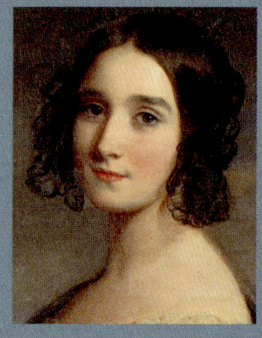

CHAPTER 17

The Vienna Embassy I
1841–8

"Quieta non movere"

Latin maxim

fter Adelaide's death in March 1841, Margaret concentrated on her three remaining daughters and particularly on finding a suitable husband for Emily, now acknowledged as a graceful beauty. From Paris, where she kept open house for eligible men from the Faubourg Saint-Germain, she and the girls went to Ems for the summer, mixing with "a royal crowd", before spending some months at home in Brighton prior to settling in London for the season. Meanwhile, ambitious as ever, she continued to hope for a diplomatic appointment for Charles. Unofficially, Louis-Philippe and Madame Adélaïde told her that this would be difficult, even though they recognized his abilities, as did the minister for foreign affairs, M. Guizot. Not only was Marshal Soult resolutely against him but he was not acceptable to the Emperor of Russia, the King of Naples and the Queen of England, while in Austria, Prince Metternich, the chancellor, had declared, "he was not a statesman and he had no wish to do business with him".[1] This situation changed after the Austrian ambassador to France, Count Apponyi, who knew the Flahauts well, persuaded Prince Metternich to change his mind and agree to receive Charles. But the future remained uncertain and it was not until early September that Louis-Philippe finally confirmed the nomination to Vienna. Charles told Margaret how much he owed to Madame Adélaïde,[2] "who has behaved with a kindness & friendship that we ought never to forget and I certainly never shall", and went on to admit that he was "bewildered at the thought of all the arrangements I shall have to make & very sad at having so many months to pass without you & the children".

Determined that everything in his Vienna establishment should be perfect and "digne d'un grand seigneur", he set about planning for it. This meant deciding which of the family carriages he would need, ordering liveries for his servants from the tailor of the duc d'Orléans, and buying silver and bronzes from Odiot and Denière. All had to be done in a rush as the king and Guizot wanted him installed by the last week of October. He and Margaret were kept so busy that she told Emily that

> I hardly see him, and never hear a word from his lips except about orders and arrangements . . . By 8 o'clock in the morning he has a levée of tailors, shoemakers, coach makers, silversmiths & & and an audience of friends, advisers and attachés each waiting their turn amidst the usual decider of soap suds, flannel, foulards & & which goes on till he finds a moment to swallow his breakfast, after which he immediately . . . goes to the foreign affairs where he reads dispatches & documents for 3 or 4 hours, after which he hurries thro' the rest of his visits or business and returns to dinner at 7, after which he either goes out again till bed time, or sits writing or talking with our usual *habitués* who come in after dinner. We have Mr. Périer every night and I hope [he] will get Vienna, as he will be very useful to your Papa. My day is spent in shopping for him, ordering lamps, clocks, bronzes and an indescribable number of trifles which worry up all my time. I must remain for a week after him.

Her main task was finding a tenant for the Paris house, and getting it ready for a long let. Eventually it was occupied by the prince de Ligne, the Belgian ambassador, with his Polish wife, Jadwiga, and their young children. Delighted as they were with the spacious accommodation, terrace and the garden which they compared to a country mansion, the prince and princesse de Ligne were not ideal tenants. Three years later, when Margaret returned there, she complained to Emily that "The old house seems strangely inhabited, very unlike what it was. My little dressing room is turned into the principal receiving room, the walls entirely covered with small pictures of all the sovereigns of Europe, past and present. On the door of the W.C. is an oil painting of a grim warrior full length, sword drawn as if to defend the retirement of all intruders." She went on: "The Salon de l'Angle seems aban-

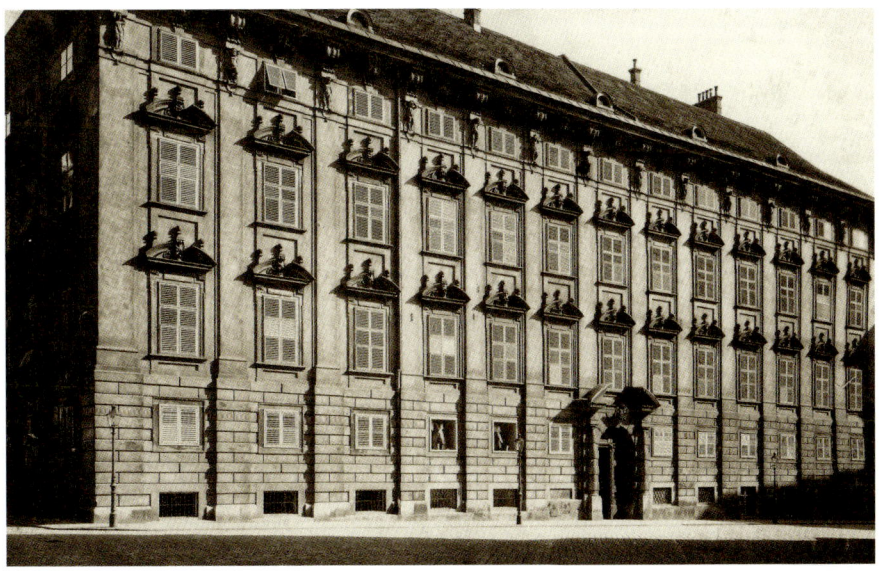

39 Palais Starhemberg, Minoritenplatz, Vienna

doned and all the sofas are taken out of the principal salon which has a pianoforte placed in it and a collection of tables from all the different parts of the house without taste or method in the arrangement. On one of the panels is hung an enormous round black frame on which is placed a collection of bronze medals making the most glaring hideous decoration in a Louis XV salon – it would hardly be acceptable in a library and could only by rights belong to a museum or the cabinet of a collector. The trees and garden have grown so immensely that there is neither air or light and of course, no flowers." A few days later, when looking for a vase for Emily, she was annoyed to find that all her china had been removed from a store cupboard and placed in an inaccessible dark corner.

On his arrival in Vienna on 19 November 1841 Charles settled into the baroque Palais Starhemberg in the aristocratic Minoritenplatz with the help of his Scottish housekeeper, Margaret Husson, and his valet, François. He was careful to follow the strict protocol prescribed for his first official engagement with the imperial family, headed by the Emperor Ferdinand I. This went well; as he informed Margaret:

> Thanks to [Prince Paul] Esterhazÿ's [*sic*] kindness in lending
> me his carriages, I had this morning my audience of the
> Emperor & Empress & was graciously received. The arrival
> was rather imposing as detachments of all the Household
> troops, German, Italian, Hungarian, lined the passage from
> the bottom of the stairs to the door of the room preceding the
> presence chamber, all presenting arms. I was introduced to
> the Emperor, no one but His. Majesty & myself being in the
> room. He is evidently very shy but extremely good natured.
> The Empress who was accompanied by two ladies, received
> me immediately after the Emperor. She was indeed very
> gracious & agreeable. Mind, that as all you say on this subject
> is repeated & comes round here back again, pray therefore say
> that I am perfectly pleased, which also I assure you is the case.
> I went there with three carriages, 2 servants & my chasseur
> behind mine, 2 behind the secretaries & 1 only behind the
> Maître de Cérémonie. I had no more liveries, my 2 coureurs
> running before my carriage.

Next, on 29 January 1842 the Empress Mother received him most graciously, followed by his presentation to all the archdukes and Archduchess Sophie. "There was no awkwardness and the Archdukes Charles and François were very cordial in spite of the war – both said it was a great distinction to have been the Emperor's ADC".[3] The final formality, his Ricevimenti for Viennese society passed off equally well and with 10 servants in livery, 2 couriers, 1 *chasseur*, 6 *valets de chambre* in attendance, he received from 12 until 2, Saturday, Sunday, Monday – Finis.

These duties over, his next worry was having the house ready for the grand embassy dinner celebrating the birthday of Louis-Philippe on 30 April. Without Margaret the difficulties seemed so insurmountable that he pleaded, "Pray get me out of this scrape". Every detail, however minute, was of importance to him. He complained that it was impossible to get anything done in Vienna, that deliveries from Paris and London took two months and often arrived damaged, that he would never have enough tea-cups for his Viennese guests, that it was impossible to find the right type of dessert plates, that the "crowns over the King's cipher on the silver dishes from Odiot were "very bad, not at all royal. It seems that all emblems of that kind in France lose their character". In view of the scale of his dinners he declared, "Taste alone will not do. Size is necessary", and he sent Margaret the exact measurements of his dinner-tables. Knowing her taste for a splendid looking table, he continued, "Do not spend our money on covers or ornamental plate everyone here is à la Russe, anything different is laughed at, so get nothing but useful plate." In the event the dinner went well, with the great Odiot plateaux arriving from the repairers just ten minutes before the first of the 58 guests was announced. As Prince Metternich, suffering from piles, had to cancel, the Nuncio stepped in to propose the king's health and Charles reported that "Prince Cobourg [father-in-law of the duc de Nemours, second eldest son of Louis-Philippe], who never comes, did me the honour to come, the table looked magnificent, everything compared advantageously with the dinners of my predecessors".

When Margaret joined him in the autumn of 1842 she completed the decoration and furnishing of the Throne Room, the four handsome drawing-rooms, each hung with a different coloured silk, and the private living quarters.[4] To obtain this grand effect they had exceeded their means and in 1844 Charles admitted to Emily that they might have done just as well at a third of the cost. However, their guests agreed that this blend of "Austrian magnificence with English comfort set off by the salt and vivacity of French conversation" made a great addition to the charm of the city.[5]

Charles's priority as ambassador was to establish good relations with the all-powerful Prince Metternich (1773–1859), the first foreign minister to recognize the July Monarchy. Now an old man, Metternich's declared intention was to safeguard the Vienna Settlement, prevent the disintegration of the Austrian Empire and, as the enemy of liberalism, to maintain stability in Europe. On his nomination Charles had written him a very flattering letter and as soon as he reached Vienna paid him the first of many visits. He was impressed by Metternich's manner, "perfectly kind, perfectly simple, a great quality in one who for 36 years lived with greatest authority and had the greatest share in management and settlement of all the great affairs of Europe – facility of conversation, good nature, He has much of Talleyrand's 's quiet ways with less reserve and more talk. I wish I may please him half as much as he pleases me." Metternich's huge experience meant that he was "always interesting. He has his point de vue which would not be that of an Englishman or Minister but which is that of a great statesman placed at the head of the Austrian monarchy". The two spent hours discussing not only politics and diplomacy but many other topics of mutual interest – the natural sciences, medicine, literature – losing all sense of time.

For her part, the volatile, sharp-tongued Princess Melanie was delighted that her elderly husband had found such congenial companionship. Always interested in anything new, the prince was greatly intrigued by a pair of candlesticks recently invented in England, which Charles brought as a gift when invited to spend the New Year with them. In June, after a happy dinner party of twenty at the embassy, Melanie enthused over the excellent food and beautiful silver, which she considered worthy of a grand seigneur.[6] Charles, who accompanied the Metternichs to take the waters at Marienbad in August 1842, was impressed by the extraordinary popularity of the avowed enemy of liberalism:

> I must say it is impossible to show more good will and respect than the whole population of this place for Prince Metternich, everyone taking off his hat and trying to follow or get on his passage, all smiling kindly towards him. Everybody in this country looks up to him.[7]

Regardless of Foreign Minister Guizot's fears that this close friendship might lead Charles not to dare to disagree with any policy of Metternich's which was detrimental to French interests,[8] he maintained his assiduous attendance on the veteran statesman, and although perhaps less so in the final phase of his embassy, 1846–8, he was always convinced that "the Peace of Europe depends on his life". As for Melanie, in spite of the occasional misunderstanding, she always remembered him on 4 November, the feast day of St Charles, and as a mark of her regard she commissioned the artist Moritz Michael Daffinger to paint Charles's portrait for the album of her friends.[9] Most happily, although both were liable to lose their tempers easily, Margaret and Melanie got on well, which was fortunate as they were obliged to see much of each other. When in England Margaret undertook to shop for damasks and Chinese silks on Melanie's behalf, and the two women took an interest in each other's children.[10]

Before Margaret arrived in Vienna in the autumn of 1842, Charles warned her that his position as ambassador made life not as simple as in London or Paris. He explained that through so many intermarriages Viennese society was all one great family and consequently "Ranks are so defined and by etiquette so tyrannically limited that an acquaintance which would not belong to their proper set would become for us a serious inconvenience". As discretion was essential he asked Margaret to keep any stories to herself as "everything comes back here and the worst thing you can do is being represented by abusing what is done". He went on: "People are determined not to admire in others what they don't do themselves" and later added that "Vienna people don't like people to come here and give them lessons. There is a great love of scandal here, one must not go against old established customs".[11]

He also suggested that Margaret take advantage of her time in England to forget her political prejudices and get on good terms with the Tory government. Even though he understood how much she preferred the company of her old friends in the Whig party, it was different for him in Vienna, where he got on very well with the British ambassador Sir Robert Gordon (1791–1847), brother of the prime minister, the 4th Lord Aberdeen. Charles stated that "it would be exceptionally inconvenient to me if you were to place yourself in an attitude of opposition in England. You must be the wife of the ambassador and nothing else. Tell this to your friends, they will esteem you for it." He advised that on ordinary soirées people were quite plainly dressed, for more importance was attached to inner reality than to outward show, and so there would not be many occasions for her to show off her cashmere shawl. As for diamonds, "people who have them wear them at a ball at Court but on no other occasion, it is not the fashion"; but aware of her interest in jewellery, he pointed out that the mounting in Vienna was not only very good but cheaper than elsewhere.

Charles remembered to describe the baptism of the new baby of the Archduchess Sophie in the Imperial Chapel, when exceptionally, a great many diamonds were displayed by between twenty-five and thirty ladies, who were all magnificently dressed in gold- and silver-embroidered gowns. At her request, he went into great detail about the clothes she and the girls would need:

For your presentation to the Emperor & Empress, Empress
Mother & Archduchess Sophie you will require a train, but it
is probable that they will all receive you the same day or at all
events in 2 days; therefore two trains is all you require, for
unless some court ceremony takes place quite unexpectedly,
you never appear *en robe à queue*. With one rich & another
plain you have all that is required, but you must let them
come in the piece & get them arranged at Vienna. For your
receptions you will require 2 gowns, 1 for the 1st & 3rd day
when few people come & 1 for the 2nd which is the great day.
Emily & Georgina will appear there & must also be dressed.
Will you tell Emily that I have told M. de Marescalchi [an
attaché, married to Mathilde de Pange] to beg his wife to
execute any commissions you & the girls may give her & that
she had better write to her if she wants anything. I shall open
a credit to Emily for 3000 & Georgina 2000 francs & you must
order what you think Louisa will want. It is much better to
order everything from Paris as dress is very dear at Vienna.
Young Ladies wear white ball gowns of muslin or organdi
worked or plain with pretty ribbons & flowers. In winter
Ladies wear Silks & in spring also white gowns but the
Elégantes get almost everything from Paris & *articles de goût*
are very *recherchés*. The dress of your daughters will be
observed. The preparations you had made when that sad
mourning came on, will not be lost for the fashions take a
year to come from London & Paris, Court mourning is
observed in Vienna just as rigorously as in London.[12]

Margaret's presentation went well, as might be expected after her long
experience of court life. As the only woman, she enjoyed a half-hour gossip
with the empress, "not handsome but fresh, grand air, good humoured
expression tall good figure, similar to her sister, the Princess of Hesse
Darmstadt [whom she had met at Ems]". The empress spoke Italian to the
Nuncio, Turkish to the Ottoman ambassador and English to Juniper, the
American envoy, who was very pleased. As soon as the Palais Starhemberg
was ready she embarked on a programme of entertaining and after two great

and brilliant dances, held a big charity reception for the victims of the Guadaloupe earthquake.[13] To amuse Viennese society she put on plays acted by her friends and embassy secretaries, and Sir Robert Gordon "laughed till he cried" at a performance of *L'Artiste*. Her *thés dansants* for the young, which were another success, attended by the eldest Metternich children, Richard and Melanie, who "polk and gallop to perfection". At her large dinners her guests ate French, English and Scottish dishes: Pouding à la Chateaubriand, le Plum Pudding sauce au porto, Gelée au Sherry à l'anglaise, Cheddar cheese, Bengal chutney, and a Hotch Potch.[14] Both Margaret and Charles recognized the importance of giving attractive presents known as *étrennes*, to their staff and Viennese friends on New Year's Day and planned for them well in advance, drawing up their lists in September. As "Real English" gifts were appreciated more than any others, most were acquired in England: blotters decorated with "Landseer's dogs", needlework kits with patterns of English birds, a Scotch knitting-box, and stationery in leather cases. The attachés who dined frequently with Charles and Margaret, were given well-chosen *étrennes*, and treated as members of the family.

During her time in Vienna from 1842 to 1844, then in 1846, and finally from 1847 to 1848, Margaret received at home. She also attended the costume balls, diplomatic dinners, soirées and dances in the princely Liechtenstein, Schönburg, Schwarzenberg, Esterházy and Lobkowicz palaces, and those of the Sándor and Colloredo families. Although the imperial family did not entertain formally on more than two or three occasions each year, the various members accepted invitations from the aristocracy, and by so doing added to the importance of these events. They also appeared at the theatre, where Margaret seldom went since there were not many plays she wanted to see, except those acted by touring French players. Music was quite different, particularly light opera, and in 1847 she and Charles were greatly impressed by the voice of Marietta Alboni.[15] Occasionally there was an attraction such as a French equestrian troupe with one performer driving a team of six horses while standing on two. But in comparison with London and Paris, Vienna was so quiet as to be boring and on 30 November 1845 Charles complained of the *ennui*: "You have no idea of the dullness of this town . . . so little hospitality, no chasses except Liechtenstein who was not free to accompany me", and in a letter of 11 November 1846 to his friend the politician Edward Ellice, he explained that

> Society of Vienna is divided into small coteries to which it is
> extremely difficult to be admitted as the Ladies who preside
> are anything but tolerant. That and the little entertainment
> they afford makes the young diplomatic men little anxious to
> get into them and I dare say that your protégé will do like
> William Grey and most of his colleagues pass most of his time
> at the club or with his comrades. I believe Vienna to be the
> worst town to send a young man to, all the young aborigines
> lead an idle life. One tells the story of one of them who
> speaking to one of his friends who had complained of having
> nothing to do, 'Why, I am never idle; when I have nothing to
> do I lay myself down and smoke a cigar.' It is . . . a dangerous
> place for the fortune and health of a young man.[16]

In the last phase of her time in Vienna, from October 1847 to March 1848 Margaret tended to lead a very solitary life and felt the absence of the girls, then in England. Her inability to speak German was a disadvantage and she missed the cut and thrust of political discussions. As morning visits were not a Viennese custom, she passed the day distributing cards, taking walks by herself in the Prater, or through the gardens and wooded alleys of the ramparts encircling the city. Surprisingly, though she still continued to paint, she never mentions visiting the many art collections belonging to the imperial family and the aristocracy to which distinguished visitors were given access. Towards the end of the day: "We dine at 5 and then pass a long evening until time to pay a visit to Princess Schönberg,[17] or go to Metternich's." Her favourite companion was the kind and affectionate Countess Léontine Sándor, daughter of Metternich by his first wife, and she also got on well with the Polish countess Lanckoronska, *née* Potocka, "a very pleasing little woman". To her great regret, Lord Ponsonby, Sir Robert Gordon's successor, and Lady Grey's eldest brother, remained distant:

> We derive no benefit from English embassy except for
> William Grey who is always kind and friendly. We have not
> yet seen Lord Ponsonby, neither he nor his wife ever appear
> at Metternich's soirées – he is a very singular man, for I hear
> that in all societies he speaks in a most disrespectful manner

of his chief saying he is a madman . . . he hardly sees his own attachés and seldom invites them to dinner.[18]

As for Lady Ponsonby she caused a stir by appearing at court in a dress so décolleté that the empress was obliged to shut her eyes; ". . . her dress is laughed at by everybody", Charles told Margaret.[19]

Experienced and generous employers as they were, the Flahauts still had to contend with servant problems. Margaret's Bohemian maid was bad-tempered, wore the same dirty cotton dress every day for four months, could not be relied on to dress her for dinner and would not wash tooth and hair brushes. Another, Anna, had to be dismissed for stealing fans, clothing and jewellery. When the English coachman attempted to kill himself, Margaret noted this was the fifth mental case in the embassy. The poor coachman who had been having an affair with a widow, came to believe he was being haunted by the ghost of her husband and was driven so crazy that it took six men to lift him out of the house. There was a crisis in 1846 when the excellent housekeeper, Margaret Husson, married to a former pâtissier chef of the Flahauts, wanted to resign after twenty-five years' service and had to be persuaded to stay with them. Margaret, who blamed Charles for being too easy-going, wrote to him in 1845:

> . . . when you leave Vienna I hope that you will reduce the
> establishment and get rid of as much of the old leaves as you
> can. You will never have a well organised and respectable
> house in which there are elements who have been so long
> accustomed to bad habits and disrespectful manners.

This was aimed at Charles's valet, François, who in the opinion of Charles was not only loyal but very useful in "this cheating town" for his ability to detect dishonest tradesmen. Rather than dismiss him, a compromise was arranged so that François would never appear in her presence. This proved unworkable, as a few months later the hot-tempered François kicked the husband of Margaret's lady's maid downstairs, and informed the porter that, on the orders of His Excellency, the man was never to be admitted. The war continued until 1848, when François, named *l'Autocrate* by Margaret on account of his despotic character, finally departed.

Inevitably, during her time in Vienna (1842–4, 1846, 1848), Margaret's independent spirit and tactlessness led to other differences with Charles. On the diplomatic front there were at least two episodes which embarrassed him. As mentioned in chapter 16, when she was obliged to meet Napoleon's widow, Marie-Louise, in residence at Schönbrunn in 1843, she showed her staunchly Bonapartist disapproval of the ex-empress by adopting the most disagreeable manner, which Princess Metternich wisely pretended not to notice.[20] Then in February 1844, much to the astonishment of Viennese society, Margaret decided to support the Opposition party in the Diet at Pressburg, praising their speeches and encouraging these dissident young Hungarians to visit her.[21] In the opinion of the highly intelligent Polish countess Rosalie Rzewuska, Charles had the "reputation of an adventurer, yet people were so intrigued by his distinguished manners that he was received everywhere, on account of his desire to please"; but his wife was a positive handicap: "She made numerous blunders. A conceited Englishwoman, interested only in the getting [of] favourable comments in her country's press and acting accordingly".[22] Others disliked her too. As the baronne du Montet (7 May 1843) reported:

> The Comte de la Tour told me that Madame de Flahaut is
> disliked by high society: she is regarded as unreasonable and
> temperamental . . . and is known as Madame Fléau [i.e. plague].
> She is English, and although rich, is mean with it, frequently
> reminding her husband that she is the richer of the two.

She went on to give an example of Margaret's domineering behaviour:

> . . . this winter when she gave a ball she decided to open the
> windows and since M. de Flahaut noticed that the dancers
> objected to the draughts, he followed behind her, shutting the
> windows which she was opening so highhandedly. Mme de
> Flahaut then went up to him, shouting 'I want the windows
> open, and kindly remember that I am the person giving this
> ball.' Monsieur de Flahaut fled towards some of the ladies
> and said 'Let her do as she wants, for she might get really
> angry and then she becomes quite impossible'.[23]

Neither gave up fighting this minor war about room temperature and in February 1847 Charles complained to Georgina that he had caught a cold at Princess Clary's as "some Viennese families had adopted the custom of passing from Equator one minute to the North Pole the next, what with the excessive heat of candles and then opening windows between dances". He added: "I think your mother has introduced this to Vienna and if it continues it will kill off the aristocracy. What is wanted is a good system of ventilation." For her part Margaret, a hypochondriac brought up to stand the rigours of winters in Scotland, disliked the lack of air and heat in rooms with double doors, double windows and thick-pile Turkey carpets, and when Charles fell ill in November 1847 attributed the

> problem to the over heated atmosphere he lives in . . . but this
> is a subject I do not press as he attributes it entirely to my part
> believing that air is necessary to life! It is a positive calamity
> to me the effect produced on my head from stoves.[24]

Charles remonstrated with her in his letters, referring to painful scenes, some caused by arguments over their finances. He worried about the rents of their houses in Paris, Vienna, Brighton and London. As far as Scotland was concerned, although he thought the costs of gamekeepers high, he defended Mr Loch's management of her estates, and advised that

> when one determines on making reproaches one must be
> more than certain of being in the right considering especially
> that you pay him nothing for whatever trouble he has taken
> over your affairs. I asked you to be very calm and considerate
> in all you do or say on the business for you would do yourself
> a great damage by any unjust and especially violent language.

In September 1843, after she wrote that she felt "she no longer contributed to his happiness", he tried to reassure her, but on 2 September the following year, he spoke out quite plainly:

> . . . you cannot suffer the least observation which does not
> agree with your own ideas and I dare say that the only effect

of this letter will be to produce an answer similar to the
conversation which the observations themselves did bring on.
I can assure you that if your reflections have been melancholy,
mine have not been comfortable as to our future relations and
I felt very miserable alone.

Three weeks later relations had not improved and he replied to another accusation from her on 27 September 1844:

These repeated violent scenes are becoming so painful to me
that their recollection is very far from encouraging for the
future but accept that I do not understand what you mean by
my mind being poisoned against you and will be more every
day. No creature exercises any influence upon me in that
respect and any effect that has been produced upon me has
been your own doing. . . . when we are separated and all these
violent scenes cease, the recollection of your affection remains
and you would do better not to refer to past quarrels.

Another cause for concern was her obsession with politics and on 24 May
1847, when she was in Paris, obviously worried, he urged:

Pray do not meddle in the politics of the day. You can do no
good and only injure me and yourself. Make as much use as
one can of one's ear and as little as possible of one's tongue is
an excellent rule,

adding on 4 June:

I think you should get to London as soon as possible and
avoid all political conversation.

This habit of discussing their differences so frankly did not damage their
marriage, on the contrary it seems to have helped husband and wife come to
terms with each other, and after begging her to be very calm and avoid violent
language he might conclude: " I long to be with you again", or sadly, "I have

had no letters today which makes it a bad one".[25] Relations between them improved over the following years when their joint worry over the health of their youngest daughter Louise seems to have eclipsed any major disagreements and there are fewer complaints from either side in their correspondence, which must always have read like an enjoyable conversation between old friends.

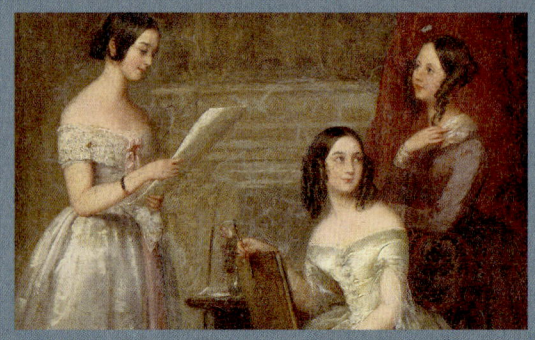

CHAPTER 18

The Vienna Embassy II

*A sense of conflict is pervading the world and not all the
wiles of politicians can suppress it*

Alexandre Thomas, *Revue des deux mondes* (1846)

C harles grieved for Adelaide with "her angelic heart": "I never get into my bed without thinking of my poor dear child's last moments. I see her, I feel her dear hand reaching for mine. Never will that sad remembrance leave me. I wake with it in the night." The deaths of two sisters made the lives of the three others, Emily, Louise and Georgina, even more precious and his love intensified during the long separations of the years in Vienna. He missed them when they were away in England: "I cannot tell you how I . . . constantly dread the long months that still separate me from you all. In three days I shall have been here a month – 7 long ones must pass before we are together again". It got worse as the years passed, and again on his own in January 1846, he told Emily, "As I am getting old, very old, I resent having to waste my remaining years far from those I love", and in the following November, "How I wish I had a magic ring to carry me to see my girls in Torquay".

He longed for their letters, their portraits were close by on his desk, he wrote to them often and sent presents: bracelets with his miniature; a parasol handle; pretty earrings from Hungary; sable for a muff for Emily; a pelisse for Georgina; he also sent old German bijoux; an emerald necklace; and Viennese enamelled blackamoor pins, a speciality of the jeweller Hermann Ratzersdorfer, who was "a terrible cheat over price". In 1846 he sent a bracelet to Louise, enclosing his miniature, "looking a bit elderly", by Alois von Anreiter and another to Georgina. So much importance was attached to these portraits which had to capture personality as well as likeness that commissions were given to several artists so as to obtain the most characteristic image. Charles thought the best Viennese miniaturist was Josef Kriehuber

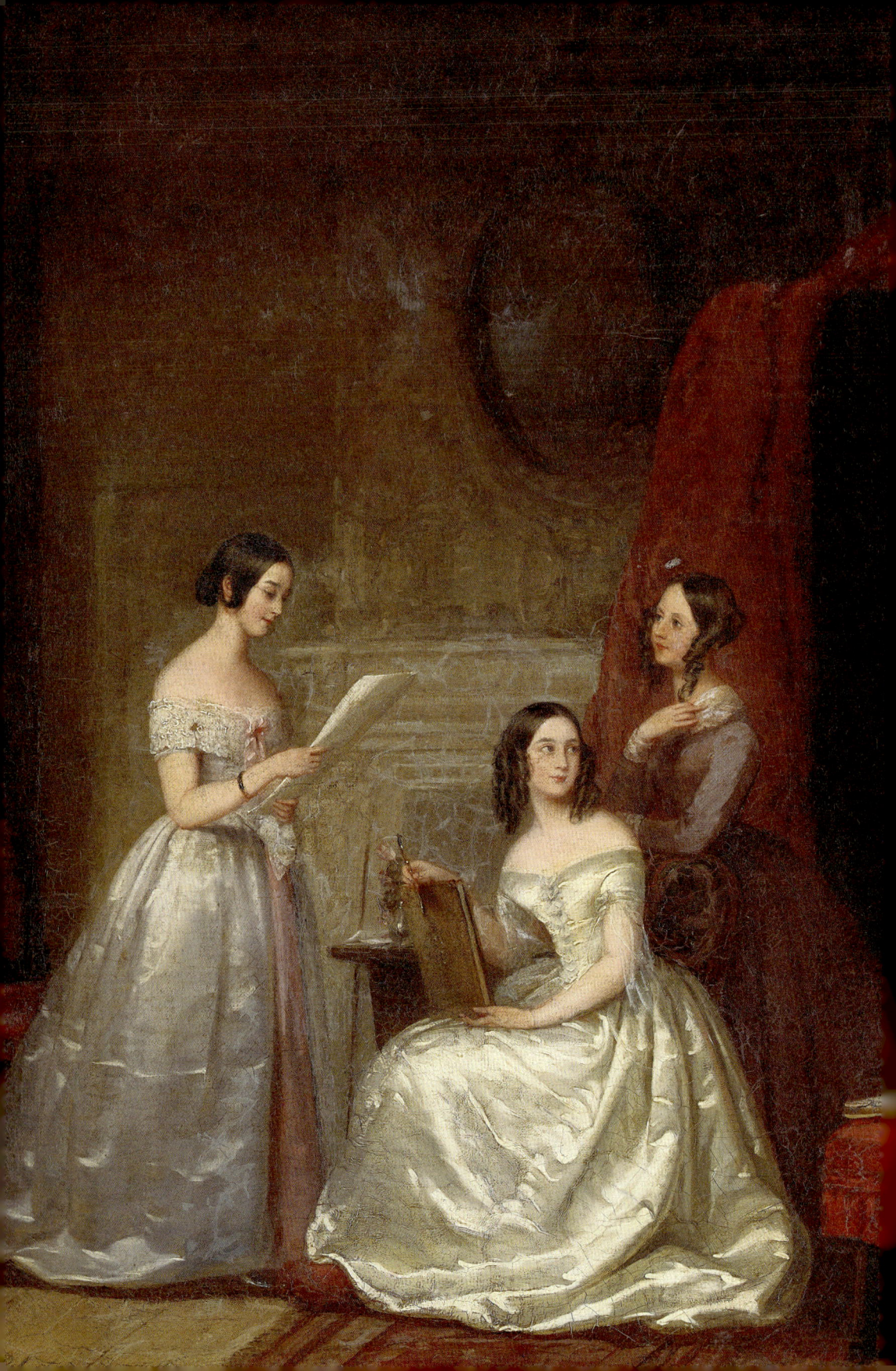

(1800–1876), who replaced the "horror" Moritz Michael Daffinger (1790–1849) had painted for Princess Metternich and asked Emily to help launch him in London by finding twenty sitters at £20 each for a portrait.[1]

When the girls stayed in Vienna, they not only went to parties, *bals d'adolescents*, rode in the Prater and at the riding schools in the winter, but also learnt German from a tutor, M. Landschütz. Although the social life of Vienna could not compare with the animation of London and Paris, the city scored musically. Emily was the most musical and an excellent pianist, but the other girls took up with the constant flow of new dances – waltzes quadrilles and polkas – composed by Joseph Lanner and then by the father and son Johann Strauss, which provided the most enjoyable aspect of life in the city. The girls' presence made a huge difference to the atmosphere in the Palais Starhemberg and Charles, who had to face three winters entirely on his own, hated coming back to an empty house after a grand diplomatic dinner. In his solitude he begged Margaret not to be too hard on them:

Do not always take them to task for some little bad habits . . .

and went on to say:

> . . . don't always think of authority but sometimes of soft and
> gentle affection. Don't let your maternal solicitude show itself
> constantly on recommendations about health, lessons,
> manners but show them that you are occupied about their
> pleasures, amusements and agreements of all sorts. We are
> now old people and should find our happiness and joy in
> those of our children . . . the first thing is not to attach
> importance [to] or make points of trifles.[2]

As long as Emily remained unmarried, relations with her mother were so strained, that in July 1842 he begged Margaret, "For God's sake, take Emily gently and friendly and depend on it you will find it succeeds much better than taking things with a high hand", for "She might rebel and you

**40 Christina Robertson (1796–1854): Louise, Emily
and Georgina de Flahaut**

fail in your object which is a good one". He then repeated the dictum of Metternich: "In affairs of this world the object is one thing, the way and manner is another and not the least important". Everything altered when, after many changes of heart, Emily decided to accept the proposal of Lord Shelburne, future 4th Marquess of Lansdowne, a favourite of Lord Macaulay, who described him as "kind, lively, intelligent, modest with the gentle manners which indicate a long intimacy with the best society and yet without the least affectation". There was a long wrangle over the settlement before the engagement was announced in April 1843, but once terms had been agreed, and the wedding had taken place that November at the British embassy in Vienna, all differences were forgotten and this marriage, apparently of reason, turned out very well.

For the Lansdownes, Emily was "a bright spot who gilds every hour of the day", sharing their life at Bowood with its wonderful works of art, the brilliant talk at table, the great concerts and large parties in Berkeley Square, and smaller gatherings at the Villa Lansdowne at Richmond. This house brought back memories to Margaret, who wrote to Emily in 1844:

> I only wish I was your neighbour at the Star and Garter for I adore Richmond where a great part of my dull childhood was passed and remember with pleasure the few gay days I passed with young people of my own age instead of old dowagers and the society of my grandmother. I little thought that when I went to play with Arabella Townshend in your present drawing-room that it would once be the habitation of my own daughter.[3]

Similarly, Charles remembered meeting Emily's father-in-law Lord Lansdowne, then little Lord Henry Petty, in 1794 "in his father's library, he was then at Westminster and I was a poor little French boy at Hounslow".

Now mother and daughter became very close, exchanging long gossipy letters. Margaret sent details of the activities of Louise and Georgina, reported on the latest Opera cloaks in Paris, and on the jewels, shawls and gowns in the dress circle of Isabelle de Praslin. She described a visit to the duchesse de Praslin at Vaux-le-Vicomte, and although impressed by the extensive restoration of the interiors, the pavilions and garden, she observed the unfortunate state of the doomed household.[4] Emily in her turn wrote about her new life, gave a full description of her sitting-room at Lansdowne House and all it contained, and assured her mother that she was very happy. Margaret replied, "What you say is all that we could wish or desire . . . after all marriage is a great lottery even to those who rush into the engagement with the most sanguine hopes."[5]

In 1845 the first of Emily's three children was born, always known as "Clan", and then came another son, Edmond, followed by a daughter, Emily. The birth of "Clan" was particularly welcomed by the Scottish housekeeper, Margaret Husson, as it "shows the nonsense of the prophecy about the Princesses of Aldie" (for instance, Margaret's heiress mother, Jane Mercer of Aldie) as being unable to produce sons. Emily's relations with Charles were also excellent, and they wrote often to each other, he in French. In an undated letter from this period he confided:

> Your letters need not contain any news of extraordinary
> events, all I want to know is what you are doing, what is
> going on around you, and details of the children's health,
> their doings – both good and naughty. . . . all this means
> much more to me than the Dardanelles and the
> Principalities.[6]

He gave her his miniature by Josef Kriehuber in return for one of her sitting-room, encouraged her to continue her singing, sent all the latest waltzes, and in December 1845 warned her to keep away from politics: "Please do not imitate Lady Jersey and the others whom I will not name. Nobody likes them, not even the men of the party the 'femme politique' adopts as her own." Happily, Shelburne was also very friendly and supported all Emily did for her parents and sisters. He shared Margaret's interest in the arts and particularly in interior decoration, and together they enjoyed looking through the plates of Thomas Chippendale's great work on furniture *The Gentleman and Cabinet Maker's Director* (1754), searching for suitable designs for door-locks, escutcheons, drawer handles etc.

It was the declining health of Louise (1825–1853) which cast the greatest shadow over the years in Vienna. At first all went well. Wearing her Paris dresses she waltzed three days in succession at the Carnival balls of 1843, she

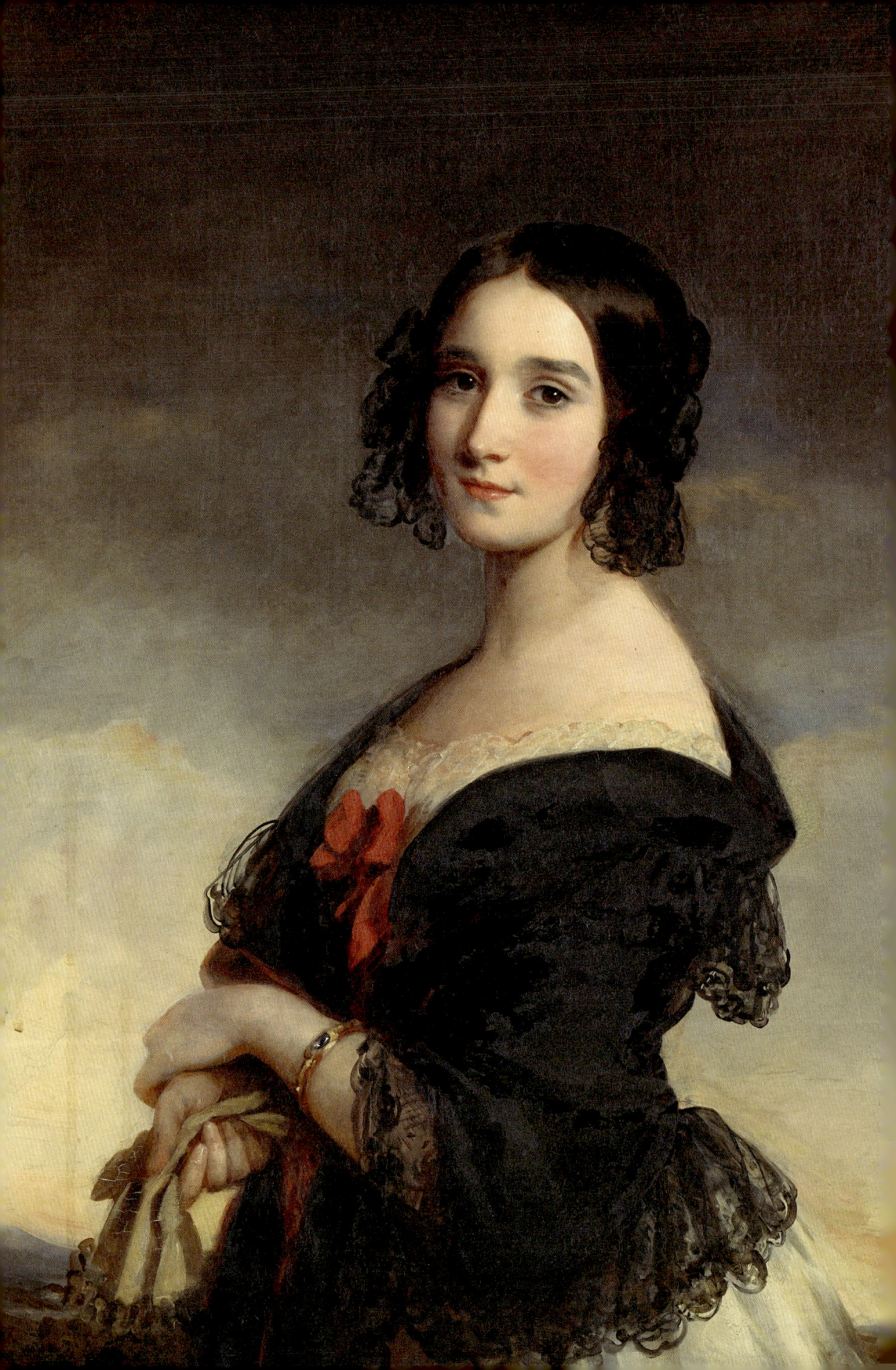

made friends with young Austrians, played the piano and learnt German with her governess "Mussy", Mlle Steinbauer. A year later she became ill, and as there was no improvement after a stay in the mountains at Ischl, Charles and Margaret decided to have her looked after in England. From Lord Lansdowne's house in Richmond Louise visited the London doctors, Seymour and Watson three times weekly, and then spent an uncomfortable winter in Hastings, leaving Charles alone and worried in Vienna. In 1845, as hopes of the pure sea air curing the chronic cough, insomnia and general weakness proved to be in vain, Margaret determined to go abroad for consultations with Dr Andral in Paris, going from doctor to doctor and from one town to another, and then on to Italy.

The warmer climate brought no improvement and in 1846 Margaret and the girls travelled from Rome to Eaux-Bonnes in the Pyrenees in the belief that "the waters are miraculous for setting up weak constitutions and giving tone to the system" under the supervision of Dr Prosper Darralde. From there Margaret decided to winter in Rome: "1) Louise says it agrees with her, 2) Georgina likes it and will see more of English society there than anywhere else except London, 3) Emily and Shelburne will be there, 4) will bring Papa to Italy to join us good for his health and our pleasure". This tiring and fruitless life on the move continued until May 1847 when Margaret finally admitted defeat: "I have hawked about the world for three years and have now come to an age to feel that one has few moments to lose for the enjoyment of being with those one loves and that a comfortable home is an everyday enjoyment that nothing can make up for – if only poor Louise had profited by all these déplacements". Having lost confidence in the doctors consulted in Vienna, London, Paris, Florence, Rome and at Eaux-Bonnes, they returned to England. In despair, Margaret formerly so sceptical, unlike Charles, now began to consider the results of homeopathy. She left Louise and Georgina with Emily, who took them to Torquay and joined Charles in Vienna in October 1847.

In these difficult years Georgina emerges as an unselfish, devoted and loving. daughter and sister. She was a good linguist who spoke German and French well, went to the balls at Carnival time, designed embroidery patterns, copied Old Masters and painted portraits, but admitted that she was

41 **Christina Robertson (1796–1854): Emily**

not so successful with landscapes. Without complaint, she accompanied her mother with Louise on her travels back to England, to France and Italy. With Margaret so preoccupied, friends such as Princess Czartoryska offered, for the sake of convention, to escort Georgina to parties, and in July 1847 Princess Grasalkowicz chaperoned her with her maid, two servants and her own carriage on the journey home from Paris. Thereafter she divided her time between Lansdowne House, Holland House, and Brighton with the Willoughby de Eresbys, always careful not to outstay her welcome in town. When Louise was in England, rather than leave her invalid sister on her own, Georgina turned down invitations to breakfasts given by the Duke of Devonshire and the ball of the Duchess of Sutherland. While Margaret worried over her missing the pleasures of the London season and having to lead such a dull life, Georgina assured her that she had absolutely no regrets. Strong and determined, she had appointed herself guardian of Louise, a difficult patient whose health was delicate both physically and psychologically.

The six-year embassy in Vienna covered the end of the old order epitomized by Metternich. As the emperor was incapable, power was divided between different factions, and there was not much for Charles to do except guard over the interests of the government of Louis-Philippe. One problem was the presence in Austria of the Legitimist branch of the Bourbons, represented by the comte de Chambord, his sister, Louise Marie, known as Mademoiselle, and their aunt, the duchesse d'Angoulême, who from 1844 were living in exile at nearby Frohsdorf. However, relations with them went smoothly, and the duchesse set a truly royal example by "weeping with them that weep" and going into family mourning after the death of the duc d'Orléans on 13 July 1842. When the imperial court attended the wedding of the Prince Charles III of Parma to Mademoiselle in November 1845, Charles, conscious of the problems Louis-Philippe's children faced in making suitable marriages, expressed his misgivings: "Nothing can be worse than the young man's reputation. His language to his friends is odious: he talks of nothing but the Princess's dot and of all he will do now he is going to be rich. They say the duchesse d'Angoulême is enchanted with the match and anxious to hurry it on while the duchesse de Berry is much less pleased, I should have expected the contrary."[7]

Another marriage, that of Princesse Clémentine, youngest daughter of Louis-Philippe, concerned him more directly, as the bridegroom was Prince

August of Saxe-Coburg and Gotha, son of a very rich family with estates in Austria and Hungary, and brother of Victoria, wife of the duc de Nemours. After successfully negotiating the financial settlement, Charles then resolved the problem of rank for the couple, a question of huge importance at a court obsessed with questions of precedence and etiquette. Eventually it was agreed that they would be received by the imperial court on the same footing as had been agreed in Russia for the Duke of Leutchenberg and the tsar's daughter Marie. All went well, and when the young couple arrived in Vienna after their marriage at Saint-Cloud, they were invited to a dance and dinner at Schönbrunn. Clémentine was welcomed by the emperor and empress in the saloon where all the imperial family joined them, and when dinner was announced Auguste was treated as a royal highness, much to the satisfaction of his French in-laws. After observing Clémentine at Schönbrunn, dancing at the Esterházy's and then at her country house Eberthal, Charles sent a glowing report:

> She is much improved in all respects and is kind and amiable as possible, full of reason and good feeling, her attention to her new family admirable and the simplicity with which she has taken her place among them shows great tact without losing dignity. Eberthal is not St. Cloud or Neuilly but it is a comfortable little chateau with a pretty garden full of flowers. Her son of 3 months is strong and flourishing and husband although a 'slow goer', has improved so much in appearance after Paris, now with his bushy whiskers and d'Orsay coat, that people are saying 'en vérité c'est un beau garçon'.[8]

As always, the high point each year was the embassy dinner of 30 April in honour of Louis-Philippe, which was always a worry when Margaret, a superb hostess, was not present. Just after an assassination attempt on the king in Paris, Charles confided his doubts to Margaret on 29 April 1846:

> All the ennui of my dinner for the King's fête tomorrow. We shall be 72. How many sincere well-wishers among them God only knows. At the same time I must say that the last execrable attempt has caused here universal sorrow and

indignation. The fact is that there is a general feeling that the
peace and tranquillity of Europe depend on the king's life
and there are many people placed in high stations legitimately
in their heart who offer God very sincere prayers for the
preservation of his days and throne.[9]

Master of *l'art de vivre*, supported by Margaret Husson, his chef, Bellot, and
valet, François, these anniversary dinners were always successful. They did
not last too long (an hour and a half only), the service and quality were excellent, good wishes for the king's health were expressed on behalf of the
emperor and empress and people said they had never seen anything better.

Although there were rumours of his appointment as tutor to the infant
comte de Paris, Charles showed no desire to leave, and on 25 April 1845
Barante reported to his son Ernest:

> Mr. de Flahaut has no desire to leave Vienna. He is in his
> element. After three and a half years away France shocks him
> and he no longer feels at home here. He prefers the
> diplomatic life in a country governed by a hierarchy, where
> order and calm prevail, and is no longer accustomed to our
> pointless and petty agitation.[10]

As far as Franco-British relations were concerned, he got on very well with
his colleague Sir Robert Gordon, but, regretting English involvement in
India and Afghanistan and the aggressive attitude towards France taken by
Lord Palmerston, and being worried about the Pritchard affair,[11] he felt he
should not leave Vienna until things settled down.[12] Unfortunately, the situation got worse, for not only was Gordon's successor, Lord Ponsonby, a much
more difficult character, but soon after his arrival in Vienna their respective
governments were divided over the question of the marriages of the Spanish
Infantas.[13] This, Charles admitted, was "a very disagreeable affair and keeps
me in hot water". However, despite a distinct lack of encouragement he succeeded in maintaining good relations with Lord Ponsonby, declaring that
"Nothing would be so painful to me as not to be seen to be friendly to a
brother of Lady Grey."

The setting up of a Polish Republic in January 1846 was followed by uprisings in Galicia (Austrian Poland) and in Posen (Prussian Poland), which were suppressed and Cracow was incorporated into the Habsburg Empire. The disappearance of this last vestige of Polish territorial independence was a great blow for Charles, who in 1831 had tried, albeit ineffectually, to support the cause when in Berlin. Sensing that Guizot thought his despatches inadequate and that he did not take a strong enough line with Metternich, he offered to resign, but this was not accepted.[14] When Tsar Nicholas visited Vienna for two days in January 1846 Charles told Margaret that he had

> made himself very disagreeable and carried away with him the ill-will of everybody. A more disdainful look and manner than his I never saw during the representation at the theatre and it was the same I hear the whole time: everything they had prepared, dinners ordered, people invited, soirées arranged, he refused everything except a military dinner after the review.[15]

Throughout 1847 trouble was brewing in Portugal, Spain, Switzerland, and, most threateningly for Austria, in Italy, where the tide of liberalism seemed unstoppable. That summer, disillusioned and lonely, Charles had had enough, telling a friend in June 1847 that a life of separation from his wife and children was odious to him, adding ruefully:

> . . . the man who tries conscientiously to get at the truth and tells it is not appreciated, while the one who lies and flatters the weaknesses and passions of the Government and country alone is valued and approved. Such approbation I will never deserve. . . .

It now dawned on him that his hopes of the long-desired London embassy would never be realized. In December 1847 Margaret told Emily that

> We hear today that Montebello is likely to be sent to England as Barante is to go to Naples but this I think will be personally hostile to your Father who has never been objected to except upon the score of having an English wife and being

a great favourite in England. Beware of your friends and
never mind your enemies! He has no regrets for he believes it
impossible at moment to do business in that quarter on fair
terms and has given up all thoughts of going there. What a
sad situation for both countries to be placed in when their
best and steadfast friends are forced to think so and where
their most serious interests are sacrificed to the vain rivalry of
two ministers.[16]

However, she refused to give up and solicited the help of the Duke of
Devonshire to use his influence on behalf of Charles, "so we can all be
together". She was right to do so, for in his heart of hearts Charles still desired
the London post: "If it were offered me I should accept it but I would not
ask for it. One must not ask for things when one is not almost sure to succeed." Aware of his father's hopes, Auguste Morny assessed the situation,
explaining that the main obstacle was that the French government believed
that the Flahauts had made too many friends and too many enemies in the
English political camps. In these circumstances he advised that they should
leave it to him and their other friends to lobby on their behalf. He also considered that on account of his excellent relationship with Prince Metternich
it was unlikely that Guizot would want to send Charles to London and
replace him with another ambassador in Vienna.[17]

In July 1847 Charles went on leave: first to Paris, then London and
Scotland until Guizot, worried about political unrest, recalled him on 8
October. He returned to Vienna where Margaret joined him later for the
final phase of his embassy, bracing themselves to face the rigours of another
Viennese winter. The signs were not good. As he told Emily in January 1848,
". . . l'horizon politique est fort sombre. Enfin espérons". Margaret agreed,
observing

> . . . that in Austria the wise and prudent are discouraged, and
> the violent and unreasonable excited. All believe that some
> change here must inevitably be the consequence for it is
> evident that a stagnant pool like this cannot remain with
> running water and raging torrents on every side without
> having its placid surface undisturbed.

She also regretted that "Lord Palmerston should inspire the whole world with terror, which seems to put confusion in all European policy and upset all former friendships and alliances".[18]

Charles's last engagement, much against Margaret's wishes, was his attendance at the funeral of Count Hardegg in February 1848. Exposed to snow and ice for three hours he followed the cortège across the city as the last honours were paid to the war chief by an immense body of troops. His presence there was considered a great mark of respect not only by the archdukes but by the military and society in general, and he was pleased by the approval showed by the crowd when his servants appeared.

As Charles and Margaret suspected, under a seemingly tranquil surface popular discontent was waiting to explode in France, Italy, Hungary and Germany when demands for reasonable reform were resisted. In an instant, governments were overturned, leading to anarchy, confusion and terror across Europe. When the news came of the abdication of Louis-Philippe on 24 February 1848 and the establishment of a Republic in France, Charles resigned immediately, handing over the embassy to the efficient first secretary Mr Gabriac, and although Alphonse de Lamartine, now in charge in Paris, wanted him to stay,[19] he refused, in spite of fearing that "Auguste will be angry that I gave up my place but I could not do otherwise". Then on 13 March, following the revolution in Austria, Metternich fled, bringing to an end a thirty-year ascendancy over European politics. Totally disillusioned, Charles told Emily, "I am heartily sick of public men & things and long for nothing but calm and repose. God grant that England may afford it to me". However, the question of his military rank meant that he could not go to England without asking for a *congé*, and resignation was a very serious step. As for Margaret, although so upset that she walked "almost like a disturbed spirit in a state of nervous agitation", she rose to the occasion, and arranged for a great auction sale of their possessions and the packing up of all that had to be transported back to England. Because of the fear of insurrection, the Viennese rich stayed away from the sale, and there were no takers for the fine furniture and *objets de prix* on offer.

With the dispersal behind them, they made their way to London where on 31 March Henry Greville met them at the Hollands: "She told me nothing could exceed the excitement in Germany which showed itself at all the railway stations as they travelled from Vienna, and in the various towns by the multitudes parading the streets, singing patriotic songs, embracing, hoisting flags and illuminations. No one knows what has become of the Metternichs." Shortly after that the prince and princess arrived, staying in a hotel until Margaret found the perfect house for them at 44, Eaton Square, "neither a cottage or a palace", though it took time for them to get used to living vertically. The Duke of Wellington called every day, and all their friends rallied round but the fog and expense of living in London became too much and they moved on to Brighton, since for Prince Metternich, "Être à Brighton c'est être à Londres, comme on est à Vienne quand on séjourne à Baden." They told their daughter, Countess Léontine Sándor, how much Margaret had done for them, and the friendship continued until Melanie died in 1854.[20]

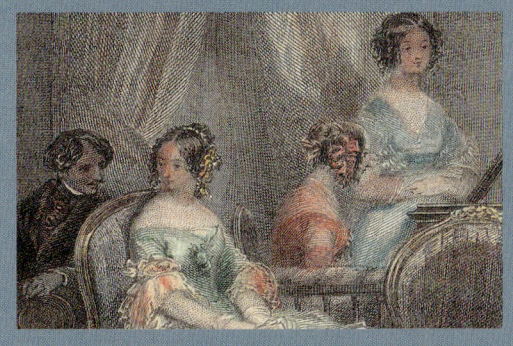

CHAPTER 19

London, 1848–64

*On pourrait appeler Londres la Babylone noire. Lugubre le
jour, splendide la nuit. Voir Londres est un saisissement.
C'est une rumeur sous une fumée. Analogie mystérieuse ; la
rumeur est la fumée du bruit. Paris est la capitale d'un
versant de l'humanité, Londres est la capitale du versant
opposé. Magnifique et sombre ville. L'activité y est tumulte et
le peuple y est fourmilière. On y est libre et emboîté. Londres
est le chaos en ordre*

Victor Hugo, *William Shakespeare* (1864)

Arriving in England in March 1848, after escaping from the calamities of revolutionary Europe, the Flahauts were relieved that Queen Victoria was still on the throne and supported by a government firmly maintaining law and order, civil and religious freedom. Charles was obliged to return to France in 1849 to settle the matter of his military pension (£270 p.a.) that had been abolished by the Second Republic, but detesting socialism, which "asserts itself by murder, plunder, fire, cruelties and brutalities showing no respect to age or sex", he had no wish to settle there. Instead, they resolved to make London their home with their unmarried daughters Georgina and the invalid Louise, and enjoying the company of the eldest, Emily, Lady Shelburne and her children. Ever practical, Margaret set about house-hunting, a daunting task since good houses were scarce in London, those available being too big, too small, too dark or in too dull a neighbourhood. From 78, Eaton Square they moved to 6, Tilney Street, "an old dirty house undergoing a scouring process, smell from kitchen all day, with radical defects except situation, a charming drawing room, gay and smart", then in 1850 they rented 19, Grosvenor Square until settling in Coventry House, no. 106, Piccadilly, easy for their friends to visit and from which Charles could walk to Brooks's Club in St James's Street. She described this mansion, built in 1761 for the Earl of Coventry with beautiful interior decoration by Robert Adam, as a "pleasant, convenient abode, albeit with great faults – no privacy, noise and a short lease!" (10 years). She also regretted that there was not one good room on the "detestable" bedroom floor, accessible only by one staircase so that "masters and servants must meet upon it", and that the steps leading up to the front door were a serious inconvenience in the rain. Since they had decided to make a permanent home in London, the Paris house was sold to Baron Roger in 1853 and inherited by his stepson, the duc de Massa, in 1880.[1]

After Margaret's customary battles with the builders, decorators and upholsterers, their beautiful possessions were installed in Coventry House so they could live in comfort and entertain in style. Visiting in 1856, the statesman Lord Granville, whom they had known as a youth in Paris,[2] approved the elegance of the women in their crinolines and the hospitality: "too gay and pretty. The society there, the refined essence of cream with a beautiful buffet laid out". Other old friends came: the diarist Henry Greville, who dined there in 1857, lists the lords Lansdowne and Ashburton, the ladies William Russell and Tankerville and M. Gabriel Delessert, formerly prefect of police in Paris.[3] Foreigners were always welcomed: the Portuguese conde de Vila Real, son of Charles's stepfather M. de Souza, and the Marquis Lavradio, the Hanoverian ambassador Eduard von Kielmansegg, the French Colonel Wimpffen, who had distinguished himself in the Crimean War and the Italian Princess Camporeale, soon to become the wife of the statesman Marco Minghetti. Always anxious to strengthen the ties between the two countries, they were close to the French ambassador, their old friend Count Alexandre Walewski (1851–5), though less so with his successors, Jean-Gilbert Persigny (1855–8, 1859–60) and Marshal Pélissier, duc de Malakoff (March 1858–April 1859). As the years went by, rather than go out, they preferred to see their friends at home, suggesting, for example, that Edward Ellice should come any evening – "we accept no invitations". This was their base, interspersed with frequent stays in Paris until Napoleon III appointed Charles ambassador in December 1860, which obliged them to live for some months at the embassy in Albert Gate, then returning to Coventry House after his resignation before leaving permanently for Paris in 1864.

London had developed since Margaret's marriage, for, as the capital of the world's richest industrial and trading nation, it had increased in scale as had its population. Although in comparison with Paris the city lacked fine monuments, the great houses of the aristocracy were magnificent, there was much bustle in the streets, where the coachmen conducted elegant equipages with dexterity, and the shops sold merchandise from all over the world.

42 **Eugène Lami (1800–1890): hand-tinted print**
of *An Evening at 6, Tilney Street* **(overleaf)**

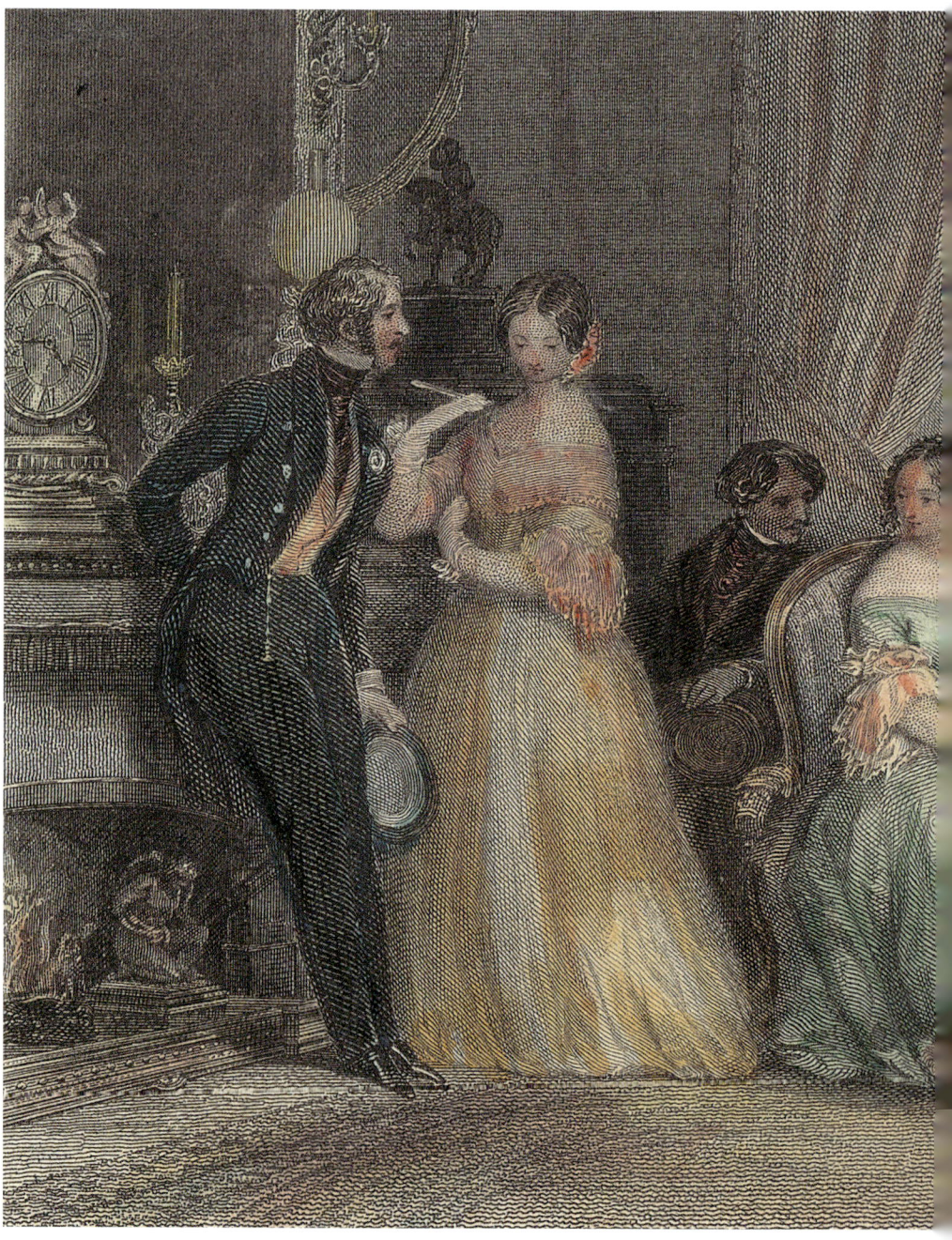

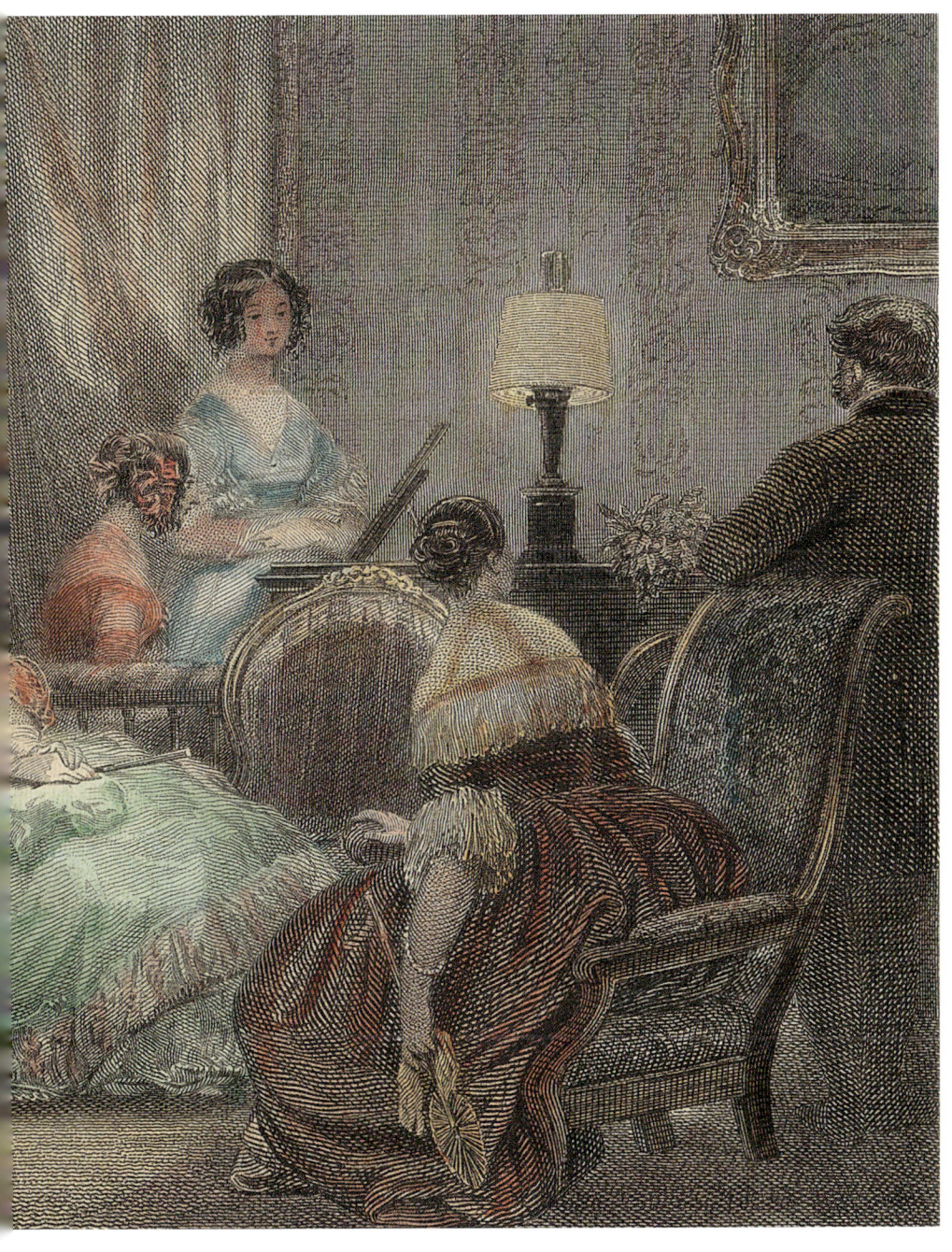

Although Margaret did not care much for the London theatre, finding the humour too coarse and exaggerated, she could enjoy concerts and opera, and the collections of art and science at the British Museum. At home she continued to draw and paint, and in 1856 sent Lord Canning in Calcutta her copy of his father's portrait by Thomas Lawrence, "one of the brightest illustrations in my collection", painted in enamel to withstand the Indian climate. Reading was a daily habit: this she did in bed, beside an oil lamp. She knew, at least by sight, everybody in society, which was then a comparatively small group of 300 to 500 persons who met at the best balls and receptions during the three-month season, when, according to Rudolf Apponyi, "the world goes mad". He described the social round thus: in the morning Hyde Park in carriage or on horseback, then dressing up, then dinner followed by a ball, and next day it begins all over again".[4] She would be unlikely to miss musical evenings and receptions for 300 guests in the great Sculpture Gallery of Lansdowne House, the finest and largest privately owned room in London. It was through her introduction that the French artist Eugène Lami was commissioned by Lord Lansdowne to depict his collection as it looked on one of these gala occasions. As Margaret was now on good terms with the young Queen Victoria, and both she and Charles admired Prince Albert, they, with Emily and Georgina attended concerts at Buckingham Palace and the inauguration of the new ballroom there in 1858.

Margaret never lost her interest in French and English politics, nor did she abandon her liberal opinions. Taking place before her eyes was a power struggle between the aristocracy and the middle class, who were demanding major amendments to the great Reform Act of 1832. Following every development, reading the papers, attending the state openings of Parliament and all the important debates, discussing and arguing every issue of the day, she deplored the rivalry between Viscount Palmerston and Lord John Russell, which divided the Liberals, and the failure of successive administrations to carry on the business of the country. It was in this mood that she wrote to Emily in February 1855, "I am in despair at the mess in England and do not see any way out of it that is satisfactory", and later, "I am ashamed of the bad figure England makes at this moment and the effect it produces à l'étranger", noting how the "disorganised cabinet, the divisions of parties, blackguard press, inefficiency of the army, from whatever cause it is attributable, makes an ensemble of humiliating circumstances." After reading Lord Grey's

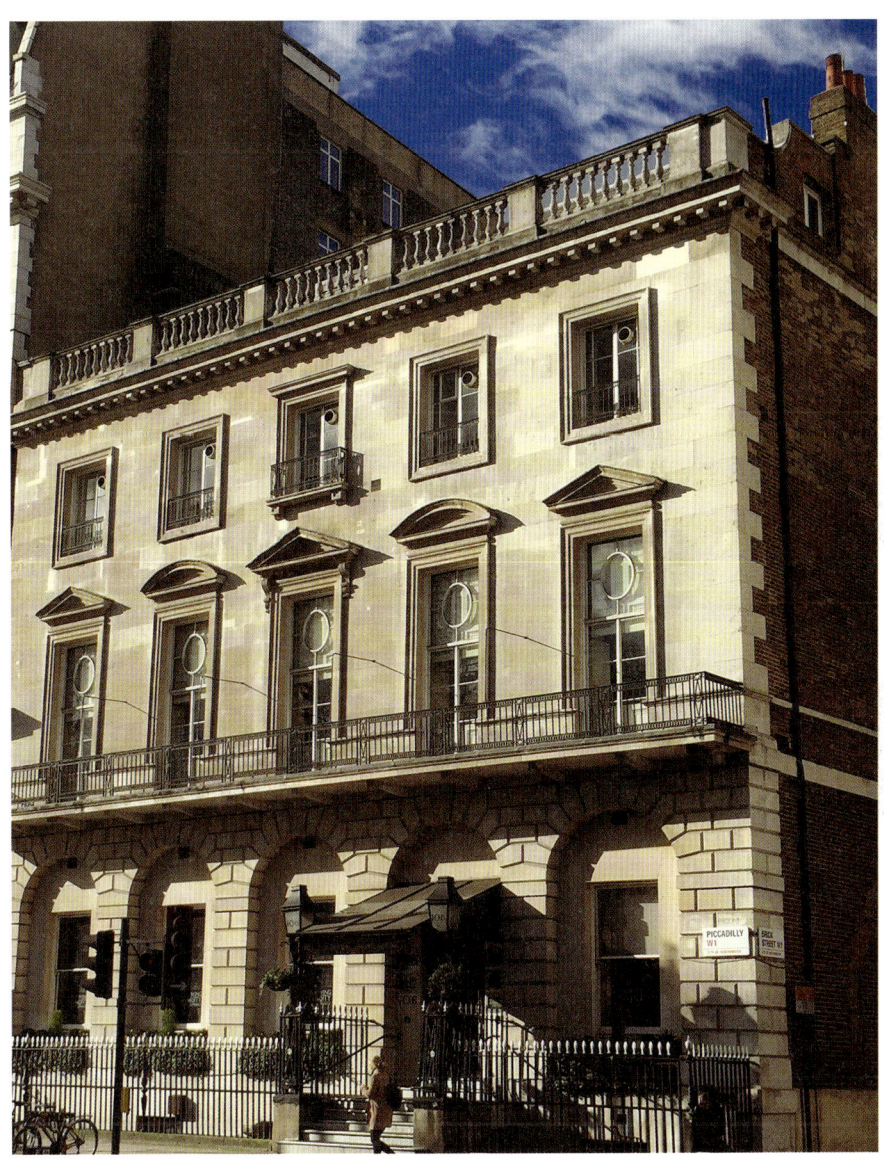

43 Coventry House, Piccadilly

correspondence upon the last Reform Bill, she compared the "high attitude of the Whigs of those days with the destructiveness of the present, Lord Derby at the head". For some time she was also scathing about the huge political influence exercised by J. T. Delane, as editor of *The Times*, suggesting in 1855 that "Mr. Delane had better be made Premier at once and divide the other offices among the correspondents of the Times."[5]

A notable public event she much enjoyed was the Great Exhibition of 1851, which some people, including Charles, thought would be a disaster, bringing demagogues of all the participating countries to preach violence and revolution. These critics were confounded by the outcome, which was a huge success, Lord Macaulay declaring the Crystal Palace "a most gorgeous sight, vast, graceful, beyond the dreams of the Arabian romances. I cannot think that the Caesars ever exhibited a more splendid spectacle".[6] Margaret agreed, and visited it many times, admiring in particular the hardstone and rock-crystal display vases exhibited by Jean-Valentin Morel of Paris which she deemed "not equalled since days of Cellini".[7]

Since Margaret was getting older, which, as she told Lord Canning, "is not an improving state" and plagued by coughs, colds, headaches and rheumatism she escaped the dense yellow London fog whenever she could. To help her recover from the death of Louise in 1853, Lord Lansdowne offered his villa at Richmond, where she had lived as a child and could meet her witty novelist friend Emily Eden. She believed walking was the best means of making "the machine work as long as the wheel will turn, or it becomes rusty and immoveable. I follow this plan and continue my walk in the morning though I come back with aching bones". Then she went as often as she could to Brighton, where she was "charmed to see and smell the sea", and "sleep, drink, walk, eat, bathe, walk and sleep again". This was a pleasure she could not share with Charles, who in April 1851 complained to Emily that he had "caught a bad throat through riding in an open fly with Margaret along the promenade in a bitter North East wind which she thought délicieux!" However, his visit in July 1852 was a "lune de miel" when she had him all to herself. They took long walks together and drives in evening before settling down to read. One of the latest books, *Journal of a Winter's Tour in India* (1852) by Francis Egerton, amused them greatly on account of his strange and extensive phraseology – on a hot day he was "pretty particularly well cooked", he never walks like other people, but is "trotted out" to see sights, the Indian servants "Knock them up a very fair dinner" and all animals are "brutes". Sometimes she varied the Brighton cure by taking the waters at Hombourg and on 15 April 1856 she went with Georgina to Bath to drink and bathe for her rheumatism. This was a success, and she claimed that living entirely for her health, the time spent drinking water, being out of doors in the lovely countryside, had restored her balance, and she felt her soul tranquil, her spirits happier and weight lighter. Back in Hombourg in 1858, she was accompanied by Charles, who reported to Emily that Margaret "was delighted, but I can't see what is wrong with her health: her appetite is excellent, she is always ready to do what amuses her and she sleeps like a log". As for his own health he was foolishly adamant: "I see no doctor having the most profound contempt for them all".

Another consequence of the advancing years was the loss of her best and oldest friends and relations. Her devoted cousin Anne Elphinstone was killed in an accident in 1850, then Fred Adam died unexpectedly in 1853, and in 1860 came the loss of Lord Elphinstone, from the effects of the climate of India, a disaster for the family as he had no children and the Cumbernauld estate was inherited by an irresponsible cousin. After the death of Lord Grey in 1845, Charles wrote that the "news has grieved us as if we had lost one of our family", and in 1861 they were equally affected by the loss of his widow, "our kindest and best friend for nearly 50 years". Lady Lansdowne died, much regretted, in 1851, and the death in 1863 of Lord Lansdowne brought to an end sixty years of uninterrupted friendship. As for the 4th and last Lord Holland, although he and his capricious wife, Augusta, had not had any contact with the Flahauts for some years, when Margaret heard that he had died at the age of 57 in Naples in 1859 she said that she had "no remembrance but of kindly acts from him since he was quite a boy". Much missed too was Lady Granville, sister of the 6th Duke of Devonshire, former ambassadress in Paris (1862), and another loss was that of a prominent Whig statesman Lord Auckland, former Governor-General of India (1849). In Scotland, Lord Rutherfurd, responsible for Margaret's business and property affairs, who shared her interests in the arts and politics, died in 1854, leaving her his "beautiful enamel gold Bonbon box".

The hardest of all these deaths to bear was that of Louise, who after years of suffering, tenderly cared for by her parents and sisters, misled by many false hopes of a cure, died of consumption on 30 May 1853. Her sweet character impressed her doctor Sir George Locock:

> I have never witnessed a more patient endurance of a long
> life of sickness cut off from the ordinary pleasures and
> pursuits of existence and it was always a delight to be able to
> diminish suffering and to make the close of such an innocent
> career as peaceful and as calm as possible.

Charles could not forget her, confiding to Emily in December 1853:

> I slept one night in my poor child's dear melancholy room –
> the little sofa where before she was so much worse she bore
> her long sufferings with so much patience and resignation
> and where I see her so grateful for any little attention any
> mark of affection.

Margaret, who was so much more reserved emotionally, remembered Louise
in her own way. In July she thanked Emily for planting her gift of a rose tree:
"I was sure that if I brought it here it would be lost in the multitude, – poor
child, it was the last rose of her summer and the last little pleasure I could
give her, and I should have been sorry if it had been neglected".[8] The family
were grateful to Louise's Austrian governess Mlle Steinbauer, who was then
engaged by Emily for her children, and much beloved by them.

The loss of the three sisters, Clementina, Adele and Louise, bound
Margaret, Charles and their two remaining daughters more closely together.
Georgina (1823–1907) chose to stay at home, devoting herself to her parents
and sister, and making herself useful to Emily's elderly father-in-law, Lord
Lansdowne. She accompanied Margaret everywhere and acted as secretary
to her father, reading the newspapers to him at breakfast every morning. By
no means a recluse, she was a great favourite of the Duke of Devonshire and
participated in the social life of London and Paris, though without ever showing much enjoyment.[9] Unlike her mother and Emily, clothes did not interest
her, and she succeeded in looking dowdy and comfortable rather than fashionable in the latest Paris toilettes. She was a mystery to Margaret, who noted
that from childhood she was always "of a close disposition", never confiding
in anyone, not even Emily and there was no way of knowing what she liked

but only what she disliked. The family hoped that she would find someone to whom she could attach herself, but she was too reserved to encourage timid men and indifferent whenever an eligible suitor presented himself. She refused a French duke, a Spanish nobleman and Maurice Cottier, an art lover from a Protestant banking family, with an income of £12,000 a year, much approved by her parents, who thought it impossible to be more "comme il faut" and gentlemanlike. Margaret, who met him at a dinner given by Auguste Morny in Paris, was taken by his looks, "as if he had stepped down from the frame of a portrait of one of the last generation of Elphinstones at Tullyallan." In 1871, after the death of both parents, Georgina married their close friend Félix de Lavalette, wit, diplomat, statesman, bon vivant, and a cousin of the Flahauts, now a widower.[10]

Emily, with her husband, the Earl of Shelburne, heir to the marquessate of Lansdowne, and her three children gave her parents and Georgina great happiness. They confided in her as she did with them, exchanging letters almost every day. When Emily told Charles how difficult she found her father-in-law, the distinguished Whig statesman, he assured her, "although Lord Lansdowne is cold and distant, he is an excellent man who approves of you", that the late Lady Lansdowne had counted on Emily to console him, and after reminding her that no family was without its problems, urged, "please overcome your shyness and DON'T be frightened of him – that puts people off!" As the closest of friends, who enjoyed each other's company, she spent as much time as possible with her parents in London and in Scotland, accompanied by her husband and children, Clanmaurice, or "Clan", born in 1845, Edmond in 1846 and Emily, known as Emmy or Kitty, in 1855. Margaret, who adored "Clan", devoured his letters, was proud of his cleverness and was relieved when he grew to a good height, "as I like to have a tall grandson and until lately he did not give much promise of becoming so". Similarly, she was delighted when the younger son, Edmond, also did well at school and she encouraged his interest in books and botany. Every Shelburne family visit to Tulliallan was a success and Charles told Emily, in October 1853 that he missed them every single minute of the day, and again in 1856, "I can't describe the gap you have left. Your presence – the boys and little Kitty in the mornings, you at lunch and Shelburne in the smoking room – made us so happy."

In their turn, Charles, Margaret and Georgina often stayed at Bowood, the Lansdowne country house in Wiltshire, not only for the annual Christmas house party but at other times during the year, sometimes for as long as a month. Ever ambitious, Margaret wanted her son-in-law to succeed, and on his appointment as Under Secretary for Foreign Affairs in 1856, told Lord Canning how pleased she was that "fitted by nature, excluded by habit", a career of usefulness would be the means of his developing abilities and riveting his attention on important matters – "therefore fewer carriages will be built, fewer horses bought and sold, less time wasted on minor details, earlier hours kept, already parties of picquet at Whites given up, fewer Holydays, less time to spend at Tulliallan and Bowood".[11] Her letters evoke the atmosphere of the house parties at Bowood, shrine of the Whig aristocracy. Not all the fellow guests were to her liking and she took against the much-admired American Ellen Twisleton and her sister, "though more inoffensive than most of their country women".[12] Lord Lansdowne's infatuation with Lady Somers amused her: "[H]e is as much in love with her as if he was 20! She more beautiful than ever, good natured, aimable, exercises sufficient dignified coquetry to feed his flame more than is quite necessary."[13] In 1861 she admitted to the awkwardness of speaking to Lord Lansdowne, who was now stone deaf, and how his family "say little to him as they will not speak loud". Describing herself now as "an old and ragged remnant of the old Whig stuff", her *politicomanie* was as strong as ever. She therefore hoped when staying with Lord Lansdowne, Lord President of the Council in the government of Lord John Russell, to hear the latest political gossip, but to her disappointment, Bowood was always "full with people who know everything but say nothing". Books were another matter, and she noted how "Everyone is talking about the Macaulay History and all agree that the siege of Londonderry is finest specimen of historical narrative ever written".

Railways made Margaret's visits - sometimes accompanied by Charles and Georgina – not just to Bowood, but to other stately homes – much easier, and her letters record the hospitality and luxury of the aristocracy of the mid-Victorian period. She complained about the dangers of travel, and in 1861 declared that more caution was required, that the stationmasters should be more exact in their timekeeping and that there should be longer intervals between trains. In her view parliamentary legislation was needed to make it less "*chanceux*" but, ever the realist, she admitted that official laws could not prevent individual carelessness. After the usually uncomfortable journey, perhaps in the fog and cold, it was always a pleasure to arrive in one of those great Whig country houses for tea beside a blazing fire and meet her fellow guests.

Travelling south from Edinburgh she could ask the superintendent of the express train to stop at Chesterfield in time to dine at Chatsworth with her old friend the Duke of Devonshire, and going north she might break the journey at York to visit the Carlisles in the great Vanbrugh mansion of Castle Howard. She was asked to stay at Tottenham Park and Beaudesert by the marquesses of Ailesbury and Anglesey respectively, at Wentworth Woodhouse by Earl Fitzwilliam, at Worsley by the Ellesmeres, at Downham by the Asshetons, at Hickleton by Sir Charles and Lady Wood. From each, her sharp eyes missing nothing, she reported on the different attractions, especially the gardens and the picture collections. She described how Lady Cowper's house parties at vast castellated Gothick Panshanger were enlivened by dancing and by the ever-popular theatricals or vaudevilles, with star performances from Lord Granville and a charming and popular couple, Augustus Craven and his French wife, Pauline, before an audience of 150 guests. Similarly, in June 1852 she wrote from Wrest Park, "a busy house with so much to do, see and hear in an immense party", that "all the young set, not rehearsing, are noisy – singing, dancing and playing les petits jeux all day long". The theatricals were held in a "theatre perfect behind a move-able panel in dining room which disappears after the performance leaving no break in carved gilt ornaments or speck on white walls". She added that besides these amusements "the whole house and garden is a study of every-thing that is most tasteful, comfortable, as in an old French château – Champlatreux".[14]

That same summer at Arundel Castle as the guest of the Duke and Duchess of Norfolk, in a large party with the Bedfords, Beauforts and Foleys, Margaret was taken by the "magnificence of the old castle, the splendour of the new establishment, the excessive good nature of inhabitants, the nice daughter of the hosts, the long drives every day across downs, and the deer". She reported from Keele Hall in Staffordshire that Ralph Sneyd (1793–1870), with whom she carried on a long correspondence, had "the nicest, best kept establishment I ever saw everything perfect, the smelliest mutton, thickest cream, largest peaches, best beds, floors with highest polish". The routine at Bletby Hall in Derbyshire with Lady Chesterfield in 1860 is evoked in detail:

hunting, shooting for gentlemen, followed by billiards, with needlework and tea for the ladies, then dinner at a long table for 22 covers with beautiful racing cups down the centre. There were games in the evening of which post seemed the favourite and whist for Lady Chesterfield, who won everything and played better than Lord Derby, Lord William and Charles who made up her party. She was pleased that it was her "destiny to sit by Lord Derby every day at dinner, so amusing, so easy to talk to, his spirits never flag", and watch him teasing Princess Edward of Saxe-Weimar, who could give as good as she got.[15] Other pleasures at Bletby included reading the "charming original letters of Lord Chesterfield to his cub of a son" and visiting Lady Sophia Des Vœux "a good natured jolly old soul" at Drakelow Hall, an Elizabethan house, furnished in that style and full of historical associations.[16] From Bletby she went on to visit Lord Wilton at Egerton Lodge, Melton Mowbray, after a short journey of an hour and a half. This was hunting country and she did not miss out on its excitements. For three hours, in a low barouche, she followed the hunt of several hundred horsemen and a few ladies in pursuit of fox and hounds over hill and dale, passing through every field and gate. Although the atmosphere in the house was definitely not intellectual she found it an agreeable change, and, as if the maxims of Lord Chesterfield on the art of pleasing had truly been absorbed, "certainly was never in a society where there was more good humour and more genuine politeness".[17]

At Woburn in January 1859, the considerate Duchess of Bedford put the Flahauts in "warm comfortable rooms, with no stairs to climb nor cold passages to pass through" in a house party of eighteen. Although everything was "très soignée", there was positively no talk of politics to interest Margaret and she also regretted the presence of so many old family members "not to be seen in general society". Ever observant, she went on to mock a rich old clergyman in the Woburn house party as a caricature of an "incroyable of 1815 with a nose like a ploughshare and a pair of legs like kitchen tongs". In contrast, she hardly ever criticized her cousins Lord and Lady Willoughby de Eresby in Torquay, where "they have a large comfortable house and garden looking down on the port which suits him [a keen fisherman] as *The Leopard* is always in the foreground, both in sight and mind and is as much pleased with the command of his lugger and boat crew as any young officer would be with his first ship".

Yet, after one of her regular visits she described Drummond Castle in 1861 as

> . . . so beautiful that it puts one out of conceit with all other places and it really is the case, for everything looks flat beside it and it combines all that can make a country place perfect – the garden is magnificent this year, and really the vegetation surpasses all imagination.

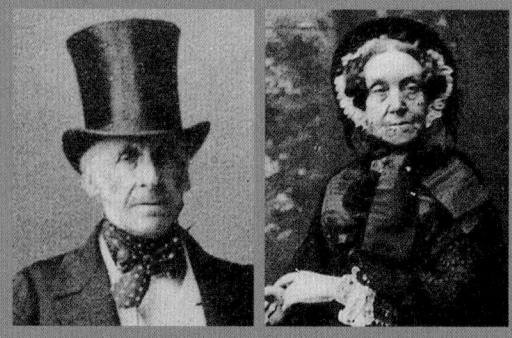

CHAPTER 20

Tulliallan and the London
Embassy, 1848–64

*Every day it rains in flintmaking showers . . . A deplorable
country, – good for the Painter with its fine lights, misty veils,
rainbows, cliffs[,] lochs and bursts of sunshine; – good also for
the deerstalker . . . but for no other person whatever . . .*

Thomas Carlyle, *Collected Letters*

The lessons she learnt from staying with others were put to good use when Margaret organized her own parties in Scotland, where every summer and autumn until November she kept open house for family, friends, sportsmen, diplomats and politicians. Her formula was not for large or "monster" parties, likely to split into separate cliques, but a judicious mix of around twelve well-chosen people, known to like each other, who could be pulled together into a team for their mutual enjoyment. These invitations were sought after not only for the society, for as the French antiquary and traveller Pierre Trabaud commented in 1853, "Of all the places visited by tourists Scotland is the pearl. They discover the grand and royal cities amidst a country abounding in souvenirs of a tragic and turbulent past with picturesque scenery striking the imagination and appealing to the heart."[1] As the train journey from London was now reduced to eighteen hours, Scotland was much more accessible, and Margaret liked to meet her guests in her phaeton when they arrived by train at Kincardine station, though rarely on Sundays, owing to the strict Scottish observance of the Sabbath.

There were family members old and young: Lord Lansdowne and the Shelburnes; the Willoughby de Eresbys, their cousin Lord Clare, and daughter Elizabeth with her husband, Sir Gilbert Heathcote; Lord Elphinstone on leave from India, Admiral Fleeming; Georgina Villiers; and Lady Louisa Howard, Emily's sister-in-law. Always included were old friends, such as the Earl and Countess of Ellesmere, the 3rd Earl Grey with his wife and sister, the Viscount Emlyn, the ladies Abercorn, Abercromby, Dunsmore and the French-born Countess Tankerville and her daughter Lady Malmesbury,

Colonel and Mrs Erskine and Mr Sneyd. There were friends from the Whig aristocracy: the Duke of Bedford; Lady Cowper and her children; Earl Granville; Lord and Lady Canning before they left for India in 1856; and Sir Charles Wood, chancellor of the exchequer, future Viscount Halifax. Always expected, but invariably called back to London on business was the politician Lord John Russell (prime minister 1846–52, 1865–6) and his parents-in-law, the Earl and Countess of Minto. Neighbours such as Edward Ellice and the de Mauleys, Lord Lynedoch, Lord Rutherfurd and Lord Murray came for short stays. The diplomats included the Persignys, with the French embassy attachés, Count Pahlen of Russia and Count Károlyi from Hungary. The most frequent visitors from France, who could always be relied on to amuse each other, were Auguste Morny, the Lavalettes, the Delesserts with their daughter Cécile de Nadaillac, the duc de Caumont, and the writer Prosper Mérimée.

Margaret's guests would have recognized the routine organized for guests in Scotland as described by Mérimée:

> An agreeable life going from one mansion to another where the hospitality is on such a scale that I despair of ever finding the right adjective for it, and which is unique to this aristocratic country. We eat like ogres and drink like Templars, starting in the morning with a hearty breakfast of meat and fish dishes with tea or coffee, then the ladies clad in red or blue check stockings, heavy shoes, short skirts set out to jump over bushes, hop over walls without touching them much to my surprise and amusement. We go on excursions by boat and pony in the same day, always to places where we can be sure to find a substantial lunch waiting for us at around 2 o'clock. Then we make our way back to the house around 7 when we change for a dinner which never seems to end. Eating well seems to be the great pleasure. The best part of the day is the morning when one is left free, the only drawback is a beast called the midge, microscopic insects but as venomous as vipers which eat people – my hands are swollen, ears bitten – but nonetheless people still go out. One gets used to the rain and as long as it is not pouring torrents

one is expected to walk. Even though the paths are streaming with water and the mountains are almost invisible one always returns to the house saying 'What a beautiful walk'. In the evening after dinner everyone reads books, writes letters, for conversation and entertaining each other is not an English custom.[2]

In this respect Tulliallan was different, for conversation was so important to Margaret that she cast her net wide to provide "new talk" for her guests. High on her list was Lady Ellesmere, always "en première ligne" for good conversation, while Félix de Lavalette, "éminemment français", could be relied on to animate a party, and two other popular talkers were Caroline Norton, the granddaughter of the playwright Richard Brinsley Sheridan, who "tells stories in a beautiful whisper, which amuses the gentlemen" and Richard Monckton Milnes, future Lord Houghton, wit, politician and man about town, whom Margaret had greatly disliked when they first met at Rossie Priory in 1848, but, as happened often with her, had subsequently become a friend. Since so many people visited Tulliallan on their way to or from other houses, there was always plenty of gossip from royal Balmoral, the ducal Inverary (Argyll), Dunrobin (Sutherland), Hamilton Palace (Hamilton), Drumlanrig Castle (Buccleuch), and from Dalmeny, Keir and Glenquoich, respectively the mansions of Lord Rosebery, William Stirling and Edward Ellice. As there was so little talk of politics in other people's houses, Margaret tried to encourage her own guests to discuss the issues of the day, but she records few revelations except, very unexpectedly from Lady Malmesbury, wife of a minister, who described Benjamin Disraeli as a "dangerous man" and talked quite openly about the divisions in the Tory government, kept together by Lord Derby.

However, since the diarist Henry Greville was such a frequent visitor, as was from 1863 the Flahauts' former enemy, the redoubtable J. T. Delane, editor of *The Times*, the subject of politics must surely have come up in their company. Certainly Delane was charmed by his stay: ". . . this is one of the finest places I ever saw. Beautiful terraced gardens, glorious woods reaching down to the Forth, and fine views of Stirling and the Ochils and Grampians. The house full of fine things."[3] Ever sympathetic to the cause of Poland in 1858 they invited the Zamoyskis. Margaret described them to Emily:

> . . . she seems a most devoted wife to a very suffering
> husband, very natural and très comme il faut. The sister is the
> ugliest girl I ever saw, her face half Chinese, half Calmuck
> but with the sémillantes [sparkling] graces of the Poles which
> she exercised upon your Papa for whom she professed a sort
> of culte saying she admired him more than any young man.
> She carried off his photograph and said his image was
> engraved on her heart. All perfect specimens of the Polish
> character and seem to have one idea, one interest, one subject
> of conversation, their nationality.

Lady Ellesmere, Henry Greville's sister, was delighted with the hospitality, which, she said, "combined the warm-heartedness of the English with the courtesy of the French".

The weather, so often abominable, with continual rain and violent storms did not affect the enjoyment of the good air and exercise. The excellent sport – fishing perch, shooting hares, grouse, wild ducks, rabbits – was the main attraction, and not only for adults. Since she considered a taste for sport the attribute of a real gentleman, nothing delighted Margaret more than to see her grandson, "Clan", wearing the kilt and enjoying estate life accompanied by the gamekeepers, "good as gold, gay as a lark, full of mischief, the pleasantest compound for his age". However, she warned him to keep away from cultivated land: "I think that young Gentlemen would do better not to trespass upon the fields in culture" and recalled that "it is the interest of Landlords to respect the property of farmers! The *sports* of the *aristocracy* are in great measure the cause of *democracy* in England, and such offences should be carefully avoided. One *gallop* may destroy a whole crop!" In July 1867, when too ill to travel from Paris to Scotland she rejoiced to hear that he was established happily at Tulliallan and longed to have his news.

She planned excursions to famous beauty spots. One of the most successful was the 5½ hour trip to Lake Katrine in September 1854 with Henry Greville, who was so enthusiastic about scenery that he "didn't seem to mind missing his comforts, coat flew open, his hat blew off, and his hair flowing, alternated shouts of admiration with extracts of operatic airs". They slept in a comfortable inn, much appreciated by another member of the party, Count Károlyi, who showed more interest in his cigar and luncheon, dinner and bed than in the scenery. From there they saw the lake to great advantage, "on a soft, clear, grey day with gleams of light on the distant hills and with every tree and rock reflected in lake as in a mirror of silver", and rowing on the water in the morning "our boat seemed to float on air".

Excellent company as she was, Margaret was often a guest in other Scottish houses, and her experiences come to life in her letters. Staying with the Kinnairds at Rossie Priory in September 1848, she was affronted by the "insufferable conceit and vulgarity" of Richard Monckton Milnes, "who lords it over the whole society . . . and whose musical powers resemble those of a bull bellowing out song after song in German, French, Italian, English so pronounced they might have been in any unknown tongue".[4] However, he was not intimidated by the disapproval of this very grande dame, and rather disarmingly, presented her with some letters written by the Duke of Atholl in the eighteenth century to ladies of her mother's family. She was particularly pleased with an anecdote about Lady Perth, her father's sister, in which she had admitted, "When I canna spell a word right I just make a scratch under the word that they may take it for wit!" At Fingask Castle, home of the Murray Threiplands, she "admired exceedingly many curious relics of exiled Stuarts", such as miniatures, the rock-crystal watch of Mary Queen of Scots, the camp bed of Prince Charles Edward, old dresses and weapons. Steeped in hopes and illusions for the future her fiercely Jacobite hosts had become involved with two imposters claiming to be the Sobieski Stuarts, but did not disagree when Margaret suggested that all their stories could not be true.[5]

From Fingask she went on to the Breadalbanes at Taymouth Castle, then to William Stirling of Keir, near Dunblane, a house full of interesting pictures, books and china. Her host had "a rage for proverbs, mottoes and sentiments which pervade the house and you are not allowed a minute repose from literary occupation. Even the doyloy [sic] on your plate at dinner conveys a precept not always confined to temperance". Interested in livestock, Margaret inspected the magnificent animals, though she could "not say so much for their keeping, for I never saw more filthy places and even their food did not look clean or their coats smooth". She then described the strange contrasts in the house:

> . . . all his purchases are in the best possible taste and

everything is comfortable, and well arranged downstairs but the bedrooms seem very little cared for with dirty chintz and few comforts. There is gaz in all the bedrooms, however I did obtain a pair of candles but no oil for my night lamp.

During this visit to Keir, the presence of another house guest, Mr Brookfield, a clergyman, "a very agreeable man, with no humbug about him, no church millinery in his ideas, preached an excellent sermon on the conversion of St. Paul", provided a rare glimpse of her attitude to religion, and dislike of High Church Puseyites.

At home, although Charles had to remind her that their "fortune is not like that of the Willoughby d'Eresby's or the Ellesmere's" she found she could afford not only to entertain but also to improve the house and its surroundings. This was her own province, although she complained to Emily in July 1853 that Charles would no longer look after the farm and kitchen garden and "will do nothing, only reserves to himself the privilege of finding faults with everything that is done and never giving an opinion when he is asked d'avance". Overgrown trees were moved, others planted to good effect and more peach and pear trees of the best sort introduced, the flower garden redesigned and the kitchen garden well stocked. She took over the farm, which became an absorbing interest, especially her chickens which she bred to prize-winning standard and housed in clean, warm, well-sanded quarters, protected from foxes. Exhibiting at home and abroad, she proudly informed Emily in 1858: "Last year I got three prizes from the Highland Society and this year I expect the French creatures to be still more admired for they are very rare specimens which gained the prize at the French agricultural show". The next year she tried to show them at the Crystal Palace Poultry Show and was annoyed when they arrived too late for admission.

In addition, she improved her other livestock, buying Alderney Bulls, stocking the park with "black faced" sheep and building a model dairy, with prints hanging on the walls. Always wanting the best, from Paris in April 1858 she asked Emily to help find a man and wife to manage the cows and dairy between them, from Somerset or Wiltshire where the cheese was so much better than in Scotland. While in Paris she took a great interest in the Agricultural Exhibition of 1857[6] and used her influence to see that a plough invented by Lord Willoughby de Eresby was well shown. Whatever she did, whether furthering her husband's career, raising poultry or making cheese and butter, was done thoroughly and she found these country pursuits far better suited to her years and tastes than all the amusements of London. Of course, ownership of Tulliallan was not all pleasure. Besides which, obtaining a good tenant for Meikleour proved almost impossible; plagues of rabbits devoured everything; storms brought down hundreds of trees; fifteen head of cattle were lost in the epidemic of 1860. It was never easy to replace staff and farmworkers; the route of the new railway proposed in 1861 had to be argued out between the trustees and neighbours, and there was not enough money to pay for all Margaret's schemes.

Another difficulty was the endless wrangling over her father's settlements which her stepmother and half-sister wished to overturn. Charles, who saw the irony of this, remarked to Lord Murray in May 1855 that it amused him that he and Margaret "should respect Lord Keith's settlement and that old Lady Keith and Mrs. Villiers should attack them". Yet, in spite of the protracted demands from Queeney and Georgina's lawyers and further battles with the trustees, the Flahauts managed their affairs so well that in 1858 Charles wrote, again to Lord Murray:

> I only laugh at the blindness of mankind. Poor Ld Keith
> enraged at his daughter choosing to marry me disinherits her
> for fear an extravagant & profligate Frenchman should
> dissipate his & her fortune & it turns out that after 41 years
> her fortune is in perfect order, while by the act of his widow
> & of his favoured other daughter all his plans of creating a
> great property are completely annihilated.

He might have also added that he and Margaret had greatly improved her Scottish estates for the benefit of posterity, as her father might have wished. There is no doubt that Margaret, as a true Scotswoman, was at her best at Tulliallan, making it a comfortable, attractive and happy home, offering generous hospitality to her many friends, and enjoying its amenities in full measure while confronting the problems with staff, livestock, climate, finance, with all the force of her shrewd and stubborn character.

As long as France was a republic, Charles had refused to accept an official appointment and, in April 1851, turned down an invitation from the president, Louis Napoleon, to become ambassador in London.[7] His attitude changed with the establishment of the Second Empire, and he then accepted the various offices offered by Napoleon III. This meant that after the death of Louise in 1853, he and Margaret were obliged to spend increasingly long periods in Paris. The journey was now shorter thanks to the introduction of new steamers such as *The Empress* which crossed from Dover to Calais in 1 hour 18 minutes. During these years they doggedly upheld the importance of an alliance between France and England, and in April 1859 Charles affirmed, yet again, ". . . what interests me more than anything is that the relations between my two countries should continue to be friendly".

However, neither the English monarchy nor the government – whether led by Viscount Palmerston, Lord John Russell or Lord Derby – trusted Napoleon III, although he had declared himself in 1852 to be "very reasonable, pacific and friendly to England". Led by J. T. Delane, the redoubtable editor of *The Times,* the British press was particularly hostile, publishing throughout 1852 a series of anonymous letters from Paris signed by "An Englishman". Incensed by a particularly strong attack, "detestable, like everything else which appears in its columns", Charles rose to the defence of French policies, and the emperor stated in 1853 that if England did not wish to produce a league of all the powers of Europe against her, she should stop harbouring revolutionaries. Although the two countries allied with Turkey against Russia during the Crimean War from October 1853 until 1856, the relationship was never easy, and feelings continued to run high. Once again, the French felt they were justified in their complaints against the misuse of English hospitality when it emerged at the trial of Orsini for attempting to assassinate the emperor in 1858 that the plot had been arranged in London and the bombs made in Birmingham.[8] Whenever England had reason to dislike French policies, such as the annexation of Savoy in 1860, all Charles could do was to urge the British minister to remonstrate in a friendly not hostile spirit since the emperor was entitled to be treated as an ally, not an enemy. The attacks from the British press continued. *The Times* on 6 July 1859 condemned Napoleon III as "a suspicious fraud and a most dangerous enemy",[9] then, after publishing a letter from the emperor in August 1860 to Persigny, his ambassador in London, declaring his desire for a "new era of peace", Delane commented sarcastically that "The Emperor's letter will be read with interest by all and with satisfaction by those who can forget the logic of facts."[10]

By October 1860 diplomatic relations had reached such a low point that Charles was invited, at first informally, through Auguste Morny, to replace Persigny as ambassador in London in the hope of repairing the damage and preserving peace between the two countries. Although he was now 75 years old, this time Charles accepted, as indeed had Talleyrand at the same age in 1830. Lord Granville, now in the Foreign Office, applauded this decision, writing that "Charles's eventful and chequered career made him essentially the most international man of his day. He seemed marked out to be natural mediator between angry passions and suspicions of two countries in each of which he was equally at home."[11] On 2 December 1860 Charles went to Windsor to present his credentials and on 6 December his appointment was welcomed in an article in *The Times*.

Margaret, who thought Edward Ellice had used his influence with the newspaper, wrote to thank him for his congratulations on 5 December. She explained that Charles

> . . . had no wish to re-enter public life and in any other circumstance would have declined the proferred honour, but when he was assured of the Emperor's ardent desire to be on friendly terms with England and to develop to the utmost his liberal measures at home as well as in our commercial relations he could not refuse to associate himself with such honourable measures and contribute as powerfully as he could to maintain the good relations between the two countries which has always been the dearest object of his life. And which he sincerely believes to be so necessary for the prosperity of both France and England. It is very gratifying to him to see how his appointment has been received here by all classes and he seems to be hailed like the dove with the olive branch. The Queen has received him very graciously, the Government has accepted him without hesitation, the Press has been more than civil, the corps diplomatique professes to be enchanted at the change and the society (both Whigs and Tories) have been aimable in their sayings and doings, so what is there left to wish for except youth and strength to fulfil the duties of a high position which alas! is

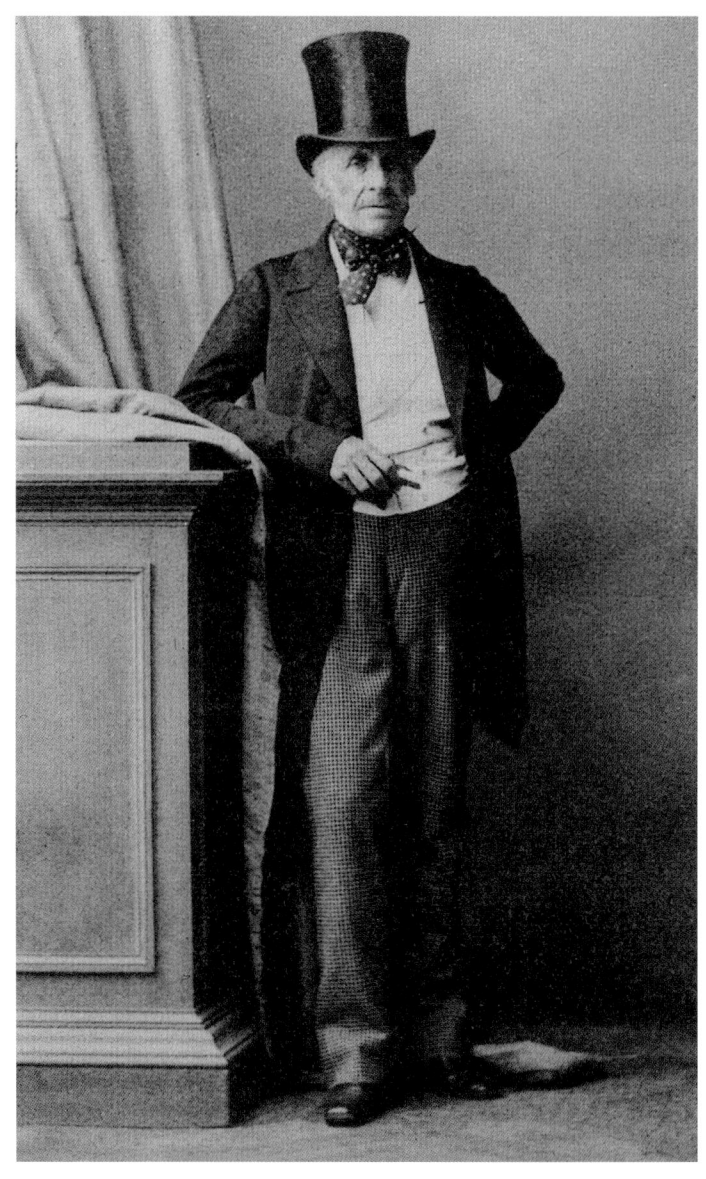

44 Photograph of Charles de Flahaut in 1862 by Disdéri

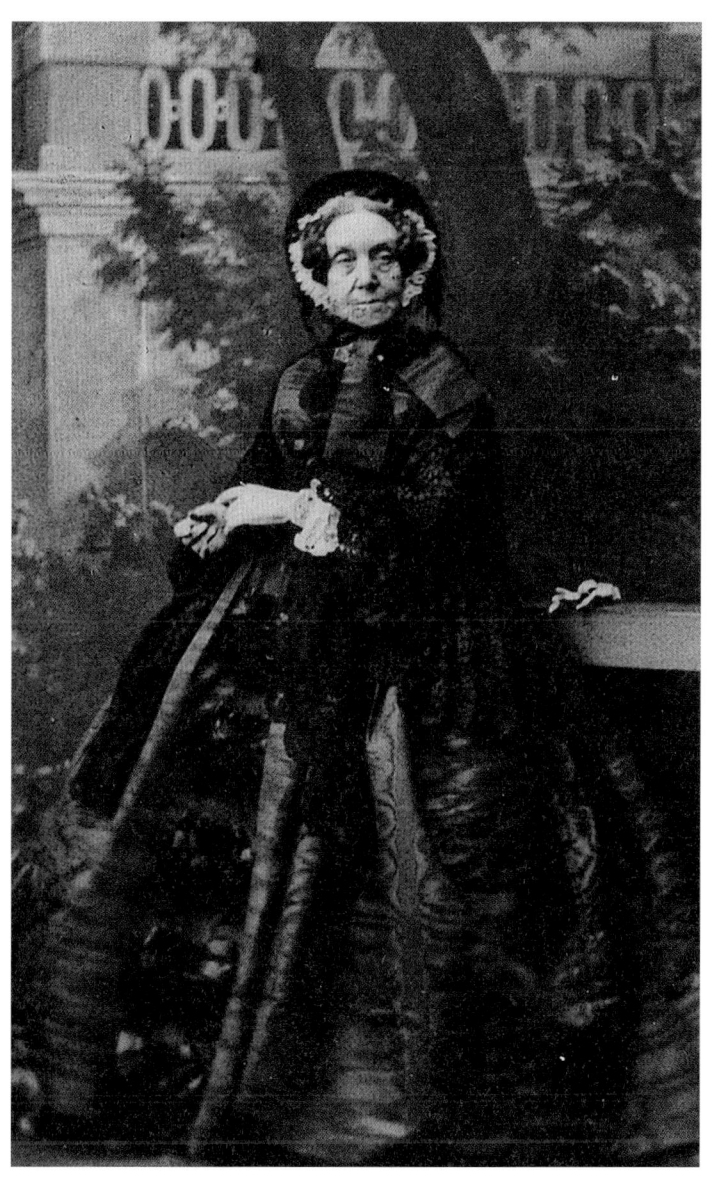

45 Photograph of Margaret de Flahaut in 1862 by Disdéri

not to be got and I therefore feel that the social part will be a signal failure. However we must do our best and trust to the indulgence of our friends where there are deficiencies! The only dissenting voice has come from poor Emily from anxiety about his health but she is reconciled now seeing he is quite well and much pleased with his very flattering reception. He himself says it is so far beyond what he expected that he now feels tempted to resign immediately to carry off his laurels before a withered leaf has time to appear.[12]

Whereas his mission in Vienna had been more social than political, now it was the other way round, and he declared himself ready to obey all the instructions coming from the foreign minister, M. Édouard Thouvenel, who told him, "By your presence alone you make a great difference." This was not so easy. Napoleon III was regarded with suspicion by Queen Victoria and Prince Albert, and politicians such as Lord Clarendon believed that "Nobody will ever be at rest as long as that Conspirator is at the head of that nation of brigands."[13] The presence of the Orléans family in exile caused difficulties and the emperor was irritated by Queen Victoria's friendship with them. There was further awkwardness at the time of the International Exhibition of 1862 when the widowed Lady Holland offered the hospitality of Holland House to Queen Marie-Amélie, making it a place of pilgrimage for Orleanists. In these circumstances Charles thought it best to leave them alone, so when they attended the same events the princes never looked in his direction, neither did he in theirs.

Charles disagreed with the emperor's policy of founding a Latin Empire in Mexico ruled by the Austrian prince Maximilian and disapproved of his handling of the problem of the Papal States, and of the activities of Garibaldi in Italy. He hoped to see both France and England reduce their expenditure on weaponry through a closer understanding. Always an admirer of Prince Albert, whom he had defended against the calumnies of various people in high places, he regarded his premature death in December 1861 as a European calamity. Had the prince lived he might have helped Charles smooth over many of the difficulties between the emperor and the queen.

While Charles established good relations with the Foreign Office, and was on such friendly terms with Lord John Russell, that he could "do business with him under all circumstances", Margaret took some time to assume her responsibilities. In March 1861 she told Lord Canning that

> I take my new duties easy for the present as my health does not allow me to go out at night as long as the weather is cold so except for a few more dinners and some 'shilling' nights as you used to call them I have had no additional exertion. After Easter I shall be obliged to give some horrible routs but in the meantime the death of Duchess of Kent has plunged us into such deep mourning that there will be nothing at court – a relief.

She was in no hurry to exchange Coventry House for the ambassador's residence at Albert Gate, where Madame Persigny had stayed on for some months and the interiors were not only dirty but needed redecoration.

After much expense and trouble the embassy, furnished to a very high standard, was ready in June 1862 for the International Exhibition. Whether entertaining there or at Coventry House, Margaret as an experienced hostess always rose splendidly to the occasion, giving not only exquisite dinners but "handsome and splendid banquets". The most assiduous attentions were paid to members of the dynasty, such as Louis-Lucien Bonaparte, who Charles thought represented the real Bonaparte type, with his high forehead, deep-set eyes and intelligent expression, unlike his cousin, Napoleon III. When Prince Murat and his American wife arrived for the banquet held in their honour, the Flahauts received them at the foot of the staircase, and everyone arose as they entered the salon as for reigning royalty. Diplomatic success came in February 1862 when Charles told Lord Clarendon that "the relations between the 2 countries are now on a satisfactory footing"; though if they had continued as they were a few months ago he had meant to resign and give notice of his intention to Palmerston and to Lord Russell;[14]

He continued in office until October 1862 when he resigned on hearing that Thouvenel had been replaced as foreign minister by Édouard Drouyn de Lhuys. Although asked to remain, he stood firm and returned to Coventry House, leaving Albert Gate free for his successor, Baron Gros. Yet his career was not over, for in 1864 he was appointed Chancellor of the Legion of Honour and he and Margaret once again took up residence in Paris.

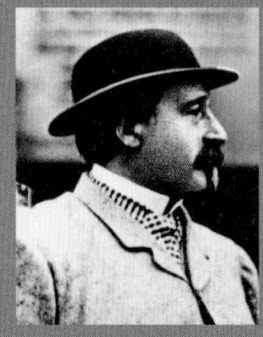

CHAPTER 21

The Final Phase:
Paris I

Paris c'est surtout cet esprit vif, léger, rapide,
. . . cette causerie où se joue à ravir ce jeu de raquettes
de la conversation . . . l'œil charmé se porte sur les groupes
de femmes qui, en agitant l'éventail, écoutent les causeurs
inclinés à demi ; les yeux scintillent comme des diamants,
les épaules luisent comme le satin, les lèvres s'ouvrent
comme les fleurs

Théophile Gautier

In this final phase of their lives Charles and Margaret stayed often in Paris, and both were to die there. The return to France came about through their close relationship with Auguste Morny, who was now very influential. Collaborating with his rich mistress, the Belgian comtesse Le Hon, Morny had made such profitable investments in a paper business, a sugar beet refinery, in railways and mines that he could afford to live in a fine house on the Champs-Élysées, and, as a member of the Jockey Club and art collector, was a well-known man about town. Elected deputy in 1842 for the Puy-de-Dôme, he was also involved in politics.[1] Since witnessing the deplorable civil and economic consequences of the Revolution of 1848, Charles, like millions of French voters, welcomed the election as president of Louis Napoleon Bonaparte, son of Queen Hortense, solely on account of his name. After calling on the new president at the Elysée (30 October 1849), he wrote to Margaret that "nothing could exceed the kindness of the reception I met with, he took me by the hand and told me I was mixed up with his oldest recollections and hoped he might consider me as an old friend."[2]

Although very taken with the president's apparently straightforward manner, Charles turned down his offer of the London embassy in 1851, saying he could not serve a republic. His refusal disappointed Morny, who as the son of Queen Hortense was the natural half-brother of the president, a relationship he signified by displaying a hydrangea flower, or hortensia, in his buttonhole. At first he and the president got on well, and from January 1849 met twice daily for private discussions about people and events, and as the Austrian diplomat Rudolf Apponyi observed rather mischievously:

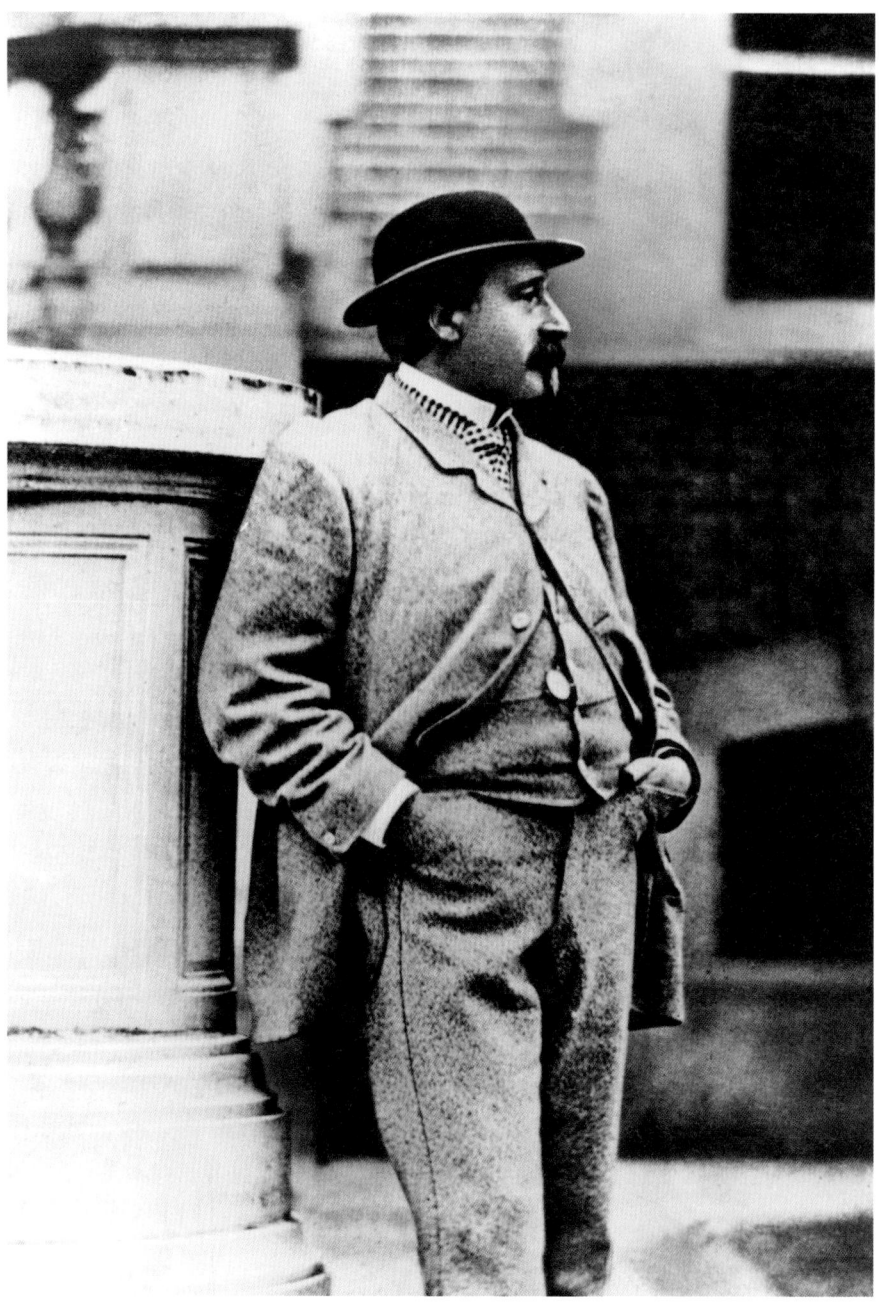

> Ever since winning the confidence of Prince Louis, the
> magnificent Morny has assumed even grander manners: and,
> as if he was the brother of the king at the court of Louis XIV
> he is now known by the title of 'Monsieur', so we are
> informed that 'Monsieur attended the salon of Madame X,' or
> 'Monsieur is not feeling well'.[3]

Morny was determined to avoid civil war and put an end to the uncertain political situation in which the extremists threatened to overthrow the president. With the support of Jacques Leroy de St Arnaud, Jean-Gilbert Victor Fialin de Persigny, Charlemagne Émile de Maupas, Jean François Mocquard, and Charles he plotted the coup d'état which took place on 2 December 1851."The coup d'état was a political drama produced by M. de Morny as brilliantly as in any play by Eugène Scribe. Like M. Scribe, with his watch key alone he unlocked the great doors of a palace for his hero."[4] It was a tremendous gamble which necessity alone could justify, but which succeeded. The assembly was dissolved, political opponents imprisoned or exiled, and the army and police overcame the resistance at the barricades with a surprisingly small loss of life.

When all was over, Margaret, who must have been consulted about the plot, received the news from Morny by electric telegraph, one of the first telegrams transmitted across the Channel,[5] followed next day by a letter from Charles:

> Never was a secret better kept and plan better executed.
> Auguste has been heroic, nothing can exceed his courage,
> firmness, good sense, prudence, calm, good humour,
> gentleness and tact during all that was going on and at the
> same time so simple and a total absence of vanity and conceit.
> All those who love him may be proud of him.[6]

Appointed minister of the interior on 17 December 1851, Morny set about clearing Paris of trouble-makers and reforming the administration of his ministry.

46 Photograph of Charles Auguste de Morny

Present at the proclamation of the Second Empire, Charles was the first to receive an embrace from the emperor. This distinction was accorded him as the last surviving officer on whom Napoleon conferred a similar honour on his departure from Malmaison in 1815.[7] In further recognition of this precious link with the First Empire official appointments followed, first as senator, next as a member of the Club Impérial, both accepted after much hesitation, then in 1860 as ambassador to London and finally in 1864 as Grand Chancellor of the Legion of Honour. Morny, who had resigned as minister of the interior in 1852, now returned to political life. He was made President of the Chamber (the Corps législatif, whose members were elected for a term of six years by universal suffrage), put in charge of the Lottery to raise funds for the Exposition Universelle of 1855, and in 1856 went to Russia as the brilliant representative of the emperor at the coronation of Alexander II. His rise to power was observed by Barante, who commented, "Morny's star is burning brightly. It is rumoured that if the Emperor took over the command of the army in the next campaign the Empress would be Regent and Morny would preside over her cabinet."[8] However, contentious issues soon surfaced, and one of the first was the imperial decision to confiscate the Orléans property. Although this measure was strongly opposed by Charles,[9] Morny[10] and Alexandre Walewski, the emperor refused to change his mind.

Even before Charles had accepted an official appointment, his alignment with the Second Empire was criticized by Emily, who had remained friendly to the Orléans family in exile. – Margaret therefore did her best to justify his position – and her own – in a long letter to Emily of June 1852:

> I have heard of no intention on the part of your father to take office at present and, as far as I personally am concerned, I should much prefer remaining in our independent situation to living in a fusty ministère in Paris surrounded by vulgar people and lauding d'obligation the joys of absolute government. In fact the only official position that would suit our present circumstances would be the embassy here which we would not like to have (even were it offered) on account of displacing our friend Walewski. However all this is for you alone, as I have never said as much to your Papa I think he should be left to exercise his own judgment in circumstances

which so nearly touch his country, his honour and his interest. Politically speaking, I do not see any reason why he should not accept office or serve the government in any way that suits him for having once made le plongeon that connects him with the present order of things I think he is almost bound to support it as usefully as he can and I believe that most people would think it a duty to do so looking back to his antecedents as well as to the part he took on December 2nd.

I am afraid, dear Emily, that you do not take the just and patriotic view of your father's political conduct which it really deserves, which makes me wish to put it before your eyes in the light in which he has always appeared to me – noble and elevated! When I married he was only 30 years of age, a Bonapartist to the bone, and high in military reputation and social estimation. Every advance was made to him by the governments of the Restoration who would have purchased his services at any price if he would have adopted their flag: but as he considered that government as a stain upon the national honour and in opposition to the will and welfare of the country he sacrificed every motive of ambition or interest that might have swayed a man of his age and his position and remained 15 years in retirement without any connection with the governments of Louis XVIII or Charles X. In 1830 when the tricolour flag reappeared and a new era opening up which promised great prosperity and happiness to his country, he then considered it as the duty of every honest man to serve the new dynasty and did so faithfully and zealously until its last hours without however ever giving up his character as a Bonapartist. Having always honoured the name of the Emperor he showed the greatest respect to his family when he had an opportunity of seeing them and promoted their interest whenever it was in his power to serve them.

After the calamitous events of 1848 when France fell into the impure hands of anarchists and socialists you know how he spurned the republic and its vicious constitution and remained almost the solitary instance among his countrymen and friends who refused to acknowledge a government which he considered a disgrace and would be the ruin of his country and he carried this feeling so far that even after Prince Louis Napoleon became President he never left a card upon the ambassador of the Republic till the arrival of our old friend, Walewski, made it impossible to abstain from doing so any longer. Here again his conduct has been guided entirely by feelings of patriotism and I now ask you how can he refuse his full allegiance to the Prince when he has the deep conviction that he has saved France from the dreadful fate which was threatened in 1852? That he has confidence in him for governing the country with a firm hand and a wise head and that the chief of state called to power by 7 millions of the French people is the nephew and heir of Napoleon with whom he had served so gloriously and from whom he had received every mark of approbation favour and distinction?

The only objection that could be brought forward to his entire liberty of action is our respect and attachment to the family at Claremont which remains in full force but you must recollect that in the first instance it was, as your father has always said, un marriage de raison pas d'inclination, and tho' afterwards it became one of great affection as long as the duc d'Orleans lived. Yet with him and Madame we lost our only real friends in the family and have never had any marks of confidence from them ever since. Had Mr de Flahaut been allowed to remain in the household of course every other sentiment would have been sacrificed to that duty. This is a long story which I'm afraid will bore you but I am anxious to reassure you about the anxiety you seem to feel that he may be inclined to do something you and your friends would be ashamed of and I think you need have no apprehension on that score if you look back on his past life.[11]

As Emily continued to attack her father, Morny – always close to her – explained that he really had no choice, for "since he owed everything to the

Emperor, was his aide de camp, remaining loyal to the very last, and ever since has devoted himself to his memory, would it not be strange if he had nothing to do with his nephew?" He then pointed out that it was not Louis Napoleon who had dethroned Louis-Philippe, and that his election as president had saved France from anarchy.[12] When Charles, who also sent her a full justification of his actions, pleaded with her not to let politics spoil their family life, he seems to have convinced her, as they remained as close as ever.

Charles soon came to regard the Second Empire as no more than a charade. While admitting that the emperor was good-natured he thought him lazy, slow to come to a decision and inconsistent, in total contrast to his uncle, Napoleon I.[13] With his innate sense of diplomacy he was alarmed in 1854 when he heard him accuse the Emperor of Russia of iniquity, for such words were "never forgiven or forgotten and the era of conquest over". As for his own position, he was plagued by place hunters, hated by political opponents – Legitimists, Orleanists and Republicans – and felt ill at ease in the increasingly vulgar new rich Second Empire society. Morny, who felt the same about Louis Napoleon, confided his dislike:

> . . . incapable of friendship: – only happy in the company of flatterers and toadies. He used me because he couldn't find anyone else for the coup d'état of December 2nd. But once I had risked my life and done what was required, then he got rid of me.[14]

Disillusioned with the Empire, but still remaining part of it, father and son depended on each other for advice and encouragement. From their correspondence it is clear that they were very close, and Morny admitted his need for "a true friend" like his father. Just as Talleyrand used the "tu" with the young Charles, and then the "vous" in his later years, so Charles did the same with the adult Auguste, using the "vous" and addressing him either as "mon cher Auguste", or "mon cher ami". For his part, Morny wrote "Mon cher ami" to his father and "Chère Madame de Flahaut" to Margaret, who had made him welcome at her homes in Paris, London and Scotland, and shared his interest in art. There can be no doubt that Margaret and Charles did everything to smooth over the disadvantages of his illegitimate birth, and he acknowledged their concern in a letter to Emily of March 3, 1851: "I love my father and sisters, that is my real family, more than anything else in this world." He showed his attachment by giving jewellery to the Flahaut girls and encouraged Charles to invite them to stay and occupy "Auguste's apartment. It would have made him very happy and he has begged me to say so." The elderly Charles was touched when, to mark his birthday, usually forgotten at this stage of his life, Morny bought him an expensive gold snuff-box. Now that the Flahaut Paris house had been sold, he offered to build another, which they could rent, but instead, Charles, sometimes accompanied by Margaret, lived with him at the Hôtel de Morny, 15, avenue des Champs-Élysées, and used his carriages. The two men, who clearly enjoyed each other's company, talked politics incessantly, played piquet at home, dined out in restaurants, visited the theatres together and Charles declared that Auguste and a bright coal fire were the two most comforting sights in Paris.

Morny's life as a *grand seigneur* and the dubious methods he used to pay for it inspired two contemporary novels. In Émile Zola's *Son Excellence Eugène Rougon,* he is Monsieur de Marsy,[15] and the character of Monsieur Mora in the *Le Nabab* by Alphonse Daudet is also a faithful portrait. Besides his political position as President of the Corps législatif he was actively investing in industry, speculating in property, and seizing every opportunity for making money, taking full advantage of the current economic upsurge. Two of his most successful business ventures were the race course at Longchamp and the resort of Deauville, and these still flourish as proof of his financial acumen and vision.

Margaret, who followed his financial, political and social success and referred to him, tongue-in-cheek, as "the great man", was amused when with "the illusion of becoming a country gentleman" he restored a huge château at Nades in the Auvergne. He also bought a retreat at Viroflay near Versailles, where he stabled his horses, and lived in great luxury at the Hôtel de Lassay, his official residence as President of the Corps législatif, where he held balls, concerts, theatricals and receptions. Henry Greville, who had known him since 1829, described dinner in the grand manner with Morny, now covered with orders and crosses, for the Flahauts, ambassadors, and the imperial noblesse: "a very handsome repast and fine plate, heaps of servants, two in bag-wigs and swords stationed at entrance of the saloon, besides an enormous porter in the hall armed with a halberd."[16] From his grandmother, Adèle de Souza, as well as from Charles and Margaret he had acquired a taste for collecting works of art which impressed connoisseurs, Eugène Delacroix among them:

> Never have I seen such luxury. His pictures looked much
> better in his own house. There is a magnificent Watteau; I
> was struck by the wonderful skill it displayed. Flanders and
> Venice are united in this painting, but one or two of the
> Ruysdaels, especially a snow scene, and a very simple seascape
> where there is little to be seen except a grey sea and a few
> small boats, seemed to me the very summit of art because the
> art is entirely concealed . . . To have pictures like these always
> before one's eyes in one's own home must be the most
> exquisite pleasure.[17]

They were shown to great advantage in the Gallery at the Hôtel de Lassay.[18]

The director of the Beaux Arts, M. de Chennevières, admired not only his taste in pictures and the manner in which they were shown but the man himself: "the most perfectly polite, the most elegant, the best bred man of his time".[19] Chennevières certainly seems justified in hinting that Morny modelled his pose of "gentleman of the old school" on M. de Flahaut, "who has so much class". His calm, courtesy, charm, easy manner and tact, recalled his father, whose aristocratic way of living he copied, including the liveries for his footmen and valets. From his first visit in 1829 he was enthralled by Scotland and when he had his own children talked to them about Tulliallan. It is unlikely that they ever went there as Margaret doubted whether his wife "with her irregular habits and temper could ever accommodate herself to English life and that it would vex him if she were to exhibit all her capricious fancies in a country where they would not be tolerated".[20] Morny met his wife, Princess Sophie Troubetskoy, during his mission to Moscow for the coronation of Alexander II, and the news of their engagement came as a surprise, as in his letters he complained that Russia "is not fit for a dog, the women are hideous, the courtiers servile, the pavements bad and no theatre is worth going to".[21]

Whereas the passionate relationship between Charles and Margaret became a successful partnership, the marriage of Morny was far from that. When he married Sophie the Flahauts were pleased, since this would mean

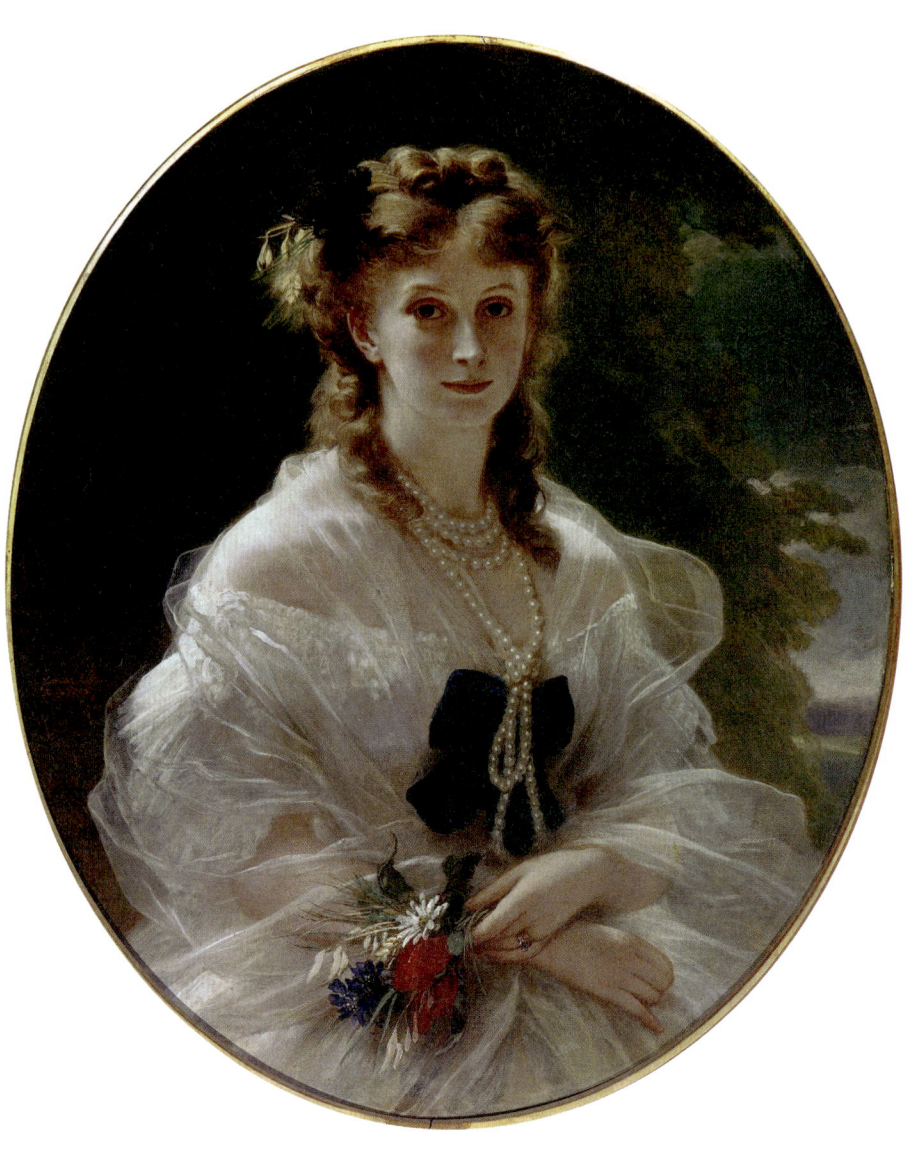

47 Franz Xaver Winterhalter (1805–1873):
Princess Sophie Troubetskoy, duchesse de Morny

a break from his longstanding, tyrannical mistress Fanny Le Hon, and they looked forward to meeting the bride. Margaret sent her first impression to Emily in February 1858:

> . . . she looks very delicate and seems quite transparent, like a *bergère* in *Saxe, pâte tendre blanc et rose* . . . and scarcely eats enough to keep her alive. No soup, no fish, no vegetables, no sweet things, only a small bit of meat or chicken.[22]

Her behaviour was not as refined as her looks, for she was very independent, did as she pleased, refused to eat the Présidence dinners, left her guests abruptly to smoke cigarettes "like a trooper" and sometimes, without taking leave, slipped off to the Opera with a friend. No-one could call her gracious, and, given her youth, all were amazed at her extraordinary aplomb and self-possession. Georgina, who had expected to make friends but was rebuffed, reported back to Emily on 8 April 1858 that she had never met

> anybody who had so little le désir de plaire & I hear she has no success, which is a great pity, for she might have been of use to Auguste. When people are introduced to her she hardly looks at them & often spends her whole evening without uttering, which is thought très maussade [sullen] & as you know French people expect *des frais*.[23]

Knowing how important details of dress and jewellery were to Emily, Margaret described the fairy-like appearance of Madame de Morny at a Tuileries dinner:

> . . . [she looked] pretty in a most ethereal dress, and appeared like a silvery vapeur passing over a starry firmament! To descend from Parnassus, her gown was of white tulle with a shower of small silver spots over a light blue tulle, which 2 petticoats were *bouillonné* together in festoons like the waves of the sea, and on her head she had a small tiara of diamond stars, with which her braided hair in front, and large golden curls hanging behind, made a very picturesque costume. She

only wanted a silver wand in her hand to look like the beneficent spirit in the last act of a mythological Ballet![24]

On 25 May 1858, Margaret deplored

> the sad avenir, which awaits poor Auguste – it is painful that having escaped from a virago, he should have fallen into the hands of one who in point of temper is I believe ten times worse, and a fool into the bargain. She does not even read a newspaper, so as to be able to follow the occurrences of the day, and only the night before last when somebody mentioned that explanations from Ld Canning had arrived, she asked 'But who is this Lord Canning and where is he? I've never heard anything about him.'[25]

By 17 September 1860 Margaret had not changed her mind, and, when to her great relief, Madame de Morny had cancelled a visit to London, declared:

> I never had any favour for the Russian, he [Morny] is *garde malade* and seems *très contrarié* and I've no doubt she troubles him as much as she can. I am afraid that her ways are not ignored in the world for Monsieur Pahlen [Russian ambassador] told me that she was said to be a wayward thing and so *mécontente* that she was likely to make her husband very unhappy. Pahlen gave me a deplorable account of the morals and manners of all the breed.

Later she opined:

> I never had any favour for the Russian Alliance and what I saw of her did not tend to dispel my prejudices but on Auguste's account I always felt anxious to be on friendly terms with her.

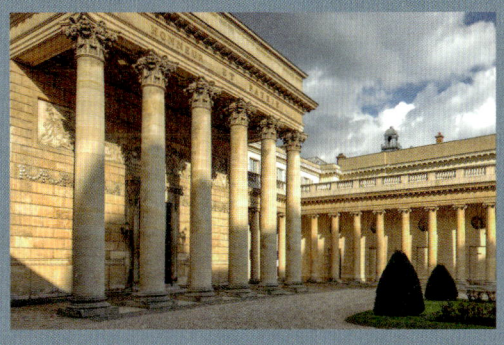

CHAPTER 22

The Final Phase:
Paris II

*Tout cela est beau aujourd'hui, pourtant je ne donnerais pas
deux sous du dernier acte*

Alfred de Musset on Empress Eugénie

W hen Napoleon III was proclaimed Emperor of the French, Charles felt obliged to spend more time in Paris to give Morny his support. Until his appointment as ambassador in London in 1860, Charles attended the Senate or Upper House when it was in session. Having served under Napoleon and shaken the world with him, he could never face idleness, and needed the excitement of daily occupation which came with an official life. Another incentive was his involvement in the publication of the correspondence of Napoleon, supervised by a commission set up under Marshal Vaillant in 1853. As a self-appointed guardian of the emperor's memory he believed he had a duty to make "it more illustrious than if the Emperor himself had been consulted on the publication".[1] From the first he disapproved of the undiscriminating selection and tried to reverse some of the resolutions adopted which did not show the emperor at his best. Each meeting of the commission, held in the Luxembourg Palace took at least four hours, sometimes longer, and, by thus slowing up the project, Charles displeased Napoleon III.

When Margaret remained in London with the invalid Louise, his letters describe how he spent his time. He renewed his friendships with the Bonaparte family – breakfasting with the Grand Duchess of Baden, and dining with Princess Mathilde, "a good hearted creature, but I am afraid must constantly get into hot water from the looseness of her tongue. Alexandre Dumas came there after dinner & also 2 Abyssinian Princes, perfectly black but very handsome, one a model for an Othello to Titian [7 April 1859]."[2] He and Margaret felt differently about the princess's brother, the clever, ambitious radical Prince Jérôme, whom they regarded with suspicion as the evil genius of France, "who might, if listened to, plunge the country into war to be succeeded by anarchy and probably a new revolution".[3] Because of his many connections Charles was hardly ever free from official engagements at the Tuileries, for dinners, balls and concerts at the Mornys and at the residence of Alexandre Walewski, now the minister for foreign affairs. He also got on well with the English ambassador Lord Cowley, who invited him to all important celebrations such as the dinner celebrating Queen Victoria's birthday on 24 May every year. For him "a rather active day was a long sitting of the committee for Napoléon's correspondence, 40 people to dinner here & afterwards ball. It was for the Plénipotentiaires (who I believe have arrived to the term [reached the end] of their labours). The dinner was well served & excellent & the ball quite charming: charming toilettes with a blaze of light to show them. I did not get to bed before 3 & left before supper".[4]

The Paris of the Second Empire maintained its reputation as the centre for luxury and elegance and Charles never grudged spending his time shopping for Margaret. He bought stockings, camisoles, caps, chose patterns for a gown from Madame Palmyre, warned her of imminent mourning for the King of Hanover in April 1851, sent patterns for her to choose from and then had her dresses made, and, advised by Morny, informed her that the "number of volants [frills] is now a minimum of nine". There were other commissions too: strawberry seeds for John Murray, rose bushes for Bowood, and bronze wall lights for Sir Charles Wood.

As long as Morny remained unmarried, Charles could live very happily with him, but Margaret was more demanding. When in Paris she missed the comfort of her London homes, especially in 1856 when they had to leave their pleasant apartment in 15, Champs-Élysées after Morny gave the house to his daughter by Madame Le Hon on her marriage to Prince Stanislas Poniatowski. Upset, Margaret complained to Emily "This makes me VERY VERY LOW as I am afraid Mr. de Flahaut will not give up Paris altogether." Worried about his health, she decided to stay as there was no one else to look after him. Her attempt to rent temporary accommodation in a modern building in Avenue Gabriel was not a success. She complained that the "chimney pieces are too narrow for our bronzes, the ceilings are very low, and everything is in proportion with that". Even worse, their kitchen had been placed in "an empty bedroom by a narrow passage BRINGING the SMELL DIRECT INTO the SITTING ROOM!", Emily sympathized, for the grandeur of Lansdowne House was pervaded by a permanent smell of Irish stew. Staying with Morny, at the Hôtel de Lassay, which saved the expense of having her own kitchen, was not satisfactory either, as his splendid apartments were too overheated and dark for Margaret: feeling the cold, he had stoves and braziers in all the "padded" rooms while she, brought up in chilly Scotland, craved for light and fresh air.

Nonetheless, true to her character, she made the most of her life in Paris. It was a different city from the one she had known during the reign of Louis-Philippe, with the Baron Haussmann supervising the broadening of the boulevards, improvements in street lighting and sanitation, and the erection of new public monuments, but against this background she remained as active as her age and health permitted. She participated in fairs organized to raise funds for charity, and taking advantage of the French craze for all things Scottish, especially tartan, she stocked her stalls with items ordered from Edinburgh. Politics remained an absorbing interest, and she observed that Morny was "having difficult time keeping unruly deputies in order – more vicious than ever. French politicians not suited for liberty of speech and that gag was useful. I blush for such a thought!" and was aware of the dangers faced by Napoleon III, not only from assassination attempts but the ever-present possibilities of anarchy and revolution. At the time of the empress's confinement in 1856 she was impressed by the Paris churches full of men, women and children praying for a safe delivery and for a prince, indicating their hopes for the dynasty. She seems to have agreed with French foreign policy telling Emily, "I would like the idea of Lombardy free of Austrians, and would not weep over a deposed king of Naples, or a Pope shorn of his power".

At home she and Charles played games of patience and enjoyed long walks in Paris, "more beautiful than ever". In the hot weather they drove to the Bois de Boulogne, "arranged in the most perfect taste and kept like a garden – carriages there every evening, the crowds remain till midnight, water illuminated by numerous boats gliding about with coloured lanterns – a very pretty scene". They saw Rachel in *Adrienne Lecouvreur*, and again in the part of the tsarina in Scribe's drama, attended dinners and balls given by the emperor and empress at the Tuileries and at Saint-Cloud and by the élite of the various groups in Parisian society. Margaret's descriptions of these occasions and impressions of her fellow guests, such as those at a reception given by Madame Walewska at the Quai d'Orsay in 1856 show no signs of her wicked tongue mellowing with age: one lady had grown "as fat as a porpoise", another had become "a grey, overdressed old woman", a third "as obsequious as she used to be impertinent", the duchesse de Trévise "quite affectionate and tender", and two more described respectively as "the prettiest of the pretty", and "smiling and agreeable". The social success of American women in England and in France remained a mystery: in her opinion they were "very pushing and impertinent", and she was alarmed when Morny showed an interest in a Miss Annie Hutton.

She never gave up painting, copying pictures in the Morny collection and obtaining a permit to wander round the galleries of the Louvre to sketch whatever she liked, sometimes on her own but often accompanied by Cécile de Nadaillac. Shopping remained a pleasure, as she reminded Emily in 1858,

> ... getting up at 9, walking the Boulevards until 10.30,
> peering into all the shop windows reading the titles of old
> volumes at bookstalls and diverting myself with such polite
> amusements as one can only indulge in at such an early hour.
> It is a very convenient hour for shopping as there are no
> visitors to interfere with you – if you have any commission to
> give me I am your woman – I like to have such an object on
> my daily walks.

One such, a lapis lazuli watch, was bought from Mellerio in the rue de la Paix at the request of Lady Palmerston. She continued to see her old friends: the Polish Madame Lanckoronska; the Russian Princess Lieven, who called nearly every day; and the Duchess of Galliera. She was delighted when Richard Metternich with his wife, Pauline, daughter of her Viennese friend Madame Sándor, were appointed to the Austrian embassy.

Margaret approved unreservedly of Eugénie de Montijo whom the emperor married in January 1853. The Flahauts and the Willoughby de Eresbys who were friends of the empress, her Scottish mother and family, thought her good and generous and therefore likely to have a beneficial influence over her husband. She also behaved well at grand representations at the Opera, at all her official entertainments and made the imperial court the centre of fashionable society. Meeting her at the Tuileries in February 1854, Margaret observed that "except for a necklace of enormous diamonds, she showed no change from what she was formerly" and remembered all her old friends. The following year, on January 26th she reported, again from the Tuileries, that the

> ... Empress was graceful and gracious and does the honours
> with more ease and simplicity as well as dignity than most of
> those who have been brought up to the metier. As she sat in
> her chair of state looking and smiling and bowing to all those
> that passed before her I could not help thinking how
> awkward our best bred English girl would have been placed
> in the same situation.

At another dinner, in spite of having a very bad cold, the empress chatted away happily on all sorts of subjects, and again Margaret was struck by "her air comme il faut and perfect grace, particularly incorporated in a curtsey she made in taking leave which called forth the admiration of Lord Hertford and all the men who were standing by".[5]

Always friendly, the empress asked for news of the Willoughby de Eresbys, and of their son, Alberic, and listened sympathetically while Margaret enlarged on the trials of living in the cramped conditions of rented accommodation. Margaret continued to admire her, and in 1866 described

> ... the opening of the Chambers by the Emperor which was
> really a very fine sight from the size of the Hall, filled with so
> many brilliant costumes, cardinals, Generals, Senators and
> *Cent Gardes* not least tho' last. I always come away from these
> ceremonies more impressed than ever with the grace of the
> Empress, who made her *entrée* in procession up the centre of
> the Chamber and then turned to make a *reverence* [révérence]
> to the assembly, in which *she looked a Queen all over*! She
> wore a very pale lilac satin high gown, with a Bruxelles lace
> écharpe crossed with long ends hanging down behind and a
> whole bonnet![6]

48 Lily-of-the-valley diamond brooch belonging to Margaret

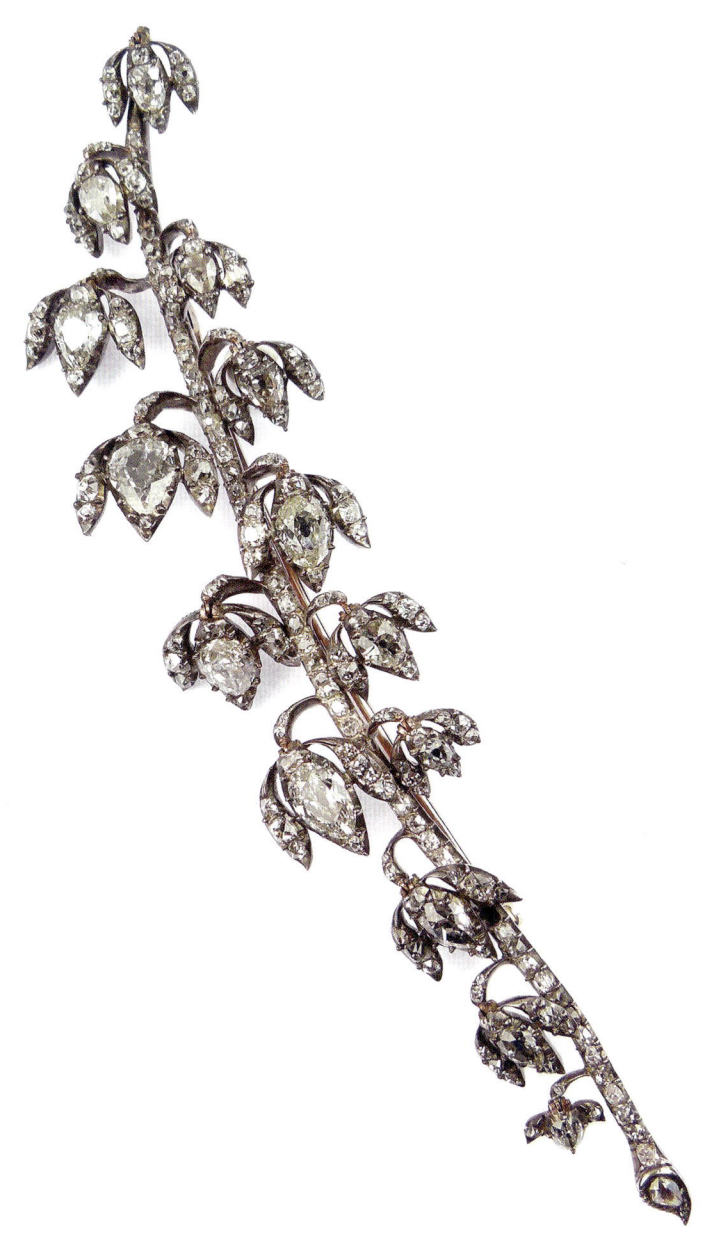

Margaret, who owned beautiful jewellery, enjoyed another evening at the Tuileries at the time of the Exposition Universelle of 1867. After dinner, at the request of Prince Charles of Prussia, the empress showed the 120 guests her jewels, considered second only in importance to those of the empress of Russia. As Margaret quipped, this was a "More innocent an amusement than inspecting instruments of war which is supposed occupation of France at this moment".[7]

Increasingly alarming reports of Morny's decline in health turned out to be justified, and on 10 March 1865, Margaret sent this account to her half-sister Georgy:

> All is over. At about 5 this morning, suddenly at last for Mr. de F. who had been called there at 3 o'clock in the morning, had only left his bedside 10 minutes before, having been told by the Doctors that there would be no change during the day. Yesterday I had given up all hope, but his position was not considered dispensary [?], so we came home at five o'clock but when we were at dinner (or rather sitting round the dining table) a message came to say that Auguste wished to see us all, so we went immediately and he received us most affectionately but seemed suffering much from fever & restlessness. About eight both the Emperor and Empress came and seemed much affected and they remained till after the consultation of the Doctors after nine. The result of this meeting was that they thought they saw some improvement in the symptoms, and wished him to be left perfectly quiet, so we all came home, but at three he became worse and Mr. de F., Emily and Georgina went. They did not call me till it was too late to go with them and as I told you before they left him only ten minutes before he expired quite unexpectedly. I went to the House immediately to take my last leave of him and was glad to bring away a happier impression of him than the painful one of last night. All beauty & peace instead of pain & suffering! I have brought here poor little Marie, who was pale and sad, and had not recovered from the impressions she received when he sent for the children last night to give them

a last embrace. After Mme de Morny *took in* the extent of the danger she has behaved very well and passed all last night on her knees by his bedside, giving him drink and attending to him. I have seen her today in a restless state and not crying but looking ill and watching about the House like a distracted spirit. The House is thronged with sorrowing people, for no one was more beloved by all indoors and out. Mr. de Flahaut is calm and taking some rest in his armchair, is much tired but not ill. We are all very miserable.[8]

In a dramatic gesture, the widow cut off all her hair to place in his coffin and Margaret, Emily and Georgina wept for the loss of a son and brother. In recognition of his services to the Second Empire and his closeness to the emperor, Morny was given a magnificent funeral. The procession of the coffin from the Hôtel de Lassay to the Madeleine to the accompaniment of Chopin's funeral march was watched by a huge crowd. Most agreed that his death was a great loss to the régime, and an English diplomat, Lord Kimberley, who disliked him intensely, declared that "When the secret history of these times [Second Empire] is known I think it will be found that Morny pulled all the strings in all the most critical moments of Louis Napoleon's strange career."[9]

After Charles had accepted the appointment as ambassador in London he and Margaret concentrated on that assignment and left Paris. Although they resumed their visits from 1863, it was not until 1864 when Charles took over the Hôtel de Salm as Grand Chancellor of the Legion of Honour that the old couple returned permanently. As this meant living in one of the most beautiful houses in Paris, Margaret with her excellent taste, felt happy there, and pleased by this further recognition of her husband's abilities, and found it fitting that he should be bestowed with the privilege of presiding over the highest French order of merit founded by Napoleon Bonaparte in 1802. Others, such as the artist Charles Bonnegrace, saw in his success her influence as wife, political partner and confidante, for the portrait exhibited in 1866 depicted the 81-year-old Charles, not only as the distinguished soldier and

49 **Photograph by Antonio Martinelli of the courtyard of the Hôtel de Salm, Paris (overleaf)**

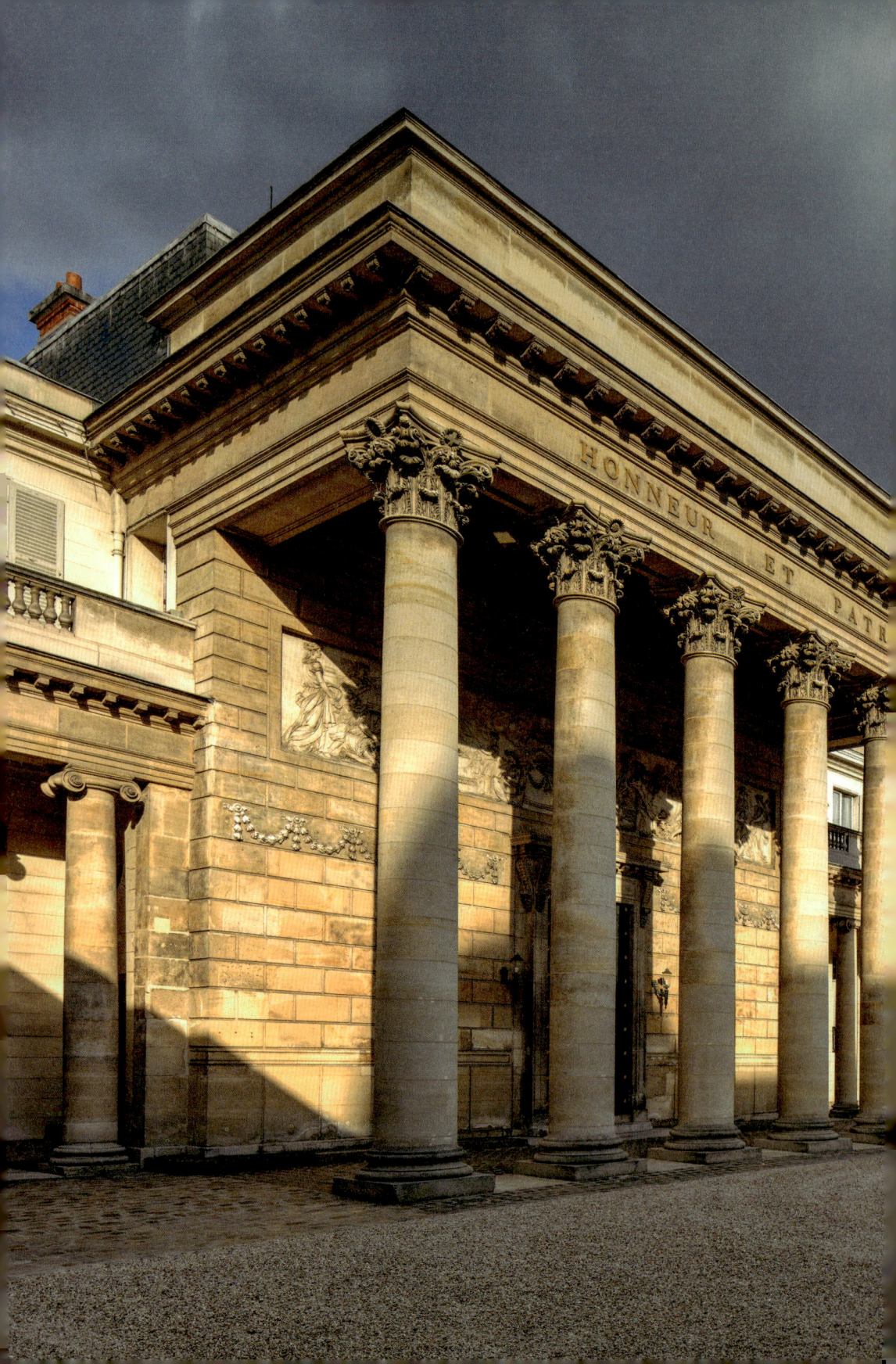

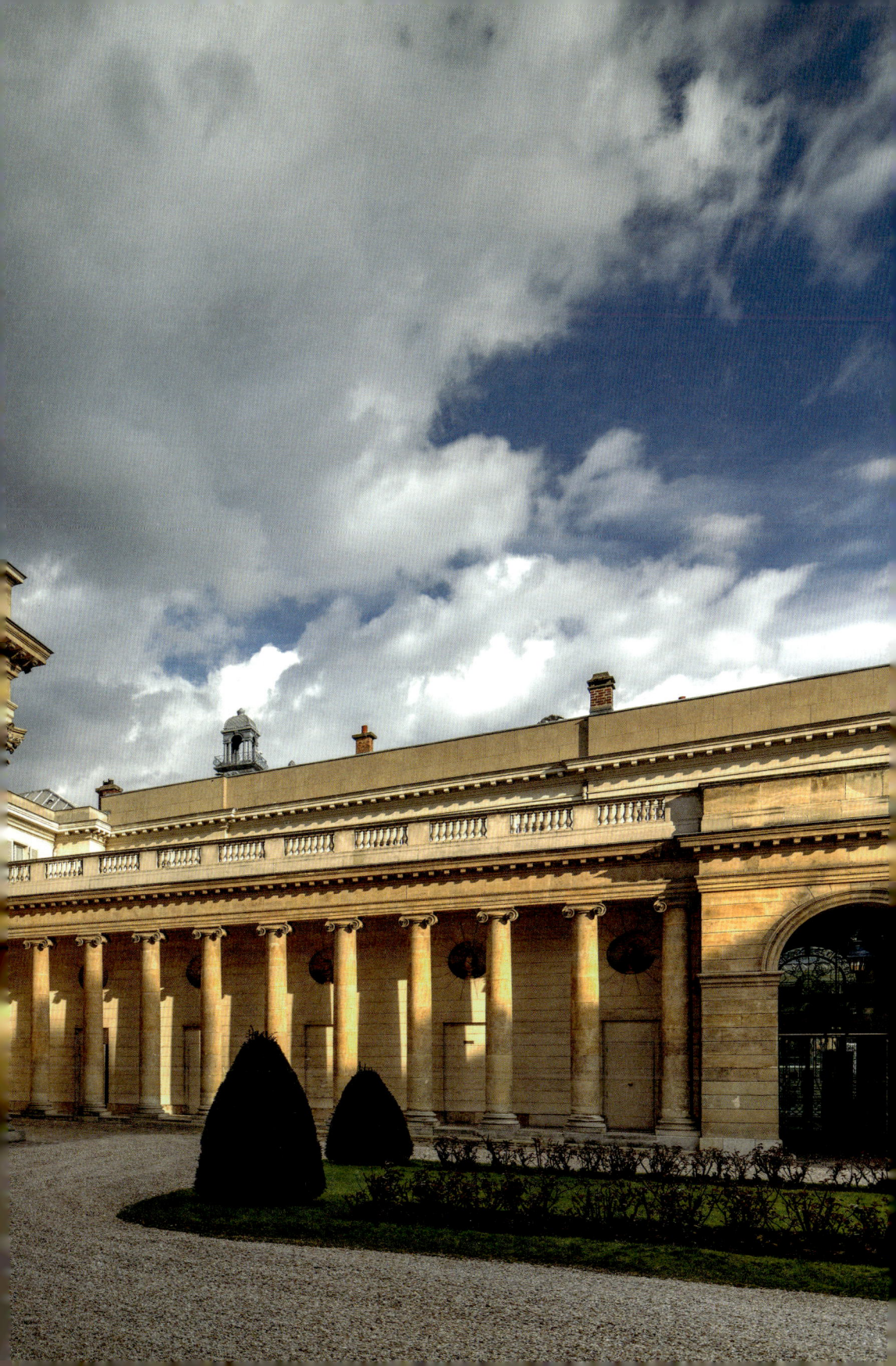

diplomat but also as a patriarchal grandfather.[10] Active to the end, the Flahauts inevitably encountered new problems, one of which brought about the end of their long and close friendship with Alexandre Walewski. This unexpected situation arose after a new commission to publish the *Correspondence* of Napoleon I was set up under Prince Napoleon and Walewski. The work which turned out to be even more disagreeable than under the previous chairmanship of Marshal Vaillant, led to irreconcilable differences of opinion. Georgina explained to Emily that Walewski not only behaved very badly to Morny, his political and social rival, but also "wrote an impertinent letter to Papa". When Charles, exasperated, told Napoleon III that he could no longer serve on the commission with Walewski, he was asked to resign. The quarrel continued; although Morny attempted to reconcile them, neither couple cared to be in the same room with the other and even Margaret turned against Walewski, now regarded as an enemy.

Having been close to Morny for so many years, they remained friendly with his young widow and, as she seemed indifferent and brought them up badly, they took the four children to their hearts. Charles regaled them with stories about their father, Queen Hortense, Napoleon, Talleyrand and Madame de Souza, linking them with the history of France.[11] He and Margaret visited the family at the Palais Morny in Deauville, watching the children play on the beach, and keeping an eye on their progress. From England, news of Emily's children always gave their grandparents immense pleasure. On the birthday of Emmy, the youngest, Margaret wrote, "[S]he has been such an addition to our happiness that I only wonder how we could even live without the sight of her bright face among us. Give her 1000 kisses from old Granny which I expect to return when we meet again." When the boys came to stay in Paris the grandparents bought them the smartest shirt studs and cuff-links and organized a programme of steeplechases, theatres, races and balls for their enjoyment.

Yet even in this seemingly tranquil period of her life Margaret was still ready for a fight and declared that her "old naval spirit which is not yet extinguished in spite of years, a change of country and more prudence and reason . . . was only lying dormant until she needed to call upon it". Her passion for politics continued undiminished and she begged Emily to keep her informed of events from her side of the Channel. In one of her last letters she hoped Gladstone would succeed in introducing further parliamentary reform, fearing that the intransigence of the Tories might bring about a revolution. She summed up the situation by quoting a favourite old Scottish proverb of her father: "Having swallowed the cow, why choke on the tail?" meaning that when performing a great task, one should persevere to see it through to the end, and not give up half way.[12]

As was their custom, they kept open house at the Hôtel de Salm, entertaining visitors – expected and unexpected – to Paris and seeing much of their relations and old friends, especially Félix de Lavalette, appointed guardian to the Morny children. Charles refused to cut down on his official and social activities and Margaret told Emily in January 1866 that "After a heavy day's business on Wednesday (beginning with a visit to the Emperor at 10 o'clock and ending with the Senate & Club till six) he came home for a hurried dinner to go to see the Le Lion amoureux at the Français [play by François Ponsard] where he became so giddy & ill that he gave us a sad fright".

When he was obliged to slow down she continued to worry, writing to Emily on New Year's Day 1867:

> I only wish that I could persuade him to go out a little
> oftener, and see a few people, for except the Lavalettes we see
> no one, and I do not think that he has sufficient exercise
> either for his body or his mind! A novel in the morning, and
> écarté or patience in the evening is not sufficient distraction
> for anybody who has been accustomed to *stronger mental food*.

He recovered in time to attend the functions organized for the Exposition Universelle, which opened in Paris in April:

> Your Father is wonderful, for tho' he was more than an
> hour at the exhibition yesterday morning, he persevered in
> his intention of passing his respects to the King of Prussia and
> went *alone* to the Prussian Ball – he did not get home till
> 12 o'clock, and not having found his servant to call the
> carriage, *walked* home by himself without a *paletot*! All
> very imprudent, but he does not seem the worse and went
> to the Emperor this morning at 11 o'clock.

She went on to say:

> ... the King of Prussia has made himself more popular here
> than the Emperor of Russia, who has not the same art of *saying
> nothings*, and failed in attentions and cordiality even to his own
> country women, who are not pleased with his manners.

She continued on 4 July [1867]:

> ... you will be glad to hear that your Papa did not suffer
> from the heat and fatigue of the great ceremony and dined
> out the same day at Mr. de Lavalette, and went to the
> exhibition with Georgina the next morning.

As for herself, Margaret, now aged 80, admitted: "I am not so valiant and still feel tired and languid, but that has been the case for some time." She was now deaf, her eyesight was failing, and though she suffered from headaches, coughs, colds, rheumatism and gastric problems, she continued to plan for her summer cure of fresh air, sea or mineral waters. Her doctors, the English Sir Charles Locock and Dr Gull, the French Dr Andral and Dr Chepnell could not agree. Carlsbad was too far away, so was Homburg, and they could not find a suitable house in the country near Paris. For some time Charles refused to leave the Hôtel de Salm which was a great blow, as in Margaret's opinion it "was not a very wholesome residence from smells and drains in the hot months". Finally, they decided on Deauville for they would be near the Morny children and Dr Oliffe, his doctor. Although neither food nor lodgings were satisfactory, the sea air certainly seemed to agree with Margaret. Yet this turned out to be only a brief respite, for in September, soon after returning to Paris she collapsed, and never to recover from a stroke, died on 11 November. Thereafter, Charles, always cordial and courteous, carried on his duties as Grand Chancellor for another three years without her, but supported by their daughter Georgina. For him death came on 1 September 1870, coinciding with the defeat at Sedan of the army of Napoleon III by the Germans which sounded the death knell of the Second Empire. Significantly, and according to their wishes, he was buried close to Margaret in Scotland, where they had spent the happiest years of their long and momentous partnership.

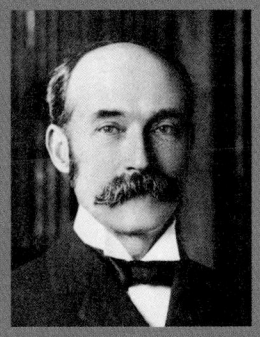

Epilogue

But the story was by no means over, for not the least remarkable aspect of the life of Margaret de Flahaut is that all her ambitions were realized by her grandson, "Clan", 5th Marquess of Lansdowne. Patriotic, clever, cultured and courteous, as heir to the family Whig tradition he had a passion for governing. After appointments to the highest public offices – Governor-General of Canada 1883–8, then Viceroy of India 1888–93, Secretary of State for War 1895–1900, Secretary for Foreign Affairs 1900–5, he negotiated the Anglo-French Entente with Paul Cambon and Théophile Delcassé, thus achieving the goal that had always eluded the Flahauts. Moreover, with the marriage of "Clan" Lansdowne's daughter Evelyn and the future 9th Duke of Devonshire in 1895, Chatsworth and Devonshire House obtained a hostess in the mould of Margaret, who herself had once dreamed of becoming the wife of the 6th Duke. Devoted to his mother, Emily, he also carried on the Flahaut letter-writing tradition, confident that everything he did and saw would be of interest to her, his closest friend, until her death in 1895 brought their lively correspondence to an end.

50 Detail from a photograph by Elliott & Fry of "Clan",
Henry Petty-Fitzmaurice, 5th Marquess of Lansdowne

NOTES

Key to Archives
Archives Nationales, Paris,
Archives Privées: 565 AP

British Library: BL Holland
House Papers Add.Mss.

Devonshire MSS, Chatsworth:
CS

National Library of Scotland,
Edinburgh: Flahaut/Ellice
Papers; Rutherfurd Papers Ms.

Chapter 1
THE ADMIRAL'S AMBITIOUS
DAUGHTER *pp. 9–16*

1 Ganière, p. 73, quoting the
   comte de Las Cases: "un très
   beau vieillard, et de manières
   parfaites".
2 A strong Whig, he was
   elected MP for co.
   Dumbarton from 1781 to
   1790 and subsequently for
   co. Stirling from 1796 to
   1801.
3 The Nairnes were Jacobites
   and Margaret's cousin,
   William, married Carolina
   Oliphant (1766–1847), who
   anonymously collected old
   Scottish airs, some with
   strong Stuart associations,
   and also composed new
   songs in that tradition such
   as "Will ye no come back
   again".
4 Her father was the fourth
   son of the 10th Lord
   Elphinstone, by Clementina
   Fleming (1719–1799),

daughter of John Fleming,
6th Earl of Wigtoun, and
Mary Keith, daughter of
William Keith, 9th Earl
Marischal. On the death of
her uncle George Keith, the
last Earl Marischal (1778),
Clementina became heir of
the family of Keith. The
10th Earl Marischal spent
most of his career in Prussia,
where he became a great
friend of Frederick the
Great and an admirer of
J.-J. Rousseau.
5 Lloyd, no. 85, plate 18.
6 BL HH Papers Add.Mss.
   86499.
7 Almack's was a famous suite
   of assembly rooms
   established in King Street, St
   James's, London, where
   weekly balls were given,
   managed by a committee of
   high-ranking ladies, who
   operated a very exclusive
   admission policy.

Chapter 2
FRIENDSHIP WITH PRINCESS
CHARLOTTE *pp. 18–30*

1 Havelock, 1814, LXXXII,
   p. 222.
2 Aspinall. These papers are
   now in the British Library.
3 Charles Hesse (1792–1832);
   as the reputed natural son of
   the Duke of York and a
   German lady of rank, his
   parentage brought him in
   contact with Charlotte,
   Princess of Wales. An officer

in the 18th Hussars, he
served in the Peninsular War
as ADC to the Duke of
Wellington and was
wounded at Vitoria. He was
killed in a duel with Count
Léon in Paris after a dispute
over cards.
4 565 AP 27 dossier 4 pièces
   146–7.
5 On 18 June 1814 the
   engagement with Prince of
   Orange being at an end, as
   "our tempers did not agree",
   Miss Knight asked him to
   return portraits, letters, any
   other remembrances and
   three rings.
6 Greville, pp. 379–82.
7 565 AP 31 dossier 19 pièce
   277.
8 565 AP 27 dossier 4 pièce 33.
9 Hester Maria Elphinstone
   Keith Papers (Ms. Hyde 1-5),
   Houghton Library, Harvard
   University.
10 565 AP 27 dossier 4 pièces
   85–6, and 565 AP 10, dossier
   34 pièces 192 and 193.
11 Aspinall, pp. xxii–xxiii.
12 Benson & Esher, vol. 2, p. 39.
13 565 AP 28 dossier 8 pièces 21
   and 22.

Chapter 3
MARGARET'S MAN FRIENDS
AND SUITORS *pp. 32–44*

1 *Don Juan*, Canto XII, 32, ll.
   255–6: 33, ll. 263–4: 34, ll.
   265–6.
2 Marchand, vol. 2, 29 July
   1812, pp. 183–4, 186–7.

3 Marchand, vol. 4, pp. 112–3.
4 W. Hazlitt, *Conversations of James Northcote*, No. 15, cited in Marchand, vol. 5 (1976), p. 64, note 1; Quennell, pp. 369–70.
5 Marchand, vol 5, p. 64.
6 Guiccoli, p. 184, cited in Marchand, vol. 5, p. 64, n. 1.
7 Marchand, vol. 7, p. 54.
8 565 AP 31 dossier 25 pièce 374.
9 Masson, *Napoléon*, pp. 136–8.
10 565 AP 26 dossier 4 pièces 6–10.
11 Kerry, *Napoleon*, pp. 188–9.
12 565 AP 26 dossier 6 pièce 21, written 3 April 1816.
13 Askwith, p. 90.
14 CS6/188.
15 Boigne, p. 170.

Chapter 4
CHARLES DE FLAHAUT BEFORE HIS MARRIAGE *pp. 46–55*

1 BL HH Papers Add.Mss. 51718.
2 Bernardy, p. 13 note, letter from the comte d'Angiviller to the comtesse de Neuilly, 2 September 1804.
3 Idem, p. 18. Charles was proud of his name and wished it was the Billarderie blood and not that of Talleyrand in his veins. After his death, his daughter Georgina, Madame de Lavalette, asked the biographer, Frédéric Masson, not to mention Talleyrand, as requested by her father.

4 BL HH Papers Add.Mss. 51718. Another admirer was the writer Stendhal, who quotes from the novel in his journal for 1 August 1801.
5 Staël, p. 197.
6 Carpenter.
7 Kerry, *Napoleon*, p. 219.
8 565 AP dossier 2 pièce 10.
9 Kerry, op. cit., p. 77.
10 565 AP 21 dossier 1 pièce 24.
11 Stryienski, pp. 203–4: Anna Potocka *née* Tyszkiewicz (1776–1867).
12 Hanoteau, vol. 2, pp. 110–11.
13 Kerry, op. cit., p. 239; Masson, *Impératrice Marie-Louise*, pp. 372–3, describes the priestesses of the sun in the Quadrille des Incas.
14 Barante, vol. 2, p. 159.
15 Hanoteau, vol. 3, pp. 86–7.
16 Ibid., pp. 131–3.

Chapter 5
CHARLES IN ENGLAND: NOVEMBER 1815–DECEMBER 1816 *pp. 57–63*

1 Letter from Charles to his mother, 21 November 1815, 565 AP 5 dossier 6, pièce 206.
2 565 AP 11 dossier 5 pièce 28: letter from Lord Kinnaird.
3 Montaigne, *Essais*: "Parce que c'était lui, parce que c'était moi" [Because it was he, because it was I], the words Michel de Montaigne uses to explain the mystery of his love for his friend La Boétie. Lamartine borrowed

the same formula.
4 The ring on Lord Holland's finger representing Brutus, assassin of Caesar, was regarded by Republicans as a sacred effigy, heroic virtue itself.
5 565 AP 5 dossier 14 pièce 234.
6 565 AP 5 dossier 7 pièce 213.
7 Alain-René Lesage, *Gil Blas*, the adventures of a young man who in several episodes of the novel practises medicine, guided by two quack doctors Sangrado and Cuchillo.
8 Marchand, vol. 5, p. 14 (6 January 1816).
9 565 AP 9 dossier 4 pièce 85: Adèle to Charles, 31 May 1817.
10 565 AP dossier 3 pièce 54.
11 Sir Robert Wilson and General Michael Bruce. Sir Robert Wilson was greeted everywhere on the boulevards as liberator of Lavalette.

Chapter 6
A MUTUAL ATTRACTION *pp. 65–9*

1 Surtees, p. 96.
2 Boigne, p. 171: "pour cacher sa déconvenue".
3 Ultras, or ultra-royalists, now returned to France with the Restoration of the Bourbon monarchy, resented a Bonapartist making a marriage with a close connection to the heiress to the throne of

England.

4 565 AP 21 dossier 1 pièces 2–84 (for letters from Charles to Margaret from March 1816 to April 1817).

5 565 AP 9 dossier 15 pièces 213 and 565 AP 31 dossier 5 pièce 31.

6 He resumed military life by participating in the siege of Antwerp with the duc d'Orléans in 1832.

Chapter 7
WEATHERING THE STORM
pp. 71–81

1 565 AP 21 dossier 1 pièce 7.
2 565 AP 20 dossier 1 pièce 2.
3 565 AP 20 dossier 1 pièce 4: Lord Keith to Margaret April 1817.
4 565 AP 10 dossier 32 pièce 104: letter of 2 April 1817, and dossier 34 pièce 143 April/May 1817.
5 Hester Maria Elphinstone Keith Papers (Ms. Hyde 5), Houghton Library, Harvard University.
6 As above.
7 As above.
8 565 AP 9 dossier 4 pièce 84.
9 565 AP 21 dossier 1 pièce 82.
10 Pélissier, p. 323.

Chapter 8
EARLY MARRIED LIFE IN SCOTLAND *pp. 83–97*

1 Hester Maria Elphinstone Keith Papers (Ms. Hyde 5), Houghton Library, Harvard University.

2 Hon. William George Grey born 15 February 1819, eighth son of 2nd Earl Grey. 565 AP 27 dossier 4 pièce 54: Margaret to Lady Grey, "cargo" containing: "une pièce de baptiste, 23 aunes de Valencienne, 6 petits bonnets brodés, trois très beaux, trois fort jolis, plus votre modèle ; une robe d'enfant à coqueluchon telle que nous les fesons [*sic*] ici, un fourreau de votre baptiste d'Ecosse et pris, pour la façon, sur un de ceux de lady Elisabeth, mais pour les enjolivements sur un de ceux de la duchesse de Berry, car c'est sa lingère qui travaille pour vous, et 12 chemises d'enfant".

3 See letters from Adèle to Margaret "ma fille" 1817–1823, 565 AP 24 dossiers 1–6.

4 Wilson, p. 49 and Mameluck Ali, p. 112. The counters for the game of ombre are in the Museo Napoleonico, Rome.

5 Wilson, *passim*.
6 Custine, p. 266.
7 Ticknor, p. 277.
8 "He hates sitting after dinner, and I am told that Lord Qu(eensberry) [. . .?] Tweeddale &c &c who are to be there never get up from table till daylight." Lord Lyndoch (1748–1843), brilliant soldier, Peninsular War veteran. James, 4th Earl of Fife (1776–1857), of Duff House, co. Banff, also Peninsular War veteran,

fine art collector, married the daughter of the Countess of Dysart.

9 565 AP 31 dossier 2 pièce 13.
10 Comte Casimir de Montrond (1769–1843), wit, man about town, longstanding friend of Charles de Flahaut and the *âme damnée* of Talleyrand.
11 1830. From Brighton, Margaret to Lord Holland: "Mr. de F only obtained his privilege as an English subject from the purchase of stock in the BOS [Bank of Scotland] taking advantage of a late 17th century Scottish law according to which a foreigner with shares in the BOS became automatically a British citizen, but he obtained them in a more regular way from Mr. Peel who gave him letters of denization when he was in Scotland with the King some years ago [i.e. 1822 Charles went to Edinburgh to thank George IV for being so obliging as to grant him letters of denization (also Mr Peel)], rendering an important service." BL HH Papers Add.Mss. 121, 17 August 1830, no. 121 and 565 AP 27 dossier 4 pièce 77, Margaret to Lady Grey on the subject.
12 Grant, vol. 2, pp. 98–100.

Chapter 9
COUNTRY LIFE IN SCOTLAND: MEIKLEOUR AND TULLIALLAN *pp. 99–110*

1 AP 565 26 dossier 17 pièces 82–3: Captain Hall, letter sent from Madras to Miss Minto.

2 Custine, p. 320.

3 Mrs Ferguson, *née* Elizabeth Nisbet, was the divorced wife of Lord Elgin.

Chapter 10
THE GREAT WORLD: PARIS I
pp. 112–27

1 Waller.

2 Raikes, vol. I, pp. 215 and 225.

3 British ambassadors in this period: Lord Stuart 1825–4, Lord Granville 1824–8, Lord Stuart 1828–30 and 1831–5, Lord Cowley 1835, Lord Granville 1835–41, Lord Cowley 1841–6.

4 Raikes, entry for 18 January 1836, vol. 2, p. 309.

5 Lady Glengall, married to an Irish peer, was the co-heiress of a government contractor, said to have left a fortune of £3,000,000. For French criticism of the behaviour of English women, see Sartory, p. 40.

6 Raikes, vol. 2, entry for 5 October 1843, p. 300; Daniel 12:4.

7 Guillaume Dupuytren, surgeon at the Hôtel-Dieu.

8 Alexandre-Pierre-Edmé Klor taught French and Italian language, literature, history and geography at the Conservatoire impérial de musique during the Empire.

9 C. Harmand was the author

of the *Manuel de l'amateur des arts dans Paris, contenant la description complète des musées et galeries . . . et de tout ce qui a rapport aux arts du dessin* (1824).

10 Henriette Sontag (1806–1854); in *Donna al Lago* she is Elena with Pisaroni: ". . . il y avait une telle union dans les voix qu'on aurait pu croire qu'elles n'en formaient qu'une seule . . . beau idéal du chant ensemble".

11 Giulia Grisi (1811–1869) made her Paris debut in *Semiramide*, a triumph repeated over the next 25 years.

12 In *L'Aiglon* by Edmond Rostand she is the mistress of the duc de Reichstadt, son of Napoleon and of Marie-Louise, Duchess of Parma.

13 Zamoyski, pp. 114–15.

Chapter 11
HOME AND GARDEN: PARIS II
pp. 129–40

1 Le Strange, vol. I, p. 410. He writes: "Lady Keith's letter is long, full and so admirably written that I wish I could show it to you. I wish I could depend on her opinion! I am sure it is sincere but you know how strong her feelings are . . . and I cannot quite believe in her representation of the moderate views of the Liberal party."

2 565 AP 21 dossier 2 pièces

87–8, Perregaux, who was hoping to separate from his wife, accused her rather than Charles, who did not agree to a duel. All three were reconciled.

3 Armaillé. Léontine, widow of vicomte Albert de Noailles, p. 112.

4 Kozmian, pp. 329–33.

5 Leveson Gower, vol. 1, pp. 431 and 435.

6 Castellane, vol. 2, p. 201.

7 565 AP 21 dossier 9 pièce 196.

8 565 AP 21 dossier 8 pièce 149.

9 Daudet, vol. 2, p. 348.

10 Raikes, vol. 2, p. 361. Entry for 4 May 1836. For the pioneering English taste for objects and furniture from the past, see Grand Palais, no. 55, p. 151. Early in her marriage Margaret asked her mother-in-law to buy her "du vieux Sèvres". Adèle, whose taste was purely neo-classical, considered such pieces "vieilles et vilaines". Similarly, although she undertook to buy a Watteau for Lord Murray, Adèle did not want it known – "cela me ferait tort".

11 565 AP 24 dossier 2 pièce 10, copy of original letter.

12 The archbishop's house in the île de la Cité was pillaged and burnt by insurgents on 29 July 1830.

13 565 AP 12 dossier 4 pièce 61, for letter to Margaret, and see also Dion-Tennenbaum. Her article also refers to

"deux grands divans à rampe d'appui, copiés par Jacob sur ceux du comte de Flahaut", in the grand salon of the duc d'Orléans.

Chapter 12
THE ORLÉANS MONARCHY: PARIS III *pp. 142–56*

1 AP 565 21 dossier 1 pièce 43.
2 Huart, p. 236; "Il est grand, bien fait, a une figure agréable, bien qu'un peu fanée. Il est très soigné et aimable en société, mais l'on voit qu'il a trop de suffisance, ayant été gâté par les dames." Diary entry for 4 December 1816.
3 Daudet, vol. 1, p. 293. Madame de Flahaut "a sauté de plaisir au reçu de la nouvelle de la révolution".
4 BL HH Papers Add.Mss. 51720/171.
5 The son of the Emperor Napoleon and the Empress Marie-Louise, then in Vienna and known as the duc de Reichstadt.
6 565 AP 21 dossier 8 pièce 149.
7 Daudet, vol. 1, p. 293.
8 565 AP 21 dossier 8 pièce 149.
9 565 AP 21 dossier 9 pièces 163–9.
10 565 AP 21 dossier 9 pièces 176–240.
11 Daudet, vol. 3 (1914), pp. 309–12, asserts that Louis-Philippe was in favour of retaining Baudrand, and that settled the dispute.

12 Le Strange, vol. 3, pp. 258–9.
13 Greville, p. 261.
14 Price, p. 203. Madame Adélaïde used the term "very July" for supporters of Louis-Philippe.
15 Letter from Charles de Flahaut to Lady Grey, Grey Papers, Borthwick Institute, University of York: ". . . his being short sighted gives him often an air of embarrassment and makes him averse to moving in a room", and caused a fall from a cabriolet in March 1836 and perhaps his death in 1842. Margaret considered it "really dangerous for him to drive as he does not see obstacles in his way".
16 Barante, vol. 5, p. 60, letter from Alexis de Guignard, comte de Saint-Priest.
17 565 AP 21 dossier 2 pièce 12.
18 Naville, vol. 2, p. 203.

Chapter 13
MARGARET AND TALLEYRAND *pp. 158–70*

1 Bernardy, p. 156.
2 Bowood Archives.
3 BL HH Papers Add.Mss. 51719/ 21.
4 Barante, vol. 3, p. 466.
5 Bowood Archives.
6 Haussonville, pp. 165–6.
7 Barante, vol. 4, p. 167.
8 Greville, p. 117. Talleyrand told Margaret that "Parmi tous c'est Palmerston qui est le véritable homme d'État".
9 565 AP 21 dossier 9 pièce 168.

10 Grey Papers, Borthwick Institute, University of York.
11 Grey Papers, Borthwick Institute, University of York.
12 Waresquiel, p. 1003.
13 Ibid. p. 1083.
14 Grey Papers, Borthwick Institute, University of York.
15 Grey Papers, University of Durham Library, GRE/B15/2/32/1.
16 Grey Papers, Borthwick Institute, University of York.
17 Parturier, vol. I, 1822–35, p. 365.
18 565 AP 28 dossier 35 pièce 222. Flahaut had become a British citizen at time of marriage through his purchase of stock in the Bank of Scotland. Also see note 21 below.
19 Le Strange, vol. 3, pp. 262, 265.
20 Grey Papers, Borthwick Institute, University of York.
21 For the reasons why Charles was not accepted by the British monarchy: 565 AP 28 dossier 6 pièces 16–17. Letters of Margaret to Lord Melbourne, March, April 1838; 565 AP 28 dossier 3 pièce 5. Letter of Margaret to Lord Granville; 565 AP 27 dossier 4 pièce 9. Letter from Lady Grey to Margaret, April 1838.
22 Grey Papers, Borthwick Institute, University of York. Talleyrand, like the devil, was lame. Pozzo di

Borgo was a Corsican, an enemy of Napoleon who was appointed Russian ambassador in Paris and in London from 1835.

23 Beau, p. 56.

24 Grey Papers Borthwick Institute, University of York.

25 Letter from Pauline de Talleyrand-Périgord to Emily: in June 1838 "Monsieur votre Père vous aura raconté ses derniers moments combien ils ont été à la fois beaux et déchirants", and Madame Adélaïde wrote to Margaret: "La mort de ce pauvre M. de Talleyrand m'a fait beaucoup de peine et mal vous en aurez eu tous les tristes détails par votre mari qui y est toujours resté."

Chapter 14
MARGARET'S FRIENDSHIPS
pp. 172–86

1 Leveson Gower, vol. 2, p. 433.

2 Haussonville, pp. 145–6.

3 Kozmian, p. 325.

4 Mansel, p. 335, n. 34.

5 Le Strange, vol. 2, p. 143.

6 Naville, vol. 2, p. 210.

7 Durham University Library, Grey Papers: GRE/B15/2/4: ". . . no one can be more interested in everything that concerns your happiness than I am".

8 565 AP 27 dossier 4 pièce 23.

9 565 AP 27 dossier 4 pièces 146–7.

10 Grey Papers, Borthwick Institute, University of York.

11 Durham University Library, Grey Papers GRE/B15/2/5/1.

12 Grey Papers, Borthwick Institute, University of York.

13 565 AP 27 dossier 4.

14 Sudley, p. 46.

15 Macaulay, essay in the *Edinburgh Review*, July 1841.

16 See Chapter 16: Margaret's Cult of Napoleon.

17 BL HH Papers Add.Mss. 51719, 51720, 51721.

18 Trevelyan, p. 153.

19 NLS Rutherfurd Papers MS 9693.

20 565 AP 30 dossier 10 pièce 100.

21 CS2/210/10.

Chapter 15
MARGARET'S TRAVELS
pp. 188–202

1 565 AP 31 dossier 8 pièce 73.

2 Angeli.

3 565 AP 27 dossier 4 pièce 275.

4 565 AP 31 dossier 7 pièces 63, 64.

5 In 1831 Georgina Elphinstone had married the Hon. Augustus John Villiers. Horse racing and gambling were a mutual passion.

6 Her will, drawn up in 1859, bequeaths to her daughter, Lady Shelburne, future Marchioness of Lansdowne, her drawing books "with portraits of my friends and contemporaries of my own painting and the album of copies of pictures done by myself at Rome and from de Morny's collection".

7 CS2/210/7.

8 CS2/210/4.

9 565AP 31 dossier 9 pièce 83.

10 565 AP 27 dossier 4 pièce 219.

Chapter 16
MARGARET'S CULT OF NAPOLEON *pp. 204–15*

1 Custine, p. 363.

2 Maillé, p. 234.

3 The portrait cannot have been taken from life as Lord Keith disliked the sightseeing attracted to Napoleon at Torbay and even forbade his wife, Queeney, from attempting to see him there. There is no evidence to suggest that Margaret succeeded in so doing.

4 Translated thus in the *Eclectic Magazine*, vol. 10, April 1847, p. 528, and in earlier publications.

5 Chaumet Archives, Paris.

6 565 AP 26 dossier 14 pièce 74.

7 University of Durham Library, Grey Archives, GRE/B15/2/3A.

8 BL HH Papers Add.Mss. 51719/103.

9 Grey Papers, Borthwick Institute, University of York.

10 Armaillé, pp. 65–6.

11 CS2/210/11; letter to Duke of Devonshire: ". . . this horrid tragedy which came home to me from having so long inhabited the apartment. For five years I slept upon that bed and sat on the causeuse on which she died! The whole scene has haunted me night and day with every object before my eyes with a frightful reality." Earlier, en route to Rome she called at Vaux-le-Vicomte, recently restored by the duc and duchesse de Praslin – "a fortune has been spent to return it to appearance of days of Fouquet in its original magnificence, including a new roof so that they can hold a fete in honour of Louis Philippe". However, she sensed that something was very wrong with the marriage, which she attributed to the poisonous influence of the governess recommended, after being with Lady Hislop, by herself and by Anne Elphinstone.
12 CS6/1448.
13 Metternich, vol. 6, p. 656.
14 Cars, p. 154.
15 565 AP 27 dossier 4 pièces 175–7.
16 NLS Flahaut/Ellice Papers Ms. no. 114.
17 AP 565 31 dossier 7 pièce 54.
18 Castellane, vol. 2, p. 198.
19 Kozmian, p. 325.
20 BL HH Papers Add.Mss. 51719.
21 BL HH Papers Add.Mss. 51720.

22 Ibid., 51720.
23 565 AP 30 dossier 9 pièce 91.

Chapter 17
THE VIENNA EMBASSY I, 1841–8 *pp. 217–31*

1 565 AP 29 pièces 12–13.
2 565 AP 21 dossier 16 pièces 438–9.
3 Neither the Emperor Ferdinand I, an epileptic, nor his wife, the empress, was capable of governing. His brother the Archduke Francis Charles was also of very limited abilities, but was married to the ambitious Archduchess Sophie, the mother of the future Emperor Franz Joseph. She dominated the Archduke Louis, the emperor, empress and dowager empress. The most able Habsburgs were the uncles Archduke Charles, of military distinction, John, a Liberal, and Louis. All these factions disliked each other.
4 From the outside the Palais Starhemberg, built by the family of that name 1661–7, appeared like a monument of Viennese baroque architecture, but the interior had been completely refashioned in the severe neo-classical style of 1783, and then made brighter and more welcoming in 1820. Visitors walked up a monumental staircase flanked by allegorical statues in niches.

5 565 AP 28 dossier 21 pièce 153.
6 Metternich, vol. 6, pp. 600–1.
7 565 AP 30 dossier 6 pièce 3.
8 Naville, vol. 3, 1, 8 August 1843, p. 70.
9 This album, containing 248 portraits "des invités du Chancelier Metternich et de son épouse la princesse Mélanie". was sold in Paris at the Drouot Richelieu by Beaussant Lefèvre, 4 May 2012.
10 565 AP 33 dossier 12 pièces 162 and 310, letters, and 311, portrait drawing of Princess Melanie Metternich by Georgina de Flahaut.
11 565 AP 21 dossier 16 pièce 455; 565 AP 21 dossier 16 pièce 454; 565 AP 21 dossier 16 pièce 456; 565 AP 21 dossier 16 pièce 464.
12 565 AP 22 dossier 1 pièce 81.
13 565 AP 10 dossier 29 pièce 19: Bal à l'ambassade de France à Vienne, 30 janvier 1843; list of subscribers includes comte de Blacas; Margaret took 34 tickets, Esterházy 20, the Metternichs 19.
14 "Pouding à la Chateaubriand". Served for first time at the embassy in Rome when Chateaubriand was ambassador, 1822–4, it was a variant of the *diplomate* theme, consisting of sponge fingers sugar, eggs, fresh or candied fruit, raisins, milk, *crème anglaise*, rum or maraschino. Information kindly supplied

by Étienne Grafe. Hotchpotch is a broth of carrots, turnips, lettuce, parsley, green peas, beans and cauliflower in lamb stock.

15 565 AP 23 dossier 1 pièce 26; Charles enjoyed Donizetti's "Maria de Rohan" sung by Tadolini and the new tenor Gaetano Fraschini, but, in 565 AP 23 dossier 1 pièce 27, was not impressed by Jenny Lind.

16 National Library of Scotland, Ellice Papers, nos 160–1.

17 Princesse Aloïse Schönburg (1803–1884) welcomed Charles warmly on his arrival in Vienna, and was very friendly with Margaret.

18 565 AP 31 dossier 9 pièce 95.

19 565 AP 23 dossier 2 pièce 73.

20 Metternich, vol. 6, p. 656.

21 Radziwill, p. 313.

22 Caetani Grenier, vol. 1, p. 499.

23 Montet, p. 395.

24 565 AP 31 dossier 9 pièce 95.

25 565 AP 22 dossier 4 pièce 150.

Chapter 18
THE VIENNA EMBASSY II
pp. 233–46

1 565 AP 30 dossier 10 pièce 120.

2 565 AP 22 dossier 1 pièce 78.

3 565 AP 31 dossier 6 pièce 37.

4 565 AP 31 dossier 7 pièce 51.

5 565 AP 31 dossier 6 pièce 24.

6 565 AP 30 dossier 28 pièce 256.

7 565 AP 22 dossier 1 pièce 187.

8 565 AP 31 dossier 6 pièce 43. Queen Marie-Amélie thanked Margaret when congratulating her on Emily's marriage: "Je profite de cette occasion pour remercier M. de Flahaut de l'obligeant empressement avec lequel il s'est occupé des arrangements pour le mariage de notre chère Clémentine" (565 AP 28 dossier 12 pièce 33, 10 July 1843) and letter from Madame to Margaret: ". . . j'ai donné à lire votre lettre à mon cher Roi, tous ces détails lui ont fait grand plaisir et il a ajouté il est impossible de faire mieux qu'eux, j'aime à vous le redire et combien il est satisfait de toute la manière d'agir et de faire de votre mari, notamment dans la délicate et importante affaire du contrat de mariage pour Clémentine", 565 AP 28 dossier 17 pièces 80–1, 24 February 1843.

9 565 AP 23 dossier 1 pièce 38.

10 Barante, vol. 7, p. 134. Letter to Ernest-Sébastien de Barante, 25 April 1845.

11 Anglo-French rivalry over Tahiti came to a head when Pritchard, a Protestant missionary who settled in Tahiti from 1825, was arrested in 1844 by a French admiral, who formally annexed the island to France, leading to an outcry from England.

12 565 AP dossier 4 pièce 202.

13 Aware that the British government did not want a union between the crowns of Spain and France, especially after the French occupation of Algeria, and after months of discussion, Louis-Philippe announced the betrothal of his son the duc de Montpensier to the sister of Queen Isabella of Spain and of the Queen to her cousin Don Francis, unlikely to have children. Led by Lord Palmerston the British public resented this fait accompli, by which, in the end, the French gained nothing.

14 Naville, vol. 3 (1964), p. 220.

15 565 AP 23 dossier 1 pièce 2.

16 565 AP 31 dossier 9 pièce 111.

17 565 AP 28 dossier 16 pièce 43, letter of 30 April 1847.

18 565 AP 31 dossier 10 pièces 115–16.

19 565 AP 30 dossier 12 pièce 142.

20 565 AP 28 dossier 26 pièce 175, letter from Countess Sándor: "Mes parents m'ont assez pu me dire combien vous avez été bonne pour eux." Margaret continued to send well-chosen presents such as a "Lenticular telescope" to Prince Metternich then in Brussels in December 1849.

Chapter 19
LONDON, 1848–64 *pp. 248–61*

1 The Hôtel de Massa was removed to no. 38, rue du Faubourg Saint-Jacques, Paris, and is now the headquarters of the Société des gens de lettres.
2 The 2nd Earl Granville was the son of the ambassador to France, 1824–8, 1830–5, 1835–41, and well known to the Flahauts, as was his mother, Harriet, sister of the 6th Duke of Devonshire.
3 Greville, pp. 80–1.
4 Daudet, vol. 2 (1926), p. 158.
5 565 AP 31 dossier 17 pièce 220.
6 Trevelyan, p. 551.
7 565 AP 31 dossier 13 pièce 163.
8 565 AP 31 dossier 15 pièces 115–6.
9 Margaret wrote to Emily: "Georgy doesn't enjoy herself but on the contrary walks through mazes of the games and dances with the greatest gravity and composure, and makes me regret I'm too old to show her how much more I would enjoy it all".
10 As the third wife of Félix de Lavalette, Georgina was 50, he 56. Widowed in 1881, she retired to England where she remained close to the Empress Eugénie.
11 565 AP 26 dossier 10 pièces 50–1.
12 Twisleton. In spite of Margaret's prejudice, Ellen Twisleton made many friends in England

including Thomas Carlyle and his wife, Jane.
13 Lord Lansdowne's bequest of £10,000 to Lady Somers was honoured by his heirs, who said it was their great pleasure to do so. 565 AP 30 dossier 13 pièce 153.
14 565 AP 31 dossier 14 pièce 183. Champlâtreux, a country house near Épinay north of Paris, built for the Molé family, 1751–7.
15 565 AP 31 dossier 21 pièce 299.
16 Drakelow Hall was the seat of the Gresley family.
17 565 AP 31 dossier 21 pièce 306.

Chapter 20
TULLIALLAN AND THE LONDON EMBASSY, 1848–64 *pp. 263–75*

1 Trabaud.
2 Parturier, Série 2, vol. 3, pp. 551–2, Série 2, vol. 2, pp. 95–6, and Taine, pp. 112–3.
3 Dasent, vol. 2, p. 71.
4 565 AP 31 dossier 10 pièces 129–30. DNB entry says he was a sweet and graceful singer!
5 During the 19th century two brothers, John and Charles Hay Allen, falsely claimed descent from Prince Charles Edward Stuart, the Young Pretender, whose mother was Clementina Sobieska. John died in 1872, Charles in 1880.
6 Delacroix, 6 June 1856, p. 315: "For my own part, I

felt unutterably wretched in that extraordinary agglomeration – those poor animals, unable to make out what the stupid crowd wanted of them, or to recognize the keepers who have been allotted them at random."
7 Charles's refusal of the offer of London embassy in 1851 was perhaps influenced by Emily. She held strong opinions like her mother, was very pro-Orléans and did not want problems between her father and father-in-law, Lord Lansdowne, President of Council in the Cabinet of Lord John Russell. Morny, who tried to make him change his mind with the full agreement of Margaret, protested to Emily, ". . . j'avais cru que ce projet serait utile pour lui, agréable pour vous et que votre refus était motivé par des scrupules que je trouvais de votre part fort exagérés".
8 565 AP 31 dossier 19 pièce 258.
9 Dasent, vol. 1, p. 319.
10 Kennedy, p. 109.
11 Fitzmaurice, p. 62.
12 National Library of Scotland, Edinburgh, Manuscripts Division, Flahaut/Ellice Papers, nos 135–8.
13 Kennedy, p. 138.
14 Ibid., p. 185.

Chapter 21

THE FINAL PHASE: PARIS I
pp. 277–88

1 Dufresne; D'Angio-Barros.
2 Kerry, *Coup d'État*, p. 73.
3 Daudet, vol. 4, pp. 263–4.
4 Goudemare, p. 6.
5 Kerry, op. cit., opp. p. 120. The telegram read: Assembly dissolved. The President of the Republic Makes an Appeal to the Country.
6 Idem, p. 121, letter from Charles to Margaret, 3 December 1851.
7 Greville, p. 19, 10 December 1852.
8 Barante, vol. 8, p. 93.
9 565 AP 30 dossier 16 pièces 172–3.
10 It was in protest against this decree that Morny had resigned as minister of the interior.
11 565AP 31 dossier 14 pièce 179.
12 565 AP 30 dossier 17 pièce 175.
13 Greville, p. 118. It is a great thing to find a sovereign who sucks in the truth even if he spits out a part of it afterwards.
14 Kerry, op. cit, pp. 201–2 and p. 207.
15 Émile Zola: M. de Marsy "... avant l'empire ... était alors entretenu par sa maîtresse, une baronne dont il avait mangé les diamants en trois mois. M. Kahn prétendait que pas une affaire véreuse ne traînait sur la place de Paris, sans qu'on trouvât dedans la main de Marsy. Et ils s'échauffaient l'un l'autre, ils se renvoyaient des faits de plus en plus forts : dans une entreprise de mine, Marsy avait touché un pot-de-vin de quinze cent mille francs ; il venait d'offrir, le mois dernier, un hôtel à la petite Florence, des Bouffes, une bagatelle de six cent mille francs, sa part d'un trafic sur les actions des chemins de fer du Maroc ; il n'y avait pas huit jours enfin, la grande affaire des canaux égyptiens, lancée par des créatures à lui, s'était écroulée avec un immense scandale, les actionnaires ayant su que pas un coup de pioche n'avait été donné, depuis deux ans qu'ils opéraient des versements. Puis, ils se jetèrent sur sa personne elle-même, s'efforçant de rapetisser sa haute mine d'aventurier élégant, parlant de maladies anciennes qui lui joueraient plus tard un mauvais tour, allant jusqu'à attaquer la galerie de tableaux qu'il réunissait alors."
16 Greville, p. 335.
17 Delacroix, 3 April 1847, p. 74.
18 D'Angio-Barros, p. 180.
19 Chennevières, pp. 123–4.
20 565 AP 31 dossier 19 pièce 261.
21 565 AP 26 dossier 10 pièce 43.
22 565 AP 31 dossier 19 pièce 237.
23 565 AP 31 dossier 19 pièce 255.
24 565 AP 31 dossier 19 pièce 253.
25 565 AP 31 dossier 19 pièce 277.

Chapter 22

THE FINAL PHASE: PARIS II
pp. 290–302

1 "... sa mémoire plus illustrée qu'il aurait publié lui-même s'il eût pu être consulté". In addition to his duties as member of the committee charged with the publication of Napoleon's correspondence, Charles defended his memory from any criticisms raised in new books such as *Mémoires* (1857) by the Maréchal duc de Raguse, whom he accused of attacking his benefactor, betraying him during his lifetime and calumniating him when dead, and in article on the 1815 campaign by Edgar Quinet, *Revue des Deux Mondes* (October 1861). See Kerry, *Napoleon*, pp. 313–23.
2 565 AP 23 dossier 14 pièce 310.
3 565 AP 31 dossier 20 pièce 293.
4 The dinner was for representatives negotiating the peace settlement with Russia.
5 565 AP 31 dossier 17 pièce 223.
6 565 AP 20 dossier 3 pièces 22–3.

7 565 AP 31 dossier 26 pièce
402.

8 565 AP 20 dossier 3 pièce
26.

9 Hawkins & Powell,
Camden 5th Series, vol. 9
(1997), p. 272 and p. 50
"Morny – type of
Imperialist French
adventurer, cold cunning
man of the world, vulgar,
insolent, and intensely
conceited."

10 *L'Artiste* (1866), vol. 1 (Jan.–
Sept.), p. 181, ". . . une idée
pensive de patriarche, qui
reflète la famille, le foyer
heureux, la quiétude
intime, l'ascendant
affectueux, l'autorité
domestique et charmante".

11 D'Angio-Barros, p. 181.
Although the Morny
children turned out very
badly they were not
neglected by the Lavalettes
nor by Emily Lansdowne.

12 National Library of
Scotland, Manuscripts
Division, Ellice/Flahaut
Papers.

BIBLIOGRAPHY

Angeli
Diego Angeli, *Roma Romantica*
(Milan, 1935)

Armaillé
Comtesse d'Armaillé, *Quand on
savait vivre heureux, 1830–1860*
(Paris, 1933, reprint, Paris, 1999)

Askwith
Betty Askwith, *Piety and Wit: A
Biography of Harriet, Countess
Granville, 1785–1862* (London,
1982)

Aspinall
Arthur Aspinall, ed., *The Letters
of The Princess Charlotte, 1811–
1817* (London, 1949)

Barante
Claude de Barante, ed.,
Souvenirs du baron de Barante,
8 vols (Paris, 1890–1901)

Beau
André Beau, *Talleyrand.
L'Apogée du sphinx. La
Monarchie de Juillet* (Paris, 1998)

Benson & Esher
Arthur Christopher Benson &
Viscount Esher eds., *The Letters
of Queen Victoria, 1837–1861*, 3
vols (London, 1908)

Bernardy
Françoise de Bernardy, *Charles
de Flahaut, 1785–1870* (Paris,
1954)

Boigne
Comtesse de Boigne, *Mémoires*
(Paris, 1907–8)

Caetani Grenier
Giovannella Caetani Grenier,
ed., *Mémoires de la comtesse
Rosalie Rzewuska 1788–1865*,
3 vols (Rome, 1939–1950)

Carpenter
Kirsty Carpenter, *The Novels of
Madame de Souza in Social and
Political Perspective* (*French
Studies of the Eighteenth and
Nineteenth Centuries*, book 24)
(Oxford & Berne, 2007)

Cars
Jean des Cars, *La Princesse
Mathilde* (Paris, 1988)

Castellane
*Journal du maréchal de
Castellane, 1804–1862*, vol. 2
(Paris, 1895)

Chaumont
Chaumont, Jean-Philippe, ed.,
*Archives du général Charles de
Flahaut et de sa famille. 565 AP*
(Paris, 2005)

Chennevières
Philippe de Chennevières,
*Souvenirs d'un directeur des
Beaux-Arts* (Paris, 1883, reprint,
Paris, 1979)

Custine
Marquis de Custine, *Mémoires
et voyages, ou Lettres écrites à
diverses époques : pendant des
courses en Suisse, en Calabre, en
Angleterre et en Écosse* (reprint,
Paris, 1992)

D'Angio-Barros
Agnes D'Angio-Barros, *Morny. Le Théâtre du pouvoir* (Paris, 2012)

Dasent
Arthur Irwin Dasent, *John Thadeus Delane: Editor of "The Times"* (London, 1908)

Daudet
Ernest Daudet, ed., *Vingt-cinq ans à Paris, 1826–1850. Journal du comte Rodolphe Apponyi, Attaché de l'Ambassade d'Autriche à Paris*, 4 vols (Paris, 1913–1926)

Delacroix
Hubert Wellington, ed., Lucy Norton, trans., *The Journal of Eugène Delacroix* (London, 1951)

Dion-Tennenbaum
Anne Dion-Tennenbaum, "Le Sanctuaire du Pavillon de Marsan" in Hervé Robert, ed., *Le Mécénat du duc d'Orléans 1830–42* (Paris, 1993)

Dufresne
Claude Dufresne, *Morny. L'Homme du Second Empire* (Paris, 1983)

Fitzmaurice
Lord Edward Fitzmaurice, *The Life of Granville George Leveson Gower, Second Earl Granville K.G., 1815–1891,* 2 vols (London, 1905)

Ganière
Ganière, Paul, *Napoléon à Sainte-Hélène. Le Dernier*

Voyage de l'empereur de Malmaison à Longwood (Paris, 1957)

Goudemare
Sylvain Goudemare, *Mémoires de Monsieur Claude* (Paris, 1999)

Grand Palais
Un Âge d'or des arts décoratifs (Paris, 1991)

Grant
Elizabeth Grant of Rothiemurchus, *Memoirs of a Highland Lady,* 2 vols (reprint, Edinburgh, 1988)

Greville
Viscountess Enfield (Alice Byng, countess of Strafford), ed., *Leaves from the Diary of Henry Greville* 2nd Series (London, 1884)

Hanoteau
Jean Hanoteau, ed., *Mémoires de la reine Hortense* 3 vols (Paris, 1927)

Haussonville
Comte d'Haussonville, *Ma Jeunesse,* 1814–1830. *Souvenirs* (reprint, Brionne, 2011)

Havelock
Scenes of Russian Court Life: Being the Correspondence of Alexander I. with his Sister Catherine, trans. Henry Havelock (London, 1917)

Hawkins & Powell
Angus Hawkins & John Powell, eds., *Journal of John Wodehouse, 1st Earl of Kimberley, 1862–1902,*

Camden 5th Series, Book 9 (Cambridge, 1997)

Huart
Suzanne d'Huart, ed., *Journal de Marie-Amélie. Reine des Français* (Paris, 1981)

Kennedy
Aubrey Leo Kennedy, ed., *"My dear Duchess": Social and Political Letters to the Duchess of Manchester, 1858–1869* (London, 1956)

Kerry, *Coup d'État*
Earl of Kerry (Henry William Edmund Petty-Fitzmaurice), *The Secret of the Coup d'État: an unpublished correspondence of Prince Louis Napoleon, MM. de Morny, De Flahault, and others, 1848–1852* (London, 1924)

Kerry, *Napoleon*
Earl of Kerry (Henry William Edmund Petty-Fitzmaurice)*, The First Napoleon: Some Unpublished Documents from the Bowood Papers* (London, 1925)

Kozmian
André-Édouard Kozmian [Andrzej Edward Koźmian], "Le Carnet d'un mondain sous la Restauration", *Revue de Paris*, Jan.–Feb. 1900, pp. 311–52

Las Cases
Las Cases, Emmanuel de, *Le Mémorial de Sainte-Hélène. Le Manuscrit retrouvé* (Paris, 2017)

Le Strange
Guy Le Strange, ed. and trans., *Correspondence of Princess*

Lieven and Earl Grey (London, 1890)

Leveson Gower
Frederick Leveson Gower, ed., *Letters of Harriet*, *Countess Granville, 1810–1845* (London, 1894)

Lloyd
Stephen Lloyd, *Portrait Miniatures from Scottish Private Collections*, exh. cat., National Portrait Gallery of Scotland (Edinburgh, 2006)

Macaulay
Thomas Babington Macaulay, "The Late Lord Holland", essay, *Edinburgh Review*, July 1841

Maillé
Duchesse de Maillé, *Souvenirs des deux Restaurations* (Paris, 1984)

Mameluck Ali
Mameluck Ali (Louis-Étienne Saint-Denis); Christophe Bourachot, ed., *Souvenirs sur l'empereur Napoléon* (Paris, 2000)

Mansel
Philip Mansel, *Paris between Empires, 1814–1852* (London, 2001)

Marchand
Leslie A. Marchand, ed., *Byron's Letters and Journals*, 12 vols (London, 1973–82)

Masson, *Impératrice Marie-Louise*

Frédéric Masson, *L'Impératrice Marie-Louise, 1809–1815* (Paris, 1902)

Masson, *Napoleon*
Frédéric Masson, *Napoleon at St. Helena, 1815–1821* (Oxford, 1949)

Metternich
R. Metternich, ed., *Mémoires. Documents et écrits divers laissés par le prince de Metternich, Recueil des Documents (1835–1848), Journal de la Princesse Mélanie*, vol. 6 (Paris, 1883)

Montet
Baronne Alexandrine Prévost de la Boutetière de Saint-Mars du Montet, *Souvenirs de la baronne du Montet,1785–1866* (Paris, 1904)

Naville
Jacques Naville, ed., *Lettres de François Guizot et de la princesse de Lieven* (Paris, 1963)

Parturier
Maurice Parturier, *Prosper Mérimée. Correspondance générale*, vol. 1, 1822–1835 (reprint, Toulouse, 1956)

Pélissier
Léon-G. Pélissier, *Le Portefeuille de la comtesse d'Albany, 1806–1824* (Paris, 1902)

Price
Munro Price, *The Perilous Crown: France between Revolutions, 1814–1848* (London, 2007)

Quennell
Peter Quennell, *Byron: The Years of Fame* (New York, 1935)

Radziwill
Princess Radziwill, ed., *Chronique de la duchesse de Dino, 1831–1862* (Paris, 1909)

Raikes
Thomas Raikes, *A Portion of the Journal of Thomas Raikes, Esq. from 1831 to 1847* (London, 1856)

Sartory
Madame de Sartory, *Petit Tableau de Paris, pour 1818*, vol. 1 (Paris, 1818)

Staël
Madame de Staël, *Corinne*, trans. Isabel Hill (London, 1838)

Stryienski
Casimir Stryienski, ed., *Mémoires de la comtesse Potocka* (Paris, 1897)

Sudley
Lord Sudley (Arthur Paul John Charles James Gore Sudley, Viscount), trans. and ed., *The Lieven-Palmerston Correspondence, 1828–1856* (London, 1943)

Surtees
Virginia Surtees, ed., *A Second Self: The Letters of Harriet Granville, 1810–1845* (Salisbury, 1990)

Taine
H. Taine, intro., Prosper

Mérimée: *Lettres à une inconnue*, vol. 2 (Paris, 1908)

Ticknor
G. Ticknor, *Life, Letters and Journals* (reissue, Boston, 1909)

Trabaud
Pierre Trabaud, *D'Inverness à Brighton. Notes et sentiments sur les Îles Britanniques* (London & Paris, 1853)

Trevelyan
Sir George Otto Trevelyan, ed., *The Life and Letters of Lord Macaulay* (London, 1882)

Twisleton
Ellen Dwight Twisleton, *Letters of the Hon. Mrs. Edward Twisleton Written to her Family 1852–1862* (London, 1928)

Waller
David Waller, *The Magnificent Mrs Tennant* (New Haven & London, 2009)

Waresquiel
Emmanuel de Waresquiel, ed., *Mémoires et correspondances du prince de Talleyrand* (Paris, 2007)

Wilson
Sir Arthur Wilson, ed., *A Diary of St. Helena, 1816, 1817: The Journal of Lady Malcolm* (London, 1929)

Zamoyski
Adam Zamoyski, *Chopin: Prince of the Romantics* (London, 2010)

PICTURE CREDITS

agefotostock/Alamy Stock Photo: fig. 17

Alinari/Topfoto: fig. 39

Bignor Park, West Sussex. Photographs by Prudence Cuming Associates Ltd: frontispiece; figs. 4–6, 8, 15–16, 23, 32

Bridgeman Images: fig. 46

Eaton Square Mayfair: fig. 43

Einsiedeln Abbey. Photo National Museum, Switzerland: fig. 11

Paul Fearn/Alamy Stock Photo: fig. 7

Galleria Francesca Antonacci, Rome: fig. 36

Trustees of the Grimsthorpe and Drummond Castle Estates:
fig. 14 (courtesy Ray Biggs); figs. 18–19, 44–5

Hirarchivum Press/Alamy Stock Photo: fig. 50

Antonio Martinelli: fig. 49

Meikleour House, Perthshire. Photographs by John McKenzie: figs. 2, 10, 20–1, 24–8, 30–1, 37, 40–1

The Metropolitan Museum of Art. Purchase, Mrs Charles Wrightsman Gift, in memory of Jacqueline Bouvier Kennedy Onassis, 1994: fig. 29

Musée national du Palais de Compiègne. Diomedia/Universal Images Group/Christophel Fine Art: fig. 47

Courtesy Lord Robert Mercer Nairne: fig. 13

National Maritime Museum, Greenwich, London. The Picture Art Collection/Alamy Stock Photo: fig. 3

National Portrait Gallery, London: fig. 12

S. J. Phillips Ltd: fig. 48

Photo 12/Alamy Stock Photo: fig. 22

Private collection: figs. 33–5, 38, 42

Carla van de Puttelaar: back jacket flap

Rijksmuseum, Netherlands: fig. 9

Royal Collection Trust © Her Majesty Queen Elizabeth II, 2018: fig. 1

INDEX

AUTHOR'S ACKNOWLEDGMENTS

As I discovered Margaret at Drummond Castle I must first thank Baroness Willoughby de Eresby for her longstanding support, and the Drummond Foundation for so generously sponsoring publication of the biography. I am also greatly indebted to Isabelle Lucas in Paris, who accurately transcribed so many relevant documents in the Archives Nationales over several years and commented perceptively on the first draft of my text. Thanks are also due to the descendants of Margaret and Charles: the Marquess of Lansdowne; his brother, Lord Robert Mercer Nairne, with Sam and Claire Mercer Nairne; the Viscount Mersey; and the Duke of Devonshire, who have given me access to objects, paintings and documents associated with Margaret in their possession. Friends and colleagues who have encouraged me to persist with what has been a very long term project include: Francesca Antonacci; Kirsty Carpenter; Charles Cator of Christie's; the late Count Andrew Ciechanowiecki; Julia Clarke of Sotheby's; Étienne Grafe; Roselyne Hurel; Arthur Macgregor, who kindly introduced Ed Gordon and Robert Seaton in Scotland; Philip Mansel; Jonathan, Nicolas and Francis Norton of S. J. Phillips; Béatrice de Plinval of Chaumet; Christopher Rowell of the National Trust; Nabil Saidi; Jeremy Warren; and Haydn Williams. Invaluable support has come from my assistant, the many-talented Judith Kilby Hunt, from Guy Penman and Amanda Corp in the London Library, and from the archivists Andrew Peppitt and Fran Baker at Chatsworth, and Kate Fielden and her successor Catherine Spence at Bowood.

Special thanks are due to the prize-winning photographer Carla van de Puttelaar, to the Prudence Cuming team in London, to John McKenzie in Scotland and to Antonio Martinelli in Paris for supplying high-quality illustrations. Finally, I have benefited from the talents of my indefatigable picture researcher Jo Walton, from the imagination and taste of the layout designer Christine Jones, and from the wide-ranging literary and historical knowledge of John Adamson, my publisher. My heartfelt thanks go to all three for so enthusiastically adopting Margaret as a friend and using their professional skills to help me recreate her life and world. To any others whose names I have inadvertently omitted from this list of acknowledgments, I send my apologies.